Preparing Foreign Language Teachers for Next-Generation Education

Chin-Hsi Lin
Michigan State University, USA

Dongbo Zhang
Michigan State University, USA

Binbin Zheng
Michigan State University, USA

A volume in the Advances in Higher Education and Professional Development (AHEPD) Book Series

Information Science REFERENCE
An Imprint of IGI Global

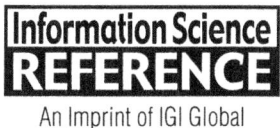

Published in the United States of America by
> Information Science Reference (an imprint of IGI Global)
> 701 E. Chocolate Avenue
> Hershey PA, USA 17033
> Tel: 717-533-8845
> Fax: 717-533-8661
> E-mail: cust@igi-global.com
> Web site: http://www.igi-global.com

Copyright © 2017 by IGI Global. All rights reserved. No part of this publication may be reproduced, stored or distributed in any form or by any means, electronic or mechanical, including photocopying, without written permission from the publisher. Product or company names used in this set are for identification purposes only. Inclusion of the names of the products or companies does not indicate a claim of ownership by IGI Global of the trademark or registered trademark.
                    Library of Congress Cataloging-in-Publication Data

Names: Lin, Chin-Hsi, 1979- editor. | Zhang, Dongbo, 1978- editor. | Zheng,
  Binbin, 1985- editor.
Title: Preparing foreign language teachers for next-generation education /
  Chin-Hsi Lin, Dongbo Zhang and Binbin Zheng, editors.
Description: Hershey : Information Science Reference(an imprint of IGI
  Global), [2016] | Includes bibliographical references and index.
Identifiers: LCCN 2016012752| ISBN 9781522504832 (hardcover) | ISBN
  9781522504849 (ebook)
Subjects: LCSH: Foreign language--Training of. | Language and
  languages--Study and teahing. | Language and languages--Computer-assisted
  instrucation. | Language and lanugages--Technological innovations.
Classification: LCC P53.85 .P64 2016 | DDC 418.0071--dc23 LC record available at https://lccn.loc.gov/2016012752

This book is published in the IGI Global book series Advances in Higher Education and Professional Development (AHEPD) (ISSN: 2327-6983; eISSN: 2327-6991)

British Cataloguing in Publication Data
A Cataloguing in Publication record for this book is available from the British Library.

All work contributed to this book is new, previously-unpublished material. The views expressed in this book are those of the authors, but not necessarily of the publisher.

For electronic access to this publication, please contact: eresources@igi-global.com.

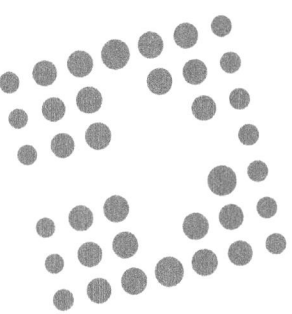

Advances in Higher Education and Professional Development (AHEPD) Book Series

Jared Keengwe
University of North Dakota, USA

ISSN: 2327-6983
EISSN: 2327-6991

Mission

As world economies continue to shift and change in response to global financial situations, job markets have begun to demand a more highly-skilled workforce. In many industries a college degree is the minimum requirement and further educational development is expected to advance. With these current trends in mind, the **Advances in Higher Education & Professional Development (AHEPD) Book Series** provides an outlet for researchers and academics to publish their research in these areas and to distribute these works to practitioners and other researchers.

AHEPD encompasses all research dealing with higher education pedagogy, development, and curriculum design, as well as all areas of professional development, regardless of focus.

Coverage

- Adult Education
- Assessment in Higher Education
- Career Training
- Coaching and Mentoring
- Continuing Professional Development
- Governance in Higher Education
- Higher Education Policy
- Pedagogy of Teaching Higher Education
- Vocational Education

IGI Global is currently accepting manuscripts for publication within this series. To submit a proposal for a volume in this series, please contact our Acquisition Editors at Acquisitions@igi-global.com or visit: http://www.igi-global.com/publish/.

The Advances in Higher Education and Professional Development (AHEPD) Book Series (ISSN 2327-6983) is published by IGI Global, 701 E. Chocolate Avenue, Hershey, PA 17033-1240, USA, www.igi-global.com. This series is composed of titles available for purchase individually; each title is edited to be contextually exclusive from any other title within the series. For pricing and ordering information please visit http://www.igi-global.com/book-series/advances-higher-education-professional-development/73681. Postmaster: Send all address changes to above address. Copyright © 2017 IGI Global. All rights, including translation in other languages reserved by the publisher. No part of this series may be reproduced or used in any form or by any means – graphics, electronic, or mechanical, including photocopying, recording, taping, or information and retrieval systems – without written permission from the publisher, except for non commercial, educational use, including classroom teaching purposes. The views expressed in this series are those of the authors, but not necessarily of IGI Global.

Titles in this Series

For a list of additional titles in this series, please visit: www.igi-global.com

Handbook of Research on Professional Development for Quality Teaching and Learning
Teresa Petty (University of North Carolina at Charlotte, USA) Amy Good (University of North Carolina at Charlotte, USA) and S. Michael Putman (University of North Carolina at Charlotte, USA)
Information Science Reference • copyright 2016 • 824pp • H/C (ISBN: 9781522502043) • US $310.00 (our price)

Administrative Challenges and Organizational Leadership in Historically Black Colleges and Universities
Charles B. W. Prince (Howard University, USA) and Rochelle L. Ford (Syracuse University, USA)
Information Science Reference • copyright 2016 • 301pp • H/C (ISBN: 9781522503118) • US $170.00 (our price)

Developing Workforce Diversity Programs, Curriculum, and Degrees in Higher Education
Chaunda L. Scott (Oakland University, USA) and Jeanetta D. Sims (University of Central Oklahoma, USA)
Information Science Reference • copyright 2016 • 398pp • H/C (ISBN: 9781522502098) • US $185.00 (our price)

Handbook of Research on Transforming Mathematics Teacher Education in the Digital Age
Margaret Niess (Oregon State University, USA) Shannon Driskell (University of Dayton, USA) and Karen Hollebrands (North Carolina State University, USA)
Information Science Reference • copyright 2016 • 679pp • H/C (ISBN: 9781522501206) • US $235.00 (our price)

Handbook of Research on Engaging Digital Natives in Higher Education Settings
Margarida M. Pinheiro (University of Aveiro, Portugal) and Dora Simões (University of Aveiro, Portugal)
Information Science Reference • copyright 2016 • 500pp • H/C (ISBN: 9781522500391) • US $300.00 (our price)

Exploring the Social and Academic Experiences of International Students in Higher Education Institutions
Krishna Bista (University of Louisiana at Monroe, USA) and Charlotte Foster (Missouri Western State University, USA)
Information Science Reference • copyright 2016 • 363pp • H/C (ISBN: 9781466697492) • US $185.00 (our price)

Handbook of Research on Global Issues in Next-Generation Teacher Education
Jared Keengwe (University of North Dakota, USA) Justus G. Mbae (Catholic University of Eastern Africa, Kenya) and Grace Onchwari (University of North Dakota, USA)
Information Science Reference • copyright 2016 • 418pp • H/C (ISBN: 9781466699489) • US $285.00 (our price)

Handbook of Research on Effective Communication in Culturally Diverse Classrooms
Katia González (Wagner College, USA) and Rhoda Frumkin (Wagner College, USA)
Information Science Reference • copyright 2016 • 477pp • H/C (ISBN: 9781466699533) • US $295.00 (our price)

www.igi-global.com

701 E. Chocolate Ave., Hershey, PA 17033
Order online at www.igi-global.com or call 717-533-8845 x100
To place a standing order for titles released in this series, contact: cust@igi-global.com
Mon-Fri 8:00 am - 5:00 pm (est) or fax 24 hours a day 717-533-8661

Table of Contents

Preface xiv

Section 1
The Status Quo and Standards of Technology

Chapter 1
Technology Instruction in Language Teacher Education Programs 1
Yining Zhang, Michigan State University, USA
Matthew Deroo, Michigan State University, USA

Chapter 2
EFL Teachers' Knowledge of Technology in China: Issues and Challenges... 23
Yanjiang Teng, Michigan State University, USA

Chapter 3
Technology Standards for Chinese Language Teacher Education 38
Wenxia Wang, Florida State University, USA
Liying Feng, Florida State University, USA

Section 2
Language Teachers' Perceptions and Uses of Technology

Chapter 4
Language Teachers' Perceptions of External and Internal Factors in Their Instructional (Non-) Use of Technology 56
Haixia Liu, Beijing Normal University Zhuhai Campus, China & Michigan State University, USA
Chin-Hsi Lin, Michigan State University, USA
Dongbo Zhang, Michigan State University, USA
Binbin Zheng, Michigan State University, USA

Chapter 5
Identifying the Contributors to Improve Mobile-Based TPACK Competency of Elementary School Teachers in China 74
    Zhong Sun, Capital Normal University, China
    Jiaxin You, Capital Normal University, China
    Wei Song, Capital Normal University, China
    Zheng Qu, Capital Normal University, China
    Liming Luo, Capital Normal University, China

Chapter 6
Teaching Foreign Languages in the Twenty-First Century: Lessons from Spanish Hybrid Education 92
    Sarah Gretter, Michigan State University, USA
    Ager Gondra, State University of New York – Purchase College, USA

Chapter 7
Implementing a Flipped Classroom in Teaching Second Language Pronunciation: Challenges, Solutions, and Expectations 114
    Kazuhiro Yonemoto, Tokyo Medical and Dental University, Japan
    Asami Tsuda, Columbia University, USA
    Hisako Hayashi, Carleton University, Canada

Chapter 8
Divergent Teacher Viewpoints of Technology Integration in the Language Classroom 130
    Andy D. Halvorsen, University of Oregon, USA

Section 3
Technology in Language Teacher Preparation and Learning

Chapter 9
Learning to Teach for Next-Generation Education: A Careful Blend of Action and Reflection 153
    Muriel M. Grosbois, Université Paris – Sorbonne, France
    Cédric G. Sarré, Université Paris – Sorbonne, France

Chapter 10
Mentoring Preservice EFL Teachers for Technology Integration: A Cloud-Based Internship Project 175
    Mei-Hui Liu, Tunghai University, Taiwan

Chapter 11
A TL-TPACK Model on CSL Pre-Service Teachers' Competencies of Online Instruction 198
    Hsiu-Jen Cheng, National Kaohsiung Normal University, Taiwan

Chapter 12
The Technology Segment of a Methods Course: Its Impact on Teaching Realities and Imagined Needs 226
    Jason D. Hendryx, University of Wyoming, USA

Chapter 13
Mentoring Teacher Assistants to Use Online Tools 245
    Grisel M. Garcia Perez, University of British Columbia – Okanagan, Canada

Chapter 14
Social Media and Foreign Language Teacher Education: Beliefs and Practices 261
    Jiahang Li, Michigan State University, USA

Compilation of References 278

About the Contributors 307

Index 311

Detailed Table of Contents

Preface xiv

Section 1
The Status Quo and Standards of Technology

Chapter 1
Technology Instruction in Language Teacher Education Programs 1
    Yining Zhang, Michigan State University, USA
    Matthew Deroo, Michigan State University, USA

It is important to examine how prospective teachers were prepared with integrating technology in their teaching. This study explored the integration of technology instruction among ten top world language teacher preparation programs in the United States. Data collection included document analysis of syllabi and interviews with program directors and instructors. The findings revealed that technology instruction were provided to language pre-service teachers through general technology courses, methods courses, and a series of technology-related courses infused throughout the entire program. In addition, technology courses organized a variety of approaches to enrich students' experiences with technology. We also generated four main themes to reflect some key elements in current technology instruction for pre-service teachers. The study enriches our knowledge of the current situation for how different world language teacher education programs prepare their pre-service teachers.

Chapter 2
EFL Teachers' Knowledge of Technology in China: Issues and Challenges... 23
    Yanjiang Teng, Michigan State University, USA

Through the lens of teachers of English as a Foreign Language (EFL) in China, this chapter aims to examine what knowledge of technology EFL teachers at all levels possess and how they apply their technological knowledge in teaching practice. The reviewed literature indicated that most EFL teachers hold positive attitudes towards technology. However, there still exists a gap between the curriculum requirement and the reality in terms of technological pedagogy in EFL teaching context. EFL teachers' use of technology in teaching varies in terms of personal preferences, school levels and locations, and administrative support. In addition, this review revealed that several factors influence EFL teachers' integration of technology into their practice and some challenges are still on the way: 1) EFL teachers' knowledge of technology is insufficient; 2) Lack of resources for schools and teachers at less developed areas, and 3) Lack of specific support for EFL teachers' technological needs.

Chapter 3
Technology Standards for Chinese Language Teacher Education 38
    Wenxia Wang, Florida State University, USA
    Liying Feng, Florida State University, USA

Guided by the TPACK theory (Mishra & Koehler, 2006), this chapter reviews and compares the technology standards related to and designed for teachers of Chinese as a Foreign Language (CFL) from the entry level to the accomplished level in the United States and China. It has found that the technology standards are often included in the comprehensive standards for teachers and parallel the standards about other aspects of teaching. The technology standards related to CFL in the two countries share some similarities but also differ in important ways. Several important and critical understandings are identified, including the needs for CFL technology standards, the theoretical foundations for CFL technology standards, and a more solid and comprehensive infrastructure for CFL education. Recommendations are made to address the needs, and research is called for to study the development and implementation of CFL technology standards.

Section 2
Language Teachers' Perceptions and Uses of Technology

Chapter 4
Language Teachers' Perceptions of External and Internal Factors in Their Instructional (Non-) Use of Technology 56
    Haixia Liu, Beijing Normal University Zhuhai Campus, China & Michigan State University, USA
    Chin-Hsi Lin, Michigan State University, USA
    Dongbo Zhang, Michigan State University, USA
    Binbin Zheng, Michigan State University, USA

Prior studies (e.g., Li & Walsh, 2011) found that language teachers did not use technology fully despite its possible facilitating function in language teaching. Through a survey and group discussions, this study explores pre-service Chinese-language teachers' perceptions of the internal and external barriers to their instructional technology use. The respondents (N=47) expressed five main types of external barriers: a) lack of technology, b) difficulty in accessing the available technology, c) lack of technical support, d) lack of proper assessment, and e) negative parental attitude. The two main internal barriers identified in this research were a) negative attitude originating from teachers' pedagogical beliefs, and b) lack of technology-related knowledge. The findings of this study should be of practical use in the future design and implementation of professional development aiming at improving language teachers' use of technology in teaching.

Chapter 5
Identifying the Contributors to Improve Mobile-Based TPACK Competency of Elementary School Teachers in China... 74
    Zhong Sun, Capital Normal University, China
    Jiaxin You, Capital Normal University, China
    Wei Song, Capital Normal University, China
    Zheng Qu, Capital Normal University, China
    Liming Luo, Capital Normal University, China

Self-Efficacy (SE) and technology acceptance are two contributors related to Technological Pedagogical and Content Knowledge (TPACK). Many studies have indicated that TPACK is correlated with SE and the level of technology acceptance in both traditional and online learning environments. Studies using mobile learning devices in the classroom, however, are yet to be established. The authors conducted an empirical study by investigating mobile-based TPACK, SE, and technology acceptance of more than 500 English teachers from about 220 elementary schools in China, who used Android system-based pad in classrooms for one year. As a result, SE and technology acceptance had indirect positive effects on mobile-based TPACK, while no significant difference was observed in gender for TPACK. However, younger teachers and teachers with higher levels of education showed superior TPACK levels than other participants in the study. Finally, several implications for teacher professional development, limitations, and future research plans are presented.

Chapter 6
Teaching Foreign Languages in the Twenty-First Century: Lessons from Spanish Hybrid
Education 92
    Sarah Gretter, Michigan State University, USA
    Ager Gondra, State University of New York – Purchase College, USA

This chapter explores the case of a hybrid Spanish program where technology, standards, and teacher expertise in foreign language education are merged to bolster students' learning. The chapter identifies the instructional elements relevant to 21st century foreign language education, and depicts the transactional relationship between technology, standards and teacher experience in a Spanish hybrid teaching environment. Finally, we provide a set of recommendations for current and future Spanish educators, as well as foreign language educators in general based on the experiences shared by students, educators, and administrator in the program.

Chapter 7
Implementing a Flipped Classroom in Teaching Second Language Pronunciation: Challenges,
Solutions, and Expectations 114
    Kazuhiro Yonemoto, Tokyo Medical and Dental University, Japan
    Asami Tsuda, Columbia University, USA
    Hisako Hayashi, Carleton University, Canada

While the philosophy of flipped classroom has recently been drawing much attention of second language teachers, integrating technology into pedagogy is often an issue. This is also the case in pronunciation teaching. Second language pronunciation teaching has been largely dependent on teachers' intuition and beliefs, realized by repetition. Although recent technology developments in the field of linguistics, namely ultrasound imaging, enable visualization of movement and motion inside the mouth, it has not yet been widely used in second language education. In this chapter, taking a self-learning website for Japanese language pronunciation, the authors explore what makes teachers stay away from technology integration into language learning and how this barrier can be overcome to implement a flipped classroom. Specifically, the authors address the importance of taking initiative in planning how technology can be integrated into pedagogy while closely collaborating with and involving other fields of study, like linguistics, as well as information technology.

Chapter 8
Divergent Teacher Viewpoints of Technology Integration in the Language Classroom 130
    Andy D. Halvorsen, University of Oregon, USA

This chapter presents a qualitative analysis of the beliefs and practices of three language teachers in Thailand vis-à-vis their integration of technology in the classroom as well as their views regarding social networking site participation as a facilitative tool for instruction. The study brings together research on the identity development work of teachers and Computer Assisted Language Learning (CALL). Through the analysis of extensive teacher interview data and classroom observations, the study demonstrates how these teachers self-identify as users of technology, and how this sense of self interacts with and shapes various aspects of their teaching practice. The three teachers in this study represent a range of divergent viewpoints related to technology use and integration in the classroom, and the analysis of these viewpoints helps to illustrate the specific factors underlying how and why they choose to make pedagogic use of technology.

Section 3
Technology in Language Teacher Preparation and Learning

Chapter 9
Learning to Teach for Next-Generation Education: A Careful Blend of Action and Reflection 153
    Muriel M. Grosbois, Université Paris – Sorbonne, France
    Cédric G. Sarré, Université Paris – Sorbonne, France

This chapter examines how pre-service teachers specializing in English Language Teaching (ELT) in secondary schools can learn to teach for Next-Generation Education by developing professional skills that are in line with today and tomorrow's technology-mediated environments. To face this challenge, some specific CALL-based ELT training combining action and reflection has recently been introduced in the Education Department at Paris-Sorbonne University. In order to examine the specific CALL-based ELT training offered in light of the set objective, its theoretical underpinnings will first be considered. The design and content of a CALL-based ELT course and of an online tutoring module will then be studied. The pre-service teachers' perception of this CALL-based ELT training will then be explored through the results of online surveys. Conclusions will be drawn from these results and future directions will be outlined.

Chapter 10
Mentoring Preservice EFL Teachers for Technology Integration: A Cloud-Based Internship
Project 175
    Mei-Hui Liu, Tunghai University, Taiwan

This chapter proposes an integrated mentoring model in the context of established and emerging Information and Communications Technology (ICT) tools to be applied into teacher professional development. Twenty preservice English as a Foreign Language (EFL) preservice teachers participating in a Cloud-based internship project were involved in a series of training activities, including virtual technology training workshops, in-class methods instruction, design and implementation of teaching projects on a Cloud platform, and subsequent face-to-face and online discussions on teaching practices. Multiple qualitative data collected offers evidence to examine the potential of employing this mentoring mechanism to make amends for what has been rarely exploited in the extant technology teacher training models in the foreign language education field. Based on the research findings, a revised mentoring model is suggested for further investigation.

Chapter 11

A TL-TPACK Model on CSL Pre-Service Teachers' Competencies of Online Instruction 198

Hsiu-Jen Cheng, National Kaohsiung Normal University, Taiwan

This chapter aims to introduce the integration of TPACK into a Chinese pre-service teacher training program and discuss its outcomes and challenges. First, the concept of TPACK was introduced and relevant TPACK research and its constraints in the previous studies were discussed. Through the partnership between a Chinese pre-service teacher training program in Taiwan and a Chinese learning program in the States, the author developed a Teaching and Learning Model, entitled TL-TPACK model, integrating practicum, course design, advisors, peer cooperation, and reflections—five training strategies to ensure the training and learning outcome. At the end of the chapter, an empirical Chinese pre-service teacher training study applying the TL-TPACK model was conducted to investigate pre- service teachers' seven TPACK competences and Chinese learners' learning performance. Finally, research implications and suggestions for future studies were discussed.

Chapter 12

The Technology Segment of a Methods Course: Its Impact on Teaching Realities and Imagined Needs 226

Jason D. Hendryx, University of Wyoming, USA

This chapter reports a case study with survey data collected from one residency Spanish language teacher completing the final phase of a modern languages education program as well as two current in-service Spanish language teachers who completed the same program the year previously. Specifically, the study examined 1) what the three teachers recall of an overarching framework for embracing technology they were introduced to in their methods course, 2) what technologies they currently employ for language instruction and why, and 3) what characteristics they imagine the model modern language educator of the future will require. Findings revealed that these teachers did not recall in detail the overarching system for embracing technology introduced to them, they utilized a very broad range of technologies for teaching which would prove difficult to train them all in effectively during a methods course, and they saw flexible, engaging, patient, and content-prepared professionals as the future of the profession.

Chapter 13

Mentoring Teacher Assistants to Use Online Tools 245

Grisel M. Garcia Perez, University of British Columbia – Okanagan, Canada

This chapter indicates how a group of Teaching Assistants (TAs) was trained in the use of technology to help students enrolled in large first year Spanish classes excel in learning of Spanish as a foreign language. Framed by the Communities of Practice theory proposed by Wenger (1998), this study supports the theory that by examining their practices, trainees may become more effective in what they learn. Six TAs participated in the study and their reflection-on-action logs were examined and compared to the trainer's personal observations. Interpretation of the results was then carried out by comparing parallel and dissimilar ideas which were then used as focus for discussion. Outcomes support the theory that communities of practice and reflective inquiry are valuable teacher training tools.

Chapter 14
Social Media and Foreign Language Teacher Education: Beliefs and Practices 261
   Jiahang Li, Michigan State University, USA

This chapter will focus on examining how instructors who are preparing foreign language teachers, both pre-service and in-service, integrate social media in their teaching practices to gain more insights on what beliefs these instructors hold and what differences and similarities between their beliefs and actual teaching practices about social media integration in foreign language teacher education. The chapter will first provide a literature review about the general beliefs that instructors held on the integration of social media and foreign language teacher education. Next, promising examples of the integration of social media in foreign language teacher education will be provided. Last but not least, affordances and challenges of the integration of social media and foreign language teacher education will be discussed, followed by implications and future directions.

Compilation of References 278

About the Contributors 307

Index 311

Preface

TECHNOLOGY, TEACHING, TEACHER EDUCATION, AND TEACHER LEARNING

Background

The unprecedented growth of Information and Communication Technologies (ICT) is redefining not only how students learn, but also how teachers teach. Self-directed learning outside of school, particularly with the support of mobile devices, has never been more possible. On the other hand, school-based technology integration is maintaining its critical role in the place where students spend most of their learning time each week. Teachers, as pedagogical decision-makers, are on the front line of technology integration in any school system: pivotal players in fulfilling ICT's potential to engage students in meaningful learning, promote multiliteracies among them, and develop their critical thinking skills. Teacher preparation and standards often require that teachers integrate ICT to promote students' engagement in learning and maximize learning effects (Council of Chief State School Officers, 2011; International Society for Technology in Education, 2007).

Language teaching is no exception. For example, the American Council on the Teaching of Foreign Languages (ACTFL) highlights in its Program Standards for the Preparation of Foreign Language Teachers that "programs of foreign language teacher preparation must demonstrate that they include 'opportunities for candidates to experience technology-enhanced instruction and to use technology in their own teaching'" (ACTFL, 2013, p. 2).

Technology integration, however, comes with conditions (Zhao & Frank, 2003; Zhao et al., 2002). Research has consistently found that a myriad of factors may affect ICT integration in education. Ertmer (1999) named these factors first-order and second-order barriers/enablers. The first-order factors are extrinsic to teachers, and include the educational system, policy initiatives, curriculum mandates, individual school policies (e.g., heavy workloads or lack of time for innovation), leadership, and the availability of resources (e.g., appropriate software and instructional materials), as well as technical, administrative and peer support. The second-order factors are intrinsic to teachers: their cognitive systems (e.g., knowledge, beliefs, and perceptions) or "mental lives" (Borg, 2006, p. 1). These two broad categories of factors work together to drive teachers' pedagogical decisions on technology integration.

Despite the clear affordances of digital technologies for language teaching and frequent calls for teachers to integrate technology into their teaching (e.g., ACTFL, 2013; Egbert et al. 2009), teachers' actual practice with respect to technology use appears to be limited (Hubbard, 2008). This unexpected outcome, in light of heightened investment in educational technology, seems partly attributable to a failure to understand teachers. Empirically, scholars still know little about what technologies language teachers

Preface

use, how they use them, or what factors influence their use (or non-use) of these technologies – to say nothing of how and how well teachers are prepared and supported in this area.

This volume brings together original research studies and reviews specifically to address this gap in the literature regarding second/foreign language teachers, teaching, teacher education, and teacher learning in the digital era. Specifically, the 14 original chapters report on a range of issues related to language teacher cognition (e.g., beliefs, identity, and knowledge base) and technology use, as well as how teacher education and teacher learning impinge on technology integration. Taken together, the research presented provides an up-to-date, in-depth inquiry into language teachers' perceptions of technology integration, the factors that have shaped these perceptions, the influence of these perceptions on their pedagogical (non-)use of technology, and the role of technology in the preparation and professional learning of language teachers.

ORGANIZATION OF THE BOOK

The current volume places the teacher at the center of its examination of language education in the digital era. In particular, it aims to build an innovative knowledge base about technologies, second/foreign language teaching, and language teacher education and teacher learning. To achieve this goal, the book's collection of original theoretical and empirical studies covers three major areas: 1) the status quo and standards of technology in language teacher education, 2) language teachers' perceptions and uses of technology, and 3) technology in language teacher preparation and learning.

Section 1: The Status Quo and Standards of Technology

This section focuses on technology and language teacher education in its broad social and educational context, and includes three chapters. Chapters 1 and 2 examine and synthesize our current understanding of technology in foreign language teacher education in the different contexts of the United States and China, respectively. Chapter 3 then compares the technology standards of Chinese as a second language teachers in China against those applied to world language teacher education in the United States.

Chapter 1, "Technology Instruction in Language Teacher Education Programs," by Yining Zhang and Matthew Deroo, offers a comprehensive overview of technology instruction in world language teacher education programs in the United States. Though many national and international educational entities highlight the importance of technology training and propose various guidelines for language teacher education, the prior literature has had very little to say about how pre-service teachers are prepared in actual practice. Using document analysis of the syllabi of the U.S.'s top ten world language teacher education programs, Zhang and Deroo found major variations in the technology training that was provided, which can be divided into three main types, with nine categories of learning activities – prominently including attendance at educational technology conferences. Zhang and Deroo further identified four themes that summarize the prevailing objectives of technology instruction: 1) understanding issues about technology, teaching, and learning, 2) integrating technology into teaching, 3) developing positive attitudes and greater confidence towards technology, and 4) documenting professional growth and reflection. The authors argue in favor of adding digital portfolios to technology-related courses to help situate technology training in authentic scenarios.

Preface

Chapter 2, "EFL Teachers' Knowledge of Technology in China: Issues and Challenges," by Yanjiang Teng, systematically reviews English as a foreign language (EFL) teachers' knowledge of technology across different school levels in China. This chapter first provides an overview of ICT use in education; technology-related EFL curriculum reforms; and the development of teachers' technology training in China during the last several decades. It goes on to review what kind of technology knowledge is needed for EFL pre- and in-service teachers, and points out the need for more professional development targeted at integrating technology into pedagogy for EFL teachers, in order to meet the pedagogical needs of EFL teachers in China. By way of conclusion, this chapter identifies three major challenges that Chinese EFL teachers face when integrating technology into their instruction: 1) insufficient technology knowledge; 2) lack of resources in rural areas; and 3) limited support for EFL teachers' technological and pedagogical needs, and makes a series of specific recommendations based on these findings.

Chapter 3, "Technology Standards for Chinese Language Teacher Education" by Wenxia Wang and Liying Feng, reviews and compares the technology standards of Chinese-language teacher education in China against those of world language teacher education in the U.S., using the framework of Technological, Pedagogical, and Content Knowledge (TPACK, see Mishra & Koehler, 2006). TPACK postulates that teachers' technology knowledge should be interactive and integrated with pedagogical content knowledge, and standards promulgated by the International Society for Technology in Education include all TPACK components and require U.S. teachers to be able to apply TPACK in their teaching. But in the next stage, licensing and re-certification, the Interstate New Teacher Assessment and Support Consortium (InTASC) does not specifically include technological knowledge among its core standards. Nor does the last stage or the stage of advanced professional certification by the National Board for Professional Teaching Standards has direct coverage of technological content; instead, technology is treated as an integral part of teachers' knowledge. Using TPACK as the guiding framework for comparison, Wang and Feng find that technology is included in the standards of world/Chinese-language teacher education in both China and the United States. On the other hand, the Chinese standards are comparatively brief and mainly focus on technology knowledge as a single distinct component that does not link to other elements the American standards are more aligned with TPACK and highlight the connections between technology knowledge and pedagogical and content knowledge. Wang and Feng call for more detailed technology standards to guide Chinese-language teacher education in China.

Section 2: Language Teachers' Perceptions and Uses of Technology

Whether or not language teachers use technology, what types of technologies they use, and how they use them are subject to the influence of various factors extrinsic and intrinsic to teachers. Around these issues, the five chapters that make up Section 2 examine how first- and second-order factors (Ertmer, 1999) drive language teachers' actual use of technology. Chapters 4 and 5 investigate the reasons that teachers use or do not use technology, with the former focusing on the uptake of ICT by Chinese-language teachers in the United States, and the latter on the use of mobile technology by English-language teachers in China. Chapter 5 also links these teachers' use of technology to TPACK. Chapters 6, 7, and 8 are case studies documenting which technologies teachers use and how they use them to meet their pedagogical needs. Chapter 7 focuses on Spanish-language teachers' and students' experience in a hybrid environment. Both these groups of respondents identified challenges during this implementation. Chapter 8 portrays the challenges of designing an effective flipped lesson for teaching Japanese pronunciation to English native speakers, and Chapter 9 examines Thai English teachers' views of technology integration in Thailand.

Preface

Together, these three chapters present a consistent picture of the requirements and challenges of the technology integration process in second/foreign language education.

Chapter 4, "Language Teachers' Perceptions of External and Internal Factors in Their Instructional (Non-) Use of Technology," by Haixia Liu, Chin-Hsi Lin, Dongbo Zhang, and Binbin Zheng, examines the reasons behind teachers' use or non-use of ICT in language classes. Drawing upon two frameworks that identify factors affecting technology use in general – the technology acceptance model (TAM) and the unified theory of acceptance and use of technology (UTAUT) – Liu, Lin, Zhang, and Zheng examine how internal and external factors affect pre-service K-12 Chinese-language teachers' use of technology in the U.S. Based on the results of a questionnaire and group discussions among 47 teachers who were completing their certification while teaching full-time in K-12 schools, the authors report that many first-order barriers have been greatly reduced in most schools (see Ertmer et al., 2012). On the other hand, the authors identify five external barriers to Chinese-language teachers' use of technology, including a) lack of technology, b) difficulty in accessing the available technology, c) lack of technical support, d) lack of proper assessment, and e) negative parental attitude, as well as two main internal barriers: negative attitudes originating from teachers' pedagogical beliefs, and lack of technology-related knowledge, which are only likely to be remedied by ongoing professional development.

Chapter 5, "Identifying Contributors to Improved Mobile-Based TPACK Competency of Elementary School Teachers in China," by Zhong Sun, Jiaxin You, Zheng Qu, Wei Song, and Liming Luo, reports on a study of more than 500 EFL teachers in a mobile-based learning environment in China that examined these teachers' self-efficacy, technology acceptance (including perceived usefulness and perceived ease of use), and TPACK. Using structural equation modeling, the authors determined that teachers' self-efficacy has an indirect significant positive effect on TPACK, mediated by technology knowledge and technological pedagogical knowledge; that teachers' perceptions of technology's usefulness significantly predicted their TPACK through technological pedagogical knowledge; and their perceptions of ease of use significantly predicted TPACK through mobile-based technology knowledge. Younger teachers with higher educational attainment also tended to have higher TPACK. Based on these findings, the authors suggest improvement in EFL teachers' TPACK could be achieved via more professional development aimed at building confidence in technology use and technology integration into instruction.

Chapter 6, "Teaching Foreign Languages in the Twenty-First Century: Lessons from Spanish Hybrid Education," by Sarah Gretter and Ager Gondra, examines the experiences of language teachers teaching and students learning in hybrid environments, based on an instructor survey and student course evaluations, respectively. The online component of these courses featured an online lab that provided students with abundant learning resources as well as opportunities to continue using Spanish outside the classroom, such as language exercises and interactive blog-based activities. Student feedback was very positive, especially with regard to greater engagement, enhanced opportunities, and rich resources for learning Spanish. The instructors, meanwhile, indicated the benefits of the online lab for both students' course preview and reinforcement through independent learning, and reported that the availability of rich online resources had freed them up from looking for such materials, thus allowing more time to prepare their classroom teaching and refine pedagogical approaches. The teachers also liked that the technology allowed for easy monitoring of students' progress. On the other hand, both students and teachers reported challenges associated with the hybrid environment. There were also gaps between the teachers' and the students' perceptions: for example, in contrast to the instructors' view of the benefit of online lesson previewing, some students found it a major challenge to complete some online assignments (as part of their lesson previewing) without the lesson having been taught at all by the instructor.

Also, many students simply ignored the online resources. The authors recommend that the rationale of technology use be clearly defined, and that better guidance and support be provided to teachers. In addition, the perception gaps between the instructors and their students suggest that teachers may need to be strategic, flexible, and adaptive users of technology, rather than constrained by the technology that is available to them.

The learning of Japanese pronunciation by American students is very challenging due to a lack of effective pedagogical approaches, teaching resources, and in-class instruction time. Chapter 7, "Implementing a Flipped Classroom in Teaching Second Language Pronunciation: Challenges, Solutions, and Expectations," by Kazuhiro Yonemoto, Asami Tsuda, and Hisako Hayashi, reports on a flipped classroom called *eNunciate!* designed and implemented by the authors to address these problems. The flipped-classroom concept can extend students' learning outside of class, thus improving the quality and effectiveness of the lessons. Bringing together Japanese-language instructors, linguists, instructional designers, and programmers, the project included animations created from ultrasound images to visually show the movement inside speakers' mouths, and instant-feedback quizzes, as well as instruction in Japanese phonetics and phonology. The results showed a high acceptance of this project among the instructors, who were given video tutorials on how to implement the flipped lesson. The design also increased instructors' confidence in giving feedback on students' pronunciation. Students reported increased awareness of their Japanese pronunciation, while the connection between in-class and online instruction also increased their satisfaction and improved their pronunciations. Based on these findings, Yonemoto, Tsuda, and Hayashi highlight the importance of connecting online and in-class learning and provide recommendations for designing and implementing flipped learning.

Chapter 8, "Divergent Teacher Viewpoints on Technology Integration in the Language Classroom," by Andy Halvorsen, was based on a three-month observation of and face-to-face interviews with three high-school teachers of EFL in Thailand. Specifically, the chapter focuses on teacher self-identification and social networking site (SNS) participation, and these factors' impacts on the teachers' use of SNSs as tools for facilitating language learning and instruction. Guided by grounded theory and the constant comparative method (Corbin & Strauss, 2008), the author coded and analyzed the transcribed teacher interviews and classroom observation notes. Five code groups were generated based on the interviews: personal SNS use, instructional SNS use, cultural context, institutional context, and identity development (e.g., views of the self and on personal privacy). These codes were then examined against classroom observation codes to make sense of relationships among teacher beliefs, perceptions, self-identification, and classroom use of SNSs. The three teachers, who were purposefully selected to represent a range of experiences, presented divergent viewpoints related to SNSs and their classroom integration, reflecting their diverse positions and beliefs about these sites; their personal orientations toward the future or past; and a nexus of cultural and institutional factors (e.g., Internet connectivity in the classroom and curricular mandates). These findings shed considerable light on the complex interplay between contextual factors, teachers' self-identification as users of technology, their perceptions of technology in education, and their use of educational technology to build and shape classroom practices.

Section 3: Technology in Language Teacher Preparation and Learning

In contrast to the previous two sections' focus on language teachers' perceptions of technology and practice of technological use, this final section concentrates on their preparation, professional development, and learning with regard to technology. It consists of five empirical studies that examine technology in

Preface

both pre-service and in-service teacher education. Drawing upon different theoretical and methodological perspectives, these five chapters present a wide range of possibilities for better preparing language teachers for next-generation education.

Chapter 9 documents a technology-enhanced English-language teaching course in France, aimed at enabling teachers to assess the potentials of technology and design tasks that involve it. Chapter 10 proposes a new type of English-teacher preparation course for Taiwan, based on online field experience. Chapter 11 proposes a teacher training program for Chinese-language teachers in Taiwan, using TPACK to assess their perceptions and knowledge. Chapter 12 investigates how a methods course with technology training for Spanish teachers impacted their teaching. Chapter 13 examines mentoring of Spanish-course teaching assistants in the use of online tools, and Chapter 14 looks at social-media use in pre- and in-service teacher training.

In Chapter 9, "Learning to Teach for Next-Generation Education: A Careful Blend of Action and Reflection," Muriel Grosbois and Cedric Sarre examine the effects of a technology-enhanced English-language teaching course at the Paris-Sorbonne University. The French Ministry for Education requires language teachers to have ICT skills, including computer-assisted language learning. When designing a course to respond to these requirements for certification, Grosbois and Sarre set three objectives that pre-service teachers needed to achieve: 1) to be able to assess the potentials and limits of technology for language learning, 2) to be able to handle basic technological tools, and 3) to be able to design appropriate tasks involving technology. Over the two-year period of design and implementation, survey results suggested that the course met pre-service teachers' needs and expectations, and their course projects reflected the skills they had acquired and the confidence they had gained with respect to English-class technology integration. The study's findings are consistent with TPACK. Grosbois and Sarre show that, through a combination of action and reflection, pre-service teachers are likely to adapt to change and to develop the technology skills they need for 21st-century language teaching.

In Chapter 10, "Mentoring Pre-Service EFL Teachers for Technology Integration: A Cloud-Based Internship Project," Mei-Hui Liu argues for the importance of field experience in training pre-service teachers to teach with technology, and that a major drawback of existing technology training is its narrow focus on the acquisition of technological skills, rather than on linking technological skills to pedagogy. Liu therefore designed a language-teaching methods class that incorporated a required online internship project designed to strengthen the link between technological skills learned in the course and specific teaching practices. Following their 10-month internship projects, 20 Taiwanese undergraduate participants showed significant progress. Multiple sources of qualitative data indicated that these pre-service teachers appreciated the inclusion of this online internship project in their training, had learned a wide range of technological skills, and were able to apply them. In addition, the participants showed increases in both their technological confidence and their attainment in technology skills. Some of the participants, however, noted challenges, including uncertainty about how to choose an appropriate teaching approach to meet their pedagogical needs. The author identifies several areas in need of improvement, and suggests that the inclusion of micro-teaching activities and more role models might help to strengthen pre-service teachers' pedagogical knowledge. Together with the broadly similar project by Grosbois and Sarre, this chapter points to the importance and effectiveness of online field experience and how it might be used to prepare pre-service teachers for technology-enhanced language teaching.

Chapter 11, "A TL-TPACK Model of CSL Pre-Service Teachers' Competencies in Online Instruction and Learners' Learning Proficiency," by Hsiu-Jen Cheng, is a case study of a Chinese-language teacher education program. Amid an increasing demand for Chinese instructors in the world, and the growing potential for technology use in Chinese-language learning, it is essential to examine an effective way to promote Chinese language teachers' technological knowledge. Having reviewed technology and Chinese teacher education in Taiwan, Cheng suggests that there has been insufficient training in instructional technology in that country, and proposes a new program based on TPACK and involving five research-oriented training strategies: practicum, technology-integrated course design, advisors, peer collaboration, and reflection. In the semester-long implementation of this training program, 11 pre-service teachers made notable progress, especially through its online practicum (with American learners of Chinese) and reflection components. Moreover, the survey results suggested that the training had improved the participant teachers' pedagogical knowledge (PK), technological content knowledge (TCK), and TPACK, but that while TCK and PK improved significantly, TPACK performance remained low. These results indicate the need for further strengthening of pre-service teachers' PCK performance, especially through ongoing professional development.

Chapter 12, "The Technology Segment of a Methods Course: Its Impact in Relation to Teaching Realities and Imagined Future Needs," by Jason D. Hendryx, is a case study of middle- and high-school Spanish teachers who were either on the verge of completing or had recently completed a modern languages education program in a U.S. college of education. A survey consisting of a small number of open-ended questions asked how a methods course the teachers had taken, which had technology training embedded, might have impacted on their teaching; what technologies they actually used and for what purposes; what essential characteristics future modern language educators should possess; and how the methods course they took could be improved. The methods course in question adopted the approach of "3Ds": directional ("the language being conveyed by the technology relevant to the students"), developmental ("teachers not allowing the limits of the technology […] to take away from the richness of the language being taught"), and decisive (teachers regulating "the pace of the technology" to "enhance their overall teaching effectiveness"). While the participant teachers appeared to have embraced the tenets of the 3D approach, they did not seem to remember them when the course content shifted to technology training: all tended to prioritize traditional tools (e.g., PowerPoint and online videos) or technologies that were immediately available to them (e.g., SMART boards and projectors), and rarely used emerging technologies that would allow students to work collaboratively or interactively. While no teacher seemed to give a direct indication of the impact of their training on their pattern of technology use, their imagined qualities and traits of modern language teachers showed that they were all aware of the critical import of technology in language learning, and the importance of keeping abreast of new technological developments and changing teaching environments. This chapter's findings shed light on the gap that has often been found between pre-service teacher preparation and teachers' actual teaching using technology (or teaching in general), and further points at the importance of professional development that takes into consideration teachers' opinions and evolving needs.

In Chapter 13, "Mentoring Teacher Candidates to Use Online Tools," Grisel M. Garcia Perez reports on a study that examined how the teaching assistants (TAs) of the Spanish program at the University of British Columbia's Okanagan Campus (UBCO) became effective users of technology through participation in a learning community. Guided by Wenger's (1998) work on community of practice, the training of the TAs was divided into several stages in which they attended workshops on how to use learning management system (LMS) as well as an online learning center (OLC) to handle course materials and provide students with individualized feedback. They also took a course in Spanish applied linguistics, in which they had opportunities to discuss issues arising from their use of technology to support student learning. During the 10-weeks training period, the TAs were asked to keep personal

Preface

logs to document their perceptions of using the LMS and OLC and the support they had received from the learning community. Based on analysis of these logs, all the TAs had experienced considerable positive learning effects. Particularly noteworthy was the TAs' increasingly active use of technology; in other words, there was a "feedback mechanism" embodied in the training that allowed the TAs to adjust how the technology should be used. Despite these positive effects, the author – who participated in the project as a trainer – noted a number of challenges. For example, due to budgetary limitations, the TAs worked for a relatively low number of hours, and this seemed to have placed constraints on their levels of interest in the professional development activities that were studied. In addition, the unavailability of certain technologies in physical classrooms seemed to have prevented the TAs from working closely with course instructors to bridge gaps between classroom instruction and online learning outside of the classroom. These findings contribute strongly to our understanding of the importance of TA training and collaboration between TAs and instructors in technology-assisted language learning in university-based foreign language programs.

Chapter 14, "Social Media and Foreign Language Teacher Education: Beliefs and Practices," by Jiahang Li, examines pre- and in-service foreign-language teachers' social media use during a teacher training program in U.S. Following a thorough review of the literature on the use of social media in teaching, Li points out the relative scarcity of research on teachers' beliefs and practices regarding the uses of social media in the field of foreign-language teacher education. Adopting a qualitative case-study design, the author interviewed an instructor from a teacher program three times during the summer of 2013, and triangulated the interview data via online observation and teaching material data. The instructor's teacher program was designed to improve the standards-based teaching experience of elementary-level Chinese-language teachers. Li found that, despite not purposefully including social media in her course design, the participant instructor spontaneously used YouTube, Facebook, and a Chinese social media site called QQ to engage learners, access and share information, connect formal and informal learning, and build a learning community. This may have been related to the instructor's positive beliefs about the use of social media for preparing foreign language teachers. Based on these findings, Li concludes that when teachers' beliefs about technology align well with their actual teaching practices, their instructional goals will be more likely to be achieved. Conversely, teachers' beliefs can be reinforced by their teaching practices. This chapter suggests that considerable further research is needed to explore the relationship between foreign-language educators' beliefs about technology and their teaching practices; and that more specific/targeted instructional plans are needed when integrating social media into foreign-language teacher education.

REFERENCES

American Council on the Teaching of Foreign Languages (ACTFL). (2013). *Program standards for the preparation of foreign language teachers (initial level – undergraduate & graduate) (for K-12 and secondary certification programs)*. Alexandria, VA: ACTFL.

Borg, S. (2006). *Teacher cognition and language education: Research and practice*. London: Continuum.

Corbin, J., & Strauss, A. (2008). *Basics of qualitative research: Techniques and procedures for developing grounded theory* (3rd ed.). Thousand Oaks, CA: Sage. doi:10.4135/9781452230153

Council of Chief State School Officers. (2011). *Interstate teacher assessment and support consortium (InTASC) model core teaching standards: A resource for state dialogue*. Washington, DC: Author.

Egbert, J., Huff, L., McNeil, L., Preuss, C., & Sellen, J. (2009). Pedagogy, process, and classroom context: Integrating teacher voice and experience into research on technology enhanced language learning. *Modern Language Journal*, *93*, 754–768. doi:10.1111/j.1540-4781.2009.00971.x

Ertmer, P. A. (1999). Addressing first- and second-order barriers to change: Strategies for technology integration. *Educational Technology Research and Development*, *47*(4), 47–61. doi:10.1007/BF02299597

Ertmer, P. A., Ottenbreit-Leftwich, A. T., Sadik, O., Sendurur, E., & Sendurur, P. (2012). Teacher beliefs and technology integration practices: A critical relationship. *Computers & Education*, *59*(2), 423–435. doi:10.1016/j.compedu.2012.02.001

Hubbard, P. (2008). CALL and the future of language teacher education. *CALICO Journal*, *25*, 175–188.

International Society for Technology in Education. (2007). *ISTE standards for teachers*. Retrieved from http://www.iste.org/docs/pdfs/20-14_ISTE_Standards-T_PDF.pdf

Koehler, M. J., & Mishra, P. (2005). What happens when teachers design educational technology? The development of technological pedagogical content knowledge. *Journal of Educational Computing Research*, *32*(2), 131–152. doi:10.2190/0EW7-01WB-BKHL-QDYV

Mishra, P., & Koehler, M. J. (2006). Technological pedagogical content knowledge: A framework for teacher knowledge. *Teachers College Record*, *108*(6), 1017–1054. doi:10.1111/j.1467-9620.2006.00684.x

Wenger, E. (1998). *Communities of practice: Learning, meaning, and identity*. Cambridge, UK: Cambridge University Press. doi:10.1017/CBO9780511803932

Zhao, Y., & Frank, K. (2003). Technology uses in schools: An ecological perspective. *American Educational Research Journal*, *40*(4), 807–840. doi:10.3102/00028312040004807

Zhao, Y., Puge, K., Sheldon, S., & Byers, J. L. (2002). Conditions for classroom technology innovations. *Teachers College Record*, *104*(3), 482–515. doi:10.1111/1467-9620.00170

Section 1
The Status Quo and Standards of Technology

Chapter 1
Technology Instruction in Language Teacher Education Programs

Yining Zhang
Michigan State University, USA

Matthew Deroo
Michigan State University, USA

ABSTRACT

It is important to examine how prospective teachers were prepared with integrating technology in their teaching. This study explored the integration of technology instruction among ten top world language teacher preparation programs in the United States. Data collection included document analysis of syllabi and interviews with program directors and instructors. The findings revealed that technology instruction were provided to language pre-service teachers through general technology courses, methods courses, and a series of technology-related courses infused throughout the entire program. In addition, technology courses organized a variety of approaches to enrich students' experiences with technology. We also generated four main themes to reflect some key elements in current technology instruction for pre-service teachers. The study enriches our knowledge of the current situation for how different world language teacher education programs prepare their pre-service teachers.

INTRODUCTION

The potential of teaching and learning foreign language with technology has been well documented in previous studies (e.g., Egbert, Paulus, & Nakamichi, 2002; Kessler, 2006; Warschauer & Meskill, 2000; Zhao, 2003). As Egbert et al. (2002) revealed, technologies can be beneficial for a variety of purposes, such as supporting experiential learning and practice through a number of modes, providing space to give feedback to learners, allowing for pair and group work, enhancing student achievement, granting access to authentic learning materials, facilitating greater interaction, promoting both exploratory and global

DOI: 10.4018/978-1-5225-0483-2.ch001

learning, and motivating learners. The effectiveness of technology was proved to be powerful and has positive effects on improving foreign language learning (Liu, Moore, Graham, & Lee, 2002; Zhao, 2003).

The promising future brought up by teaching foreign languages with technology calls for a strong and systematic training in technology for foreign language teachers (Fuchs & Akbar, 2013; Hubbard & Levy, 2006; Luke & Britten, 2007; Moeller & Park, 2003). Teachers play important roles in teaching with technology, as it is the teachers that "select the tools to support their teaching and determine what CALL (Computer Assisted Language Learning) applications language-learners are exposed to and how learners use them" (Hubbard, 2008, p. 176). Pre-service teachers with adequate technology skills are more likely to apply these skills in their future teaching (Moeller & Park, 2003).

Despite the important need to prepare foreign language teachers with knowledge and skills in teaching with technology, pre-service teachers are often not well-prepared to use technology in their teaching (Egbert et al., 2002; Hegelheimer, 2006). The literature suggests two possible reasons. First, there is insufficient instruction in teaching with technology as a part of many language teacher education programs (Hong, 2010; Hubbard, 2008; Kessler, 2006; Tondeur, van Braak, Sang, Voogt, Fisser, & Ottenbreit-Leftwich, 2011). Second, the quality of the technology-related courses in these programs is not satisfactory (Dooly, 2009; Dooly & Sadler, 2013; Egbert et al., 2002; Peters, 2006; Schmid & Hegelheimer, 2014). That is, due to the two aforementioned issues, there is a gap between what is offered in pre-service training for technology and teachers actual implementation of technology in everyday teaching. As a result, many language teachers are found to learn little or nothing in terms of using technology in language teaching after graduating from their program (Hubbard, 2008).

To help pre-service teachers better use technology in their instruction, it is important to examine how prospective teachers were prepared to integrate technology in their teaching (Goktas, Yildirim, & Yildirim, 2008). Our current study investigated how ten undergraduate foreign language teacher education programs across the United States prepared their pre-service teachers for the skills of integrating technology into their teaching.

The following research questions were used to guide our study:

1. What technology-related courses were provided at some of the top, world language teacher education programs? How do they compare and contrast with each other?
2. What learning activities were organized in these technology-related courses?
3. What are some key themes for technology instruction among different programs?

BACKGROUND

For most foreign language teacher education programs, there are three common approaches to delivering technology-related instruction: (1) through a *TECHNOLOGY* course; (2) through *LANGUAGE-TEACHING METHODS* courses; and (3) through a succession of technology-related coursework across the program.

The first approach for teacher candidates to receive training in technology is through taking an introductory course in educational technology. Generally, this applies to all education major students, regardless of their content concentration. An introductory-level technology course is important, as it equips students with some prerequisite technical skills that enable them to further integrate technology into their language teaching (Peters, 2006). In the past, many teacher education programs have attempted to develop such technology courses to improve pre-service teachers' technological skills (Polly, Mims,

Shepherd, & Inan, 2010). Students were expected to transfer what they have learned in these technology courses to their future teaching (Tondeur et al., 2011).

The second way to implement technology in teaching language is through language-teaching methods courses. In language based pre-service teacher training programs, methods courses are those that target expanding students' knowledge in second language acquisition theories, teaching strategies, and usage of teaching materials for teaching a foreign language; the methods courses also serve to foster students' abilities to design world languages curriculum (Huhn, 2012; Luke & Britten, 2007, Moeller & Park, 2003). The technology component in a methods class thus refers to the instruction of what technology means for language learning, how technology can be integrated to meet national standards for language teaching, and how to connect technology to language teaching methods (Luke & Britten, 2007). Technology was found to connect second language acquisition theory and pedagogy in method classes through motivating students' learning and building learning communities (Moeller & Park, 2003). Technology has become one of the prevailing topics covered in methods courses in foreign language teacher education programs (ACTFL, 2012). In addition, a number of studies advocated for offering methods courses that integrate technology components during the language teacher education program (Fuchs & Akbar, 2013; Hegelheimer, 2006; Dhonau, McAlpine, & Shrum, 2010). As Dhonau et al. (2010) stated, "use of technology has been often taught in a generic course in a teacher education program and may not represent best practices in foreign language instruction" (p. 85).

Several empirical studies have demonstrated how technology instruction was tied to language education. Wildner (1999), for instance, described how technology integration was carried out in pre-service language teacher education at the University of Northern Iowa through a technology course with an emphasis of teaching foreign languages. In this course, students had the opportunity to assess the use of technology in foreign language teaching. They also learned to explore various technologies to design foreign language lesson plans. There were six phases of learning: demonstration, exploration, critique, design, implementation, and reflection. Similarly, Moeller and Park (2003) investigated how technology use was modeled in methods courses at the University of Nebraska-Lincoln. During the two-semester methods courses, based on their knowledge of language acquisition, pre-service teachers were asked to design language-learning activities with the use of technology (i.e., PowerPoint or Web-page based listening task). They were also encouraged to develop their own webpage embedding lesson plans that reflected the Intentional Society for Technology in Education (ISTE)'s National Educational Technology Standards for teachers (NETS-T).

A third approach for allowing technology-related teaching experiences for pre-service teachers is by providing them with a series of technology-related coursework, instead of only focusing on any single course as a part of their teacher preparation program (Fuchs & Akbar, 2013; Luke & Britten, 2007). Luke and Britten (2007) introduced how technology can be integrated as a "cohesive programmatic component" (p. 254) throughout the entire teacher education program at a mid-major university in the Midwest. In this program, multiple methods courses were offered with aims to integrate technology into foreign language teaching. The first course introduced students to foreign language education. A second methods course emphasized instructional approaches, and allowed students to investigate how technology can be used in language classes. The third, and final methods course focused on developing students' technology skills in foreign language education, including designing web pages, making digital materials, and working with applications that are related to language teaching and instruction.

Table 1. A synthesis of learning activities and related technologies in language teacher education courses

Learning Activity	Technology	Authors
Lecture	E-textbook, online reading material	Hegelheimer (2006); Hubbard (2008); Rilling et al. (2005)
Classroom Discussion	*Blackboard* system, email	Hegelheimer (2006); Moeller & Park (2003); Rilling et al. (2005)
Presentation	Microsoft PowerPoint, digitized media, hyper studio	Moeller & Park (2003)
Learning Software	Basic teaching applications (i.e., word processing, spreadsheet, presentation tools), database management tools, video-making applications, research tools	Egbert et al. (2002); Hegelheimer (2006)
Creating a WebQuest	Web creator, photo editing	Egbert et al. (2002); Moeller & Park (2003)
Creating Webpage/Website	Personal website, blog	Egbert et al. (2002); Hegelheimer (2006); Rilling et al. (2005)
Developing Lesson Plans	Personal website, blog	Egbert et al. (2002)
Digital Project	Personal website, blog	Egbert et al. (2002); Hubbard (2008); Moeller & Park (2003); Rilling et al. (2005)
Electronic Conferencing System		Egbert et al. (2002); Rilling et al. (2005)
Digital Portfolio	Personal website, blog	Hubbard (2008); Moeller & Park (2003)

Learning Activities in Technology Courses

Exposing pre-service teachers to learning activities that make use of technology is beneficial. As pre-service teachers see this modeled for them in the instruction they receive, it allows them opportunities to integrate technology based activities in their future language teaching (Rilling et al., 2005). Hubbard (2008) summarized eight types of learning processes that were successful: (1) lecture/demonstration; (2) project-based; (3) situated learning; (4) reflective learning; (5) portfolio based; (6) mentor based; (7) communities of practice; and (8) self-directed learning. After examining previous studies about learning activities and related technologies for language educators (Egbert et al., 2002; Hegelheimer, 2006; Hubbard, 2008; Moeller & Park, 2003; Rilling et al., 2005), the researchers present a synthesis of them in Table 1. The wide range of these activities provided students with numerous chances for exploring different kinds of technology related to teaching. Technology offers venues for pre-service teachers to integrate language knowledge into their teaching.

Key Themes in Technology Instruction

While there are a variety of approaches for how teacher preparation programs assist their students in using technology in their teaching, a synthesis of the key themes found across programs provides insight for both theory and practice. In the area of general educational technology, Tondeur et al. (2011) conducted a study among 19 articles that described how pre-service teachers were prepared to integrate technology into their lessons. They found seven key themes that are common among these technology courses: (1) aligning theory and practice; (2) using teacher educators as role models; (3) reflecting on attitudes about the role of technology in education; (4) learning technology by design; (5) collaborating with peers; (6) scaffolding authentic technology experiences; and (7) moving from traditional assessment to continuous feedback.

Although a similar categorization of key themes related to teacher training in foreign language teaching is lacking, the review of previous empirical studies that showed approaches of technology integration in preparing for language teachers (e.g., Debski, 2006; Dooly, 2009; Dooly & Sadler, 2013; Egbert, 2006; Egbert et al., 2002; Fuchs & Akbar, 2013; Guichon & Hauck, 2011; Rilling et al., 2005; Schmid & Hegelheimer, 2014; van Olphen, 2007) are somewhat consistent with Tondeur et al. s' (2011) classification. Each of the themes described below has been proved to be effective in delivering technology education in foreign language teacher education programs.

Bridging Theory and Practice

Theoretical knowledge means the understanding of the underlying theories and content knowledge that are required and related to teaching and learning; while practical knowledge is the reflection of previous experiences as a language learner or language teacher (Rilling et al., 2005). As Debski (2006) showed in his study about theory and practice integration in a technology course, discussion of cultural stereotypes enabled students to develop a webpage introducing fun facts about Australia. Rilling et al. (2005) also found that by grounding practical technology experience in theoretical instruction, students were able to get access to authentic language materials and act more autonomously in their learning.

Situating Learning in Authentic Scenarios

Some researchers addressed the need to situate technology instruction for pre-service language teachers in authentic contexts, to provide them with opportunities to practice what they have learned in real school settings (Egbert et al., 2002; Fuchs & Akbar, 2013; Schmid & Hegelheimer, 2014). If technology instruction is not situated in authentic teaching scenarios, students' practice with technology may not be able to be directly changed (Erben, 1999). Egbert (2006), for instance, reported on two solutions to situate language teacher learning. The first approach is through a web-based course that focused on creating learning tasks in real-life situations. The second approach is through a series of online discussions on reality-based cases to help pre-service teachers handle different contexts that may occur in the future. Both approaches were demonstrated to successfully prepare language teachers in using technology in their instruction.

Developing Positive Attitude towards Technology

Teachers' attitudes towards using technology in teaching, and their confidence in using certain technologies, to a large degree, can decide whether teaching content can be efficiently transferred to students through technology (Dooly, 2009; Guichon & Hauck, 2011). Studies have shown that pre-service teachers' attitudes towards enacting technology in their teaching increased after taking technology instruction courses (Hong, 2010, Fuchs & Akbar, 2013). Dooly & Sadler (2013), for instance, found that pre-service teachers reporting increased confidence to use technology in teaching language, after working on a required virtual world software project.

Collaborating with In-Service Teachers and Peers

Meaningful learning with technology has been identified to by effective when learning occurs through cooperation with others (Jonassen, Howland, Marra, & Crismond, 2008). Schmid and Hegelheimer (2014) proposed a program that facilitated pre-service teachers' understanding of technology use in teaching through connection with in-service teachers. Workshops given to pre-service teachers by in-service teachers demonstrated how current teachers used technology in language teaching. Additionally, pre-service teachers had opportunities to work with in-service teachers through research projects. Other studies have shown students working collaboratively to build websites or work on class projects to be central for training pre-service language teachers (Debski, 2006; Rilling et al., 2005; van Olphen, 2007).

MAIN FOCUS OF THE CHAPTER

Given the review above, it is found that although past studies demonstrate evidence in the effective integration of technology for language teaching programs, most of these studies only focused on discussing one particular technology, course, or program (e.g., Debski, 2006; Egbert et al., 2002; Wildner, 1999). Although they have value for contributing unique approaches to teaching with technology, there is a lack of a comprehensive understanding for how technology instruction is carried out among different language teacher preparation programs. In addition, most previous studies have focused on graduate-level technology instruction in language teacher education programs (Egbert et al., 2002; Hubbard, 2008; Johnson, 2002; Kessler, 2006; Rilling, Dahlman, Dodson, Boyles & Pazvant, 2005), instead of at the undergraduate-level. To fill in this research gap, the objectives of the present study are threefold. First, we examine how technology instruction, including types of technology courses, learning activities in technology courses, and key themes of technology courses were positioned among some top, world-language teacher education programs in the United States. Second, we are interested in exploring the similarities and differences among each of these programs in order to provide a more comprehensive picture of the current situation of technology instruction in language teacher education programs. Third, we focus on examining undergraduate programs only, in order to enrich the current literature of technology instruction in language teaching.

METHODOLOGY

This research utilized content and discourse analysis (Merriam, 2009; Yin, 2009). Although content analysis can take two forms, quantitative and qualitative, given the size of our research sample, we primarily employed the later approach to identify key themes within and across the textual materials we analyzed instead of counting the number of times that certain words, phrases, or expressions occurred. We also interviewed three individuals associated with one of the teacher preparation programs that we analyzed to better understand their university's philosophy for preparing pre-service teachers to use technology in their teaching. Below is a description of the data collection and analysis utilized for this study.

Table 2. Ten Language teacher education programs selected for the study

University	Program	Technology-Related Course Syllabi	Program Requirement
Indiana University	World languages education (Chinese, French, German, Japanese, Latin, Russian, Spanish)	Yes	Yes
Arizona State University	Secondary education (English, French, German)	Yes	Yes
Iowa State University	Secondary education	Yes	Yes
Michigan State University	Secondary teaching	Yes	Yes
Ohio State University	Foreign language education		Yes
Pennsylvania State University	World language (French, German, Latin, Russian, Spanish)	Yes	Yes
University of Michigan	World language (French, German, Latin, Spanish)	Yes	Yes
University of Iowa	Teacher education (Russian, Chinese, French, German, Italian, Japanese, Latin, Spanish)	Yes	Yes
University of Virginia	Foreign language education (French, German, Latin, Spanish)	Yes	Yes
University of Georgia	World language education (French, German, Latin, Spanish)		Yes

Data Sources

Content analysis was conducted by examining college of education websites for programs ranked in the top 10 for secondary education by US News and World Report according to the magazine's 2014 report, and by investigating the top, foreign language programs at peer and aspirant universities affiliated with the large mid-western research based university from which the authors of the chapter were writing (specifically those not already included in the US News and World Report rankings). Course descriptions, program/degree requirements, and class syllabi were collected for coding in early 2015. In cases where the above information was not publically posted, contact was made with the university to gain access to the documents. We restricted data collection to universities that had undergraduate programs, excluding any program that only offered an MA in teaching. Our final data set included class syllabi, program/degree requirements, and course descriptions for ten different universities. These include: Indiana University, Arizona State University, Iowa State University, Michigan State University, Ohio State University, Pennsylvania State University, University of Michigan, University of Iowa, University of Virginia, and the University of Georgia (see Table 2).

Interviews were conducted with three individuals from one teacher preparation program, including the director of teacher preparation at the university, a subject area course leader for world languages instruction at the college, and a graduate student who provided instruction for a methods course. The interview with the program director was done over e-mail. The interview with the subject area leader was held via Skype, while the interview with the methods course instructor was held face to face. Both were audio-recorded.

Data Analysis

Data was analyzed using open coding techniques in which both researchers examined the course syllabi, program/degree requirements, and course descriptions for each of the universities. First, we independently read through the collected materials for a single university to establish codes. Then each researcher compared codes and combined them to develop a coding scheme for analyzing the rest of the textual documents. Following the first round of coding, both researchers compared codes for each of the ten schools to resolve differences. This process allowed us to revise and enrich our coding scheme. A second round of coding followed in which the researchers collectively collapsed codes to focus specifically on the ways in which each school's technology specific course was enacted-- including course objectives, course topics, class activities, method of instruction, and instructor's role in delivering instruction.

Each interview followed a semi-structured protocol. Following each interview, the researchers transcribed the audio recordings of the interview. Next, we compared what was stated in the interviews with the codes and themes that emerged from the content analysis to look for similarities and differences between the two methods of data collection. We recognize the limitations of our interviews, in the fact that they reflect the work and beliefs of individuals from just one of the ten universities that we examined, but we believe that the statements and claims they made serve to reinforce the ideas we encountered in our content analysis.

Researcherss memos were kept throughout the data collection process in order to monitor progress of the project and track the ideas and changes that took place as the data were analyzed.

RESULTS

The following findings represent how our analysis reveals an alignment/misalignment with the current literature regarding how to best prepare pre-service teachers to utilize technology in their world languages instruction.

Approaches to Deliver Technology-Related Instruction

To answer our first question regarding the types of technology-related courses provided by each world language program, we reviewed syllabi and program descriptions of each of these ten programs, and categorized technology-related instructions according to the type of each of the courses. Interview data also factored into our analysis.

Instruction through Technology Course

Nine out of ten (90%) programs offered general technology courses for pre-service teachers from all education majors to enroll. Titles of these courses vary from: *Instructions to Computer to Teachers, Using Computers in Education, Problem Solving with Digital Technology Apps, Principles and Practices of Digital Learning, Learning Technologies in the PK-6/7-12 Classroom, Learning/Teaching with Technology, Media & Tech Education, Teaching with Digital Technologies, Technology in the Classroom, and Instruction to Computer to Teachers.* Among these nine technology courses, six are listed as three credit classes, and five are required by the program. Regarding the timeline to take the course, five university

Table 3. Technology courses among ten teacher education programs

		Number	Proportion
Technology course	Offer a technology course	9	90%
	List the course as required	5	50%
Credits	3 credits	6	60%
	2 credits	1	10%
	1-3 credits	2	20%
Timeline	First year	3	30%
	Third year	2	20%
	Not specified	4	40%

programs have explicitly stated the required/recommended time to take the course. Three programs asked students to take the technology course at the beginning of their teacher education program, either in the first or second semester, while two programs explicitly required students to take the course during their third year (see Table 3 for a summary).

Instruction through Language-Teaching Methods Courses

A second approach to integrate technology into teaching is through language-teaching methods courses. That is, courses that are specifically designed for language teachers to provide knowledge in second language acquisition and teaching. From the data we collected, four out of ten programs (40%) explicitly stated that they have included technology components in their methods courses. These technology components were reflected in the format of assigning readings regarding teaching with technology, discussing the benefits/challenges associated with the use of technology, and designing lesson plans with technology.

The interview with an instructor from a methods course at one university revealed that some teacher educators believe it is important and helpful to integrate technology in methods courses, rather than in a general technology course. She expressed:

I think, um that it's helpful to have it integrated in the methods course. I think there are some applications of technology use and questions about methodological or philosophical approaches to technology use that are general enough, but there are many that are so much more valuable when you look at it within an existing content, within a content area framework. (course instructor - interview)

A similar opinion was also reflected by the subject area leader in the interview:

What I heard most subject area leaders thought we should integrate technology as a part of the content, like we don't spend time teaching technology per se we just integrate it (subject area leader - interview)

Instruction through a Succession of Technology-Related Coursework across the Program

The third approach of technology instruction in teacher education programs ensures technology instruction occurs over time. For example, several courses taken throughout the entire teacher-preparation program increase students understanding of how technology could be used in language teaching. From our data, three programs have explicitly shown this trend in their program descriptions. For example, one program offered four technology courses for students to take during the course of their undergraduate studies. The first two courses (*Learning Technologies in the PK-6 Classroom, and Learning Technologies in the 7-12 Classroom*) mainly focus on the introduction of educational technology, and the familiar uses of technology (software, multimedia, web page development, etc.). Students who have taken these two courses are then eligible to take a follow-up course *Pre-student Teaching Experience: Learning Technologies* with a primary focus of learning to teach with technologies in real school settings. Students who have taken the two introductory technology courses are also eligible to take another advanced level course, *Principles and Practices of Learning with Technology*, in which students will explore more use of learning technologies in K-12 classrooms and delve into issues and trends in classroom technology teaching.

In another program, the succession of taking technology-related courses is explicitly stated in the syllabus: "In the summer, we focused primarily on you as a learner with technology; in Fall, the focus shifted to the use of technology for student learning. This term, as you bring technology into your classroom during student teaching (or at least contemplate doing so), our focus is on "self as professional" as we examine potential involvement with educational technology beyond the classroom via professional publication, attendance at a professional conference, and the use of technology to connect with parents and organize your classroom."

For some, the integration of using technology in language teaching is viewed as something that cannot be achieved through only taking one technology course. As the program director stated in the interview:

Our program has a strong commitment to the idea that learning to teach is always about learning to teach some content. This means that preparing to use technology in teaching is always in service of teaching particular content and that, therefore, learning to teach with technology is not a separate course in our program, but is instead a set of ideas and practices infused throughout the program. (program director - interview)

Learning Activities

Table 4 presents a list of activities that were commonly found among technology courses for language pre-service teachers. We distributed them into nine categories based on the process described in the syllabi we collected. They are: Project, Unit/Lesson Plan, Presentation, Reading, Discussion, Reviewing, Portfolio, Tool Learning, and Conference.

Project

Project-based activity is one of the most common approaches for students to have a hands-on experience with technology integration in classroom teaching. Some of these projects include designing activities using Twitter, blogs, wiki, movie/animation, Mindmaps, Ebook, grant-proposal writing, digital storytelling, web-quests and so forth. The two most frequently used projects are Blog and Movie/Animation

Table 4. A summary of activities in technology courses among ten language teacher education programs

Activity	Detail
Project	Twitter project
	Blog project
	Movie/Animation project
	Wiki project
	Mindmaps project
	eBook project
	Digital Footprint project
	Grant proposal writing
	Digital story telling
	WebQuest project
Unit/Lesson Plan	
Presentation	
Reading	Articles related with technology in teaching
Discussion	Reading response
Reviewing	Teachers' websites
Portfolio	Digital portfolio
Tool/Software learning	Word processing software (e.g., Microsoft Word, Google Doc)
	Spreadsheet software (e.g., Microsoft Excel, Google Spreadsheet)
	Presentation software (e.g., Microsoft Powerpoint, Slideshare, Prezis)
	Web development software (e.g., Google Sites, WordPress, Weebly)
	Social media
	Screencast (e.g., Jing)
	Graphic design software
	Graphic organizer software
	Curriculum-specific software
	SMART board technology
	Digital video
	Mobile apps
	iPad as an alternative to whiteboard
	Cloud computing (e.g., Dropbox, Google Drive)
	Games and simulations
Conference	MACUL (Michigan Association of Computer Users and Learners)
	Virtual Conferences

project. For instance, in the course description of *Instruction to Computers for Teachers,* the instructor required all students to create a blog using WordPress and post articles related with their teaching interests. Before creating the site, the teacher provided students with examples of top education blogs for them to review. Students also had the chance to review exemplary websites from previous semesters.

In addition, it was required that each student make comments on their peers' blogs, in order to build a blogging community. In the Movie/Animation Project from the same course, students were asked to create an educational TED talk-style video that showcase their interests and passion about education in one specific area. Students were encouraged to clarify the audience of the talk, and help the audience understand why they should care about the topic. The teacher stated in the activity description that she hopes students can "demonstrate their ability to explore meaningful learning with technology with an emphasis on creativity and innovation."

Unit/Lesson Plan

The second most common activity is to allow students to design unit or lesson plans that are relevant to the teaching content, with the integration of technology. As stated in the course *Teaching with Technology,* "the mini-unit should consist of designing a mini-unit that appropriately incorporates several of the technologies that we have discussed this semester." For instance, in a methods course *Crafting Teaching Practices*, students were asked to design a technology-integrated activity that they planed to implement in the unit. In the unit plan, they should clearly state the content, language skills, modes of communication, structure, procedure, and learning objective of learning. In addition, the students should also describe the rationale for integrating technology in the activity. Particularly, in what ways does the technology use enhance learning, and what practical and ethical considerations need to be considered in designing the activity.

Reading

A number of technology courses (either general technology courses, or methods courses) have assigned readings for students to complete before class. However, we found that none of the courses in our data have a required technology textbook. Instead, all of these courses used online resources, book chapters, or journal articles as reading assignments. Readings were also found to be tightly connected to the topic of the week.

Discussion

There are two common approaches to organize class discussions. The first way is through online discussion. This approach was found to be conducted in a couple of courses. Students were often required to post their reflections to one question on a discussion forum before or after the class. Many courses also required students to make comments on each other's post. Another format for discussion takes place in the classroom. For example, in the course *Problem Solving with Digital Technology Apps*, each student was asked to lead the class discussion related to that week's reading. The student did not need to summarize all the readings. Rather, they were expected to bring questions, or show relevant materials such as video clips to elicit class discussion.

Reviewing: The activity of reviewing included (1) review a certain software/technology, to explore its benefits and costs, and whether the software or technology was appropriate for fulfilling the teaching purposes in the class; and (2) review of educational websites that described how technology was used in the classroom. For instance, in the course *Teaching/Learning with Technology*, students were asked to locate an article on the Internet in which the use of technology by a teacher is described in detail. The students were then asked to review the International Educational Technology Standards for Teachers, and choose at least one specific standard that they think best matched the use of technology in that article.

ePortfolio: Several courses also used ePortfolio websites to document students' progress during class. For example, in the course *Using Computers in Education*, Students were required to create their own ePortfolio website to showcase all of their work, including a home page with a welcome message and stated purpose for the website, an about me page that contained professional information, a gallery that includes at least five samples of their best work, a project page with details about several of the projects in the class, and a professional development page that provides reflections about their portfolio.

Tool/Software Learning: Students had opportunities for exploring and learning various types of tools, or software, that are related with teaching for many courses, especially during the introductory or general technology courses. These tools include: word processing software, spreadsheet software, presentation software, web development software, social media, screencast tools, graphic design software, graphic organizer software, curriculum-specific software, SMART board technology, digital video, mobile apps, iPad, cloud computing tools, and games/simulations. Some of the courses we encountered have lab sessions or in-class demonstrations to showcase the use of certain technologies. Others require students to self-explore the new tools before or after class, and integrate the technology into their assignments or class projects.

Presentation

Teachers in technology-related courses used presentations as opportunities for students to showcase their work, as well as receive feedback from others. For instance, the course *Using Computers in Education* asked students to present their ePortfolio at the end of the semester. A second and more innovative approach of presenting is through self-made videos. As in the course *Teaching/Learning with Technology*, students were asked to create a narrated video tour of their ePortfolio describing all the pages, features, and how they will use the website in their classroom to potential audiences, including future students, parents, and administrators. In doing so, the audience expands beyond peers and course instructors. In fact, since students posted the video on their websites, they actually presented their work to a larger population of individuals, and more importantly, to a real audience– future students, their parents, other teachers, and administrators.

Conferences

Two of the courses in our data specifically encouraged students to explore educational technology conferences. In one course, all students were required to attend the MACUL (Michigan Association of Computer Users and Learners) Conference. In another, students were encouraged to attend conferences virtually. That is, attending a conference through the exploration of conference websites, finding keynote speakers that are of interest to them, viewing keynote presentations online, and writing down their reflections.

Key Themes

After examining syllabi from both language-teaching methods courses and technology courses across ten different world language teacher preparation programs, we found that they share similarities that can be generalized into some main themes. These themes reflect the needs for pre-service teachers to understand theoretical-based information about integrating technology in teaching and learning, as well as knowing how to apply specific software-based or web-based applications in their future classroom teaching. We generated four themes to summarize the major goals that each of the courses intends to achieve.

Theme 1: Understanding Issues about Technology, Teaching, and Learning

A common theme across all technology-related courses syllabi relates to understanding theoretical issues around the use of technology in student learning process and classroom teaching. Under this theme, we establish four different topics or sub-themes that are common to many courses.

Theme 1.1: Analyzing and Discussing Social and Ethical Issues Related to Technology in Education

A number of courses have explicitly stated in their syllabi that one of the goals of the course is to analyze and discuss social and ethical issues related to the increased use of technology in education. In specific, copyright-related issues of digital content and using digital content in a fair and responsible manner were made as the focus of such discussions. For example, in the methods course *Crafting Teaching Practice*, students had discussions about ethical issues related to teaching language with technology, such as plagiarism, cheating, and intellectual property.

Theme 1.2: Understanding Current Teaching/Learning Trends and Research around Technologies

This topic was involved in almost all the courses in our collected data. Teachers usually assigned readings about current research for the use of technology in educational settings, in order to let their students have a better understanding about the role and scope of technology in supporting learning, especially to form concrete ideas about how technology can be used to enhance instruction. In one methods course, before starting to design lesson plans, teachers asked students to read articles about what educational technology is for language learning, and to think about factors that influence teachers to use technology in language teaching.

Theme 1.3: Understanding Technology Standards for Teachers

Several programs introduced students to technology standards that define teacher's roles and skills with the use of technology in teaching. The importance of understanding technology standards for language teachers also got confirmed in our interviews.

As is true for all of the teacher prep courses, our curriculum is accountable to State certification requirements, so as subject area leader, I have to make sure all of the state requirements are filled in. One of them is technology. (subject area leader - interview)

In particular, we are responsive to state and national standards that require teacher candidates to be able to use technology in their teaching in a variety of ways, including as a tool for instruction and assessment, as well as a management and organizational tool. (program director - interview)

In one methods course, the instructor required students to read a set of standards for world language education that were created by ACTFL (American Council on the Teaching of Foreign Languages) with the partnership for 21st Century Skills. Students then needed to design an activity under the use of one specific technology resource that incorporated the teaching standards. In our interview, the instructor explained the rationale for this:

There have been some brand new changes to the ACTFL standards that actually do kind of emphasize more multimedia learning and 21st century skills so we looked at those and the shifting standards... ACTFL partnered with an organization to set partner standards involving technology and second language learning. So design an activity that is aligned with both the 21st century skills also the current State world language standards and then integrate technology.... not just... tech is how I am presenting it or formatting it, but where the tech was integral to the learning and communication. (course instructor - interview)

Theme 1.4: Understanding Different Learning Styles and How Technology can meet the Needs of Diverse Learners

Students learn according to various learning styles and they also adopt different learning strategies in regulating their learning. Thus, another common theme among the technology-related courses is to first define and understand various types of learning styles and strategies, and then explain how technology can serve to support the needs of the diversity in the classroom.

The instructor also encouraged students to think about the diversity of learners, when trying to introduce technology in class. For example, the instructor pointed out:

New teachers might think they've got this great technology-based lesson plan and they might not always think of issues like.. what do I do with a student who doesn't have access at home... How do I define what is appropriate and inappropriate technology use? (course instructor - interview)

Theme 2: Integrating Technology into Teaching

The second common theme is the instruction of integrating technology in teaching. There are usually two ways for students to gain technology-related knowledge: through teacher's instruction and demonstration, or through self-exploration of the new technology. After learning the specific use of each type of technology, students were often required to design the class activity by implementing the technology that they had just learned in order to meet the specific teaching goals that are aimed at a targeted audience.

There are generally three types of sub-themes that were addressed among the data, under using implementing technology-based activities:

Theme 2.1: Being able to use Educational-Related Technologies Easily

Students have opportunities to learn and be familiar with a variety of technologies that are related to classroom teaching. Types of technologies can be found from Table 4, under the list of tool learning.

Theme 2.2: Being able to Choose the Most Appropriate Technology to Teach in Classrooms

In addition to the mastery of a wide selection of technologies, most syllabi emphasize the importance of knowing how to select the most appropriate technology for instructional purposes, given certain learning goals, audience, and strengths and weaknesses of various technologies.

Theme 2.3: Developing Lesson/Unit Plans that Integrate Technology to Content-Learning

A majority of courses paid great attention to encouraging students to integrate technology into their teaching through developing their own lesson/unit plans. Students are asked to demonstrate their knowledge of the learned technology through completion of these projects. Lesson/unit plan contains various components including lesson objectives, teaching materials, philosophy of teaching, teacher thinking, activities that reflect lesson objectives, and pre-service teachers need to organize the lesson/unit plan in a clear, efficient, and consistent format, as well as make it detail-oriented so that another teacher could follow the plan and teach the lesson with the way it meant to be taught. In specific, students need to design the lesson/unit plan with one particular type of technology or a combination of several technologies that have been discussed in class.

Theme 3: Developing Positive Attitudes and Greater Confidence towards Technology

Half of the courses explicitly address one of the learning goals for the course as helping pre-service teachers to develop positive attitudes toward approaching new technologies and building confidence in integrating technology to their content-based teaching. For the rest of the courses, although such a teaching goal is not explicitly stated in the syllabi, we also found that one of the course goals was to help these pre-service teachers to become confident in exploring educational technologies for teaching and learning purposes. All class activities and learning content across the data we have collected are about addressing issues in technology use and designing classroom technology-based lessons.

Theme 4: Documenting Professional Growth and Reflection

Finally, we found that one third of the syllabi aimed at encouraging students' professional growth as a teacher through using technology in different ways. First, an E-portfolio is a major way to document pre-service teachers' professional growth. For example, in a course which placed great emphasis on developing one's digital portfolio, the instructor believed that the e-portfolio not only presents students' work in the course as well as presents their vision of how they plan to use technology when they begin teaching, the digital portfolio is also designed to give the students an advantage when they begin their job search. The instructor encouraged students to continually update their work on the website, even beyond this course and after graduation, to reflect their online identities as professional teachers. Second, attending conferences is recommended by some teachers. One instructor believed that "through attending conferences, students are able to mingle with professionals in the field and learn about what work is being done at the present time". A third way is having guest speakers during class. In one class, *Teaching with Technology*, the instructor invited alumni guests visit to talk about making professional connections, teacher as entrepreneur, and building personal learning networks.

DISCUSSION

Technology Instruction in World Language Teacher Education Programs

The first objective of this study is to examine how technology instructions were delivered among ten world language teacher preparation programs in the country. From the literature review, we synthesized three types of technology-related courses in these programs: (1) through *TECHNOLOGY* courses; (2) *through LANGUAGE-TEACHING METHODS* courses; and (3) through a number of technology-related assignments and coursework across the program. The findings from document analysis revealed that a vast majority of the programs (90%) provided educational technology courses for pre-service teachers in world language programs, and many programs make the course required. The findings reflected a growing agreement of the use of technology in the improvement of teaching (Egbert et al., 2002). The large proportion of technology courses also supported previous findings about the large acceptance rate of technology integration instruction in many teacher education programs (Polly et al., 2010).

A second way of delivering technology instruction is through language-teaching methods courses. Previous studies have found a disconnection between technology integration and methods courses (e.g., Dhonau et al., 2010). In our study, we found less than half of the programs explicitly address technology integration in their methods courses. At the same time, we also found that the effectiveness and importance of using technology in language teaching has been acknowledged among those methods courses that included technology components. The finding supported the need of developing technology integration in methods course (e.g., Fuchs & Akbar, 2013; Hegelheimer, 2006; Huhn, 2012). Dhonau et al. (2010) pointed out that general technology course may not represent the real needs in foreign language instruction. Findings from the interview also confirmed this belief, as it is important for students to learn teaching with technology in a methods course, given the unique context of foreign language learning.

Besides the aforementioned two types of technology instruction, the recent trend for technology instruction proposes a shift away from an isolated course to a sequence of situated tech courses (Egbert et al., 2002; Luke & Britten, 2007). We found similar pattern of training world language teachers in our study. In one program, introductory technology courses mainly focused on getting students familiar with technology, and advanced courses aimed at developing students' abilities to design courses with technology use. Our interview with the program director at one university also revealed that language teacher education programs are treating technology not as a separate element in the program, rather, that it should be emphasized throughout the entire course of study.

Discovering Learning Activities in Technology Courses

The second objective of the study is to explore types of learning activities that were employed in technology courses in world language teacher education programs. Nine major types of activities were identified: Project, Unit/Lesson Plan, Presentation, Reading, Discussion, Reviewing, Portfolio, Tool Learning, and

Conferences. The variety of learning activities reflects the enrichment of the current technology instruction for language pre-service teachers.

Previous findings denote that learning activities such as lecture/demonstration, project, portfolio, classroom discussion, presentation, learning software, and website design, are combined by instructors in various ways to create an effective learning situation for pre-service language teachers (Egbert et al., 2002; Dhonau, 2010; Hegelheimer, 2006; Hubbard, 2008; Moeller & Park, 2003; Rilling et al., 2005). Findings from our study confirmed these types of activities as major ways for teacher to organize learning in class. These activities enable pre-service foreign language teachers to learn language, teaching, and technology skills in a combined manner (Luke & Britten, 2007).

Different from previous studies, we also found that attending technology-related conferences is becoming a requirement in some technology instruction courses. In one course, students were asked to attend a technology conference, and in another course, such attendance was required to be completed virtually. Regardless of the format, we believe this is becoming a new trend in technology instruction. Students are able to integrate knowledge learned in class with practical teaching (Rilling et al., 2005), both theoretically and practically.

Key Themes in Technology Courses

The third objective of this study is to identify some key themes among technology courses in world language teacher education programs. Previous studies demonstrated some common and effective key themes for training technology integration among language pre-service teachers, including (1) bridging theory and practice, (2) situating learning in authentic scenarios, (3) developing positive attitude towards technology, and (4) collaborating with in-service teachers and peers (Debski, 2006; Dooly, 2009; Dooly & Sadler, 2013; Egbert, 2006; Egbert et al., 2002; Fuchs & Akbar, 2013; Guichon & Hauck, 2011; Rilling et al., 2005; Schmid & Hegelheimer, 2014; van Olphen, 2007).

In this study, we found similar themes existing among most of the syllabi that we collected as well as in the interviews we conducted. We generalized theses into four main themes and some subthemes under the main themes. A summary of our findings are listed below:

Theme 1: Understanding issues about technologies, teaching, and learning.
1.1: Analyzing and discussing social and ethical issues related to technology in education.
1.2: Understanding current teaching/learning trends and research around technologies
1.3: Understanding technology standards for teachers.
1.4: Understanding different learning styles and how technology can meet the needs of diverse learners
Theme 2: Integrating technology into teaching
2.1: Being able to use educational-related technologies easily
2.2: Being able to choose the most appropriate technology to teach in classrooms.
2.3: Developing lesson/unit plans that integrate technology to content-learning
Theme 3: Developing positive attitudes and greater confidence towards technology.
Theme 4: Documenting professional growth and reflection

Our findings, on the one hand, support themes identified in previous studies. On the other, reveal a new theme that becomes prevalent in many technology-related courses: document professional growth and reflection for pre-service language teachers. Professional development in education is defined as activities that promote professional growth, and it helps teachers to keep updated with the newest and the most productive teaching practices (Mouza, 2003). Technology is regarded as a potential tool for teaching and learning to increase professional development opportunities (Lawless & Pellegrino, 2007). In this study, digital portfolios, conferences, and guest speakers are some major approaches to helping pre-service teachers with their professional growth. The use of digital technology makes it possible for pre-service teachers to document their professional development around real problems of practice. It also supports pre-service teachers to grow through communication and collaboration with peers, in-service teachers, and the whole community (Mouza, 2003).

FUTURE RESEARCH DIRECTIONS

We acknowledge that the data collected in the current study only represent a small sample of world language teacher education programs across the country. Thus, readers need to be cautious when trying to generalize our findings to a larger number of programs in the country. We recommend including more world language programs in future comparative studies. In addition, since no outcome data were available in our study, it is hard to judge the effectiveness or weakness of each approach in different programs. Future studies may examine the courses or approaches together with learning outcomes, in order to generate a better understanding of the effectiveness of these approaches.

CONCLUSION

In order to help pre-service language teachers to better use technology in their teaching, it is critical to examine how world language teacher education programs are preparing their pre-service teachers. This study explored the integration of technology instruction among the ten top world language teacher preparation programs in the country. Specifically, we found that technology instruction were provided to language pre-service teachers through general technology courses, language-teaching methods courses, and a series of technology-related courses infused throughout the entire program. In addition, we found that technology courses organized a variety of classes to enrich students' experiences with teaching under technology. We also generated four main themes to reflect some key elements in current technology instruction. They are: (1) Understanding issues about technologies, teaching, and learning; (2) Integrating technology into teaching; (3) Developing positive attitudes towards and greater confidence in use of technology; and (4) Documenting professional growth and reflection. The study enriches our knowledge of the current situation for how different world language teacher education programs prepare their pre-service teachers and calls for a more comprehensive understanding of such issues through comparative studies in the future.

REFERENCES

American Council on the Teaching of Foreign Languages. (2012). *ACTFL proficiency guidelines*. Alexandria, VA: Author.

Debski, R. (2006). Theory and practice in teaching project-oriented CALL. In P. Hubbard & M. Levy (Eds.), *Teacher education in CALL* (pp. 99–114). Amsterdam: John Benjamins. doi:10.1075/lllt.14.10deb

Dhonau, S., McAlpine, D. C., & Shrum, J. L. (2010). What is taught in the foreign language methods course? *NECTFL Review*, *66*, 73–95.

Dooly, M. (2009). New competencies in a new era? Examining the impact of a teacher training project. *ReCALL*, *21*(3), 352–369. doi:10.1017/S0958344009990085

Dooly, M., & Sadler, R. (2013). Filling in the gaps: Linking theory and practice through telecollaboration in teacher education. *ReCALL*, *25*(1), 4–29. doi:10.1017/S0958344012000237

Egbert, J. (2006). Learning in context: Situating language teacher learning in CALL. In P. Hubbard & M. Levy (Eds.), *Teacher education in CALL* (pp. 167–190). Amsterdam: John Benjamins. doi:10.1075/lllt.14.15egb

Egbert, J., Paulus, T. M., & Nakamichi, Y. (2002). The impact of CALL instruction on classroom computer use: A foundation for rethinking technology in teacher education. *Language Learning & Technology*, *6*(3), 108–126.

Erben, T. (1999). Constructing learning in a virtual immersion bath: LOTE teacher education through audiographics. In R. Debski & M. Levy (Eds.), *WORLDCALL: Global perspectives on computer-assisted language learning* (pp. 229–248). Lisse, The Netherlands: Swets & Zeitlinger Publishers.

Fuchs, C., & Akbar, F. S. (2013). Use of technology in an adult intensive English program: Benefits and challenges. *TESOL Quarterly*, *47*(1), 156–167. doi:10.1002/tesq.80

Goktas, Y., Yildirim, Z., & Yildirim, S. (2008). A review of ICT related courses in pre-service teacher education programs. *Asia Pacific Education Review*, *9*(2), 168–179. doi:10.1007/BF03026497

Guichon, N., & Hauck, M. (2011). Editorial: Teacher education research in CALL and CMC: More in demand than ever. *ReCALL*, *23*(03), 187–199. doi:10.1017/S0958344011000139

Hegelheimer, V. (2006). When the technology course is required. In P. Hubbard & M. Levy (Eds.), *Teacher education in CALL* (pp. 117–133). Amsterdam: John Benjamins. doi:10.1075/lllt.14.12heg

Hong, K. H. (2010). CALL teacher education as an impetus for L2 teachers in integrating technology. *ReCALL*, *22*(1), 53–69. doi:10.1017/S095834400999019X

Hubbard, P. (2008). CALL and the future of language teacher education. *CALICO Journal*, *25*(2), 175–188.

Hubbard, P., & Levy, M. (2006). The scope of CALL education. In P. Hubbard & M. Levy (Eds.), *Teacher education in CALL* (pp. 3–21). Amsterdam: John Benjamins. doi:10.1075/lllt.14.04hub

Huhn, C. (2012). In search of innovation: Research on effective models of foreign language teacher preparation. *Foreign Language Annals*, *45*(1), 163–183. doi:10.1111/j.1944-9720.2012.01184.x

Johnson, E. M. (2002). The role of computer-supported discussion for language teacher education: What do the students say? *CALICO Journal, 20*(1), 59–80.

Jonassen, D., Howland, J., Marra, R., & Crismond, D. (2008). *Meaningful learning with technology* (3rd ed.). Upper Saddle River, NJ: Pearson.

Kessler, G. (2006). Assessing CALL teacher training. In P. Hubbard & M. Levy (Eds.), *Teacher education in CALL* (pp. 23–42). Amsterdam: John Benjamins. doi:10.1075/lllt.14.05kes

Lawless, K. A., & Pellegrino, J. W. (2007). Professional development in integrating technology into teaching and learning: Knowns, unknowns, and ways to pursue better questions and answers. *Review of Educational Research, 77*(4), 575–614. doi:10.3102/0034654307309921

Liu, M., Moore, Z., Graham, L., & Lee, S. (2002). A look at the research on computer-based technology use in second language learning: A review of the literature from 1990–2000. *Journal of Research on Technology in Education, 34*(3), 250–273. doi:10.1080/15391523.2002.10782348

Luke, C. L., & Britten, J. S. (2007). The expanding role of technology in foreign language teacher education programs. *CALICO Journal, 24*(2), 253.

Merriam, S. B. (2009). *Qualitative research: A guide to design and implementation*. San Francisco, CA: Jossey-Bass.

Moeller, A. J., & Park, H. (2003). Foreign language teacher education and technology: Bridging the gap. *Faculty Publications: Department of Teaching, Learning and Teacher Education.* Retrieved from http://digitalcommons.unl.edu/teachlearnfacpub/175/

Mouza, C. (2002). Learning to teach with new technology: Implications for professional development. *Journal of Research on Computing in Education, 35*(2), 272–289.

Peters, M. (2006). Developing computer competencies for pre-service language teachers: Is one course enough? In P. Hubbard & M. Levy (Eds.), *Teacher education in CALL* (pp. 153–165). Amsterdam: John Benjamins. doi:10.1075/lllt.14.14pet

Polly, D., Mims, C., Shepherd, C. E., & Inan, F. (2010). Evidence of impact: Transforming teacher education with preparing tomorrow's teachers to teach with technology (PT3) grants. *Teaching and Teacher Education, 26*(4), 863–870. doi:10.1016/j.tate.2009.10.024

Rilling, S., Dahlman, A., Dodson, S., Boyles, C., & Pazvant, O. (2005). Connecting CALL theory and practice in preservice teacher education and beyond: Processes and products. *CALICO Journal, 22*(2), 213–235.

Schmid, E., & Hegelheimer, V. (2014). Collaborative research projects in the technology-enhanced language classroom: Pre-service and in-service teachers exchange knowledge about technology. *ReCALL, 26*(3), 315–332. doi:10.1017/S0958344014000135

Tondeur, J., Van Braak, J., Sang, G., Voogt, J., Fisser, P., & Ottenbreit-Leftwich, A. (2011). Preparing pre-service teachers to integrate technology in education: A synthesis of qualitative evidence. *Computers & Education, 59*(1), 134–144. doi:10.1016/j.compedu.2011.10.009

van Olphen, M. (2007). Digital portfolios: Balancing the academic and professional needs of world language teacher candidates. In M. Kassen, R. Lavine, K. Murphy-Judy, & M. Peters (Eds.), *Preparing and developing technology-proficient L2 teachers* (pp. 265–294). San Marcos, TX: CALICO.

Warschauer, M., & Meskill, C. (2000). Technology and second language learning. In J. Rosenthal (Ed.), *Handbook of undergraduate second language education* (pp. 303–318). Mahwah, New Jersey: Lawrence Erlbaum.

Wildner, S. (1999). Technology integration into preservice foreign language teacher education programs. *CALICO Journal, 17*(2), 223–250.

Yin, R. (2009). *Case study research: Design and methods* (5th ed.). Los Angeles, CA: Sage.

Zhao, Y. (2003). Recent developments in technology and language learning: A literature review and meta-analysis. *CALICO Journal, 21*(1), 7–27.

KEY TERMS AND DEFINITIONS

ePortofolio: A website/blog that a student creates to showcase his/her work and progress.

Language-Teaching Methods Course: A course that teaches students' knowledge about second-language learning theories and help them with designing their own language-teaching classes.

Situative Learning: Learning knowledge that is related with students' everyday life.

Chapter 2
EFL Teachers' Knowledge of Technology in China:
Issues and Challenges

Yanjiang Teng
Michigan State University, USA

ABSTRACT

Through the lens of teachers of English as a Foreign Language (EFL) in China, this chapter aims to examine what knowledge of technology EFL teachers at all levels possess and how they apply their technological knowledge in teaching practice. The reviewed literature indicated that most EFL teachers hold positive attitudes towards technology. However, there still exists a gap between the curriculum requirement and the reality in terms of technological pedagogy in EFL teaching context. EFL teachers' use of technology in teaching varies in terms of personal preferences, school levels and locations, and administrative support. In addition, this review revealed that several factors influence EFL teachers' integration of technology into their practice and some challenges are still on the way: 1) EFL teachers' knowledge of technology is insufficient; 2) Lack of resources for schools and teachers at less developed areas, and 3) Lack of specific support for EFL teachers' technological needs.

INTRODUCTION

Nowadays, Information and Communication Technologies (ICT) are evolving at an astonishing speed which has dramatically revolutionized almost every aspect of our lives. In educational settings, technology offers new ways of teaching and learning and has the potential to enhance students' learning outcome (Cabanatan, 2003; Felix, 2005; Kozma & Anderson, 2002). Scholars hold that ICT is increasingly playing a significant role in school curriculum reform across the nations (Kozma & Anderson, 2002; Li & Walsh, 2011; Li, 2014; Pelgrum, 2001).

Internationally, from 1990s, ICT has been regarded as an indispensable literacy skill for global competition (Tsui &Tollefson, 2007) and as the catalyst to promote educational reform and development (Cabanatan, 2003; Li, 2014). In 1996, the U.S. government issued its first National Educational Tech-

DOI: 10.4018/978-1-5225-0483-2.ch002

nology Plan (NETP, 1996; revised version on 2000, 2004, 2010, US Department of Education, 2010) aiming at getting American students ready for the 21st century through training and supporting teachers and their students with computer and Internet access. Similarly, the U.S. National Educational Technology Standards (NETS), also known as International Standards for Technology in Education (ISTE) were released in 1998 (for students), in 2000 (for teachers), and in 2002 (for administrators) respectively. In 1998, the ICT Standards for UK teachers was issued (Office for Standards in Education, 1998), aiming at encouraging teachers to demonstrate their ICT skills in a wide range of contexts. In the same vein, the Japanese government also issued the Science and Technology Basic Plan (1996-2000, 2001-2005) to increase technology competitiveness in the world (Cabinet Decision, Japan, 2005). Since 2000, the Australia government decided to increase teachers' budget on ICT training. All these efforts by policymakers and educational experts believe that ICT has a direct impact on the nations' competiveness and economic growth, and the use of ICT can increase the effectiveness of teachers' teaching and students' learning compared with the traditional way of instruction (Kozma & Anderson, 2002). ICT integrated teaching in this chapter is defined as a process of using any ICT tools to enhance teaching and facilitate students' knowledge construction.

Research studies suggest that, the benefits of ICT integrated teaching in English as a Foreign Language (EFL) settings lie in its potential to engage learners and support their autonomous learning (Chambers & Bax, 2006; Chapelle, 2003; Hu & McGrath, 2011; Li & Walsh, 2011), provide EFL teaching with authentic language environment (Xie, 2005), and establish new roles of teachers and learners (Stepp-Greany, 2002). Overall, ICT can benefit both language teachers and learners by creating a more interactive language classroom, motivating learners, and providing authentic language input from real life situations (Warschauer & Healey, 1998). On the other hand, the successful realization of ICT integrated teaching depends on teachers' technology knowledge (Cabanatan, 2003; Gu, 2012); teachers' technological pedagogical content knowledge (TPACK; Mishra & Koehler, 2006), which involves teachers' competence to combine knowledge of technology, pedagogy, and content; and teachers' attitudes or beliefs towards ICT integration into the curriculum (Bitner & Bitner, 2002). In reality, EFL teachers still report that they are slow to adopt ICT integrated teaching productively in their practice (Li & Walsh, 2011; Li, 2014). Therefore, it's critically important to understand what technology knowledge EFL teachers possess, how they use technology in their practice, and what influential factors affect their applications. In this chapter, teachers' technology knowledge refers to the knowledge necessary for teachers to conduct ICT integrated teaching to facilitate students' learning. This requires teachers to have the competence to integrate different methods, approaches, and pedagogies, together with the medium of technology, to improve teaching and enhance learning effectively.

Similarly, China also witnesses its advancement in technology and its application in education. China's steady rise in the world economy over the past few decades has brought the country more interactive opportunities with the outside world. English, a medium of international communication, has received more attention from the Chinese government and its citizens. In China, English is one of the compulsory subjects at all levels of school curricula. The update of the New English Curriculum (NEC; Ministry of Education, 2001, 2012) in elementary and secondary schools is a result of such corresponding thrust. At the higher education level, in 2004 (Revised version in 2007), Chinese Ministry of Education released the College English Curriculum Requirements (CECR, 2007) in an effort to improve non-English majors' communicative language skills, particularly oral communication competence. Among all these efforts to innovate EFL teaching efficacy in NEC and CECR, the use of technology in EFL teaching is being especially highlighted in these curriculum reforms. Both curricula require the EFL teachers to possess the technology knowledge to obtain information and resources online, design courseware and carry out ICT integrated teaching in the classroom.

Under such curriculum reform context, there is a need to examine EFL teachers' technology knowledge and practice in China, particularly focusing on how EFL teachers address their pedagogical needs. Thus, this chapter takes the EFL teachers in China as a case to examine how teachers' technology knowledge are mandated at different levels of schools; what kind of knowledge EFL teachers is needed for conducting ICT integrated teaching; and what factors and challenges EFL teachers encounter in the process of integrating technology into their teaching.

CHINA'S EDUCATION TECHNOLOGY AND EFL TEACHING CONTEXT

As many other countries, Chinese government acknowledges that technology renovation is the key to China's economic growth in the 21st century, and the integration of ICT into teaching is a striking feature of the educational landscape in China (Li & Walsh, 2011). "Education informatization is viewed as a driving force for modernization and quality education by the Ministry of Education" (Li & Ni, 2011, p.70). As far as the teachers' technology knowledge is concerned, Song (2004, pp. 75-76) held that teachers' technology knowledge training had undergone three phases of development in China. (1) The Initial Stage (1984-1995): Immediately after the implementation of the opening up policy in the early 1980s, Chinese government realized there was an urgent demand for talents with modern technological skills. Chinese officials held that the country's computer literacy should start from the infants, which expressed the country's determination in technology innovation. (2) The Development Stage (1996-2005): In 1996, the Continuing Education Regulations for Elementary and Secondary School Teachers was issued by Ministry of Education (MOE). In 1999, the Action Plan for Invigorating Education Towards the 21st Century was released. According to these policies, teachers need to possess the basic ICT skills for educational modernization. 3) The Comprehensive Development Stage (2005 afterward): From 2005 onward, China has witnessed its easy access to educational technology to its citizens. The National ICT Development Strategy (2006–2020) and China Educational Informatization Plan (2011-2020) were issued in 2006 and 2012 respectively. These documents realize that ICT has a dramatic impact on educational development reform by providing schools with technology-enhanced learning environments. All these policy documents acknowledge the power of educational technology and encourage the use of ICT for educational innovation and modernization.

As stated by Li (2014), the social-cultural context plays a key role in influencing teachers' use of technology. In addition to the macro level policies on the promotion of ICT in education, the examination system is another factor needs to be taken into account. In China, high stakes test is one of the striking features of its educational system. Both students and teachers are under great pressure to prepare for the examinations of all kinds at different levels. The EFL classes are typically characterized by "teacher-centered, textbook-directed, and exam-oriented" (Li, 2014, p. 108). The EFL classes are usually structured in the "presentation-practice-production" format in a large-group class (Thomas, 2015, p. 4). Students receive their language input from the teachers and the textbooks with teachers' explicit linguistic knowledge instruction. Meaning-focused instruction and practice is limited and students feel inadequate in communication competence. In other words, students acquire the language in a decontextualized way and have little confidence in speaking (Peng & He, 2007). In regard to the use of technology, PowerPoint is the most popular form of technology used in EFL context (Li, 2014). In summary, the EFL teachers' use of technology is monotonous, mostly for the instructional delivery purpose under the traditional teacher-dominated model (Li, 2014; Li & Ni, 2011).

The English curriculum reforms in China at all levels of schools is a response to this low efficiency in teaching and learning (Li, 2014; Mao, 2007). The core principle in these curriculum reforms is to encourage student-centered, communication-based classroom instruction with the aim to enhance students' communicative skills in real life. This requires EFL teachers to focus more on students' "participatory and collaborative learning" (Li, 2014, p. 108) than on too much practice on linguistic forms. In addition to the pedagogical shift requirement in these new curricula, the integration of ICT into EFL teaching pedagogy is another point being highlighted in these documents: EFL teachers should possess some ICT knowledge and make full use of such knowledge to improve students' learning efficiency (MOE, 2012); EFL teachers should adopt the ICT integrated teaching to create a student-centered learning environment so as to facilitate students' independent learning (CECR, 2007). In particular, the new teaching pedagogy mandated by CECR is not only a change in pedagogy but also a renovation in teaching philosophy: teachers should explore new teaching pedagogy with the support of ICT.

EFL TEACHERS' TECHNOLOGY KNOWLEDGE

As discussed above, ICT integrated teaching can benefit both teachers' teaching and students' learning despite its challenges. This section examines what kind of technology knowledge an EFL teacher needs to possess for working at different levels of schools in terms of pre-service teacher and in-service teachers. The rationale to focus on these two categories of teachers is to investigate what technology knowledge EFL pre-service teachers get from the teacher education program; does it get to align with the new mandatory curriculum requirement? What technology knowledge do in-service teachers possess in practice, and what professional development opportunities do in-service teachers have for technology knowledge enhancement? For the first category, due to the scope of this chapter, this chapter only focuses on the four-year teacher education program preparing elementary and secondary school teachers. For the second category, for the convenience of discussion, this chapter focuses on EFL teachers at schools and universities to demonstrate their teaching practice.

Pre-Service Teachers' Technology Knowledge

Generally, normal universities and teachers' colleges in China are responsible for the preparation of teachers at the elementary and secondary schools in the country. Students who are in the department of foreign languages and literature with English education as their majors are expected to work as EFL teachers after graduation. These institutions offer four-year teacher education programs which lead to a bachelor degree. Currently, the majority of the elementary and secondary school teachers obtain their academic qualifications from such programs or their equivalents.

Most EFL pre-service teachers get their training about technological and pedagogical knowledge from these teacher education programs. By examining the teacher education curriculum and courses offered to pre-service teachers, we can get what knowledge pre-service teachers have acquired in the program. Without a thorough and coherent examination of the teacher preparation curriculum, little profound change can take place in qualified teacher supply. In fact, some scholars (Anderson & Nunan, 2003; Marinova-Todd, Marshall & Snow, 2001) asserted that a high level of proficiency in the computer application is desirable for EFL pre-service teacher preparation.

Based on the scholarly work done so far, the situation of EFL pre-service teachers' technology knowledge is not satisfactory in China. Zhong, Wang, Huang, and Shi (2003) held that courses related to ICT in EFL pre-service teacher education curriculum are "marginalized": there are limited or no courses specialized in ICT integrated teaching based on an investigation of the course components of EFL teacher education programs (Wu, 2002). In the curriculum, there are a few information and technology courses; however, these technology courses are some general courses, such as Public Computer Basics, Computer Application, and Internet Technology and Educational Technology. All these courses are technology oriented without any connection to EFL teaching context. In response to this limited knowledge of technology in EFL teacher education programs, some universities began to add a few courses on technology and EFL teaching; however, technology courses related to language teaching within EFL context are still peripheral (Zhong et al., 2003). This resonated with Yang, Zhang and Yi's (2004) study: Based on a survey of over 3,000 elementary and secondary school teachers in ten provinces across China, that study revealed that the technology courses in the teacher education programs could not meet the ICT needs at elementary and secondary schools. There is still a gap between technology and pedagogical practice, and the practice of TPACK in EFL pre-service teacher education is still rare.

In-Service Teachers' Technology Knowledge

The updated New English Curriculum (MOE, 2012) and CECR (2007) require EFL teachers to possess adequate technological knowledge for their teaching. In fact, ICT integrated teaching can engage students to learn the content, improve students' motivation, develop their associative thinking and make content becomes more dynamic and accessible to students (Kozma & Anderson, 2002). On the other hand, as Xie (2005) asserted, ICT integrated teaching also poses challenges for EFL teachers: teachers should not only have the capacity to get information, but also have the ability to creatively deal with the information in their teaching. In addition, at the current information age, the ICT has changed the "role" of teachers and students (Xie, 2005): teachers are no longer the sole source of knowledge for students; students might also bring a good answer to a question with the support of the technology. Then, what factors might affect the implementation of ICT integrated teaching in EFL context? Based on scholars' discussion (Bruce, 2004; Cabanatan, 2007; Li, 2014; Xie, 2005), the following aspects need to be taken into consideration, namely, EFL teachers' attitudes and beliefs, examination-oriented context, and the reality of unbalanced regional development.

EFL Teachers' Attitudes and Beliefs on ICT Integrated Teaching

Teachers' beliefs about technology play a significant role in their use of technology. EEL teachers' attitudes and beliefs towards technology vary according to school contexts and teachers' technology knowledge. Li (2014) held that teachers' positive attitude towards ICT integrated teaching will result in active technology use. The more active use of ICT, the more confident and competent teachers will become. At present, studies on Chinese EFL teachers' attitudes or beliefs on technology revealed that the majority of teachers hold positive attitudes towards ICT integrated teaching. According to He, Puakpong and Lian (2015), most teachers in her study were in favor of using technology in EFL teaching, a study conducted in Guizhou province, a less developed region in southwest China, with 340 EFL teachers from the ethnical minority rural areas. This study revealed that 73.8% of the participants viewed the role of ICT in EFL teaching as "assistive" and 81% of them liked to use technology in teaching because they could add notes to the courseware for recycling use in different classes.

On the other hand, some EFL teachers hold negative attitudes or beliefs towards technology use. Cao, Hu, Li and Xu's (2015) study examined the use of online resources among elementary and secondary EFL teachers, based on a survey of 510 participants and 17 semi-structured interviews at a national teacher training workshop on EFL teachers' ICT knowledge in Beijing where participants are EFL teachers from Beijing, Shandong, and Guangdong provinces, which represent the most developed areas in the country. Their study indicated that most EFL teachers have low motivations in applying technology to their teaching due to the following two reasons: 1) The use of technology is a passive reaction to fulfill the requirement of the administrations or for a higher job title promotion; and 2) Teachers have to demonstrate some technology knowledge in teaching quality contest. In contrast, teachers with high motivations on technology application in the classroom are few. Then what factors affect teachers' attitudes and beliefs on the use of technology in their practice? According to Cao et al. (2015), high-stakes test pressure is the most dominant factor to prevent teachers' application of technology in practice. This test pressure is from the stakeholders of the society: school administrators, students, parents, and peers. All these people value the test score more than the teaching paradigm shift. This will be the topic of discussion in the next subsection.

Examination and ICT Integrated Teaching

As discussed above, the examination is a common practice in China that all stakeholders regard test score as the top priority in both teachers' evaluation and student's performance. It's normal to see students doing "large amounts of exercises as examination rehearsals in a regular classroom" (He et al., 2015, p. 197). This practice prevents some teachers from adopting some new teaching approaches, including the ICT integrated teaching, for fear of grade downfall.

At universities, for a long time, the College English teaching profession has been criticized as fairly time-consuming and painstaking learning with low efficiency (Mao, 2007). Teachers mostly adopt the teacher-led spoon-feeding method, and students are confined to stay on their seats listening passively. In other words, the time-consuming but low-efficient situation is typical of EFL teaching and learning in China (Hu & McGrath, 2011).

As stated in the CECR (2007), in view of the marked increase in student enrollments and the relatively limited resources, universities should remold the existing teacher-centered pattern of language teaching by introducing new teaching models with the help of multimedia and network technology. In reality, according to Mao (2007), some EFL teachers still treat computers the same as a tape recorder or a video player. About half of EFL teachers hold the perceptions that ICT integrated teaching works well for listening and speaking practice whereas reading and writing tasks might work well through the traditional classroom practice. Under such conception, some teachers think that ICT integrated teaching is only a duplicate of the traditional classroom instruction: Teacher-dominated and test-oriented are still the norm; Most students are busy for the national English proficiency test, namely the Band IV and Band VI College English Test, which is a mandatory requirement for getting the diploma in some universities. In reality, both teacher and students are under too much pressure on preparing for the test, which might affect teachers' enthusiasm to conduct any new teaching approach (Dai & Wang, 2012; Gu, 2012; Mao, 2007).

Inequity in ICT Integrated Teaching

There is a great divide concerning EFL teachers' technology knowledge across the country. Teachers in urban areas are more confident in using technology than those from rural and less developed regions. Zhai (2008) studied EFL teachers' use of technology in the elementary and secondary schools and found that EFL teachers' technology knowledge in rural areas was generally low: 1) Although most EFL teachers hold positive attitudes toward ICT; in reality, they still have difficulty in accessing to information resources. 2) EFL teachers' knowledge of modern information in rural areas was limited, and only about 30% of the teachers had a sense of ICT knowledge. About 80% of the rural English teachers were female teachers and they didn't have very good sense of using the computer. Compared with male English teachers, female teachers' knowledge on computer, multimedia and network was significantly limited. As far as the age is concerned, newly employed teachers within their first five years were slightly better than some of the middle-aged teachers (over ten years of teaching experiences) in mastering ICT knowledge, particularly for those who are over 40 years old (He et al., 2015). 3) Teachers lacked ICT curriculum integration capability.

In the same vein, Jiao and Wei (2012) investigated the elementary and secondary EFL teachers' ICT knowledge in Hebei province of northern China, a less developed region in China. The study, based on a survey of 192 participants from the rural areas, is designed to examine participants' ICT awareness and information collection competence. The findings indicated 55. 2% of the teachers were not regular Internet users at the class preparation stage. Despite most teachers had the consciousness of Internet resources, their searching capability was relatively poor. Only 33.8% of teachers could use two or more Internet searching methods. For example, 64.6% of teachers couldn't determine keywords and 11.53% of teachers often had unrelated keywords entered. In short, at present, EFL teachers were not well prepared to use ICT in their teaching.

As discussed above, multiple factors might affect the use of technology in EFL teaching. In addition to policy, test-oriented context, teachers' attitudes and beliefs, limited computer facilities, other factors such as less administrative support, and teachers' lack of confidence in computer competency might all play a role. All these above factors seem to significantly affect EFL teachers' decisions on the use of ICT integrated teaching. This indicates the necessity of professional development for EFL teachers' ICT knowledge enhancement.

TEACHERS' KNOWLEDGE OF TECHNOLOGY IN PROFESSIONAL DEVELOPMENTS

The desired ICT integrated teaching depends on the content, teachers, and the environment (Jiao & Wei, 2012). In recent years, EFL teachers have showed high enthusiasm towards ICT training. In reality, the actual training results are far from teachers' expectations (Zhong et.al, 2003). Some people think that technology is a pre-vocational issue; others think EFL teachers suffer from phobias in the use of multimedia technology in their teaching (Pelgrum, 2001; Peng & He, 2007). Effective EFL teacher training in ICT need more attention from all stakeholders.

Studies demonstrate that many EFL teachers consider computer technology as a useful teaching tool that can enhance ways of teaching by offering students a variety of language input and expanding students' learning experiences in real and authentic contexts (Zhang & Niu, 2009; Zhao. 2013).

However, at the same time, Zhang and Niu (2009) also claimed that the practical difficulties in implementing this approach into their teaching were due to lack of professional knowledge on computer skills. Through questionnaire and interview protocol, Zhao's (2013) study on university EFL teachers' use of technology revealed that ICT resources including software and hardware, effective professional development, sufficient time, and technical support need to be provided to EFL teachers (Bingimlas, 2009; Watson, 2001).

More professional development opportunities are essential to promote teachers' competence and confidence. Through classroom observations and follow-up interviews with eight secondary EFL teachers in Beijing, Li (2014) conducted a case study to explore how ICT integrated teaching was practiced and what factors influenced teachers' technology use in the classrooms. The findings indicated that PowerPoint was the top one technological application; and "sociocultural contexts, teachers' beliefs, access to resources, and technology competence and confidence" (p. 105), are the four major factors affecting teachers' application of technology in the classroom. She further suggested that more professional development on combining teachers' ICT needs and pedagogical beliefs are needed. However, some EFL teachers still doubt the effectiveness of such workshops. As discussed by some scholars (Yang et al., 2004; Zhong et al., 2003), most ICT workshops organized by the school districts were in a top-down and lecture-based format. After the intense training in a few days usually over the weekend, EFL teachers still had some issues unsolved. Yang et al. (2004) did a survey on teachers' feedback on an ICT workshop from 53 elementary and secondary schools of Changsha city in southern China. The findings indicated that more than 56% of the participants believed that the present ICT training schedule was too tight and the participants had no time to absorb the content; 45% of the teachers thought that the training was too much theory-oriented and had little connection with their teaching practice, and over 31% of the teachers held that their takeaway from the training was below average. Cao et al.'s (2015) study got the similar findings that the effectiveness of the current teacher' professional development was very low: 1) The training was organized in a top-down approach, promoting a uniform mode of operation; 2) The training was carried out in a lecture-based, theory-oriented way with limited real practice time; and 3) the training lacks needs analysis from EFL teachers, emphasizing too much on the use of computer software, far away from EFL teaching context. As Dai and Wang (2012) stated, professional developments in the areas of such as learner-centered class design, learner autonomy, and teachers' role are greatly needed for EFL teachers.

As we know, in-service training workshops aim to improve EFL teachers' ICT competence so that teachers learn to use educational software and enhance their teaching effectively. However, technical training cannot automatically translate the ICT knowledge into real classroom teaching practice. On the contrary, this training may even increase EFL teachers' technical anxiety and restlessness. In fact, after several rounds of training many teachers still felt a very limited impact on their teaching pedagogy change in terms of class activity design and resource development (Zhong et al., 2003). As He, Puakpong and Lian (2015) mentioned, the difficulty of most Chinese EFL teachers encounter is not on how to use technology itself but on how to integrate the technology into pedagogy effectively. Thus, a situated training integrated with teachers' perspectives is highly needed. That is training in conditions close to teachers' actual teaching contexts with examples featuring real learners and real tasks, and the inclusion of teachers' real needs on technological and pedagogical issues.

CHALLENGES ON EFL TEACHERS' APPLICATION OF TECHNOLOGY INTO CLASSROOM

Advances in technology bring both opportunities and challenges to EFL teachers. On the one hand, as discussed above, ICT integrated teaching can improve teaching efficiency. On the other hand, EFL teachers still encounter many challenges to carry out this means of teaching in their practice. As Warschauer and Healey (1998) argued, teachers' adaptation of ICT integrated teaching is usually impacted by: (1) teachers' own knowledge and skills (Pelgrum, 2001; Snoeyink & Ertmer, 2001); (2) teachers' attitudes towards ICT integrated teaching (Atkins & Vasu, 2000); (3) profession development opportunities and technical support (Pelgrum, 2001); and (4) school culture and support from administrators. In the same vein, the current Chinese EFL teachers encounter similar challenges in the implementation of ICT integrated teaching at different levels of schools. This section discusses what challenges Chinese EFL teachers have in their practice and at the same time some recommendations are made for improvement.

(1) EFL teachers' technology knowledge is insufficient. As discussed above, pre-service EFL teachers' training on technology in the teacher education program is limited and unsystematic. Therefore, EFL teachers feel unconfident in applying technology knowledge, together with theories on second language acquisition, into their teaching. Today's technologies are advancing at an astonishing speed and application of technologies into education is growing at high rate. For example, teachers might never hear of the new terminologies such as flipped classroom, big data, or MOOCs (Massive Open Online Courses). Without adequate foundational technology knowledge, some teachers might fear these new technologies and get isolated from the teaching community in a digital age. Under these circumstances, the teacher education programs at universities need to pay more attention to the integration of technology with pedagogy, and more courses related to computer assisted language learning (CALL) should be offered to their teacher candidates. TPACK approach, as stated in the above section, should be highly recommended. This new approach, combining technology, teaching pedagogical knowledge, and content knowledge to train teachers the skills of technological pedagogical content knowledge, is essential for EFL teachers' implementation of ICT integrated teaching in practice.

On the other hand, lack of adequate professional training might lead to a poor ICT integrated teaching practice. The one-size-fits-all workshops in-service teachers attended are not specifically targeted in EFL teaching context and they still feel hard to transform technological knowledge into pedagogical practice. Zhang, Shi, Miao and Yang (2003) asserted that EFL teacher training on technology should go from the technology-centered training to technologically integrated teaching. The former's assumption is that once teachers have a good command of technology and then they will possess the capacity to apply the technology into teaching practice. However, this is not the case. Technology training alone is far from enough. Actually, technology is only the tool or medium of instruction. The ICT integrated teaching, in a deep sense, changes the way teachers teach, and thus is a reflection of changes both in teaching pedagogy and teaching philosophy. At present, EFL teachers who participated in the technology training complained that most training is limited to technology. The people in charge of such training believed that once our teachers possessed the technology they were competent of conducting ICT integrated teaching practice (Yang, Zhang & Yi, 2004), which resulted in the present "manual + lecture" type of training.

In fact, EFL teachers need a more problem-shooting type of support and expect a technologically integrated training pattern, which emphasizes the integration of technology into curriculum instead of technology alone. This training pattern is not only to make EFL teachers recognize the importance of the technology but also to update the philosophy of education and upgrade teaching skills at the same time. In addition to the training pattern, the current teacher training is basically conducted by some social organizations which have no specialization in EFL settings (Peng & He, 2007). The training instructors are short of current EFL subjects and teaching context, which leads to no direct link between the training and the applications. Despite most teachers welcome the technology training, the operating training model towards the "oneness" is difficult to stimulate their learning interest. In a word, there is more or less a detachment between theory, technology and practice (Song, 2004).

In short, the support for EFL teachers to conduct the ICT integrated teaching is multidimensional in terms of technology, teaching philosophy, and pedagogy. All these dimensions should be taken into account in the process of supporting teachers' professional development, so as to ensure maximum training efficiency. In fact, ICT trainers for EFL teachers should have knowledge of English subjects and get familiar with the characteristics of EFL teaching and EFL teachers' real needs. More practical work, such as group discussion, hands-on activities, projects, and reflective discussion on training are needed so that EFL teachers can work closely with the practical application of technology and increase their interests in learning new things.

2) Lack of resources for less developed area schools and teachers. The challenge of educational equity is an important topic in education. Scholars (for example, Bennett, Culp, Honey, Tally & Spielvogel, 2001) proposed that application of technology might become a way to help eliminate many educational inequity issues between urban and rural area schools and bridge the digital divide. Technology should be a tool to help educators meet the educational needs of all children. In the Chinese context, the gap exists between the more developed regions and the less developed areas. For example, teachers working in less developed rural areas need special attention for balanced education resources. Otherwise, the gap might widen especially in this information age. This is a huge challenge that the promotion of ICT integrated teaching approach has to encounter. Yang (2010) proposed that the establishment of teacher learning centers in each town was particularly necessary for EFL teachers' professional development in rural areas. Another possible way to solve this issue is through the distance education model. In the era of knowledge economy, distance education model will become a means to build a lifelong learning system. Through the network, teachers in rural areas can break the boundaries of time and space.

Generally, most rural elementary and secondary schools' hardware was good, equipped with satellite receiving systems and network connected multimedia classrooms. (Zhai, 2008) However, many teachers do not have the skills to use such advanced technological equipment. Policymaker should realize that the key point in the ICT integrated teaching is to train teachers on how to apply technology effectively into their practice. In some schools, multimedia classroom solely serves as the movie showroom (Jiao & Wei, 2012). All these phenomena showed that teachers had too little technological knowledge in teaching practice. Therefore, the government should support the relatively underdeveloped areas with technological resources to harness the best educational benefits.

3) Lack of specific support for EFL teachers' technological needs from ICT experts and administrators. In addition to the ICT training at a fixed time, some in-time support focusing on EFL teachers' practical needs is still necessary. On-demand support is highly needed for improving the relevance and effectiveness of the training. According to Hu and McGrath (2011), at present, limited technological skills and pedagogic expertise are obstacles to the use of ICT integrated teaching in EFL context. Moreover, although initially the majority of teachers had held positive attitudes towards technology use in EFL teaching, their enthusiasm might wane in the light of inadequate support (Hu &McGrath, 2011).

From the administrators' perspectives, many school leaders have misconceptions towards the English subject with the excessive pursuit of high test scores and less attention to ICT integrated teaching. Therefore, it is necessary to improve the leadership's awareness of ICT knowledge to create a digital learning environment. On the other hand, the government usually pays more attention to the modern equipment than to EFL teachers' actual use of this hardware. In reality, advanced technological equipment cannot lead to good teaching and learning efficiency automatically. More teacher support on ICT integrated teaching is still highly demanded. Meanwhile, at present in China, there are no evaluation standards on EFL teachers' technological competence like the ISTE standards. Without scientific standards to evaluate EFL teachers' performance, how can we know that EFL teachers' application of technology work effectively in practice? Thus, it is suggested that standards on EFL teachers' technology use should be established for scientific assessment.

In brief, it is important to develop teachers' ability to evaluate resources and think critically about the usefulness of technology in their own classroom in order to explore the potentials of technology and to develop their own technologically integrated pedagogy. It is important to raise teachers' awareness of the shifts in their roles in technology-integrated classrooms so that teachers can change their thinking from a teacher-centered approach to a student-centered one.

CONCLUSION

The development and widespread application of ICT has had a revolutionary impact on teaching and learning of EFL. Globally, the ICT integrated teaching has been adopted in many EFL teaching context. In the field of EFL teaching in China ICT integrated teaching has been one of the striking features of curriculum reform for renovating teaching and learning performance.

By identifying the issues and challenges EFL teachers encountered in integrating technology into instruction, this chapter could offer some implications for promoting teachers' pedagogical change in integrating technology in EFL teacher education and related continuing professional development. The process of using ICT to improve students' learning is never solely a technological matter. The effectiveness of ICT integrated teaching should focus on pedagogy design by justifying how the technology is used through incorporating appropriate pedagogy and technology. This requires teachers' pedagogical change towards the content, technology, and pedagogy. In other words, in conducting ICT integrated teaching, teachers should synthesize technology knowledge, the subject matter knowledge, the subject pedagogical knowledge and technologically pedagogical knowledge in supporting more student-centered, collaborative instruction (Jung, 2005). Therefore, the alignment among technology, curriculum and pedagogy in EFL teaching is necessary. At the same time, we must realize that it is the use of technology affects the teaching and learning instead of the technology per se. Thus, more efforts need to be paid to improve EFL teachers' technological competence for better carrying out the ICT integrated teaching practice.

REFERENCES

Anderson, N., & Nunan, D. (2003, March). *Strategies for successful listening and reading development.* Paper presented in the 37th Annual TESOL Convention, Baltimore, MD.

Atkins, N. E., & Vasu, E. S. (2000). Measuring knowledge of technology usage and stages of concern about computing: A study of middle school teachers. *Journal of Technology and Teacher Education*, *8*(4), 279–302.

Bennett, D., McMillan Culp, K., Honey, M., Tally, B., & Spielvogel, B. (2001). It all depends: Strategies for designing technologies for change in education. *Methods of evaluating educational technology*, 105-124.

Bingimlas, K. A. (2009). Barriers to the successful integration of ICT in teaching and learning environments: A review of the literature. *Eurasia Journal of Mathematics, Science & Technology Education*, *5*(3), 235–245.

Bitner, N., & Bitner, J. (2002). Integrating technology into the classroom: Eight keys to success. *Journal of Technology and Teacher Education*, *10*(1), 95–100.

Bruce, C. S. (2004). *Information literacy as a catalyst for educational change. A background paper*. Retrieved October 21, 2015, from http://eprints.qut.edu.au/4977/1/4977_1.pdf

Cabanatan, P. (2003, June). *Integrating Pedagogy and Technology: The SEAMEO INNOTECH Experience*. Proposal presented to Experts Meeting on Teachers/Facilitators Training in Technology-Pedagogy Integration, Bangkok, Thailand.

Cao, W., Hu, Z., Li, H., & Xu, X. (2015). Status quo of computer-assisted ELT in basic education in China. *Computer-Assisted Foreign Language Education*, *4*, 41–46.

CECR. (2007). *College English curriculum requirements*. Shanghai: Shanghai Foreign Language Publishing Press.

Chambers, A., & Bax, S. (2006). Making CALL work: Towards normalisation. *System*, *34*(4), 465–479. doi:10.1016/j.system.2006.08.001

Chapelle, C. (2003). *English language learning and technology: Lectures on applied linguistics in the age of information and communication technology*. Amsterdam: John Benjamins. doi:10.1075/lllt.7

Dai, W., & Wang, X. (2012). The content and approach for EFL teachers' professional development in informational technological context. *Computer-Assisted Foreign Language Education*, *6*, 8–13.

Decision, C. (2005). *Science and technology basic plan. Tokyo: The Japan Science and Technology Agency*.

Felix, U. (2005). Analyzing recent CALL effectiveness research: Towards a common agenda. *Computer Assisted Language Learning*, *18*(1-2), 1–32. doi:10.1080/09588220500132274

Gu, H. (2012). The strategic reaction to the new curriculum reform in basic education: A case of the EFL teacher education program in Henan Province. *Educational Review*, *4*, 87–89.

He, B., Puakpong, N., & Lian, A. (2015). Factors affecting the normalization of CALL in Chinese senior high schools. *Computer Assisted Language Learning*, *28*(3), 189–201. doi:10.1080/09588221.2013.803981

Hu, Z., & McGrath, I. (2011). Innovation in higher education in China: Are teachers ready to integrate ICT in English language teaching? *Technology, Pedagogy and Education*, *20*(1), 41–59. doi:10.1080/1475939X.2011.554014

Jiao, B., & Wei, H. (2012). A survey on the EFL teachers' informational literacy at elementary and secondary levels. *Journal of Heilongjiang Educational Institute, 31*(10), 35–35.

Jung, I. (2005). ICT-Pedagogy integration in teacher training: Application cases worldwide. *Journal of Educational Technology & Society, 8*(2), 94–101.

Kozma, R., & Anderson, R. E. (2002). Qualitative case studies of innovative pedagogical practices using ICT. *Journal of Computer Assisted Learning, 18*(4), 387–394. doi:10.1046/j.0266-4909.2002.00250.doc.x

Kozma, R. B., & Anderson, R. E. (2002). Qualitative case studies of innovative pedagogical practices using ICT. *Journal of Computer Assisted Learning, 18*(4), 387–394. doi:10.1046/j.0266-4909.2002.00250.doc.x

Li, G., & Ni, X. (2011). Primary EFL teachers' technology use in China: Patterns and perceptions. *RELC Journal, 42*(1), 69–85. doi:10.1177/0033688210390783

Li, L. (2014). Understanding language teachers' practice with educational technology: A case from China. *System, 46*, 105–119. doi:10.1016/j.system.2014.07.016

Li, L., & Walsh, S. (2011). Technology uptake in Chinese EFL classes. *Language Teaching Research, 15*(1), 99–125. doi:10.1177/1362168810383347

Mao, M. (2007). An investigation of college English teachers' competence on web-based teaching. *Foreign Language World, 2*, 26–31.

Marinova-Todd, S. H., Marshall, D. B., & Snow, C. E. (2001). Missing the point: A response to Hyltenstam and Abrahamsson. *TESOL Quarterly, 35*(1), 171–176. doi:10.2307/3587864

Mishra, P., & Koehler, M. (2006). Technological pedagogical content knowledge: A framework for teacher knowledge. *Teachers College Record, 108*(6), 1017–1054. doi:10.1111/j.1467-9620.2006.00684.x

MOE (Ministry of Education). (2001). *English Curriculum Standards for Fulltime Common Senior High Schools*. Beijing: Beijing Normal University Press.

MOE (Ministry of Education). (2012). *English Curriculum Standards for Fulltime Common Senior High Schools*. Beijing: Beijing Normal University Press.

Office for Standards in Education. (1998). *Information technology: a review of inspection findings 1993/4*. London: HMSO.

Pelgrum, W. (2001). Obstacles to the integration of ICT in education: Results from a worldwide educational assessment. *Computers & Education, 37*(2), 163–178. doi:10.1016/S0360-1315(01)00045-8

Peng, W., & He, J. (2007). An integrated model of technology and curriculum for EFL teacher training: Issues and Strategies. *Foreign Language World, 2*, 18–25.

Snoeyink, R., & Ertmer, P. A. (2001). Thrust into technology: How veteran teachers respond. *Journal of Educational Technology Systems, 30*(1), 85–111. doi:10.2190/YDL7-XH09-RLJ6-MTP1

Song, D. (2004). A reflection on the ICT training of elementary and secondary school teachers. *e-. Education Research, 2*, 75–77.

Stepp-Greany, J. (2002). Student perceptions on language learning in a technological environment: Implications for the new millennium. *Language Learning & Technology*, *6*(1), 165–180.

Thomas, M. (2015). Introduction. In M. Thmas & H. Reinders (Eds.), *Contemporary Task-Based Language Teaching in Asia* (pp. 1–6). London: Bloomsbury Publishing.

Tsui, A. B. M., & Tollefson, J. W. (2007). Language policy and the construction of national cultural identity. In A. B. M. Tsui & J. Tollefson (Eds.), *Language Policy, Culture, and Identity in Asian Contexts* (pp. 1–21). Mahwah, NJ: Lawrence Erlbaum Associates.

U.S. Department of Education, Office of Educational Technology. (2010). *Transforming American education: Learning powered by technology*. Retrieved December 12, 2015, from http://www2.ed.gov/about/offices/list/os/technology/netp-executive-summary.pdf

Warschauer, M., & Healey, D. (1998). Computers and language learning: An overview. *Language Teaching*, *31*(02), 57–71. doi:10.1017/S0261444800012970

Watson, D. M. (2001). Pedagogy before technology: Re-thinking the relationship between ICT and teaching. *Education and Information Technologies*, *6*(4), 251–266. doi:10.1023/A:1012976702296

Wu, Z. (2002). *Teachers' knowledge and curriculum change: a critical study of teachers' exploratory discourse in a Chinese university.* (Unpublished Doctoral dissertation). University of Lancaster, Lancaster, UK.

Xie, X. (2005). Discussion on EFL teachers' information literacy at the e-age.[谢徐萍. E 时代英语教师信息素养探论. 外语界]. *Foreign Language World*, *4*, 9–12.

Yang, G. (2010). The pattern on EFL's professional development in rural area: A perspective from the " New Curriculum Standards[Education education]. *Journal of Hebei Normal University*, *12*(4), 62–65.

Yang, P., Zhang, Q., & Yi, X. (2004). On the construction of teachers' autonomy training model. *e-. Education Research*, *2*, 25–27.

Zhai, H. (2008). Discussion on elementary and secondary EFL teachers' information literacy education at the information age. *Journal of Qiqihaer Teachers'. College*, *3*, 119–121.

Zhang, J., Shi, S., Miao, F., & Yang, W. (2003). A performance criteria study on elementary and secondary school teachers' educational informational technology. *China Educational Technology*, *2*, 104–113.

Zhang, X., & Niu, G. (2009). Strategies on improving college English teachers' professional development on information technology application. *Continuing Education Research*, *5*, 44–46.

Zhao, J. (2013). The role of network technology in the development of college English teachers. *Journal of Changchun University*, *23*(4), 483–487.

Zhong, Z., Wang, Y., Huang, Y., & Shi, H. (2003). An investigation on the elementary and secondary school teachers' information literacy. *e-. Education Research*, *1*, 65–69.

KEY TERMS AND DEFINITIONS

Computer Assisted Language Learning (CALL): CALL is an approach in which the computer and other related resources are used as an aid to facilitate language teaching and learning.

Computer Literacy: The ability to use the computer and other related technology for data entry, word processing, and Internet communications.

Digital Divide: It refers to the gap in the use and access to information and communication technologies between the privileged and the underprivileged people with regard to factors such as regions, demographics, and social economic status.

High-Stakes Test: A high-stakes test refers to a test that bears important consequences or decisions for the test takers. For example, the test result is used to enroll students in a prestigious college, for the scholarship competition, or lose funding due to the poor performance in the test.

Language Input: Language input refers to the language learners receive from their teachers, textbooks, peers, and other resources.

Linguistic Forms: A unit of language or linguistic elements, such as a morpheme, a word, a phrase, or a sentence. In English as a Second or Foreign Language context (ESL/EFL), linguistic forms refer to the linguistic elements teachers teach and students receive in the language teaching and learning the process.

Stakeholders: Stakeholders refer to people can influence or be influenced by an organization's objectives, policies, or actions. In educational settings, some examples of key stakeholders are administrators, parents, policymakers, students, experts, and other professionals related to education.

Teacher Belief: Teacher belief refers to teacher's perceptions, assumptions, implications and explicit theories, judgments or opinions towards his or her profession. Teacher belief is generally believed to plays a pivotal role in impacting teacher's decision making towards his or her instructive practice.

Chapter 3
Technology Standards for Chinese Language Teacher Education

Wenxia Wang
Florida State University, USA

Liying Feng
Florida State University, USA

ABSTRACT

Guided by the TPACK theory (Mishra & Koehler, 2006), this chapter reviews and compares the technology standards related to and designed for teachers of Chinese as a Foreign Language (CFL) from the entry level to the accomplished level in the United States and China. It has found that the technology standards are often included in the comprehensive standards for teachers and parallel the standards about other aspects of teaching. The technology standards related to CFL in the two countries share some similarities but also differ in important ways. Several important and critical understandings are identified, including the needs for CFL technology standards, the theoretical foundations for CFL technology standards, and a more solid and comprehensive infrastructure for CFL education. Recommendations are made to address the needs, and research is called for to study the development and implementation of CFL technology standards.

INTRODUCTION

Chinese as a foreign language (CFL) has been developing unprecedentedly in the world. Many countries, including the United States, have developed various Chinese programs in their K-12 schools and higher education. By 2014, the Office of Chinese Language Council International of China (Hanban) had set up 475 Confucius Institutes and 851 Confucius classrooms in 126 countries and areas in the world (Xu, 2014).

DOI: 10.4018/978-1-5225-0483-2.ch003

Such fast development of CFL in China and the world requires a large number of qualified CFL teachers. In 2014, Hanban sent 15, 500 CFL teachers and administrators to 139 countries to assist and facilitate their CFL development (Xu, 2014). Hanban and the Confucius Institutes in the world have been involved in CFL teacher education, and from 2004 to 2014, they helped prepare a head-count of approximately 200,000 indigenous CFL teachers for around 100 countries, and in 2014 alone, around 35,000 CFL teachers were prepared (Xu, 2014). However, it remains unclear how CFL teachers have been educated in China and around the world.

Meanwhile, educational standards have been implemented worldwide to provide guidance for teacher education programs and to ensure that teachers help their students to achieve desired learning outcome (Murphy-Judy & Youngs, 2006). Similarly, "in foreign language education, given the emphasis on communication and the opportunities for computer-assisted learning, technologies play an ever-increasing role in learning standards" (Murphy-Judy & Youngs, 2006, p. 45). Thus, technologies should also be increasingly important in CFL, and it is necessary to understand how technology standards guide Chinese teacher education programs and CFL teachers. For this purpose, technology standards for Chinese teacher education in China and the United States are examined in this chapter, given the key roles that the two countries play in CFL education nowadays.

BACKGROUND

While China's critical role is evident in promoting CFL education within China and around the world, a justification is needed for examining and comparing technology standards for Chinese teacher education in the United States and China. The United States is a super power where English, as a global language, is also the dominant language. Thus, English itself is a disincentive for CFL education in the United States (Lo Bianco, 2011). However, the United States has become a critical site for CFL development outside of China. By 2014, the United States has had a total of 542 Confucius institutes and classrooms, which is the largest number of Confucius institutes and classrooms in a country across the world (Xu, 2014). In U.S. higher education, its CFL enrollment grew from 51,582 in 2006 to 61,055 in 2013 (Furman, Goldberg, & Lusin, 2007; Goldburg, Looney, & Lusin, 2015). In its K-12 schools, the percentages of the elementary and secondary schools that offer Chinese rose from 0.3% and 1% in 1997 to 3% and 4% in 2008 respectively (Pufahl & Rhodes, 2011). It is very likely that the numbers will continue growing. Moreover, China has a centralized educational system, but the U.S. educational system is de-centralized. Thus, comparison and contrast of the technology standards for Chinese language teacher education in the two countries may offer important insights for CFL teacher education.

To understand and describe standards for CFL teachers and knowledge that they should have, we turn to the literature of mainstream teacher education for a theoretical framework, because second and foreign language teacher education is relatively new (Freeman & Johnson, 1998; Richards & Nunan, 1990), and much work has remained to be conducted. The theory of technological pedagogical content knowledge (TPACK) by Mishra and Koehler (2006) is thus selected and used as the theoretical framework for this chapter because it integrates knowledge of technology with other components of teacher knowledge (e.g., knowledge of pedagogy and content) and best serves the purpose of the chapter.

As Mishra and Koehler (2006) acknowledges, TPACK is based on and extends the classical concept of pedagogical content knowledge (PCK) by Shulman (1987), which refers to teacher's knowledge of selecting appropriate teaching approaches for best instruction. Despite the fast development and wide application of technology in education, knowledge of technology had been often taken separated from teacher's PCK in the field before 2000. Such an approach was also "exemplified by the plethora of state and national technology standards..." (Mishra & Koehler, 2006, p. 1031). Mishra and Koehler (2006) believes that knowledge of technology should be interactive and integrated with other components of teacher knowledge (e.g., PCK), and they emphasize the complex interplay of knowledge of technology, pedagogy, and content in their framework.

татPCK [TPACK] is the basis of good teaching with technology and requires an understanding of the representation of concepts using technologies; pedagogical techniques that use technologies in constructive ways to teach content; knowledge of what makes concepts difficult or easy to learn and how technology can help redress some of the problems that students face; knowledge of students' prior knowledge and theories of epistemology; and knowledge of how technologies can be used to build on existing knowledge and to develop new epistemologies or strengthen old ones. (p. 1029)

In this framework, altogether seven bodies of teacher knowledge have been identified. In addition to teacher's knowledge of technology, pedagogy, and content (TK, PK, and CK), the other four bodies of teacher knowledge included in the framework are PCK, technological content knowledge (TCK), technological pedagogical knowledge (TPK), and technological pedagogical content knowledge (TPCK). These bodies of teacher knowledge are interactive and integrative (Koehler & Mishra, 2009). Meanwhile, Mishra and Koehler (2006) emphasize that TPACK, especially TK, is dynamic, because technology is continually developing. Thus, TPACK requires teachers to constantly upgrade their knowledge and reconfigure the interplay of technology, pedagogy, and content for quality teaching.

Since its introduction, TPACK has attracted great attention, and it has been widely discussed and applied in mainstream teacher education. More importantly, numerous research studies have been conducted from this perspective (Bos, 2011; Chai, Koh, & Tsai, 2010; Hunter, 2015), including those on second/foreign language teacher education (Cheng, 2014). Therefore, TPACK is used in this chapter to analyze and compare the technology standards for Chinese teacher education in China and the United States.

MAIN FOCUS OF THE CHAPTER

Learning to teach is life-long, and teachers constantly learn across their careers. Thus, teacher education in this chapter includes teacher preparation at the entry level up to the accomplished or expert level. Technology standards have been set forth in the United States and China for different important points across teachers' careers, so in this section the technology standards in the two countries will be reviewed and compared.

Technology Standards in the United States

It is widely known that educational system in the U.S. is de-centralized, and the states make the major decisions on their teacher certification, licensing, and professional development. On the other hand, these different stages of teacher education have been "overseen by a variety of educational agencies in the United States" (Murphy-Judy & Youngs, 2006, p. 49). Guided by TPACK, the sections below examine

Technology Standards for Chinese Language Teacher Education

the technology standards, which are closely related to CFL teacher education, from various educational institutions and agencies, and for different stages of teachers' careers: 1) initial teacher certification, 2) licensing, and 3) professional development.

1. Initial Teacher Preparation

In the United States, technology-specific standards for teachers, students, and administrators have been written by the International Society for Technology in Education (ISTE). On July 1, 2013, the two well-known agencies that reviewed most U.S. teacher education programs, the National Council for Accreditation of Teacher Education (NCATE) and Teacher Education Accreditation Council (TEAC), consolidated under a new agency, the Council for the Accreditation of Educator Preparation (CAEP). NCATE/CAEP collaborated with ISTE for their standards for foreign language teachers (Murphy-Judy & Youngs, 2006).

ISTE standards appear discipline-neutral, and they expect all teachers to be able to apply ISTE standards and integrate technology into their instruction and professional development, and model and promote technology use to students, colleagues, and the community (ISTE Standards for Teachers, 2008). The requirements in these three areas of teachers' work are reflected in ISTE's five standards for teachers[1]:

1. Facilitate and inspire student learning and creativity.
2. Design and develop digital age learning experiences and assessments.
3. Model digital age work and learning.
4. Promote and model digital citizenship and responsibility.
5. Engage in professional growth and leadership (ISTE Standards for Teachers, 2008).

These standards model how teachers should incorporate technology in their instruction, professional development, and community responsibility, which is made more specific and clearer in the more detailed descriptions of the standards and their supporting elements. Take standards 1 for an example. Its supporting explanation, "teachers use their knowledge of subject matter, teaching and learning, and technology to facilitate experiences that advance student learning, creativity, and innovation in both face-to-face and virtual environment" (ISTE, 2008), includes expectations for teachers' content knowledge (CK), pedagogical knowledge (PK), technology knowledge (TK), and their amalgamation and interplay, technological pedagogical content knowledge (TPACK). While one of the standard's supporting components, "promote, support, and model creative and innovative thinking and inventiveness," focuses more on teachers' PK, another supporting component, "engage students in exploring real-world issues and solving authentic problems using digital tools and resources," stresses teachers' technological pedagogical knowledge (TPK). Both its third and fourth supporting components require teachers' TPACK, "promote student reflection using collaborative tools to reveal and clarify students' conceptual understanding and thinking, planning, and creative processes," and "model collaborative knowledge construction by engaging in learning with students colleagues, and others in face-to-face and virtual environments." Similarly each of the other four ISTE standards requires several of the seven bodies of TPACK framework, and overall, the ISTE standards expect teachers to not only possess TPACK, but also be able to access and apply their TPACK flexibly in their instruction.

NCATE/CAEP collaborates with the American Council on the Teaching of Foreign Languages (ACTFL) to review foreign language teacher preparation programs in the United States. In collaboration with NCATE and then CAEP, ACTFL has developed its *Program Standards for the Preparation of Foreign Language Teachers* in 2002 and revised it in 2013. However, these standards are descriptive instead of prescriptive, and during accreditation process, NCATE/CAEP and ACTFL also tend to recognize the conceptual frameworks developed by individual institutions to fit their contexts, so technology standards included in NCATE/CAEP and ACTFL intend to provide guidance rather than mandate (Murphy-Judy & Youngs, 2006).

The ACTFL program standards consists of two parts: 1) "requirements for programs of foreign language teacher preparation," 2) "content and supporting standards" (ACTFL Foreign Language Teacher Standards Writing Team, 2013, p. 2-3). The requirements in part one appear brief, and in the eight components of the requirements, Component 7 requires teacher preparation programs to provide "opportunities for candidates to experience technology-enhanced instruction and to use technology in their own teaching" (ACTFL Foreign Language Teacher Standards Writing Team, 2013, p. 2-3), but in addition to this, no further explanations are provided to give more guidance on how this should be implemented in teacher preparation programs. While this component focuses more on teacher candidates' TK and TPK, all the other seven requirements demand candidates' CK, PK, or program opportunities/resources for candidates to gain such knowledge. Moreover, few details are provided to describe how these components should interact with each other, so Component 7 appears parallel to the other components in the Part one. Thus, TK and TPK in Component 7 seem to be taken as one part of teacher knowledge which looks separated from other bodies of teacher knowledge embedded in the other components.

In the six ACTFL's content standards for reviewing language teacher preparation programs, technology is not mentioned, but a closer look at the standards' supporting elements, supporting explanations, and rubrics shows that TK and technology skills are expected in almost each standard. For example, Standard 4 expects language teacher candidates to demonstrate "integration of standards in planning, classroom practice, and use of instructional resources" (ACTFL Foreign Language Teacher Standards Writing Team, 2013, p. 2). The third key elements of Standard 4 require teacher candidates to "use the *Standards for Foreign Language Learning in the 21st Century* and their [teachers'] state standards to select and integrate authentic texts, use technology, and adapt and create instructional materials for use in communication" (ACTFL Foreign Language Teacher Standards Writing Team, 2013, p. 10). It is evident that ACTFL considers TK a necessary component interacting with other bodies of teacher knowledge and expects teacher candidates to be able to draw on such interwoven and integrated teacher knowledge when designing their instruction. This point is more evident in the ACTFL's explanation for the Standard 4, "…candidates use the principles embedded in the standards to select and integrate authentic materials and technology" (ACTFL Foreign Language Teacher Standards Writing Team, 2013, p. 10). Therefore, similar to ISTE, both NCATE/CAEP and ACTFL regard teacher candidate's TK as a necessary and integrative component of their teacher knowledge, which should not be isolated or separated from other bodies of their teacher knowledge.

However, these national standards remain generic and have not been tailored to any particular foreign languages or CFL in the United States. In 2006 when the *Standards for Foreign Language Learning: Preparing for the 21st Century* was published by the National Standards in Foreign Language Education Project, the generic national standards were adapted to the ten most commonly taught foreign languages in the United States, including Chinese. It may be possible in the future that the national teacher preparation standards will also be tailored to different languages.

Technology Standards for Chinese Language Teacher Education

2. Licensing and Re-Certification

Collaborating with state education agencies (e.g., a state's department of education) that are in charge of teacher licensing, the Interstate New Teacher Assessment and Support Consortium (INTASC) aims to standardize the licensing process in the United States. In 1992, the INTASC published its *Model Standards for Beginning Teacher Licensing and Development: A Resource for State Dialogue*. The generic model standards were translated into foreign language education, and in 2002, *Model Standards for Licensing Beginning Foreign Language Teachers: A Resource for State Dialogue* was published. The INTASC updated its generic model core standards in 2011 and re-oriented the standards as professional instead of those only for beginning teachers. Concurrently its name was changed to the Interstate Teacher Assessment and Support Consortium (InTASC). In 2013, the InTASC released its *Model Core Teaching Standards and Learning Progressions for Teachers 1.0*, which includes model core teaching standards and progressions for teachers, but this version has not been tailored to foreign language education.

The *Model Standards for Licensing Beginning Foreign Language Teachers: A Resource for State Dialogue* contains ten standards ranging from content and pedagogic knowledge to reflective practice and community. TK was neither included in the ten core standards nor their supporting explanations. In this document, technology was regarded as a tool to enhance instruction, to conduct assessment, to develop proficiency and cultural understanding, etc. Throughout the 49 pages of the document, use of technology was mentioned in only five places in the illustrations and examples for the standards for 1) "content knowledge," 2) "instructional strategies," 3) "planning for instruction," 4) "assessment," and 5) "reflective practice and professional development." The most sophisticated illustration about the use of technology is for instructional strategies:

Language teachers incorporate technology into their instruction. They are familiar with educational applications of technology and can use technology as a tool to develop and assess language proficiency, cultural understanding, and critical thinking skills. Teachers know how to embed technology into instruction, prepare students for its use, and integrate it into their lessons and curriculum. They use technology appropriately to enhance instruction and/or conduct assessments including the use of the Internet and other multimedia applications. (Interstate New Teacher Assessment and Support Consortium INTASC Foreign Language Standards Committee, 2002, p. 23)

Thus, the illustration indicates that TK was taken as an incremental skill, but not one of the essential bodies of teacher knowledge identified by Mishra and Koehler (2006), even though teachers were expected to "incorporate" technology into their teaching, and use of technology was considered an important skill for teachers. The important reasons may be that the document was written in 2002 when instructional technology was not well developed or TK was not recognized as crucial to teachers.

The importance of TK was strengthened in the InTASC's standards in 2011 and especially in the teaching standards and learning progressions in 2013. As part of the updating work to the former standards in 1992, a review of research from 1990 to 2011 was conducted on the main topics to be included in the new standards, and technology was one of the topics examined (the Council of Chief State School Officers, 2011). Seemingly TK does not appear in the new ten standards, but the term "technology" is mentioned repeatedly in the standards' components, learning progressions, and their examples in eight out of the ten standards except the two standards for learner development and content knowledge, as shown in table 1 below.

Table 1. TK and technology in the InTASC standards

No.	Standards	Standards			Progression	
		Performances	Essential Knowledge	Critical Dispositions	Components	Examples
#1	Learner development					
#2	Learning differences				×	
#3	Learning environments					×
#4	Content knowledge					
#5	Application of content					×
#6	Assessment	×				
#7	Planning for instruction				×	×
#8	Instructional strategies	×	×		×	×
#9	Professional learning and ethical practice	×			×	×
#10	Leadership and collaboration				×	×

(2013)

The table indicates that technology is expected in most InTASC standards and learning progressions, which means that TK has been taken as necessary and also an integrative part of teacher knowledge by the InTASC. For example, in the section of "performances" of the Standard 8 for instructional strategies, the InTASC expects "the teacher engages learners in using a range of learning skills and technology tools to access, interpret, evaluate, and apply information," and in its section of "essential knowledge," the InTASC requires "the teacher understands how content and skill development can be supported by media and technology and knows how to evaluate these resources for quality, accuracy, and effectiveness" (the Council of Chief State School Officers, 2013, p. 38). Thus, the InTASC requires teachers to have TK and to be able to apply their TK to actual teaching. Moreover, it anticipates that teachers' "… cross-disciplinary skills (e.g., communication, collaboration, critical thinking, and the use of technology) are woven throughout the teaching standards because of their importance for learners" (the Council of Chief State School Officers, 2013, p. 4). Therefore, TK in the InTASC standards is taken as an integrative and inseparable part of teacher knowledge that also interacts and interweaves with other parts of teacher knowledge and jointly shapes teacher's instruction.

It should be mentioned that the field of CFL education has developed specific standards for CFL teachers, even though these standards are not set forth for licensing and re-certification purposes. Instead, they reflect the expectations of the CFL profession for new CFL teachers in the United States. In 2007, the Chinese Language Association of Secondary-Elementary Schools (CLASS) published their joint work with the National East Asian Languages Resource Center (NEALRC) at the Ohio State University, *CLASS Professional Standards for K-12 Chinese Teachers*. These standards outline the knowledge, skills, and dispositions that new CFL teachers should have for teaching CFL in the United States. While the CLASS and NEALRC aligned the standards with other professional standards (e.g., INTASC's standards for foreign language teachers in 2002, ACTFL language learning standards, and the Chinese Language Specific Standards for K-12 Learners by CLASS), they also maintained that the standards should be regarded as guidance instead of regulations for new CFL teachers when they are teaching CFL in the United States (NEALRC and CLASS, 2007).

Technology Standards for Chinese Language Teacher Education

More importance was attached to the teacher's TK in the *CLASS Professional Standards for K-12 Chinese Teachers,* which consists of 12 standards describing the expectations for CFL teachers in their language proficiency and knowledge, knowledge of second language acquisition, knowledge of learners, instructional planning and assessment, professional development, etc. Different from other national standards discussed above, the CLASS and NEALRC explicitly set forth "technology knowledge and skills" as one of the 12 standards, the Standard 11, and expect that "teachers understand technology supports the teaching and learning of language and culture and provides tools, strategies and practices that motivate student interest and increase performance. They incorporate technology into lesson planning and instructional delivery" (NEALRC and CLASS, 2007). Thus, TK for Chinese language teachers is augmented to a position which parallels those of content knowledge, knowledge of students, PCK, etc. However, the document appears brief. Except a couple of sentences above, no elaborations or examples for this standard or other 11 standards are included to provide further guidance for new CFL teachers. Neither is it clear about how the Standard 11 or TK relates to other standards and/or other bodies of teacher knowledge in the CLASS standards for CFL teachers.

3. Advanced Professional Certification

At the higher end of a continuum of teacher standards are the standards set forth by the National Board for Professional Teaching Standards (NBPTS). Different from the CAEP/ACTFL, InTASC, and CLASS standards, the NBPTS target at experienced teachers who may voluntarily pursue recognition to their expertise in teaching through National Board Certification (Shrum & Glisan, 2016), which takes experienced teachers three years to complete the process (National Board Certification for Teachers: World Languages Standards, 2010). ACTFL also collaborates with the NBPTS for board certifying foreign language teachers. The generic NBPTS standards include five core propositions, which reflect NBPTS's beliefs about and expectations for accomplished teachers:

1. Teachers are committed to students and their learning.
2. Teachers know the subjects they teach and how to teach those subjects to students.
3. Teachers are responsible for managing and monitoring student learning.
4. Teachers think systematically about their practice and learn from experience.
5. Teachers are members of learning communities. (NBPTS, 2010, p. 5)

Similar to NCATE/CEAP and INTASC, the NBPTS translated their five core propositions to 14 standards into world language education and released *National Board Certification for Teachers: World Languages Standards* in 2004. In 2010 the 14 standards were consolidated into nine standards to describe different facets of accomplished world language teaching, which are listed below.

Standard I: Knowledge of students
Standard II: Knowledge of language
Standard III: Knowledge of culture
Standard IV: Knowledge of language acquisition
Standard V: Fair and equitable learning environment
Standard VI: Designing curriculum and planning instruction
Standard VII: Assessment

Standard VIII: Reflection
Standard IX: Professionalism (NBPTS, 2010, p. 19-20)

Each of these facets is followed by its succinct standard statement and detailed elaboration. The NBPTS also maintains that these standards should "…occur concurrently because of the seamless quality of accomplished practice" (NBPTS, 2010, p. 19).

Similar to NCATE/CEAP and INTASC standards, TK does not appear in the NBPTS standard statements for world language teachers, but it is explicitly required for accomplished teachers in the elaborations for the standards from IV to VIII. For example, in the elaboration for standard VIII of reflection, the NBPTS requires "teachers stay abreast of relevant technological advancement and are familiar with how technology not only assists instructional planning and delivery of instruction, but also offers ways to examine the effectiveness of lessons" (NBPTS, 2010, p. 60). Thus, TK is regarded by the NBPTS as an integrated and essential part of the accomplished world language teacher's knowledge and skills. Moreover, the NBPTS maintains that, along with advancement of technology, accomplished "teachers avail themselves of technology to update their own knowledge…" and "…integrate technology into lessons" (NBPTS, 2010, p. 60). Thus, the NBPTS expects not only integrated but also current TK of accomplished teacher's knowledge, which should be incorporated into the teacher's knowledge and actual instruction seamlessly.

Technology Standards in China

Different from the United States, China has a centralized educational system, so the Ministry of Education of China often makes educational policies and standards implemented across the country. For CFL education in China, however, Hanban, the executive body of The Office of Chinese Language Council International that is affiliated with China's Ministry of Education, has been playing a critical role in providing standards for the CFL profession. In addition, universities and professional organizations in China have been making important contributions.

CFL was not recognized as a subject until 1983, and it was associated with other disciplines, including education, psychology, and computer science in the first Chinese as a Foreign Language Education and Research Conference, but technology was not applied and researched in CFL education until the late 1980s (Zhang, 2009). The first draft of *Standards for Qualified Teachers of Chinese to Speakers of Other Languages* was jointly developed by multiple universities in China in 1985, including Beijing Language and Culture University and Beijing University (Zhang, 2009), but the document cannot be found in the literature, so it was not clear whether a technology standard was included. However, much was invested in developing technology in CFL education, and some accomplishments were achieved, which facilitated CFL development and helped pave the way for including technology in professional standards for CFL teachers in China.

Since the 21st century, Hanban has become very active in promoting CFL in China and the world. It has also been involved in developing various CFL learning and instructional resources, including multimedia products and websites for CFL learning and teaching. In 2007, Hanban released the *Standards for Teachers of Chinese to Speakers of Other Languages* (Zhang, 2009)[2], which provides comprehensive professional expectations for CFL teachers in their knowledge and skills. These standards have also been used as references for educating, assessing, and evaluating CFL teachers in China and those CFL teachers who are affiliated with Hanban.

Technology Standards for Chinese Language Teacher Education

The standards consist of five modules that introduce 10 supporting standards about being a qualified CFL teacher internationally. These five modules are: 1) "linguistic knowledge and skills," 2) "culture and communication," 3) "second language acquisition and learning strategies," 4) "teaching methodology," and 5) "teacher's advocacy and ethics" (Hanban, 2007). The ninth standard included in the fourth module is the one describing modern education technology and application. In addition to this standard for technology use, the other three standards contained in the fourth module are 1) "CFL teaching methods," 2) "assessment and evaluation," and 3) "CFL curriculum, syllabus, textbooks, and assistive resources" (Hanban, 2007).

The ninth standard about technology use consists of two supporting elements, which are further described with a list of brief statements about the concepts involved and the skills required to implement them in teaching. Within the first supporting element of the standard of technology, there is a list of eight points on Chinese educational technology and 10 teacher's abilities and skills. This supporting element requires that CFL teachers be familiar with relevant electronic devises and know how to use them and the software and multimedia relating to CFL. The second supporting element includes eight points and five types of teacher's knowledge and skills, which expect CFL teachers to be able to understand and apply their knowledge of internet into their CFL instruction. The technology standard, together with its supporting elements, offers guidance for CFL teachers and the profession in applying modern computer technologies into CFL instruction. Consistent with the standards, knowledge and application of modern education technology is also included in the *Introduction to Test for Certificate of Teaching Chinese to Speakers of Other Languages* written by Hanban, (Hanban, 2014).

However, the technology standard and the other nine standards appear brief and general in Hanban's *Standards for Teachers of Chinese to Speakers of Other Languages*. They include only concise statements, but do not provide detailed illustrations and examples about how to implement them CFL instruction, which looks similar to CLASS standards in the United States, but differs from other U.S. standards for certification, licensing, and board licensing. Meanwhile, although the technology standard is taken as one of the ten standards for CFL teachers, it is included in the fourth module of teaching methods and appears separated and parallel to the other three standards in the module. In the *Introduction to Test for Certificate of Teaching Chinese to Speakers of Other Languages*, technology is taken as one of the supporting elements for the standard of Chinese instructional methods, which remains consistent with the Hanban standards. Thus, TK in the Hanban standards is taken as part of teacher's pedagogical knowledge instead of an integrated element of teacher knowledge that is equally important as pedagogical knowledge. In addition, little information can be found on how various bodies of teacher knowledge relate to each other in the five modules of the Hanban standards for teachers, so the described CFL teacher's TK in the Hanban standards appears to be separated instead of integrated with other bodies of teacher knowledge.

Technology standards for experienced CFL teachers in China have not been found in the literature. One possible reason may be that more experienced teachers in China tend to pursue graduate studies for more recognition in the profession. Standards for CFL teachers with Master's degrees have not been found, but in 2007, the same year when the Hanban standards for CFL teachers were released, the State Council of China approved 24 universities to start their Master Programs of Teaching Chinese to Speakers of Other Languages (MTCSOL) and provided *Curriculum Guide for Master Program of Teaching Chinese to Speakers of Other Languages* (Zhang, 2009). In this guide, a course of modern technology on language education is specified, but it is not taken as a core course and also appears separated from other courses (Guidance Committee for Higher Education of the Ministry of Education of China, 2009), which looks consistent with Hanban's *Standards for Teachers of Chinese to Speakers of Other Languages*.

Meanwhile, similar to the Hanban standards for CFL teachers, this curriculum guide appears brief and generic, and no detailed illustrations and examples are included to provide more instructions. However, more and more universities in China offer MTCSOL programs. For example, another 39 universities were approved in 2009 to start their MTCSOL programs. Thus, relevant standards, including those for technology, appear necessary for more experienced CFL teachers or teachers with Master's degrees, because standards can offer a common framework for language teacher education and also provide guidance for teachers (Katz & Snow, 2009; Shrum & Glisan, 2016).

Comparison of Technology Standards in the Two Countries

Some detailed comparisons have been made in the above sections. However, comparisons at the national level can help identify similarities and differences between the countries in their technology standards for CFL teachers, and thus facilitate understanding and development of the increasingly important area of Chinese education.

Technology standards are often included in the comprehensive standards for second/foreign language teachers and CFL teachers in both countries, and few separate and stand-alone technology standards can be located from either of the two nations, so CFL teacher's TK appears to be taken as one part of their general teacher knowledge base in the standards in the two countries. Even though the standards developed by the International Society for Technology in Education (ISTE) have been in existence for a while in the United States, they target at teachers across disciplines, not second/foreign language teachers or CFL teachers in particular. While teachers of various disciplinary specialties share commonalities in their knowledge base, second/foreign language teachers' knowledge, including CFL teachers', may be different from teachers of other disciplines, because second/foreign language teachers' medium and target of instruction are the same (Freeman, 2002). Thus, research is needed to investigate how the ISTE standards are applicable to second/foreign language teachers, including CFL teachers before the standards are applied in CFL teacher education and/or new technology standards are developed to provide guidance for CFL teachers.

When technology standards for CFL teachers (CLASS and Hanban standards) are compared to those for second/foreign language and mainstream teachers (ISTE, ACTFL/CAEP, InTASC, and NBPTS), they appear more separated and parallel to content, pedagogy, and other standards and/or are taken as one part of teachers pedagogical knowledge in the CLASS and Hanban standards, whereas technology standards in the ISTE, ACTFL/CAEP, InTASC, and NBPTS are often embedded in different standards and TK in these standards is regarded integrated with other parts of teacher knowledge. Thus, the relationship between TK and other bodies of teacher knowledge in ISTE, ACTFL/CAEP, InTASC, and NBPTS standards appears more consistent and aligned with Mishra and Koehler's (2006) TPACK construct than it is in the CLASS and Hanban standards. There may be a couple of reasons for such a difference among the standards.

First, the ISTE, ACTFL/CAEP, InTASC, and NBPTS standards draw on the literature of education in the United States, especially teacher education, so insights may be gleaned from works such as Mishra and Koehler (2006) and Shulman (1987) and then embedded in these standards, so TK is taken as an integral part of teacher knowledge. While little background information is available to help understand how the CLASS and Hanban standards are developed, it is possible that they are influenced by computer-assisted language learning (CALL) in the field of second and foreign language education. Thus, the technology standards in the CLASS and the Hanban standards look important but separated from the other standards. Even though ACTFL standards focus on world language teachers, they are for accreditation and certification purposes, so are aligned with the generic CAEP standards.

Second, the cultural contexts for developing the standards are different, and the CFL teachers that the standards target at also vary. The Hanban standards are developed in the China, whereas all other standards are set forth in the United States, so the contexts for developing the standards are very different, which may have influenced how technology is viewed by the standard developers in the United States and China. Despite the similarities between the CLASS and the Hanban standards in terms of their technology standards, they are also different in important ways. TK in the CLASS standards is regarded as one part of teacher knowledge that parallels other parts of teacher knowledge, including pedagogical knowledge, whereas TK in the Hanban standards is taken as one part of pedagogical knowledge. All these differences shown in the standards in the two countries may reflect that teaching is culturally constructed (Anderson-Levitt, 2002). Moreover, the Hanban standards are designed for assessing and certifying CFL teachers in China, but the CLASS standards aim to provide guidance for new CFL teachers in the United States. Therefore, cautions have to be taken to select appropriate standards to fit the contexts and to ensure clear guidance and directions for CFL teachers.

In addition, the current available technology standards and standards for CFL education tend to be brief. Compared to the ACTFL/CAEP, InTASC, and NBPTS standards, the ISTE standards, especially the CLASS and the Hanban standards, do not offer detailed illustrations and/or examples to provide more guidance. During their implementation, teacher education programs may not interpret the standards in the same way, which may lead to misinterpretation or confusion among CFL teachers, and consequently affect CFL education negatively.

SOLUTIONS AND RECOMMENDATIONS

Review of the technology standards for CFL teachers and teacher education above has found similarities as well as differences in the technology standards in the United States and China, so some issues have to be addressed to facilitate CFL development in the United States and in China.

First, it is necessary to develop detailed technology standards for CFL teacher education to help address the current urgent need for qualified CFL teachers and fast development of CFL. The comparison above has revealed that the current technology standards for CFL teacher education (the CLASS and Hanban standards) are brief and may not be able to provide clear guidance for CFL teacher education. Research has found that teacher candidates and instructors can only use technology to present information or organize their courses when applying the ISTE standards, but they need more understanding about how to use technology for pedagogical purposes (Lewis, 2015). Thus, one way to address such an issue in CFL teacher education is to provide more explanations for the CLASS and Hanban standards, so that CFL teachers and teacher education programs are guided more effectively when implementing the technology standards included in the CLASS and Hanban standards. An alternative may be to develop detailed technology standards by drawing on the literature of CALL and mainstream teacher education because CFL teacher education may be similar to but also different from mainstream teacher education.

Second, technology standards and comprehensive standards for CFL experienced teachers should also be developed to help build a more solid and complete infrastructure for CFL teacher education. Certification does not mean completion of learning to teach; instead, learning to teach is continuous, and teachers constantly learn from their teaching and across their careers (Shrum & Glisan, 2016). The

NBPTS standards have helped recognize accomplished world language teachers and thus foster a teaching community for world language education in the United States. Thus, developing similar standards for CFL teachers should also help identify accomplished CFL teachers and facilitate CFL teacher education. This is more important for CFL education, because one of the challenges for CFL teacher education is a severe lack of CFL mentor teachers to assist CFL interns and new teachers in learning to teach in classrooms (Wang, 2012). Recognizing accomplished CFL teachers by the field of CFL not only creates more respect for these teachers, but help build mentoring resources for CFL teacher education, and thus facilitate to develop a more solid infrastructure for CFL education.

In addition, as CFL education is increasingly globalized, collaboration appears crucial among researchers in China and the United States, for a more solid and comprehensive foundation for technology standards. The comparison above reveals that CFL stakeholders and policy-makers in the two countries share some views about technology standards, but they also appear to approach technology standards for CFL teachers from different philosophical and theoretical perspectives. However, with the fast development of technology and CFL in the two countries and the world, it is critical to prepare qualified CFL teachers and help them gain solid knowledge of technology (TK). It is equally important for CFL teacher education in China to help CFL teachers understand the different expectations for them in their teacher knowledge (including TK) across different countries and prepare them for such differences, because CFL education is becoming global, and Hanban has been sending thousands of CFL teachers to different parts of the world. Thus, technology standards should be developed to provide guidance for CFL teachers for globalized CFL education. To achieve this goal, collaborations among the researchers and standard developers in the United States and China are needed to understand the similarities and differences before the technology standards are set forth for CFL teachers, so that the new technology standards can truly reflect the comprehensive expectations of CFL education.

FUTURE RESEARCH DIRECTIONS

It appears very necessary for the field of CFL to research and develop technology standards that can truly guide CFL teacher education, which may be fundamentally similar or different from those technology standards in the literature. Mishra and Koehler's (2006) TPACK theory may be able to shed light on future technology standards for CFL teacher education in China, but research should be conducted to examine whether TPACK can be applied in the Chinese context, because TPACK is based on the U.S. context, and contexts greatly influence and shape teachers' knowledge (Borg, 2003; Kang & Chen, 2014). Alternatively, research is needed to identify theoretical foundations for technology standards for CFL teachers in the Chinese context that can best capture CFL teachers' TK, because CFL teachers may need particular TK, and the Chinese context is also different from that for TPACK.

It is equally important to study the implementation of technology standards to identify and address possible challenges. Such efforts are critical to help build a solid CFL infrastructure, which is fundamental for CFL teacher education and the field of CFL. In the field of second language education, research on the implementation of ACTFL learning standards finds that the standards help promote learners' communicative competence and they have been well integrated into instructional resources and accepted by the field (Shrum & Glisan, 2016). Similar studies on standards for CFL teacher education, technology standards in particular, are needed greatly, especially nowadays when technology has been increasingly important in education and CFL has been developing so fast in the world.

CONCLUSION

From the perspective of TPACK (Mishra & Koehler, 2006), this chapter reviews and compares the technology standards for CFL teachers in the United States and China. Some conclusions can be drawn. First, the technology standards for CFL teachers are at the their early stage of development, so much work needs to be done to develop and elaborate the technology standards for CFL teachers, in order to provide a frame for CFL teacher education and direct its development. Second, a theoretical framework should be identified and/or developed for the technology standards for CFL teachers in order to be able to address the needs of globalized CFL education, given the particular characteristics of CFL education and the fast development and importance of technology in education. Third, efforts should be made to develop a continuum of technology standards to guide teachers from the entry level to the accomplished level, and thus help build a more solid and comprehensive infrastructure, which is fundamental and critical for sustained development of CFL education.

REFERENCES

ACTFL Foreign Language Teacher Standards Writing Team. (2013). *Program Standards for the Preparation of Foreign Language Teachers*. Retrieved from http://www.actfl.org/sites/default/files/pdfs/ACTFL-Standards20Aug2013.pdf

Anderson-Levitt, K. (2002). *Teaching cultures*. Cresskill, NJ: Hampton Press.

Borg, S. (2003). Teacher cognition in language teaching: A review of research on what language teachers think, know, believe, and do. *Language Teaching*, *36*(2), 81–109. doi:10.1017/S0261444803001903

Bos, B. (2011). Professional development for elementary teachers using TPACK. *Contemporary Issues in Technology & Teacher Education*, *11*(2), 167–183.

Chai, C. S., Koh, J. H. L., & Tsai, C.-C. (2010). Facilitating Preservice Teachers' Development of Technological, Pedagogical, and Content Knowledge (TPACK). *Journal of Educational Technology & Society*, *13*(4), 63–73.

Cheng, H. (2014). The study of CSL online teacher training course and the teachers' development of technological pedagogical content knowledge. *Journal of Technology and Chinese Language Teaching.*, *5*(2), 1–18.

Chinese Language Association of Secondary-Elementary Schools. (2007). *An Overview of the Twelve Professional Standards for K-12 Chinese Language Teachers.* Retrieved from https://nealrc.osu.edu/sites/nealrc.osu.edu/files/teacher-k-12-class-teachers-standards.pdf

Freeman, D. (2002). The hidden side of the work: Teacher knowledge and learning to teach. *Language Teaching*, *35*(01), 1–13. doi:10.1017/S0261444801001720

Freeman, D., & Johnson, K. E. (1998). Reconceptualizing the knowledge-base of language teacher education. *TESOL Quarterly*, *32*(3), 397–417. doi:10.2307/3588114

Furman, N., Goldberg, D., & Lusin, N. (2007). *Enrollments in languages other than English in United States institutions of higher education, fall 2006*. Retrieved from http://www.mla.org/pdf/06enrollmentsurvey_final.pdf

Goldburg, D., Looney, D., & Lusin, N. (2015). Enrollments in languages other than English in *United States institutions of higher education, fall 2013*. Retrieved from http://www.mla.org/pdf/2013_enrollment_survey.pdf

Guidance Committee for Higher Education of the Ministry of Education of China. (2009). 全日制汉语国际教育硕士专业学位研究生指导性培养方案 [Training guidance of full-time Master of Teaching Chinese to Speakers of Other Languages]. Retrieved from http://mtcsol.chinesecio.com/article/71

Hanban. (2007). 国际汉语教师标准 [Standard for International Chinese Language Teachers]. 外语教学与研究出版社 [Foreign Language Teaching and Research Press].

Hanban. (2014). 《国际汉语教师证书》考试大纲(试行) [Test Syllabus for International Chinese Language Teacher Certificate (Trial version)]. 人民教育出版社 [People's Education Press].

Hunter, J. (2015). *Technology integration and high possibility classrooms: Building from TPACK*. New York: Routledge.

International Society for Technology in Education. (2008). *ISTE standards teachers*. Retrieved from http://www.iste.org/standards/iste-standards/standards-for-teachers

Interstate New Teacher Assessment and Support Consortium. (2013). *InTASC: Model core teaching standards and learning progressions for teachers 1.0*. Washington, DC: Council of Chief State School Officers.

Interstate New Teacher Assessment and Support Consortium INTASC Foreign Language Standards Committee. (2002). *Model standards for licensing beginning foreign language teachers: A resource for state dialogue*. Retrieved from http://programs.ccsso.org/content/pdfs/ForeignLanguageStandards.pdf

Kang, Y., & Cheng, X. (2014). Teacher learning in the workplace: A study of the relationship between a novice EFL teacher's classroom practices and cognition development. *Language Teaching Research*, *18*(2), 169–186. doi:10.1177/1362168813505939

Katz, A., & Snow, M. A. (2009). Standards and second language teacher education. In A. Burns & J. C. Richards (Eds.), *The Cambridge guide to second language teacher education* (pp. 66–76). Cambridge, UK: Cambridge University Press.

Koehler, M., & Mishra, P. (2009). What Is Technological Pedagogical Content Knowledge? *Contemporary Issues in Technology & Teacher Education*, *9*(1), 60–70.

Lawrence, K. S. (1999). Standards for Foreign Language Learning in the 21st Century. *Np: Allen*.

Lewis, C. L. (2015). Preservice teachers' ability to identify technology standards: Does curriculum matter? *Contemporary Issues in Technology & Teacher Education*, *15*(2), 235–254.

Lo Bianco, J. (2011). Chinese: The gigantic *up-and-comer*. In L. Tsung & K. Cruickshank (Eds.), *Teaching and learning Chinese in global contexts: CFL worldwide* (pp. xiii–xxiv). London: Continuum.

Mishra, P., & Koehler, M. J. (2006). Technological Pedagogical Content Knowledge: A framework for teacher knowledge. *Teachers College Record*, *108*(6), 1017–1054. doi:10.1111/j.1467-9620.2006.00684.x

Murphy-Judy, K., & Youngs, B. (2006). Technology standards for teacher education, credentialing, and certification. In P. Hubbard & M. Levy (Eds.), *Teacher education in CALL* (pp. 45–60). Amsterdam: John Benjamins. doi:10.1075/lllt.14.06mur

National Board for Professional Teaching Standards. (2010). *World language standards* (2nd ed.). Retrieved from http://www.nbpts.org/sites/default/files/documents/certificates/nbpts-certificate-eaya-wl-standards.pdf

National East Asian Languages Resource Center at the Ohio State University and Chinese Language Association of Secondary-elementary Schools. (2007). *CLASS professional standards for K-12 Chinese teachers*. Retrieved from https://nealrc.osu.edu/sites/nealrc.osu.edu/files/teacher-k-12-class-teachers-standards.pdf

National Standards in Foreign Language Education. (2006). *Standards for foreign language learning: Preparing for the 21st century*. Retrieved from http://www.actfl.org/sites/default/files/pdfs/public/StandardsforFLLexecsumm_rev.pdf

Pufahl, I., & Rhodes, N. (2011). Foreign language instruction in U.S. Schools: Results of a national survey of elementary and secondary schools. *Foreign Language Annals*, *44*(2), 258–288. doi:10.1111/j.1944-9720.2011.01130.x

Richards, J. C., & Nunan, D. (Eds.). (1990). Second Language Teacher Education. New York: Cambridge University Press.

Shrum, J. L., & Glisan, E. W. (2016). *Teacher's handbook: Contextualized language instruction* (5th ed.). Boston: Heinle & Heinle.

Shulman, L. (1987). Knowledge-base and teaching: Foundations of the new reform. *Harvard Educational Review*, *57*(1), 1–22. doi:10.17763/haer.57.1.j463w79r56455411

The Council of Chief State School Officers. (2011). *Research synthesis*. Retrieved from http://www.ccsso.org/Resources/Publications/InTASC_Research_Synthesis.html

The Council of Chief State School Officers. (2013). *InTASC model core teaching standards and learning progressions for teachers 1.0*. Retrieved from http://www.ccsso.org/documents/2013/2013_intasc_learning_progressions_for_teachers.pdf

Xu, L. (2014). *2014年孔院年度报告* [2014 Hanban annual report]. Retrieved from http://www.hanban.edu.cn/report/pdf/2014.pdf

Zhang, X. (2009). 世界汉语教育史 [International Chinese education]. Beijing: Business Publishing House.

KEY TERMS AND DEFINITIONS

Accomplished Teachers: It refers to those teachers who have years of teaching experience and also excel in teaching. It is different from the term experienced teachers in that experienced teachers may not be accomplished.

Chinese as a Foreign Language: It refers to teaching Chinese to speakers of other languages. Teaching Chinese to speakers of other language is also often called Chinese as a second language, from the perspective of second language acquisition or depending on whether Chinese is spoken in the context outside of the classroom. However, in this chapter, the term Chinese as a foreign language (CFL) is used despite the different perspectives.

New Teachers: In the chapter, the term refers to newly certified teachers or who are in the first few years of their teaching careers. In the literature, the term is often used interchangeably with beginning teachers and novice teachers.

Teacher Certification: It refers to a process that a teacher candidate completes the requirements of a teacher education program and is awarded a certificate to be recognized as being qualified to teach.

Teacher Knowledge: It is one of the key concepts for studying teachers and teacher education. Researchers have argued about the differences between teacher knowledge and teacher's beliefs, but they tend to agree that it is hard to make a difference between the two concepts. In this chapter, teacher knowledge is used to refer to what teachers know.

Teacher Licensing: It is often used interchangeably with teacher certification, but it differs from teacher certification in that it is often associated with state approval in the United States—the teacher/candidate is either approved by the state to teach in that state or the institution where the candidate attend the teacher education program must be approved by the state department of education to offer teacher licenses.

Technology: The term technology can cover a wide range of instructional tools and resources in education, but in this chapter, it refers to those related to computer technology, such as computers, internet, multimedia resources, etc.

ENDNOTES

[1] Each of the five standards includes more detailed description and supporting elements. The complete version of ISTE standards can be found online.

[2] Hanban updated the Standards in 2012, but the new version is not available to the public.

Section 2
Language Teachers' Perceptions and Uses of Technology

Chapter 4
Language Teachers' Perceptions of External and Internal Factors in Their Instructional (Non-) Use of Technology

Haixia Liu
Beijing Normal University Zhuhai Campus, China & Michigan State University, USA

Chin-Hsi Lin
Michigan State University, USA

Dongbo Zhang
Michigan State University, USA

Binbin Zheng
Michigan State University, USA

ABSTRACT

Prior studies (e.g., Li & Walsh, 2011) found that language teachers did not use technology fully despite its possible facilitating function in language teaching. Through a survey and group discussions, this study explores pre-service Chinese-language teachers' perceptions of the internal and external barriers to their instructional technology use. The respondents (N=47) expressed five main types of external barriers: a) lack of technology, b) difficulty in accessing the available technology, c) lack of technical support, d) lack of proper assessment, and e) negative parental attitude. The two main internal barriers identified in this research were a) negative attitude originating from teachers' pedagogical beliefs, and b) lack of technology-related knowledge. The findings of this study should be of practical use in the future design and implementation of professional development aiming at improving language teachers' use of technology in teaching.

DOI: 10.4018/978-1-5225-0483-2.ch004

INTRODUCTION

The history of using technology such as computers, audio and video to facilitate foreign-language learning is not short. As Garrett (1991) noted, technology can "play a major role in foreign language learning and in research on that learning" (p. 95). The advent of new technologies (e.g., multimedia, mobile devices, and the Internet) has brought new opportunities for the facilitation of language learning and instruction in almost all major language areas including grammar, vocabulary, reading, writing, listening and speaking (Levy, 2009). The advantages of using technology in the classroom have also been verified as well. Warschauer and Harley's work (as cited in Li & Walsh, 2011) found that proper integration of information and communication technology (ICT) was associated with "a more interactive language classroom, motivating learners", and "authentic language output" (p. 101). Therefore, it is not surprising that there has been an increased emphasis on technology adoption in many national curriculum guidelines, including those for foreign languages (Oxford & June, 2007). The U.S. National Standards in Foreign Language Education Project (1999), for example, listed use of technology as one of the seven essential elements of curricular design. The considerably more recent 21st Century Skills Map for World Languages (ACTFL, 2011) also places particular emphasis on the integration of technology with classroom practices to enhance students' learning.

Despite this increased emphasis, the literature has shown that technology has not been used to its full potential in language teaching in U.S. (Ravitz, Becker, & Wong, 2000; Arnold, 2007). However, studies discussing *why* there had been such underuse among language teachers have been rare. Most existing research on technology acceptance or adoption mainly focused on teachers regardless of their teaching content (e.g., Ertmer, 1999; Ertmer, Ottenbreit, Sadik, Sendurur, & Sendurur, 2012; Teo, 2011, 2014). Yet more studies on how teachers from a particular academic content area use technology is in need. For an example, it is suggested that future study should look at "sector specific and subject specific barriers" (BECTA, 2004, p. 4). Given the importance of technology integration in language classrooms, and the low technology uptake by language teachers, the present study aims to find out what factors or barriers language teachers perceive as having an influence on their (non-) use of technology in their teaching.

LITERATURE REVIEW

Quite a few studies have touched on the issue of teachers' low levels of technology integration. One line of research has aimed to identify which aspects of technology-adoption models influence teachers' intentions to use technology by testing those models among teachers (e.g. Teo, 2011, 2014). Another has attempted to identify specific barriers that may prevent teachers from using technology in the classroom (e.g. Bradley & Russell, 1997; Ertmer, 1999; Ertmer et al., 2012; Veen, 1993). In spite of their seemingly divergent foci, both these lines of enquiry have aimed to explain technology (non-) use from external and internal angles.

External Factors

External factors are those that do not pertain to teachers themselves, but to resource-availability issues such as time, money, support, and training. They have been widely reported to have very substantial effects on teachers' technology adoption (e.g., Egbert, Paulus, & Nakamichi, 2002; Li, 2014; Li & Walsh, 2011),

Table 1. External barriers to technology adoption

External Barriers	Related Studies
Lack of time	(BECTA, 2004; Butler & Sellbom, 2002; Chizmar & Williams, 2001; Cuban et al., 2001; Fabry & Higgs, 1997; Snoeyink & Ertmer, 2001)
Lack of ICT resources	(BECTA, 2004; Guha, 2000; Mumtaz, 2000; Pelgrum, 2001)
Lack of reliable technologies	(Bradley & Russell, 1997; Cuban et al., 2001; Snoeyink & Ertmer, 2001)
Lack of support	(Cuban, 1999; Fox & Henri, 2005; Chizmar & Williams, 2001; Copley & Ziviani, 2004; Ertmer, 1999; Salehi & Salehi, 2012)
Lack of training	(Kirkwood, Kuyl, Parton & Grant, 2000; Snoeyink & Ertmer, 2001; Veen, 1993; Wild, 1996)

even though not all such studies used the same broad term *external factors* to describe the particular set of phenomena they were concerned with. For example, external factors are sometimes termed *facilitating conditions* in models of technology adoption and utilization such as the Technology-to-Performance Chain (TPC) model (Goodhue & Thompson, 1995) and the Unified Theory of Acceptance and Use of Technology (UTAUT) (Venkatesh, Morris, Davis & Davis, 2003). In the spherical model of second-language (L2) teachers' integration of technology into the classroom, Hong (2010) used *contextual factors* to describe resource-related issues such as "lack of computers" or "little support from school" (p. 61). External factors are sometimes also discussed as barriers that inhibit teachers' use of technology, hence the oft-used term *external barriers* (e.g., Butler & Sellbom, 2002; Chizmar & Williams, 2001; Cuban, Kirkpatrick & Peck, 2001; Snoeyink & Ertmer, 2001; Veen 1993). The different types of external barriers identified in the literature are presented in Table 1.

Table 1 sets forth the five main types of external barriers that tend to explain teachers' underuse or non-use of technology. *Lack of time* refers to the lacking of time needed to learn new technological skills, to attend technology-related professional development sessions (Fabry & Higgs, 1997), or to prepare multimedia materials by previewing websites, to plan how to integrate technology into lessons (Cuban et al., 2001), or to explore and practice using the specific technology that is available (BECTA, 2004).

Lack of ICT resources, the second major external barrier, has been found to be an important hindrance not only to good practice in the use of ICT itself, but to achievement in general (BECTA, 2004). A number of sub-factors were found to be related to this barrier, including hardware shortage, improper software, lack of proper resource organization or old and unreliable equipment (e.g. Pelgrum, 2001; Guha, 2000).

The third external barrier is *lack of reliable technology*, e.g., delays caused by equipment breaking down during class. Unreliable technology can lead teachers to fear equipment malfunctions, and thus deter them from using the equipment they have already (Bradley & Russell, 1997) and/or lead to their rejection of technology uptake (Cuban et al., 2001; Snoeyink & Ertmer, 2001).

The fourth external barrier identified in previous studies is *lack of support*, which may be technical (e.g., Cuban, 1999), institutional (e.g., Snoeyink & Ertmer, 2001), or financial (e.g., Chizmar & Williams, 2001). Scarcity of funds, a lack of skilled personnel, and inadequate technical support for ICT in schools were all also identified as major impediments to the integration of ICT into curricula (Copley & Ziviani, 2004; Ertmer, 1999; Salehi & Salehi, 2012).

The last external barrier that has frequently been reported in the literature is *lack of training* (e.g., Kirkwood et al., 2000). Specifically, teachers reported feeling that they were not adequately trained in how to solve technical problems or to understand the basic operations of technology and software applications (Snoeyink & Ertmer, 2001). Beyond training in basic technology skills, however, training in pedagogical use of those skills has also been found wanting (Snoeyink & Ertmer, 2001; Veen, 1993; Wild, 1996).

While the above-mentioned external barriers could all hinder teachers' technology implementation, they are relatively easy to identify and eliminate (Ertmer, 1999) as compared to the internal ones discussed below. As Ertmer (2012) recently noted, increasing access to technological resources has "effectively reduced and even eliminated" some external barriers (p. 424). However, even with improved access to resources such as hardware, Internet service, software, tools, training, and support, variations undoubtedly exist from school to school and region to region; and it is far from certain that the barriers faced by teachers are similar across geographic, socioeconomic and other contexts. Given the unique requirements of language learning – including but not limited to oral language practice and cultural learning – and variations between language-program types, it is worth finding out if language teachers experience special external barriers to the integration of technology into their teaching, i.e., external barriers that are *not* faced by teachers of other subject areas.

Internal Factors

Internal factors are more difficult to identify than external ones because they are closely related to individuals' attitudes toward and beliefs about technology, which according to Kerr, "may not be immediately apparent to others, or even to the teachers themselves" (as cited in Ertmer, 2005, p. 51).

Internal factors have been addressed in several theoretical frameworks covering technology adoption or use. In the Technology Acceptance Model (TAM; Davis, 1989), for example, individuals' intentions to use technology are influenced by their attitudes and their subjective norms – the latter being associated with individuals' perceptions of how other people value the use of technology. In addition, TAM holds that usage is affected by the *perceived usefulness* and *perceived ease of use* of a given technological component. Similarly, UTAUT proposes three major internal factors – *effort expectancy*, *performance expectancy*, and *social influence* – of which the first two refer to individuals' expectations of how easy to use and how useful such technology will be (which are clearly identifiable with/as the TAM's *perceived ease of use* and *perceived usefulness*). UTAUT's dimension of social influence, meanwhile, is about how other people influence individuals' use of technology, and thus can be seen as overlapping to a certain extent with the TAM's social-norms dimension. In the TPC model, the precursors to technology utilization include the following internal factors: *expected consequences of use* (beliefs), *affect toward use*, *social norms*, and *habit*. Other models that targeting at language teachers also include internal factors such as the *CALL teacher education* and *individual teacher factors* in Hong's (2010) study, or the *pedagogical beliefs*, *competence*, and *confidence* in Li's (2014) study. A careful comparison of the various rival models of technology adoption suggests that most internal factors involved are actually quite similar (see Table 2).

As in the case of external factors, many previous studies approached internal factors from a "barriers" perspective, investigating the roles played by the above-mentioned internal factors in preventing teachers' use of technology in the classroom as displayed in Table 2 below.

The first such grouping reflects *negative attitude* toward using ICT in education, which can be traced back to teachers' unfavorable perceptions of ICT's benefits and/or the level of effort required to use it. Some studies (e.g., Ertmer, 1999; BECTA, 2004) have seen this negative attitude as an essential barrier to teachers' technology use, insofar as teachers are unlikely to use technology when no evidence of usefulness can be found.

Table 2. Internal barriers to technology adoption

Internal Barriers	Related Studies
Negative attitude (e.g. Uncertainty about its worth/ Lack of belief in ICT benefits/ No perception of benefits)	(BECTA, 2004; Butler & Sellbom, 2002; Ertmer, 1999; Mumtaz, 2000)
Lack of confidence	(Bosley, Krechowiecka & Moon, 2005; Lee, 1997; Pina & Harris, 1993)
Computer anxiety	(Bradley & Russell, 1997; Guha, 2000)
Subjective norm (e.g. administrative disagreement)	(Teo, 2011; Butler & Sellbom, 2002)
Lack of incentive	(Chizmar & Williams, 1998; Schoepp, 2005)

Conversely, if teachers positively perceive that the use of technology is difficult or that technology-based methods need more effort than traditional ones, they will tend to experience *computer anxiety* (Bradley & Russell, 1997; Guha, 2000) or a *lack of confidence* in their computer competence (Bosley et al., 2005; Lee, 1997; Pina & Harris, 1993), which would in turn lead to their reduced use or complete avoidance of technology in teaching.

Subjective norm is defined as "the perceived social pressure to perform or not to perform" a specific action (Ajzen, 1991, p. 188). An internal barrier rooted in a sense that the teacher lacks support may in fact relate to real-world external barriers. When educational administrators are supportive of ICT implementation (i.e., an external factor), teachers can be motivated to use technology. However, if teachers perceive that technology use is not encouraged, this lack of support would have an unfavorable impact on their technology use. This internal barrier is also associated with the attitudes of students and colleagues.

Another internal barrier is *lack of incentives and motivations* (Chizmar & Williams, 1998; Schoepp, 2005). Teachers would feel less motivated to use technology in their teaching if no appreciation or obvious rewards can be earned for the extra efforts to learn to use technology.

Some other less frequently discussed internal barriers also exist. For example, teachers' *technology-use habits* can form internal barriers to technology implementation regardless of their attitudes or beliefs about technology use and their ICT skills (Limayem, Hirt, & Chin, 2001). Another under-studied internal factor is *subject culture*, "a general set of institutional practices and expectations which have grown up around a particular school subject" (Goodson & Mangan, 1995, p. 614), as teachers' willingness to use technology depends to a great extent on their perceptions of its compatibility with the general practices or norms of the subject in question (Hennessy, Ruthven, & Brindley, 2005).

The above literature review indicates that, while both internal and external factors (or more specifically, internal and external barriers) may affect teachers' technology adoption, it is unclear which of these factors/barriers particularly affect language teachers. Two research questions guided this study:

1. What external factors do language teachers perceive as having an impact on their integration of technology into instruction?
2. What internal factors do language teachers perceive as having an impact on their integration of technology into instruction?

METHOD

This study employed a mixed-methods approach, with quantitative data being collected via a questionnaire, and qualitative data from group discussions.

Participants

The participants in this study were 47 pre-service Chinese-language teachers enrolled in a certification program in Education at a university in the Midwestern United States. All were native speakers of Chinese and had bachelor's or master's degrees in a variety of disciplinary areas, such as Chinese Language Arts, Teaching English to Speakers of Other Languages (TESOL), Biology, Business, etc. There were 38 female and nine male participants, with 66% aged between 21 and 25 years old; 23% aged 26 to 30; and the remaining 11% aged 31 and above. The program in which the participants were enrolled was post-baccalaureate and involved an alternative route to certification. One of the features that distinguished it from traditional U.S. foreign-language teacher education programs was that, while taking courses with the program online through both synchronous and asynchronous communication, all participants were placed to teach full-time in K-12 schools.

Procedure

Data collection involved two steps. First, a researcher-developed questionnaire was administered to the participants online through Qualtrics (for details, see Instruments, below). Then, approximately one week later – as part of a required course that supported their teaching in schools – each participant attended one of several online focus-group discussions, in which they shared and discussed their views on and practices of technology use in Chinese-language teaching.

Instruments

1. **Survey:** The questionnaire consisted of three parts, designed to elicit the participants' demographic information, their perceptions of the relation of technology use to external factors, and their perceptions of the relation of technology use to internal factors. Each survey items was presented in Chinese, as a statement responded to via a five-point Likert scale, with 1 indicating strong disagreement and 5 strong agreement. The content of the questionnaire was based largely on three previously discussed technology-adoption models (TAM, UTAUT, and TPC), with the second and third components corresponding to those models' main external and internal factors, respectively. A total of 30 questions were included in the questionnaire, some of which (N=8) were adopted from Teo (2011).
    a. Demographic information: The first part of the survey consisted of four questions regarding the individual respondent's name, age group, gender, and educational background.
    b. External factors: The second part of the questionnaire included five statements focused on external factors affecting technology use in the respondents' Chinese-language teaching. An example of a statement from this section is, "The school offers a positive environment for my technology use." The Cronbach's α for these five items was 0.86.

c. Internal factors: Each of the 21 items constituting the third part of the questionnaire focused on one of three dimensions: *perceived usefulness*, *perceived ease of use*, and *subjective norms*. There were 10 items concerning perceived usefulness, of which an example is, "Information technology can improve students' interest in learning." The Cronbach's α for these 10 items was 0.91. For perceived ease of use, there were three items, including, "I think it is easy to use information technology." For these three, the Cronbach's α was 0.74. The last dimension, subjective norms, had eight items, including "My friends think that I should use information technology." For these eight, the Cronbach's α was 0.91.

2. **Focus Groups:** The participants were divided into seven groups, each with either six or seven members, to discuss issues relating to their technology use. A member of the instructional team of their course acted as the moderator for each group. All discussions were conducted in Chinese on Adobe Connect, an online meeting tool that was also used for the online course that the participants were taking, and audio-recorded using that software's recording function. Several open-ended questions were used to guide each group discussion. They covered the types of technology the participants had used; factors (pertaining or not pertaining to themselves) that had had an impact on what technologies they used and how they used them; and the types and sources of support for their use of technology that they hoped to receive in the future.

Data Analysis

All participants completed the questionnaire in full. Descriptive statistics were computed for the Likert-scale items, and a general inductive approach was used to analyze participants' responses during group discussions: with one of the researchers reviewing each one several times to identify commonalities across all responses. The same researcher was also responsible for transcribing this data and translating it into English. The other three researchers took turns reading the transcripts and the translations to ensure that both were error-free. They also reviewed the commonalities identified by the first researcher and noted areas where they had different ideas. Lastly, all four researchers met to develop a set of categories based on the commonalities, and these categories were grouped into broad themes related to the external and internal factors of interest in this study.

RESULTS

External Factors

Data from the survey and the focus groups were analyzed to answer our first research question, regarding external factors affecting teachers' technology adoption. Focus-group analysis revealed more specific information about how several external barriers had operated to negatively impact some of the respondents' technology use.

Environment

The first and second statements regarding facilitation conditions received average scores higher than 4 (see Table 3), indicating that on the whole, the respondents perceived their schools as being positive environments for technology use.

Time

Facilitation statements 3 and 4 attained average scores of 3.81 and 3.60, respectively, suggesting that the participants tended to have enough time for technology implementation in both classroom teaching and class preparation.

Resources

The last statement relating to facilitation received an average score of 3.06, indicating that the participants on the whole were not particularly confident or optimistic about the ease with which technological resources for teaching could be found. This seemed to be supported by some teachers' responses in the group discussion: for example, participant #3 compared the resources for Spanish and Chinese programs, noting that "Spanish has wonderful online programs, but not Chinese".

The group discussion revealed other themes related to limited resources, including *difficulty accessing available technology* and *devices that are not set up properly for what teachers want to use them for*. Regarding the first, many participants reported that it was not easy to reserve computer labs or mobile devices for their teaching. As one participant (#19) stated, "we need to make a reservation for using iPads." Another (#24) described a similar situation: "there are only 30 laptops in our school, but you need to make a reservation before use. Thus, we need to check the schedule of the computer lab, so we seldom use those [laptops]." Several participants reported that devices they intended to use were not ready. As participant #19 stated regarding her experience of using iPads, "Many apps [that we want to use] have not been installed, so we need to find a technician to download and install them." Several participants noted occasions on which they had failed to use technology because equipment they intended to use did not work at that time it was needed.

Table 3. Perceptions of facilitating conditions

Statements	M	SD
1. The school offers a positive environment for my technology use.	4.15	0.86
2. I can obtain technology usage help and suggestions from colleagues.	4.06	0.67
3. I have enough time in class to use technology.	3.81	0.97
4. I have enough preparation time to use technology in teaching.	3.60	1.08
5. It is easy for me to find technological resources for teaching.	3.06	1.21

Support

Though some teachers reported being able to obtain help from their colleagues, several said it was not easy to find technical support. As one participant (#5) commented, "teachers need to learn [how to operate technology equipment]. It would be very troublesome to find a technician for help." Another (#6) shared all the trouble she had gone through to solve technical problems by herself, e.g., using a search engine and reading a thick manual, and participant #19's above-mentioned negative experience with iPad apps left him feeling troubled. Some participants were unwilling to ask for help from technicians as frequently as they needed it – fearing that this would be bothersome – while others felt that too few technicians were available in their schools.

Assessment

In addition to the above-mentioned external factors, two more were revealed in group discussions: *assessment* and *parental attitude*. High-stakes testing has been identified as a main obstacle to technology use (e.g., Fox & Henri, 2005). Teachers are constantly under pressure to meet high standards in a limited amount of time, which can dis-incentivize their use of technology. However, our study's sample of Chinese-language teachers did not report experiencing any pressure of this kind, perhaps because Chinese is typically not a subject that involves high-stakes testing. Instead, the focus groups revealed a different kind of concern about assessment in relation to technology use. As one participant (#14) said, "One reason why I am against technology, maybe because I do not know it very well, is the difficulty in assessment. How do we know whether students have learned something or not [through the use of technology]? How do we know how they use technology?" Similarly, another participant (#11) indicated that because using technology to teach was a relatively new idea to her, there should be more rubrics for evaluating learning outcomes in technology-enhanced learning environments.

Parental Attitude

A few participants mentioned another external factor, *parental attitude*. As one participant (#3) explained, "maybe some parents do not want their children to spend much time on these devices after they come back from school. Some parents do not want their children to be online due to various considerations". Another participant (#16) shared a story from her school about a parent who filed a complaint about a teacher's use of the Internet to teach Chinese, because the parent believed that there was inappropriate language on the website that the teacher used.

Internal Factors

Our second research question focused on internal factors. Again, survey responses and focus-group transcriptions were both used to answer the question. The questionnaire covered three internal factors: *perceived ease of use*, *perceived usefulness*, and *subjective norms*. Our analysis of the group discussions yielded two additional factors: *pedagogical beliefs* and *technology-related knowledge*.

Perceived Usefulness

As Table 4 indicates, all the statements concerning perceived usefulness received average scores higher than 4. This finding suggests that, as a group, the respondent teachers thought that technology was useful both in their teaching and for students' learning. For example, there was a very high level of agreement with "Information technology can enhance students' interest in learning" (M = 4.57, SD = 0.54), and "The application of information technology makes my teaching more vivid" (M = 4.55, SD = 0.54).

Perceived Ease of Use

Table 5 presents the survey's three statements relating to perceived ease of use. All received average scores of 3 or above (M = 3.55, SD =0.77; M = 3.38, SD = 0.87; M = 3.51, SD = 0.75), indicating that the participants did not feel that learning to use and using technology were especially challenging. Yet their perceptions did not seem to be very positive, either, as none of the statements received average scores over 4. Compared to the other two internal factors (see Tables 4 and 6), the ratings appeared low here.

Subjective Norms

Table 6 sets forth the subjective norms perceived by the teachers in this study. The last statement in this category was rated highest (M = 4.32, SD = 0.84), which suggests that most participants tended to think positively about technology use in their future teaching. Statements 3, 4, 5, 6 and 7 were all rated close to 4.00 (M = 3.98, SD =0.61; M = 3.96, SD = 0.62; M = 4.02, SD = 0.64; M = 4.00, SD = 0.69; M = 3.94, SD = 0.73); taken together, these positive responses suggest that the participants as a group were positively influenced by others in their workplaces as well as by academic programs aimed at promoting the use of technology in Chinese teaching.

Table 4. Teachers' perceptions of technology's usefulness

Statements	M	SD
1. Information technology can enhance students' interest in learning.	4.57	0.54
2. Information technology can improve students' language ability.	4.17	0.70
3. Use of information technology can improve students' autonomic learning.	4.26	0.74
4. Use of information technology can improve students' collaborative-learning ability.	4.00	0.81
5. Use of information technology can improve students' problem-solving ability.	4.17	0.73
6. Information technology gives me inspiration for teaching design.	4.45	0.54
7. Use of information technology in teaching enriches my teaching content.	4.55	0.54
8. The application of information technology makes my teaching more vivid.	4.55	0.54
9. Using information technology gives me more confidence in teaching.	4.17	0.84
10. Using information technology improves my teaching quality.	4.30	0.78

Table 5. Teachers' perceptions of technology's ease of use

Statements	M	SD
1. I feel that it is easy to learn information technology.	3.55	0.77
2. I feel that it is easy to use information technology.	3.38	0.87
3. I feel that it is easy to use information technology in teaching.	3.51	0.75

Table 6. Teachers' subjective norms

Statements	M	SD
1. My friends think that I should use information technology.	3.70	0.83
2. My classmates think that I should use information technology.	3.74	0.85
3. My colleagues think that I should use information technology.	3.98	0.61
4. My advisor thinks that I should use information technology.	3.96	0.62
5. My professors think that I should use information technology.	4.02	0.64
6. My principal thinks that I should use information technology.	4.00	0.69
7. My school division requires that I use information technology.	3.94	0.73
8. I think using information technology is a necessary requirement for future teaching.	4.32	0.84

Pedagogical Beliefs

The results of the survey items presented in Table 6, above, showed that as a group, the participants tended to think positively about technology implementation. On the other hand, group discussions revealed that some internal barriers did exist, one being closely associated with pedagogical beliefs, particularly in relation to the learners they taught. For example, one participant who taught in a preschool (#17) said that she seldom used technology, explaining:

I rarely use technology because I am teaching preschoolers, so what I do most often is demonstration with real objects. The only things related to technology usage are some websites such as Better Chinese based on a textbook series for young learners of Chinese. I would select some of the exercises from those websites to practice with children. I can just use the abundant materials that I have to create flashcards rather than using Quizlet [a website for creating online flashcards], which seems troublesome to me.

In short, this participant did not use technology mainly because she did not think it would be appropriate for her students, and because there were low-tech alternatives to popular but "troublesome" forms of technology. Another participant (#39) thought that students should not be given technological tools such as a smartphones or iPads because these devices would distract their attention away from their studies and interfered with their learning.

Technology-Related Knowledge

Another internal factor that emerged from our focus groups is related to knowledge and skills. Previous studies revealed two main types of knowledge/skills that teachers require if they are to use technology efficiently: specific *technological knowledge*, and *technological pedagogical knowledge* (Snoeyink & Ertmer, 2001; Hughes, 2005). The group discussions indicated that our sample lacked both these kinds of knowledge. For example, when the participants were asked about what kinds of support they needed with regard to educational technology, one participant (#34) mentioned that once he failed to convert an audio file from a WMV format to an MP3 format due to his lack of knowledge of how to do so, and therefore was unable to prepare materials for students..

What concerned the participants the most in this sphere was technological pedagogical knowledge. As indicated earlier by the survey results, the participants overall felt comfortable with using technology, but lacked technological pedagogical knowledge to ensure that technology was used appropriately to meet their needs. As noted by one participant (#19), "the major problem is classroom management. It is a severe problem. Too much technology will take [students'] attention away". Another (#34) voiced a similar concern:

I agree with what the teacher said just now about how to make sure students do what they are told to do [when technology is being used in classroom], instead of goofing around. This happens in our middle school. One time I asked my students to compare China and the U.S., but they were just surfing around. So, can someone guide us on how to catch students' attention, and how to control their behavior [when we are using technology to teach]?

Another example suggested that some teachers lacked the technological pedagogical knowledge to engage students effectively. When comparing face-to-face class instruction against instruction in a computer lab, one participant (#14) said:

When students are sitting in a classroom and interacting with the teacher, they do not get bored because the instructor is teaching. There are emotions and body language. When you use technology, students are interested at first. But after 20 minutes, they no longer feel excited, so the real effective time for learning is no more than 30 minutes.

DISCUSSION

External Factors

Teachers have increasing access to technology and use computers frequently for both personal and professional reasons (Project Tomorrow, 2008). Ertmer's (2012) review of the key external barriers to technology adoption found that many external barriers (access, support, etc.) have been greatly reduced in the majority of schools. However, Ertmer's work was based on a national survey that treated teachers in the U.S. as a single group, without differentiating between subject areas. Hence, it is worth asking whether the same finding applies to language teachers.

The present study's survey results showed that our sample of Chinese-language teachers, considered as a group, had satisfactory school environments vis-à-vis the use technology, though a few of them felt that they lacked the time and/or resources to incorporate technology into their teaching. This partially confirms Ertmer's (2012) finding that increased access to technology in U.S. schools has considerably reduced first-order barriers.

On the other hand, group discussions among the same Chinese-language teachers revealed that such external barriers, though reduced, still exist. The first type of external barrier identified in this study was resources. Hew and Brush (2007) devised a four-part typology of resource limitations: 1) technology (including computers, peripherals, and software); 2) access to available technology (covering the amount, types and location of technology); 3) time; and 4) technical support. Our focus-group results showed that a lack of all four types of resources remained. Though no participants said that they did not have access to computers or the Internet, some did mention the limited availability of technology in their schools, and others reported that they still experienced a lack of access to such technology as was available. Additionally, some participants felt it was impolite to ask for help from technicians as frequently as they actually needed it; and, as a result, that they needed to learn how to troubleshoot technical-equipment problems for themselves.

Our study also identified assessment as an external barrier to the use of technology. Prior literature pointed out that high-stakes testing was the most important such factor (e.g., Butzin, 2004; Fox & Henri, 2005). While we did not find any external barriers of that exact type, we did identify a related one: participants' lack of clarity on how to appropriately assess how much their students were learning, if that learning was technology-mediated. This finding demonstrates that the technology-supported classroom has brought new challenges to language teachers when it comes to measuring student learning and the effects of their own teaching.

We identified parental attitude as another external factor, which was not a completely new finding. For example, Liu (2011) pointed out parental involvement as one of the factors influencing teachers' technology integration. Specifically, our study found that some parents opposed the use of technology due to concerns about online safety or age-inappropriate information. Such attitudes would understandably inhibit teachers' use of technology.

Internal Factors

The gap between increased computer access and technology training, on the one hand, and the continued underuse of technology, on the other, has led researchers to focus on internal factors (e.g., Ertmer & Ottenbreit, 2010; Teo, 2014). The Chinese-language teachers in our sample generally had a positive attitude toward technology integration, in that they assigned high scores to the survey dimensions *perceived usefulness* and *perceived ease of use*, and their ratings for *subjective norms* also appeared to reflect positive feelings toward technology integration. Though one might assume that the high ratings for these three internal factors would necessarily result in the use of technology in language classes, our findings did not support such an assumption. In focus groups, many of our participants explained why they did not use or were even "against" using technology. Three major reasons hindering their use of technology emerged: a lack of technological knowledge, a lack of technological pedagogical knowledge, and beliefs about their students.

A lack of specific technological knowledge could discourage teachers from using technology, and just such a barrier has been frequently reported in the literature in the case of non-language teachers (e.g.,

Hew & Brush, 2007; Snoeyink & Ertmer, 2001; Williams, Coles, Wilson, Richardson, & Tuson. 2000). Taken together, prior findings and those of the present study on Chinese-language teachers suggest that it is always necessary for teachers to acquire technological knowledge of both hardware and software and keep that knowledge up to date, if such technology is to be used effectively in the classroom.

In addition to reporting technological knowledge as an internal barrier to their technology use, several participants also stated that they lacked necessary knowledge of how to engage students with technology. Previous studies have suggested that technology has the potential to provide innovative or even transformational educational opportunities (e.g. Hughes, 2005). However, unless they are provided with professional development in technology-assisted pedagogy specific to their field, language teachers are likely to feel challenged by technology and less willing to use it in the classroom.

Lastly, a few participants said they did not use technology due to their beliefs about their students: e.g., that they were too young to be educated through technology, or too young to be disciplined in a technology-integrated classroom. Pajare (1992) defined teachers' beliefs as encompassing 1) beliefs about educational components, such as curricula and materials, 2) beliefs about students, and 3) beliefs about the role of teachers in the education process – all of which could influence what they teach and how. Thus, it was not especially surprising that beliefs about students emerged as a barrier hindering some of our participants' use of technology in their classrooms. This finding seemed to echo that of Palak and Walls (2009), suggesting that while (pedagogical) knowledge of technology can have a direct influence on teachers' technology implementation, it needs to be understood and interpreted in the context of teachers' pedagogical beliefs.

CONCLUSION

This chapter's findings demonstrate that – although access to technology has been increased greatly over the years – teachers still face various extrinsic and intrinsic barriers to the classroom use of technology. Previous studies have made suggestions as to how to overcome such barriers (e.g., Ertmer, 2005; Hew & Brush, 2007); however, overcoming internal barriers, which is likely to involve changing teachers' attitudes and beliefs, can be very challenging in comparison to overcoming barriers that do not pertain to teachers themselves. On the one hand, continuous professional development is needed to help address some if not all of the internal barriers teachers confront; on the other, more research is needed to evaluate the effectiveness of various professional-development programs/models, which would allow the optimization of teacher learning with respect to technology integration, which in turn would tend to positively impact student outcomes.

REFERENCES

Ajzen, I. (1991). The theory of planned behavior. *Organizational Behavior and Human Decision Processes*, *50*(2), 179–211. doi:10.1016/0749-5978(91)90020-T

American Council on Teaching of Foreign Languages (ACTFL). (2011). *21st Century Skills Map for World Languages*. Retrieved October 25, 2015, from https://www.actfl.org/sites/default/files/pdfs/21stCenturySkillsMap/p21_worldlanguagesmap.pdf

Arnold, N. (2007). Technology-mediated learning 10 years later: Emphasizing pedagogical or utilitarian applications? *Foreign Language Annals, 40*(1), 161–181. doi:10.1111/j.1944-9720.2007.tb02859.x

Bosley, C., Krechowiecka, I., & Moon, S. (2005). *Review of literature on the use of information and communication technology in the context of careers education and guidance.* Centre for Guidance Studies, University of Derby. Commissioned by BECTA. Retrieved September 20, 2015, from http://www.derby.ac.uk/files/icegs_review_of_literature_on_ the_use_of_ict2005.pdf

Bradley, G., & Russell, G. (1997). Computer experience, school support and computer anxieties. *Educational Psychology, 17*(3), 267–284. doi:10.1080/0144341970170303

British Educational Communication and Technology Agency (BECTA). (2004). *A review of the research literature on barriers to the uptake of ICT by teachers.* Retrieved September 17, 2015, from http://dera.ioe.ac.uk/1603/1/becta_2004_barrierstouptake_litrev.pdf

Butler, D., & Sellbom, M. (2002). Barriers to adopting technology for teaching and learning. *EDUCAUSE Quarterly, 25*(2), 22–28.

Butzin, S. M. (2004). *Project CHILD: A proven model for the integration of computer and curriculum in the elementary classroom.* Retrieved August 18, 2015, from http://www.acec-journal.org/archives_archives.php

Chizmar, J. F., & Williams, D. B. (2001). What do faculty want? *EDUCAUSE Quarterly, 24*(1), 18–24.

Copley, J., & Ziviani, J. (2004). Barriers to the use of assistive technology for children with multiple disabilities. *Occupational Therapy International, 11*(4), 229–243. doi:10.1002/oti.213 PMID:15771212

Cuban, L. (1999). The technology puzzle. *Education Week, 18*(43), 68–69.

Cuban, L., Kirkpatrick, H., & Peck, C. (2001). High access and low use of technologies in high school classrooms: Explaining an apparent paradox. *American Educational Research Journal, 38*(4), 813–834. doi:10.3102/00028312038004813

Davis, F. D. (1989). Perceived usefulness, perceived ease of use, and user acceptance of information technology. *Management Information Systems Quarterly, 13*(3), 319–340. doi:10.2307/249008

Egbert, J., Paulus, T. M., & Nakamichi, Y. (2002). The impact of CALL instruction on classroom computer use: A foundation for rethinking technology in teacher education. *Language Learning & Technology, 6*(3), 108–126.

Ertmer, P. A. (1999). Addressing first- and second-order barriers to change: Strategies for technology integration. *Educational Technology Research and Development, 47*(4), 47–61. doi:10.1007/BF02299597

Ertmer, P. A. (2005). Teacher pedagogical beliefs: The final frontier in our quest for technology integration? *Educational Technology Research and Development, 53*(4), 25–39. doi:10.1007/BF02504683

Ertmer, P. A., & Ottenbreit-Leftwich, A. T. (2010). Teacher technology change: How knowledge, confidence, beliefs, and culture intersect. *Journal of Research on Technology in Education, 42*(3), 255–284. doi:10.1080/15391523.2010.10782551

Ertmer, P. A., Ottenbreit-Leftwich, A. T., Sadik, O., Sendurur, E., & Sendurur, P. (2012). Teacher beliefs and technology integration practices: A critical relationship. *Computers & Education*, *59*(2), 423–435. doi:10.1016/j.compedu.2012.02.001

Fabry, D., & Higgs, J. (1997). Barriers to the effective use of technology in education. *Journal of Educational Computing*, *17*(4), 385–395. doi:10.2190/C770-AWA1-CMQR-YTYV

Fox, R., & Henri, J. (2005). Understanding teacher mindsets: IT and change in Hong Kong schools. *Journal of Educational Technology & Society*, *8*(2), 161–169.

Garrett, N. (1991). Technology in the service of language learning: Trends and issues. *Modern Language Journal*, *75*(1), 74–101. doi:10.1111/j.1540-4781.1991.tb01085.x

Goodhue, D. L., & Thompson, R. L. (1995). Task-technology fit and individual performance. *Management Information Systems Quarterly*, *19*(2), 213–236. doi:10.2307/249689

Goodson, I. F., & Mangan, J. M. (1995). Subject cultures and the introduction of classroom computers. *British Educational Research Journal*, *21*(5), 613–628. doi:10.1080/0141192950210505

Guha, S. (2000). *Are we all technically prepared?Teachers' perspectives on the causes of comfort or discomfort in using computers at elementary grade teaching*. Paper presented at the Annual Meeting of the National Association for the Education of Young Children, Atlanta, GA.

Hennessy, S., Ruthven, K., & Brindley, S. (2005). Teacher perspectives on integrating ICT into subject teaching: Commitment, constraints, caution, and change. *Journal of Curriculum Studies*, *37*(2), 155–192. doi:10.1080/0022027032000276961

Hew, K. F., & Brush, T. (2007). Integrating technology into K-12 teaching and learning: Current knowledge gaps and recommendations for future research. *Educational Technology Research and Development*, *55*(3), 223–252. doi:10.1007/s11423-006-9022-5

Hong, K. H. (2010). CALL teacher education as an impetus for L2 teachers in integrating technology. *ReCALL*, *22*(1), 53–69. doi:10.1017/S095834400999019X

Hughes, J. (2005). The role of teacher knowledge and learning experiences in forming technology-integrated pedagogy. *Journal of Technology and Teacher Education*, *13*(2), 277–302.

Kerr, S. T. (1996). Visions of sugarplums: The future of technology, education, and the schools. In S. T. Kerr (Ed.), *Technology and the future of schooling: Ninety-fifth yearbook of the National Society for the Study of Education* (pp. 1–27). Chicago: University of Chicago Press.

Kirkwood, M., Kuyl, T. V. D., Parton, N., & Grant, R. (2000, September). *The New Opportunities Fund (NOF) ICT training for teachers programme: Designing a powerful online learning environment*. Paper presented at the European conference on educational research, Edinburgh, UK.

Lee, D. (1997). Factors influencing the success of computer skills learning among in-service teachers. *British Journal of Educational Technology*, *28*(2), 139–141. doi:10.1111/1467-8535.00018

Levy, M. (2009). Technologies in use for second language learning. *Modern Language Journal*, *93*(1), 769–782. doi:10.1111/j.1540-4781.2009.00972.x

Li, L. (2014). Understanding language teachers' practice with educational technology: A case from China. *System*, *46*, 105–119. doi:10.1016/j.system.2014.07.016

Li, L., & Walsh, S. (2011). Technology uptake in Chinese EFL classes. *Language Teaching Research*, *15*(1), 99–125. doi:10.1177/1362168810383347

Limayem, M., Hirt, S. G., & Chin, W. W. (2001). Intention does not always matter: The contingent role of habit on IT usage behavior.*Proceedings of the 9th European Conference on Information Systems*.

Liu, S. H. (2011). Factors related to pedagogical beliefs of teachers and technology integration. *Computers & Education*, *56*(4), 1012–1022. doi:10.1016/j.compedu.2010.12.001

Mumtaz, S. (2000). Factors affecting teachers' use of information and communications technology: A review of the literature. *Journal of Information Technology for Teacher Education*, *9*(3), 319–341. doi:10.1080/14759390000200096

National Standards in Foreign Language Education Project. (1999). *Standards for foreign language learning in the 21st century*. Lawrence, KS: Allen Press.

Oxford, R. L., & Jung, S. (2007). National guidelines for technology integration in TESOL programs: Factors affecting (non) implementation. In M. A. Kassen, R. Z. Lavine, K. Murphy-Judy, & M. Peters (Eds.), *Preparing and developing technology-proficient L2 teachers* (pp. 23–48). San Marcos, TX: CALICO.

Pajares, M. F. (1992). Teachers' beliefs and educational research: Cleaning up a messy construct. *Review of Educational Research*, *62*(3), 307–332. doi:10.3102/00346543062003307

Palak, D., & Walls, R. T. (2009). Teachers' beliefs and technology practices: A mixed-methods approach. *Journal of Research on Technology in Education*, *41*(4), 417–441. doi:10.1080/15391523.2009.10782537

Pelgrum, W. J. (2001). Obstacles to the integration of ICT in education: Results from a worldwide educational assessment. *Computers & Education*, *37*(2), 163–178. doi:10.1016/S0360-1315(01)00045-8

Pina, A., & Harris, B. (1993). *Increasing teachers' confidence in using computers for education*. Paper presented at the Annual Meeting of the Arizona Educational Research Organisation, Tucson, AZ.

Project Tomorrow. (2008). *21st century learners deserve a 21st century education*. Selected National Findings of the Speak Up 2007 Survey. Retrieved March 28, 2015, from http://www.tomorrow.org/speakup/speakup_congress_2007.html

Ravitz, J., Becker, H., & Wong, Y. (2000). *Constructivist-compatible beliefs and practices among U.S. teachers*. Retrieved December 20, 2015, from http://www.crito.uci.edu/TLC/FINDINGS/REPORT4/REPORT4.PDF

Salehi, H., & Salehi, Z. (2012). Challenges for using ICT in education: Teachers' insights. *International Journal of e-Education, e-Business, e- Management Learning*, *2*(1), 40–43.

Schoepp, K. W. (2005). Technology integration barriers in a technology-rich environment. *Learning and Teaching in Higher Education: Gulf Perspectives, 2*(1), 1-24. Retrieved from http://www.zu.ac.ae/lthe/vol2no1/lthe02_05.pdf

Snoeyink, R., & Ertmer, P. A. (2001). Thrust into technology: How veteran teachers respond. *Journal of Educational Technology Systems*, *30*(1), 85–111. doi:10.2190/YDL7-XH09-RLJ6-MTP1

Teo, T. (2011). Factors influencing teachers' intention to use technology: Model development and test. *Computers & Education*, *57*(4), 2432–2440. doi:10.1016/j.compedu.2011.06.008

Teo, T. (2014). Unpacking teachers' acceptance of technology: Tests of measurement invariance and latent mean differences. *Computers & Education*, *75*, 127–135. doi:10.1016/j.compedu.2014.01.014

Veen, W. (1993). The role of beliefs in the use of information technology: Implications for teacher education, or teaching the right thing at the right time. *Journal of Information Technology for Teacher Education*, *2*(2), 139–153. doi:10.1080/0962029930020203

Venkatesh, V., Morris, M. G., Davis, F. D., & Davis, G. B. (2003). User acceptance of information technology: Toward a unified view. *Management Information Systems Quarterly*, *27*(3), 425–478.

Wild, M. (1996). Technology refusal: Rationalising the failure of student and beginning teachers to use computers. *British Journal of Educational Technology*, *27*(2), 134–143. doi:10.1111/j.1467-8535.1996.tb00720.x

Williams, D., Coles, L., Wilson, K., Richardson, A., & Tuson, J. (2000). Teachers and ICT: Current use and future needs. *British Journal of Educational Technology*, *31*(4), 307–320. doi:10.1111/1467-8535.00164

KEY TERMS AND DEFINITIONS

Assessment: To make an official evaluation of something or someone to measure the quantity and quality of (knowledge, beliefs, etc.).

External Barriers: Difficulties or obstacles that do not pertain to oneself, but are related to outside issues (such as resource availability).

Internal Barriers: Difficulties or obstacles that are originated from an individual's ideas, concepts or thoughts about something.

Pedagogical Beliefs: A state of mind in which a teacher thinks to hold true for teaching and learning, with or without evidence to support such state of mind.

Technical Support: Assistant services provided to people who use technology products including computers, Internet, mobile devices, etc.

Technology Resources: Available sources related with technology use, including financial support, technology training, access to technology such as computers, Internet and so on.

Technology-Related Knowledge: An understanding or awareness of facts, information or skill related to using technology products such as computers, Internet etc.

Chapter 5
Identifying the Contributors to Improve Mobile-Based TPACK Competency of Elementary School Teachers in China

Zhong Sun
Capital Normal University, China

Jiaxin You
Capital Normal University, China

Wei Song
Capital Normal University, China

Zheng Qu
Capital Normal University, China

Liming Luo
Capital Normal University, China

ABSTRACT

Self-Efficacy (SE) and technology acceptance are two contributors related to Technological Pedagogical and Content Knowledge (TPACK). Many studies have indicated that TPACK is correlated with SE and the level of technology acceptance in both traditional and online learning environments. Studies using mobile learning devices in the classroom, however, are yet to be established. The authors conducted an empirical study by investigating mobile-based TPACK, SE, and technology acceptance of more than 500 English teachers from about 220 elementary schools in China, who used Android system-based pad in classrooms for one year. As a result, SE and technology acceptance had indirect positive effects on mobile-based TPACK, while no significant difference was observed in gender for TPACK. However, younger teachers and teachers with higher levels of education showed superior TPACK levels than other participants in the study. Finally, several implications for teacher professional development, limitations, and future research plans are presented.

DOI: 10.4018/978-1-5225-0483-2.ch005

INTRODUCTION

Nowadays, mobile learning constructs a new learning environment different from the past. Mobile learning devices such as tablets and mobile phones with iOS or Android system are making their way into classrooms of many countries through technological integration in education. In the process of integrating mobile technology with education, teachers have become a key factor in improving the effectiveness of mobile learning (Jung & Latchem, 2011; Ng & Nicholas, 2013).

However, the frequency and level of information and communication technology (ICT) used by teachers in the classroom is still limited by multiple factors (Corbeil & Corbeil, 2007; Ozdamli & Uzunboylu, 2014). Many teachers have difficulties in managing information resources, designing learning activities, and monitoring the learning process, especially when using mobile learning devices (Ahmad et al., 2013; Embong et al., 2012a; Embong et al., 2012b). Therefore, improving teachers' specific knowledge and skills about mobile technology integration will be key in the near future (Ekanayake & Wishart, 2014; Georgina and Hosford, 2009).

Since the Technological Pedagogical and Content Knowledge (TPACK) was proposed a decade ago (Koehler & Mishra, 2005), the concept has been applied in many countries' teacher professional development. With the rapid development of mobile learning in Chinese elementary schools, teachers faced some difficulties on identifying the effective contributors of the mobile-based TPACK learning. The current study aims to explore the main contributors for mobile-based TPACK on the basis of a statewide survey.

LITERATURE REVIEW

Technological Pedagogical and Content Knowledge

Proposed by Koehler and Mishra in 2005, based on Shulman's pedagogical content knowledge (PCK), the TPACK framework comprises three parts, namely: technological knowledge (TK); pedagogical knowledge (PK); and content knowledge (CK) (Koehler et. al., 2007). Besides TK, PK, and CK, the additional four elements originated from this framework were pedagogical content knowledge (PCK), technological content knowledge (TCK), technological pedagogical knowledge (TPK), and technological pedagogical and content knowledge (TPACK), as shown in Figure 1.

Although some researchers argued that TPACK takes the concept of technology integration and packages it as a framework that is much too big (i.e., one that embodies seven distinct knowledge types) while simultaneously making it too small by dividing the "package" into so many pieces that they have become impossible to distinguish from one another (e.g., TK vs. TCK), thus might be vague to enable reasonable application (Brantley & Ertmer, 2013). However, many other researches indicated that TPACK provides a new perspective on repositioning and developing professional qualities of teachers. Many scholars emphasized the importance of TPACK application in teachers (Finger, Proctor & Albion, 2010; Harris, Grandgenett, & Hofer, 2010; Koehler, Shin, and Mishra, 2012), regarding TPACK as a framework to cultivate world language teachers (Van, 2008); a tool to design the mobile learning environment (Wong, et.al., 2015); and, an indicator of future teachers' technology integration into laptop infused classroom (Hughes, 2013). Therefore, improving TPACK capabilities has become an important research focus in IT-enabled professional development of teachers.

Figure 1. TPACK framework (Koehler and Mishra, 2005)

In order to make TPACK more effective to improve the teachers' expertise, many scholars examined the possible factors influencing TPACK such as age, gender, self-efficacy and technology acceptance. Koh and his colleagues analyzed the relative effect of age, gender, and TPACK constructs on the TPACK perceptions of pre-service teachers. (Koh, et. al., 2011). SE and technology acceptance are regarded as valuable contributors for the development of teachers' TPACK (Abbitt, 2011;Bull, 2009; Huang & Liaw, 2007; Smith & Sivo, 2012; Teo & Noyes, 2010; Wang et al., 2004).

However, only a few studies focused on contributors that impact TPACK from the perspectives of SE and technology acceptance in a mobile learning environment. To enrich this line of research, this study aims to analyze the mobile-based TPACK of elementary school English teachers in China and its relationship with their mobile-based SE and technology acceptance.

Self-Efficacy

Bandura (1996) described SE as an individual's beliefs in and expectations of his or her capability to perform a task. Bandura's theory of SE would suggest that increasing teacher knowledge would lead to increased self-efficacy beliefs and potentially to increase technology use in the classroom, as well as an increased likelihood that this technology use will be based on knowledge of pedagogy and content (Abbitt, 2001).

To connect the relationships between self-efficacy and TPACK, several correlational analyses were conducted. For instance, Sahin, Akturk and Schmidt (2009) investigated the relationship between pre-service teachers' perceived knowledge in TPACK domains and their beliefs about their abilities to teach in a classroom (self-efficacy beliefs). The study found significant differences in self-efficacy beliefs with differing levels of knowledge in technology, pedagogy, and content knowledge.

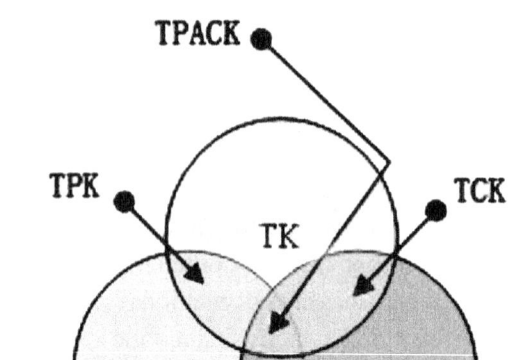

In a similar study, Abbitt (2011) investigated the relationships between TPACK and SE beliefs of pre-service teachers about technology integration. The results indicated that the SE of pre-service teachers showed a significant association with TPK, TCK, TK, PCK, and TPCK, while the correlativity do not reach statistical significance in the dimension of PK.

Furthermore, in a study of examining 25 teachers' use of technology for teaching, Wang et al. (2004) discussed factors that enabled teachers to overcome barriers and founded that teachers need more time to understand technology integration courses because of the lack of SE.

Although previous studies identified a possible relationship between self-efficacy and TPACK toward teaching, the complex nature of this relationship under mobile learning environment requires further study.

Technology Acceptance Model

According to some researches, another valuable contributor that affects TPACK is technology acceptance (Hayashi et al., 2004; Teo & Noyes, 2010; Smith & Sivo, 2012).

TAM is a theory brought up by Davis (1989) that models user acceptance of the proposed information systems. TAM contains two main determinants, namely, (1) perceived usefulness (PU), which reflects the degree of use of a particular individual's system to improve the performance of his or her work, and (2) perceived ease of use (PEOU), which reflects the individual's consideration of the ease of using a specific system level (Davis, 1989). The TAM postulates that user perception of the usefulness and ease of use is related to their attitude and behavioral intention to make use of technology (Teo, 2009b). Teacher's technology acceptance is important for successful utilization of new technology (Waheed & Jam, 2010). The perception of easy and usefulness of technology will affect teachers' attitude towards use of technology and subsequently how they use technology in classrooms (Teo, 2009a; Teo, 2010).

The usefulness and ease of use of multimedia and Internet resources have the positive effects on TPACK of pre-service teachers, while TPACK affects their attitude toward technology use and intention to integrate technology in teaching (Liu, 2011). For other informational technology, such as the ease of spreadsheet use and the use of spreadsheet template, technology acceptance has a positive effect on the teaching in academic curriculum about TPACK (Chong, et al., 2015). For blended online training, the usefulness and ease of use of technology are also effective contributors for TPACK. (Alsofyani et al., 2012)

However, most of these aforementioned studies were conducted in the context of multimedia or online learning environment. The contributors to TPACK should be examined and explored to meet the need of the emerging mobile learning environment.

RESEARCH HYPOTHESES

The current study aimed to analyze teachers' TPACK and its relationship with SE and TAM in a mobile learning environment. Hypothetical structural models are used to explore the effective indicators on mobile-based TPACK. Elements including mobile-based SE (Figure 2), PU and PEOU (i.e., TAM variables) (Figure 3) are latent variables in this study. Meanwhile, we also considered the effects of the different characteristics of teachers, particularly gender, age, and educational background, on TPACK.

To achieve the purpose of this experiment, this study proposed the following hypotheses:

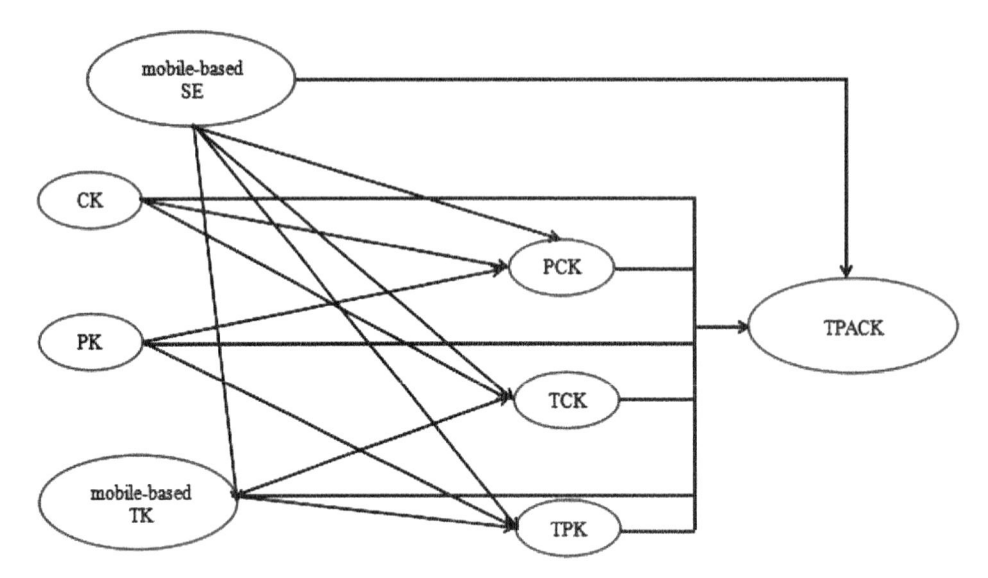

Figure 2. Proposed model for mobile-based SE and TPACK

Figure 3. Proposed model for TAM (PU and PEOU) and TPACK

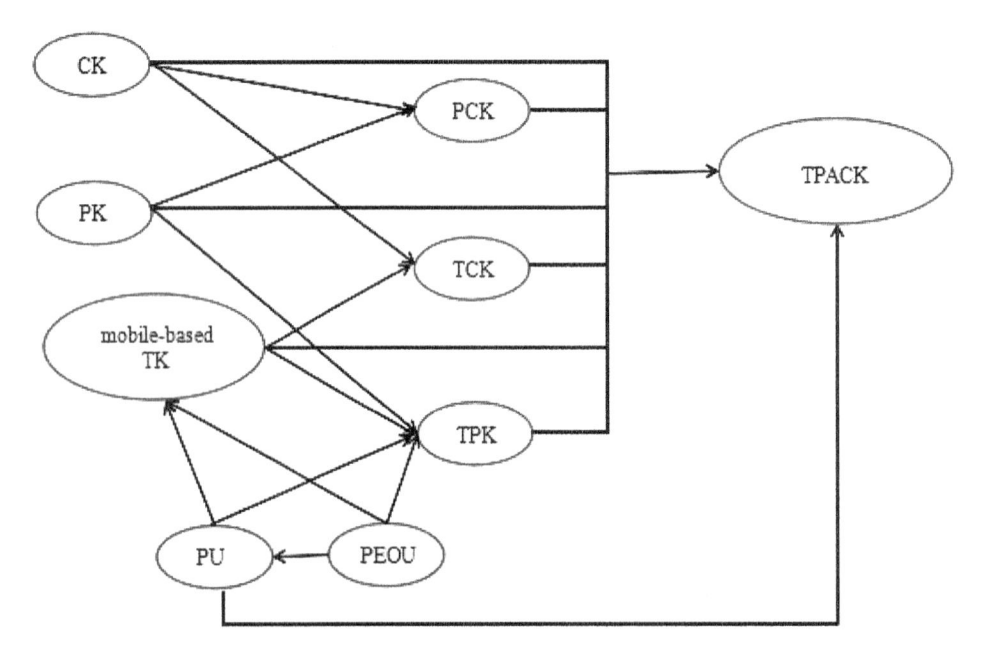

Hypothesis 1 (H1): Mobile-based SE has a positive direct effect on TPACK in a mobile learning environment.

Hypothesis 2 (H2): Technology acceptance indexed by PU and PEOU has a direct positive effect on TPACK.

Hypothesis 3 (H3): Individual characteristics of teachers (i.e., gender, age, and educational background) positively affect TPACK.

Method

The Educational Bureau of the state invited our research team to evaluate the teachers' current TPACK level and the relative contributors. This project entitled as *Evaluating the Effectiveness of Mobile EFL Schoolbags*. Data was collected through online survey that was designed by our research team. Therefore the bureau helped the authors to conduct the survey and guarantee the ethical consideration.

Participants

507 English teachers from 220 elementary schools from the middle-east part of China took the survey. The schools in this study were chosen using multistage cluster sampling, stratified by urban, countryside and rural in a specific province. And all pilot schools in the province had carried a mobile learning teaching reform for more than a year. During the reform period, the schools had introduced E-Book Package synchronous with the textbook from one of the outstanding foreign language teaching institutions in China. And teachers used E-Book Package for classroom English teaching at least half time per week. Out of 507 teachers, 108 (21.30%) were males and the remaining 399 (78.70%) were females. Moreover, 51 (10.10%) were 25 years old or younger, 140 (27.61%) were 26–30 years old, 103 (20.32%) were 31–35 years old, 78 (15.38%) were 36–40 years old, and 135 (26.63%) were 40 years old or older.

Instruments

Questionnaires were distributed and collected via an online platform since October 2013 and ended at December of the year. Out of the 507 questionnaires returned, 340 were valid questionnaires (67.06%). The questionnaire survey consisted of four main instruments, including demographic information, mobile-based SE, technology acceptance, and TPACK. The instruments were adopted from the literature, which will be discussed later, and modified by our lead author and two experts.

Demographic information includes name, school, gender, age and education background. The main results are shown as Table 1.

Mobile-based SE questionnaire. The mobile-based SE questionnaire was adopted from general SE scale (GSES) designed by Zhang and Schwarzer (1995). The GSES has been proven to have good reliability and validity. The scale has been translated into at least 25 languages and is extensively used internationally (Zhang & Schwarzer, 1995). Seven items that focus on the confidence and expectations of teachers in their use of mobile learning devices from the original 10 items of the GSES questionnaire was selected for the purpose of this study. The answer is measured by seven-point Likert scale, where 1 represents "strongly disagree" and 7 represents "strongly agree."

Technology Acceptance

To evaluate technology acceptance of mobile devices among teachers, this study adopted the scale from Davis (1989). Many researchers used Davis' scale as reference in their surveys of the acceptance of a particular technology by teachers (e.g., Gu and Fu, 2011; Smith & Stephen, 2012; Teo & Noyes, 2010). 10 questions associated with the dimensions of PU and PEOU were picked in the final draft of the questionnaire, with five questions each for PU and PEOU. The answer is measured by seven-point Likert scale, where 1 represents "strongly disagree" and 7 represents "strongly agree."

Table 1. Basic information of participants

Scale	Sample size (N)	Percentage (%)
Gender		
Female	269	79.12
Male	71	20.88
Age		
25 years old or younger	35	10.29
26–30 years old	87	25.59
31–35 years old	76	22.35
36–40 years old	51	15.00
41 years old or older	91	26.77
Educational Background		
High school	4	1.18
Two years community college	61	17.94
Bachelor's degree	265	77.94
Master's degree and above	10	2.94

TPACK

The scale of evaluating TPACK was adopted from Schmidt (2009). Given the current study focus on the teachers from English subject in the mobile setting, we defined technology as mobile devices, and modified "social studies" and "literacy" sections into "English". The final draft of the revised instrument comprised 23 questions, with each dimension comprising at least three questions. The validity and reliability of the TPACK survey is shown in Table 2. The answer is measured by seven-point Likert scale, where 1 represents "strongly disagree" and 7 represents "strongly agree."

Data Analysis

SPSS17.0 and AMOS20.0 were used to analyze the data in this study, in particular, the relationship among Teachers' SE, technology acceptance, TPACK, and demographic information in a mobile learning environment. Structural equation modeling (SEM) was used to examine the structural relationships among TPACK constructs, mobile-based SE, and TAM. Figures 4 and 5 show the final SEM models representing the relationships of SE and TAM, respectively, with TPACK constructs with a summary of the maximum likelihood parameter estimates and their significance levels. Paths without statistical significance were omitted in the final models.

Validity Analysis

This study employed exploratory factor analysis (EFA) and confirmatory factor analysis (CFA) to detect the construct validity of the instruments. 340 valid questionnaires were divided into two parts. In the first part, EFA (N_{pre} = 170) was used to reduce potential duplication problems. Only those factors with loadings greater than 0.50 were incorporated in the final questionnaire. In the second part, CFA (N_{post} = 170) was used to verify the fit degree of the structural equation model. A component analysis was conducted with orthogonal rotation (varimax) to clarify the survey structure based on the TPACK survey data. Five components had eigenvalues higher than Kaiser's criterion of 1 (Fabrigar, et al., 1999) and were grouped into five factors (TPACK, mobile-based TK, CK, TPK, and PK). TPACK, PCK, and TCK were loaded together to form the TPACK factor. Items with a factor loading value of less than 0.50 and with multiple cross-loadings were omitted. Finally, a total of 15 items were retained in the final TPACK questionnaire. Three items were retained in the final SE questionnaire and were used to measure teachers' learning and confidence expectations in a mobile learning environment. Finally, six items were retained in the final TAM questionnaire.

Reliability Analysis

Reliability refers to the measurement of consistency. Reliability coefficient measurements of objects can be measured using a range from 0 to 1.0 (Wiersma and Jurs, 2010). In this study, Cronbach's alpha was used to detect the internal consistency of the questionnaire. In general, a higher coefficient implies a higher reliability of the instrument. In an exploratory study, a reliability of 0.5 is acceptable, 0.7 to 0.98 is highly reliable, and a reliability lower than 0.5 should be rejected (Wu, 2010). The results of the reliability test are shown in Table 2, where the α values of the questionnaire items were higher than 0.8, indicating that the questionnaire of this study is reliable.

RESULTS

Mobile-Based SE has a Positive Indirect Effect on TPACK in a Mobile Learning Environment

According to Figure 4, CK, PK, and mobile-based TK were all positive direct predictors that explained the variance in TPACK (path coefficients = 0.12, 0.17, and 0.10, respectively). PK was a significant positive predictor of TPK (path coefficient = 0.48), whereas TPK was a significant positive predictor that explained a significant proportion of variance in TPACK (path coefficient = 0.74, $p < 0.001$). The latent variable mobile-based SE was a significantly positive predictor of TK and TPK (path coefficients = 0.81 and 0.40, respectively).

Since mobile-based SE had no positive direct effect on TPACK, SE had an indirect influence on TPACK through the path of TPK. Two paths showed the role of mobile-based SE on TPACK according to Figure 4.

Path 1: Mobile-based SE→TK→TPACK

Mobile-based SE had direct impact on teachers' technology knowledge. This indicates that, the more confident teachers were, the more technology knowledge they might get, and therefore they might achieve higher in terms of TPACK. This result suggests that in order to improve teachers' TPACK, they should use mobile technology more actively and confidently in their classrooms.

Table 2. Results of the validity and reliability test s

Scale		EFA	CFA	α
Mobile-based TK	TK1	0.85	0.75	0.82
	TK2	0.80	0.88	
	TK3	0.68	0.72	
PK	PK1	0.83	0.89	0.89
	PK2	0.79	0.87	
	PK3	0.76	0.83	
CK	CK1	0.60	0.73	0.88
	CK2	0.81	0.90	
	CK3	0.81	0.94	
TPK	TPK1	0.82	0.90	0.87
	TPK2	0.81	0.88	
	TPK3	0.67	0.69	
TPACK	TCK1	0.78	0.74	0.83
	PCK1	0.58	0.74	
	TPACK1	0.69	0.80	
Mobile-based SE	SE1	0.90	0.84	0.90
	SE2	0.92	0.87	
	SE3	0.93	0.90	
TAM	PU1	0.90	0.91	0.92
	PU2	0.87	0.85	
	PU3	0.91	0.91	
	PEOU1	0.85	0.82	0.87
	PEOU2	0.73	0.82	
	PEOU3	0.77	0.84	

Figure 4. Final model of mobile-based SE and TPACK (*p < 0.05, **p < 0.01, ***p < 0.001)

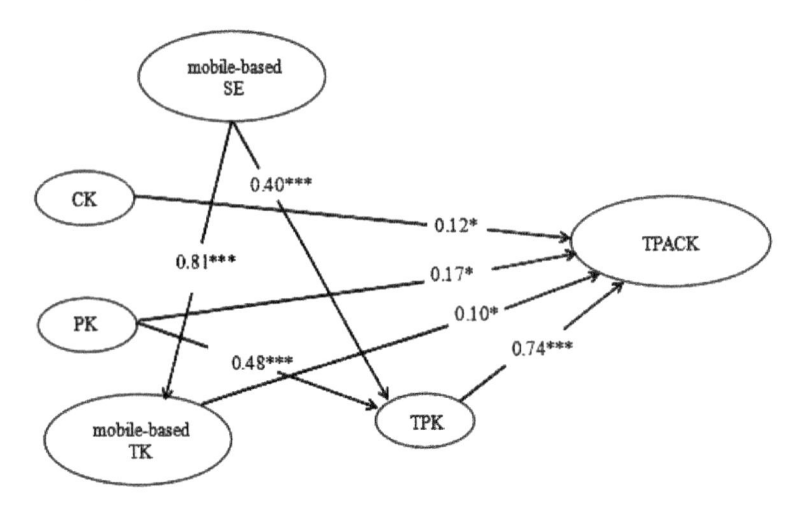

Path 2: Mobile-based SE→TPK→TPACK.

The more confidence teachers had, the better technology pedagogic knowledge they might get, the higher level of TPACK they might achieve. Pedagogic knowledge plays key roles in teaching and learning. How to integrate mobile technology into teaching strategies and methods effectively is a key to effective teaching. The results presented in Figure 4 indicated that mobile-based SE is an important factor for teachers to improve their TPK and TPACK.

Technology Acceptance Has a Positive Indirect Effect on TPACK

Figure 5 shows that CK, PK, and mobile-based TK are direct positive predictors that explain the variation of TPACK (path coefficients = 0.11, 0.18, and 0.09, respectively). Mobile-based TK and PK are significant positive predictors that explain the variation of TPK (path coefficients = 0.17 and 0.44, respectively). TPK is a significant positive predictor that explains the variation of TPACK (path coefficient = 0.74, $p < 0.001$). PU is a direct positive predictor that explains TPK (path coefficient = 0.28, $p < 0.001$). PEOU is a significant positive predictor that explains mobile-based TK (path coefficient = 0.81, $p < 0.001$). The data indicate that the model is an adequate fit for the SEM analysis.

Although PU and PEOU had no direct influence on TPACK, PU significantly predicted TPACK through TPK while PEOU significantly affected TPACK through mobile-based TK. Three paths showed the role of technology acceptance on TPACK according to the Figure 5.

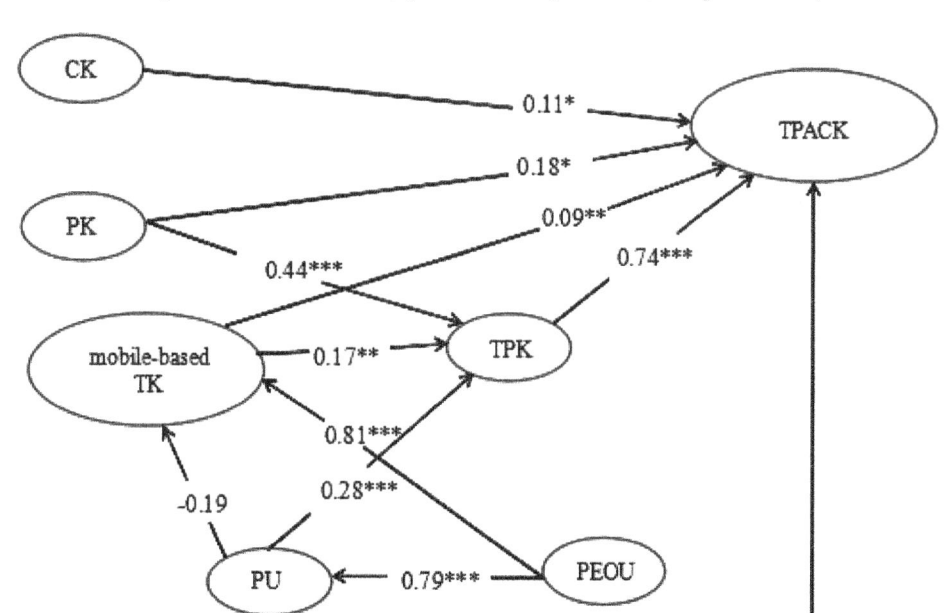

Figure 5. Final model of TAM and TPACK (*p < 0.05, **p < 0.01, ***p < 0.001)

Path 1: PEOU→PU. The result of our analysis demonstrated that teachers' perceived ease of technology use determined their perceived usefulness of technology. In another word, simple and user-friendly features are important for teachers to adopt mobile technology.

Path 2: PEOU→TK→TPACK. The perceived ease of mobile technology use also determined the level of teachers' technology knowledge, followed by the corresponding change of the TPACK. Compared with the use of desktops and laptops, mobile devices presented a better user-friendly design such as finger touching, one hand holding, and easy exploring. Therefore, teachers can get better technology knowledge than a few years ago while the desktop and laptop computers are the mainstream of technology devices. This shift offers teachers opportunities to improve their TK and TPACK level with less time and effort.

Path 3: PU→TPK→TPACK. The perceived usefulness of technology affected teachers' TPK and TPACK. This suggests that, when teachers acknowledged the usefulness of the mobile technology, they would make efforts to explore how to combine the technology into pedagogy. Technology turns into a catalyst to make the traditional teaching strategy more human-tech interactive, effective, and productive. In addition, the improvement of the TPK would result in higher level of TPACK.

Higher Educational Background Had Direct Affect on Teachers' TPACK

In this study, *T* test and ANOVA were employed to examine the impact of demographic information, such as gender, age, and education background, on teachers' TPACK. First, a series of *T* tests were conducted on gender differences of teachers' mean scores for the TPACK constructs. The results are shown in Table 3. Among all variables, no significant differences were observed between different genders. This finding indicates that gender had no significant impact on TPACK.

Then teachers were categorized into five age groups, ≤25 years old, 26–30 years old, 31–35 years old, 36–40 years old, and ≥41 years old to compare the possible differences on TPACK due to age. The ANOVA results presented in Table 4 indicate that teachers who are younger than 25 performed better than other teachers in PK (M,=7.11, SD=0.97) and TPK (M=6.82, SD=1.00).

Furthermore, another ANOVA test was conducted to examine the difference in teachers' education backgrounds. The results showed significant differences (Table 5). It was indicated that that teachers with Master's degrees or higher has better performance in TPK and TPACK than teachers with other degrees.

In summary, no significant difference existed among the TPACK of teachers based on gender. However, age affected the teachers' PK and a TPK. Education backgrounds is another factor that affect teachers' CK, TPK, and TPACK. Younger teachers' TPK were better than the older teachers'. It was then concluded the possibility to the young teachers' acceptance to new technology are easier than older teachers.

Table 3. Gender difference of teachers in TPACK

Scale	Female (*M*, SD)	Male (*M*, SD)	*T* value
Mobile-based TK	8.67 (1.21)	8.13 (1.16)	1.09
CK	6.40 (0.86)	6.99 (1.18)	−1.56
PK	5.94 (0.81)	6.39 (0.88)	−1.35
TPK	5.94 (0.83)	6.42 (0.90)	−1.34
TPACK	6.06 (0.81)	6.60 (0.98)	−1.62

Table 4. Different ages of teachers in TPACK

Scale	1 (*M*, SD)	2 (*M*, SD)	3 (*M*, SD)	4 (*M*, SD)	5 (*M*, SD)	*F* (ANOVA)	Sig.
Mobile-based TK	8.05 (0.93)	7.98 (1.01)	8.90 (1.28)	9.21 (1.39)	8.63 (1.25)	1.33	0.258
CK	6.60 (1.12)	6.15 (0.75)	6.75 (1.02)	6.61 (1.01)	6.60 (0.91)	0.53	0.709
PK	7.11 (0.97)	5.47 (0.66)	6.15 (0.89)	6.27 (0.92)	5.93 (0.77)	3.00	0.019*
TPK	6.82 (1.00)	5.35 (0.71)	6.14 (0.79)	5.94 (0.90)	6.43 (0.87)	3.08	0.016*
TPACK	7.14 (0.99)	5.77 (0.70)	6.31 (0.88)	6.11 (0.92)	6.07 (0.84)	1.91	0.108

* $p. \leq 0.05$, 1 = 25 years old and younger, 2 = 26-30 years old, 3 = 31–35 years old, 4 = 36-40 years old, 5 = 41 years old and older

Table 5. Different education backgrounds of teachers in TPACK

Scale	1 (M, SD)	2 (M, SD)	3 (M, SD)	4 (M, SD)	F (ANOVA)	Sig.
Mobile-based TK	6.75 (1.28)	9.02 (1.37)	8.44 (1.13)	9.70 (1.64)	1.10	0.350
CK	9.50 (2.39)	7.39 (1.24)	6.27 (0.81)	6.50 (0.67)	4.20	0.006**
PK	9.00 (1.83)	6.28 (0.99)	5.93 (0.78)	6.30 (0.63)	2.29	0.078
TPK	9.50 (1.91)	6.27 (1.01)	5.92 (0.75)	6.90 (1.30)	3.24	0.022*
TPACK	9.50 (1.93)	6.37 (0.99)	6.02 (0.76)	7.60 (1.25)	3.84	0.01**

** $p. \leq 0.01$, * $p. \leq 0.05$, 1: high school degree 2: Two years community college degree, 3: Bachelor's degree, 4: Master's degree and higher

DISCUSSION

This study examined the relationships among the mobile-based SE, TAM, and TPACK of elementary school English teachers by using Structural Equation Model, based on data collected from an online questionnaire. Conclusions about key factors on the improvement of teachers' mobile-based TPACK are discussed in the following paragraphs.

Confidence about Mobile Technology Helps Teachers Improve TPACK

The results showed that mobile-based SE positively affected TK and TPK, which mean that teachers with higher SE showed better performance in TK and TPK. Because TPK was a positive direct predictor of TPACK, a higher SE, thus, is an indirect positive predictor of TPACK in mobile environment. This finding indicates that improved SE of mobile technology can help teachers improve their TPACK.

This result corroborates with findings from previous studies on TPACK of pre-service teachers in the multimedia and online classroom context. Ertmer and Ottenbreit (2010) stated that teachers' changing mindset and confidence is key to technology integration. When teachers are asked to use technology to facilitate learning, the high SE on technology is desired. Hughes (2013) conducted a research on the integration of laptop usage in the teaching of pre-service teachers. The results indicated that pre-service teachers, who obtained higher SE performance in the pretest, integrate technology into the classroom more effectively than others. Lay et al. (2013) also proposed to establish teachers' confidence and understanding on new technologies to improve their TPACK. The aforementioned research proved the Bandura's theories about SE from a different perspective. Bandura (1996) considers four factors to improve SE, namely, successful past experiences, alternative role models (builds confidence when someone completes a task), verbally persuade and wake (make an individual excited, thereby driving task). Among these factors, the most important is the successful past experiences, which can also be called as task-related experience. That is, if a teacher experiences successful integration of teaching and digital learning resources related to work, then the teacher will be more confident in their future work.

However, it can be concluded from the current study that mobile-based SE of teachers had no direct relationship with their TPACK, which differs from the results of previous studies. This difference may be derived from the unique features of mobile technology compared with other technology devices. As mobile technology changes, the interaction between users and devices had been friendlier than decades ago, when basic knowledge for programming or particular learning on how to operate the computer or Internet is at its start. The difficulty for technology usage becomes abate, and consequently that will lead to a higher mobile SE effect. Nevertheless, current studies showed that improved SE is still needed for higher-level TPACK in the study. SE had positive indirect effects on the TPACK through TK and TPK in the mobile teaching and learning environment.

Ease of Use and Usefulness of Mobile Technology Help Teachers Improve Their TPACK

The SEM results show that teachers' PU had significant positive effects on their TPK. PEOU also produced significant positive contributions to their TK. Although the teachers' TAM had no direct relationship with TPACK, TPK was a direct positive predictor of the variation of TPACK. Thus, the TAM of teachers indirectly affected their TPACK. Teachers who consider mobile learning devices simple and easy to use can demonstrate a higher level of TK. On the contrary, teachers who consider mobile learning devices difficult to use would avoid integrating mobile technology into day-to-day school setting.

Alsofyani (2012) suggested similar findings in a study of online professional development of pre-service teachers. Participants who consider online educational perform easy to use could perform better in TPACK. According to the research of Lay et al. (2013), geography teachers' perception of geographic information systems will influence the practical application, and the effect subsequently influences classroom application. The present study is consistent with findings from these two studies. The easy use and usefulness of mobile technology are positive contributors to the development of TPACK.

An interesting result from our study is that, the perception of teachers on the usefulness of technology (PU) has a negative relationship with their TK, although the effect is not significant. In other words, teachers' TK will not be improved because of PU, even if they believe mobile learning devices can be useful in the classroom. Some teachers explained that the mobile devices are fairly easy to use; most of the functions could be understood without special guidance. These useful mobile technologies, however, failed to increase their technology knowledge. They might decide whether to use mobile devices in school by the easy use of mobile technology. Therefore, easy use of mobile technology played an important role for the next generation teachers' TPACK level.

Teachers with Higher Education Background Showed Higher Level of TPACK

In terms of teachers' demographic information, our study found that gender difference had no significant effect on the TPACK of teachers. Kao and Tsai (2009) concluded a similar result, saying no significant difference exists in gender on the use of Internet in educational setting.

The current study indicated that age difference significantly affected teachers' PK and TPK; that is, younger teachers' PK and TK performed better on PK and TPK. Meanwhile, ANOVA results revealed that young teachers' PEOU was significantly higher than others; part of this could be a result of young teachers accessing mobile technology more frequently. Younger teachers had weaved mobile devices into daily life more often. Most of mobile technologies were not obstacle for them. Therefore, younger teachers had the advantage to apply mobile technology into teaching. In addition, significant effect was observed on the TPK and TPACK of teachers who earned a Master's degrees or higher. Thus, teachers who are younger and have higher levels of education backgrounds may play the leading role in the later era of mobile technology.

CONCLUSION, IMPLICATIONS, AND LIMITATIONS

In this study, we investigated the contributors to the mobile-based TPACK. The major findings are 1) mobile-based SE had positive indirect impact on the TPACK through the TK and TPK, 2) TMA had positive indirect impact on the TPACK through the TK and TPK, 3) Teachers with younger age and higher education background performed better on the TPACK.

These findings can help identify the main contributors to improve teachers' TPACK in the mobile environment. The implications of this study are as follows: 1) Teachers should be more confident about the mobile technology to make teaching more effectively; 2) Mobile technology should be more user-friendly and useful, and teachers should use mobile devices more actively to integrate mobile technology into teaching; 3) "Teacher learning community" should be set. Teachers with younger age and higher education background could provide peer assistance for others.

Nevertheless, this research had some limitations. Firstly, the study was conducted solely based on survey data without face-to-face interviews or on-site observation. Secondly, the participants were all English teachers whose native language was Chinese. Therefore, the results may vary with the different cultures and educational backgrounds in other countries. Further research could involve teachers with more diversified background to identify the main influencing contributors on the mobile-based TPACK.

ACKNOWLEDGMENT

This work was supported by the Grant authorized project of Social Science Funding in China, Big data digging and searching on culture value for language learning (Project number: 14&ZH0036).

REFERENCES

Abbitt, J. T. (2011). An investigation of the relationship between self-efficacy beliefs about technology integration and technological pedagogical content knowledge (TPACK) among preservice teachers. *Journal of Digital Learning in Teacher Education*, 27(4), 134–143. doi:10.1080/21532974.2011.10784670

Ahmad, W. M. A. W., Halim, N. B. A., Aleng, N. A., Mohamed, N., Amin, W. A. A. W. M., & Amiruddin, N. A. (2013). Quantitative analysis on the level of acceptance, usage and problems of e-books among school teachers in Terengganu. *The International Journal of Social Sciences*, 7(1), 89–101.

Alsofyani, M. M., Aris, B. B., Eynon, R., & Majid, N. A. (2012). A preliminary evaluation of short blended online training workshop for TPACK development using technology acceptance model. *Turkish Online Journal of Educational Technology-TOJET*, *11*(3), 20–32.

Bandura, A., Barbaranelli, C., Caprara, G. V., & Pastorelli, C. (1996). Multifaceted impact of self-efficacy beliefs on academic functioning. *Child Development*, *67*(3), 1206–1222. doi:10.2307/1131888 PMID:8706518

Beijing Normal University Teacher Education Research Center. (2012). *Report of teachers' development of middle and elementary schools in China*. Beijing: Social Science Literature Press.

Brantley-Dias, L., & Ertmer, P. A. (2013). Goldilocks and TPACK: Is the construct 'just right?'. *Journal of Research on Technology in Education*, *46*(2), 103–128. doi:10.1080/15391523.2013.10782615

Bull, P. (2009). Self-efficacy and technology integration: perceptions of first year teaching fellows to technology integration in education. *In Society for Information Technology & Teacher Education International Conference*, *2009*(1), 1768-1776.

Chong, C. K., Puteh, M., & Goh, S. C. (2015). Framework to Integrate Spreadsheet into the Teaching and Learning of Financial Mathematics. *Electronic Journal of Mathematics & Technology*, *9*(1), 92–106.

Corbeil, R. J., & Corbeil, V. E. M. (2007). Are you ready for mobile learning? *Educase Quarterly Magazine*, *30*(2), 51–58.

Davis, F. D. (1989). Perceived usefulness, perceived ease of use, and user acceptance of information technology. *Management Information Systems Quarterly*, *13*(3), 319–340. doi:10.2307/249008

Ekanayake, S. Y., & Wishart, J. (2014). Integrating mobile phones into teaching and learning: A case study of teacher training through professional development workshops. *British Journal of Educational Technology*. doi:10.1111/bjet.12131

Embong, A. M., Noor, A. M., Ali, R. M. M., Bakar, Z. A., & Amin, A. R. M. (2012a). Teachers' perceptions on the use of e-books as textbooks in the classroom. *World Academy of Science. Engineering and Technology*, *6*(10), 580–586.

Embong, A. M., Noor, A. M., Hashim, H. M., Ali, R. M., & Shaari, Z. H. (2012b). E-books as textbooks in the classroom. *Procedia: Social and Behavioral Sciences*, *47*, 1802–1809. doi:10.1016/j.sbspro.2012.06.903

Ertmer, P. A., & Ottenbreit-Leftwich, A. T. (2010). Teacher technology change: How knowledge, confidence, beliefs, and culture intersect. *Journal of Research on Technology in Education*, *42*(3), 255–284. doi:10.1080/15391523.2010.10782551

Fabrigar, L. R., Wegener, D. T., MacCallum, R. C., & Strahan, E. J. (1999). Evaluating the use of exploratory factor analysis in psychological research. *Psychological Methods*, *4*(3), 272–299. doi:10.1037/1082-989X.4.3.272

Finger, G., Jamieson-Proctor, R., & Albion, P. (2010). *Beyond pedagogical content knowledge: The importance of TPACK for informing preservice teacher education in Australia. In Key competencies in the knowledge society* (pp. 114–125). Springer Berlin Heidelberg.

Georgina, A. D., & Hosford, C. C. (2009). Higher education faculty perceptions on technology integration and training. *Teaching and Teacher Education*, *25*(5), 690–696. doi:10.1016/j.tate.2008.11.004

Gu, X. Q., &Fu, S. R. (2011). Research of users' technology acceptance of mobile learners. *E-education*, (6), 48-55.

Harris, J., Grandgenett, N., & Hofer, M. (2010). Testing a TPACK-based technology integration assessment rubric. In *Society for Information Technology & Teacher Education International Conference* (Vol. 2010, No. 1, pp. 3833-3840).

Hayashi, A., Chen, C., Ryan, T., & Wu, J. (2004). The role of social presence and moderating role of computer self-efficacy in predicting the continuance usage of e-learning systems. *Journal of Information Systems Education*, *15*(2), 139–154.

Huang, H. M., & Liaw, S. S. (2007). Exploring learners' self-efficacy, autonomy, and motivation toward e-learning. *Perceptual and Motor Skills*, *105*(2), 581–586. doi:10.2466/pms.105.2.581-586 PMID:18065082

Hughes, J. (2013). Descriptive indicators of future teachers' technology integration in the PK-12 classroom: Trends from a laptop-infused teacher education program. *Journal of Educational Computing Research*, *48*(4), 491–516. doi:10.2190/EC.48.4.e

Jung, I., & Latchem, C. (2011). A model for e-education: Extended teaching spaces and extended learning spaces. *British Journal of Educational Technology*, *42*(1), 6–18. doi:10.1111/j.1467-8535.2009.00987.x

Kao, C. P., & Tsai, C. C. (2009). Teachers' attitudes toward web-based professional development, with relation to Internet self-efficacy and beliefs about web-based learning. *Computers & Education*, *53*(1), 66–73. doi:10.1016/j.compedu.2008.12.019

Koehler, M. J., & Mishra, P. (2005). What happens when teachers design educational technology? The development of technological pedagogical content knowledge. *Journal of Educational Computing Research*, *32*(2), 131–152. doi:10.2190/0EW7-01WB-BKHL-QDYV

Koehler, M. J., Mishra, P., & Yahya, K. (2007). Tracing the development of teacher knowledge in a design seminar: Integrating content, pedagogy and technology. *Computers & Education*, *49*(3), 740–762. doi:10.1016/j.compedu.2005.11.012

Koehler, M. J., Shin, T. S., & Mishra, P. (2012). How Do We Measure TPACK? Let Me Count the Ways. In R. Ronau, C. Rakes, & M. Niess (Eds.), *Educational Technology, Teacher Knowledge, and Classroom Impact: A Research Handbook on Frameworks and Approaches* (pp. 16–31). Hershey, PA: Information Science Reference. doi:10.4018/978-1-60960-750-0.ch002

Koh, J. H. L., & Chai, C. S. (2011). Modeling pre-service teachers' technological pedagogical content knowledge (TPACK) perceptions: The influence of demographic factors and TPACK constructs. In G. Williams, P. Statham, N. Brown & B. Cleland (Eds.), Changing Demands, Changing Directions (pp. 735-746). ASCILITE.

Lay, J. G., Chi, Y. L., Hsieh, Y. S., & Chen, Y. W. (2013). What influences geography teachers' usage of geographic information systems? A structural equation analysis. *Computers & Education*, *62*(3), 191–195. doi:10.1016/j.compedu.2012.10.014

Liu, S. H. (2011). Modeling pre-service teachers' knowledge of, attitudes toward, and intentions for technology integration. In T. Bastiaens & M. Ebner (Eds.), *Proceedings of EdMedia: World Conference on Educational Media and Technology 2011* (pp. 3350-3355). Association for the Advancement of Computing in Education (AACE).

Ng, W., & Nicholas, H. (2013). A framework for sustainable mobile learning in schools. *British Journal of Educational Technology, 44*(5), 695–715. doi:10.1111/j.1467-8535.2012.01359.x

Ozdamli, F., & Uzunboylu, H. (2014). M-learning adequacy and perceptions of students and teachers in secondary schools. *British Journal of Educational Technology, 46*(1), 159–172. doi:10.1111/bjet.12136

Sahin, I., Akturk, A. O., & Schmidt, D. (2009, March). Relationship of preservice teachers' technological pedagogical content knowledge with their vocational self-efficacy beliefs. *In Society for Information Technology & Teacher Education International Conference, 2009*(1), 4137-4144.

Schmidt, D. A., Baran, E., Thompson, A. D., Mishra, P., Koehler, M. J., & Shin, T. S. (2009). Technological pedagogical content knowledge (TPACK): The development and validation of an assessment instrument for preservice teachers. *Journal of Research on Technology in Education, 42*(2), 123–149. doi:10.1080/15391523.2009.10782544

Smith, J. A., & Sivo, S. A. (2012). Predicting continued use of online teacher professional development and the influence of social presence and sociability. *British Journal of Educational Technology, 43*(6), 871–882. doi:10.1111/j.1467-8535.2011.01223.x

Smith, J. A., & Stephen, A. S. (2012). Predicting continued use of online teacher professional development and the influence of social presence and sociability[J]. *British Journal of Educational Technology, 43*(6), 871–882. doi:10.1111/j.1467-8535.2011.01223.x

Teo, T. (2009a). Modeling technology acceptance in education: A study of pre-service teachers. *Computers & Education, 52*(1), 302–312. doi:10.1016/j.compedu.2008.08.006

Teo, T. (2009b). Is there an attitude problem? Reconsidering the role of attitude in the TAM. *British Journal of Educational Technology, 40*(6), 1139–1141. doi:10.1111/j.1467-8535.2008.00913.x

Teo, T. (2010). A path analysis of pre-service teachers' attitudes to computer use: Applying and extending the technology acceptance model in an educational context. *Interactive Learning Environments, 18*(1), 65–79. doi:10.1080/10494820802231327

Teo, T., & Noyes, J. (2010). Exploring attitudes towards computer use among pre-service teachers from Singapore and the UK: A multi-group invariance test of the technology acceptance model (TAM). *Multicultural Education & Technology Journal, 4*(2), 126–135. doi:10.1108/17504971011052331

Van Olphen, M. (2008). World language teacher education and educational technology: A Look into CK, PCK, and TPCK. In *Annual Meeting of the American Educational Research Association*.

Waheed, M., & Jam, F. A. (2010). Teacher's Intention to Accept Online Education: Extended TAM Model. *Interdisciplinary Journal of Contemporary Research in Business, 2*(5), 330–344.

Wang, L., Ertmer, P. A., & Newby, T. J. (2004). Increasing preservice teachers' self-efficacy beliefs for technology integration. *Journal of Research on Technology in Education, 36*(3), 231–250. doi:10.1080/15391523.2004.10782414

Wiersma, W., & Jurs, S. G. (2010). *Research Methods in Education*. Beijing: Social Science Literature Press.

Wong, L. H., Chai, C. S., Zhang, X., & King, R. B. (2015). Employing the TPACK framework for researcher-teacher co-design of a mobile-assisted seamless language learning environment. *IEEE Transactions on Learning Technologies*, *8*(1), 31–42. doi:10.1109/TLT.2014.2354038

Wu, M. L. (2010). *SPSS statistical analysis practice*. Chongqing, China: Chongqing University Press.

Zhang, J. X., & Schwarzer, R. (1995). Measuring optimistic self-beliefs: A Chinese adaptation of the General Self-Efficacy Scale. *Psychologia*, *38*(3), 174–181.

Chapter 6
Teaching Foreign Languages in the Twenty-First Century:
Lessons from Spanish Hybrid Education

Sarah Gretter
Michigan State University, USA

Ager Gondra
State University of New York – Purchase College, USA

ABSTRACT

This chapter explores the case of a hybrid Spanish program where technology, standards, and teacher expertise in foreign language education are merged to bolster students' learning. The chapter identifies the instructional elements relevant to 21st century foreign language education, and depicts the transactional relationship between technology, standards and teacher experience in a Spanish hybrid teaching environment. Finally, we provide a set of recommendations for current and future Spanish educators, as well as foreign language educators in general based on the experiences shared by students, educators, and administrator in the program.

INTRODUCTION

In our technology-driven and media-saturated world, foreign language educators' role is quickly evolving (Luke & Britten, 2007). Digital communication has become an essential 21st century skill for students who are exposed to an increasingly globalized and multicultural world where advances in technology are connecting them to different cultures with an ease that was unfamiliar in past centuries. Spanish language, in particular, is not only the most spoken non-English language in the United States, but is also the fastest growing one, with a 233% increase of its number of speakers since 1980 (Lopez & Gonzalez-Barrera, 2013). The influence of Hispanic cultures in the United States is indeed visible in everyday life, in the professional world, the arts, and in the entertainment industry. Twenty-first century students are aware that being proficient in Spanish is a marketable skill if they are aiming to develop a presence in a globalized world, as well as to develop an interest for their neighboring cultures (P21, 2011). But

DOI: 10.4018/978-1-5225-0483-2.ch006

how can foreign language educators be prepared to face the new challenges of teaching relevant material to students while understanding the reality of today's digital connectivity? How can the integration of technology in foreign language courses—particularly in hybrid environments—help develop students' language practices in and out of school?

The growth of information and communication technologies has generated novel opportunities while creating new challenges for foreign language education. In fact, using technology to access information about the world that surrounds us is now considered an essential 21st century skill for students (Partnership for 21st Century Skills, 2014; National Governors Association Center for Best Practices, 2010). Because of their increasing online presence (Lenhart, 2015), students' authentic exposure to foreign languages and cultures is occurring increasingly in digital environments (Kessler, 2013). Nowadays, a student has more chances to communicate with someone living abroad through the Internet than through traditional methods of communication. Students are in constant interaction with technology in their personal lives, and it is important for foreign language education to reflect this reality while reflecting goals set by national and international standards in their field.

Building upon contemporary scholarship on teaching in hybrid environments, educational standards, and teacher knowledge, this chapter therefore describes the efforts conducted in a set of hybrid (i.e., face-to-face and online) Spanish courses offered at a small Northwestern college in order to feature its experience in bolstering students' insights into the nature of Spanish-speaking cultures and languages through technology. We describe the case of these hybrid courses through surveys conducted with instructors and evaluations shared by students to highlight teachers' experiences teaching Spanish in said hybrid program. Finally, we conclude with a set of recommendations for current and future Spanish educators interested in integrating technology in their teaching. These recommendations are derived from the lessons learned from this investigation, and supplemented with an administrative perspective through an interview conducted with the course's program director. First, we describe the elements that play a role in the successful integration of technology in foreign language education, namely hybrid teaching environments, standards, and teacher knowledge.

BACKGROUND

Hybrid Environments in Foreign Language Instruction

From online programs to blended, hybrid, flipped classrooms, and MOOCS, computer-assisted language learning (CALL) has been prominent over the years in assisting students' foreign language learning, along with producing research looking at how technology shapes education in that area while enhancing learning processes (Hill, 2014; Kessler, 2009). This chapter focuses specifically on hybrid—sometimes called "flipped"—environments in CALL (Muldrow, 2013). Hybrid programs represent a mixed mode of instruction where traditional face-to-face instruction and online learning are blended (Olapiriyakul & Scher, 2006). "Flipped classroom" is a term that is now commonly used for classes that are a form of blended learning using technology with the underlying intention that the teacher will be able to interact more with students instead of lecturing during class time (Bell, 2015). Garrison and Kanuka (2004) described the flipped classroom as "an integration of face-to-face and online learning experiences—not a layering of one on top of the other" (p. 99). This model represents a mindset where learning is centered on students (Bergmann & Sams, 2012) and where instructors are responsible for maintaining a community of learning based on interaction and support.

Goertler et al. (2012) argued that institutions and students alike are inclined to favor hybrid curricula because of their flexibility in space and in time. The advantages of hybrid learning are that: it saves money and space at the institutional level while still connecting with students on campus, it improves a high quality of instruction, it allows access to a broader variety of students, and it engages the youth in a mode of communication that is familiar to them in their everyday life (Goertler et al., 2012). In fact, Kessler (2009) explained that the objective of foreign language education was to accompany students in the development of their autonomous use of the target language. This has been accomplished in hybrid education through the development of online learning labs, which was facilitated by developments in Internet-based self-access to studying languages (Kessler, 2009). While autonomy does not imply the absence of teachers, it does suggest that technology can support students' independence in learning thanks to online discussion, self-reflective or writing activities, to name a few. Technology also permits higher levels of connectivity, which can facilitate collaboration and the construction of knowledge between peers. Similarly, technology lets educators focus on a student-centered approach to learning by allowing students to explore the language in relation to their personal interests (Kessler, 2009). This student-centered approach is also determined by standards in the field of foreign education, which can serve as guidelines for both institutions implementing hybrid learning in their programs, as well as for instructors working in hybrid environments on a day-to-day basis.

Standards for Foreign Language Teaching and Learning

At the international level, the United Nations Educational, Scientific and Cultural Organization (UNESCO, 2009) has placed intercultural dialogue as a priority for the 21st century. Concurrently, a number of additional international organizations, such as the Organization for Economic Co-operation and Development (OECD) or the International Society for Technology in Education (ISTE) have published general recommendations for the integration of information and communication technology in educational settings, along with guidelines and standards aimed specifically at teachers in the area of digital skills, thus underlining the competencies that instructors need to possess to effectively teach with and through technology. We would like to highlight that due to the scope of this chapter, we only focus on standards that were appropriately relevant for foreign language education. Similarly, this chapter was written in the context of Northern American higher education and thus present standards specific to that setting.

Within said context, the American Council on Teaching Foreign Languages (ACTFL) provides the National Foreign Language Standards for Foreign Language Learning, which guide foreign language teaching. Their guidelines are composed of "5 C's:" Communication, Cultures, Connections, Comparisons and Communities. The goal of ACTFL is that students are "culturally equipped to communicate successfully in a pluralistic American society and abroad" (ACTFL, 2015). One of the standards of interest for this chapter is for students to be able to participate in communities all over the world, and more specifically to "use the language both within and beyond the school setting" (ACTFL, 2015). Today's advances in technology enable this use of language beyond the school setting. As a matter of fact, ACTFL and the Partnership for 21st Century Skills (P21) collaboratively created a 21st century skills map providing guidance for the teaching of world languages through the integration of 21st century skills while responding to increasing global economies and communication modes (P21, 2011). P21 (2011) stated that:

Teaching Foreign Languages in the Twenty-First Century

Global economies, a heightened need for national security, and changing demographics in the U.S. have increased attention to our country's lack of language capability. Every call to action to prepare our students for the 21st Century includes offering them the opportunity to learn languages other than English and increase their knowledge of other cultures. (p. 2)

In concordance with their mission to prepare 21st century students, ACTFL also provided guidance on how to train future teachers to address these aforementioned needs. In their standards for the preparation of foreign language teachers, ACTFL (2013) argued that technology should be part of teachers' toolsets for the creation and diffusion of authentic material in the classroom. They also envisioned technology being a way for teachers to help students connect to different communities online, as well as an access to tools for instruction (e.g., multimedia, web-based resources, social networks, mobile devices, etc…). Finally, the standards express that teachers should learn how to use these web-based resources or technologies "to provide authentic input to gather, evaluate, and assess learners' performance" (p. 26).

Taken together, the ACTFL standards and the 21st century map place educators at the forefront of the learning process. This collection of standards highlight teachers' role as a guide for student development, as learners become independent learners thanks to technology. Foreign language educators in the 21st century are required to not only know how to teach the language, but to also take advantage of the technological tools available for teaching, all the while understanding how to facilitate student learning. Teaching foreign languages in the 21st century has therefore become a multifaceted and complex combination of knowledge and skills that educators should possess to effectively teach in a world of connectivity and global communication.

Teachers' Technological, Pedagogical, and Content Knowledge

Mishra & Koehler's TPACK framework (2006) provides a theoretical lens to discuss the importance of integrating teachers' technological, pedagogical, and content knowledge in 21st foreign language education. The TPACK framework (Mishra & Koehler, 2006; Koehler & Mishra, 2013) is a teacher knowledge framework that describes effective teaching with technology within specific contexts. The interaction of teachers' technological, pedagogical, and content knowledge is what shapes the understanding that teachers should possess to successfully merge technology in their traditional teaching practices. The TPACK structure represented in Figure 1 highlights how technological, pedagogical and content knowledge are merged through teachers' knowledge about their subject matter, their understanding of teaching methods and practices, and their familiarity with how information technologies can assist in achieving instructional goals—all within a given context.

McGrail (2007) stated that the order in teacher knowledge should be "pedagogy before technology, rather than technology before pedagogy" (p. 81). For that reason, Van Olphen (2008) argued that professional organization such as ACTFL or ISTE play a crucial role in guiding educators to teach in our technological era. Furthermore, she asserted that teaching foreign languages through CALL required understanding how linguistic and cultural concepts could be represented with and through technology, along with pedagogical approaches from student-centered traditions and an awareness of how language competencies develop with CALL. She also added that teachers should acknowledge students' background knowledge in the subject matter and should be familiar with cognitive approaches to learning, all the while understanding how new technologies could help teaching and learning (Van Olphen, 2008).

Figure 1. The TPACK framework
From http://tpack.org

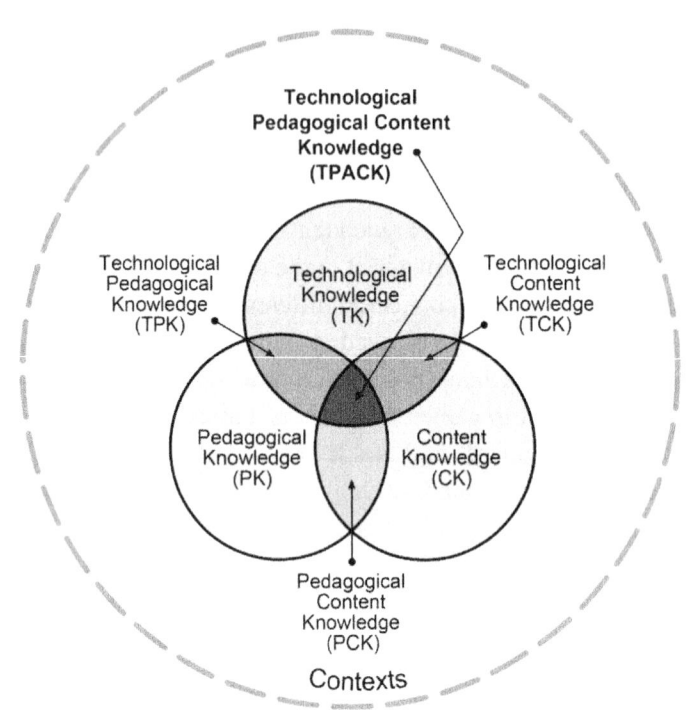

Furthermore, Zhao (2003) described the potential benefits that technology-rich instruction and curriculum could yield, including providing students with high-quality linguistic and cultural materials, more communicative opportunities, and in-time and individualized feedback. He however underlined that teachers must be adequately prepared to best integrate technology in their teaching practices and that for that purpose, it was important to remember that teachers' creativity in the use of technology was more important than technology itself. This is why the TPACK framework can inform technology use and guide teachers' practices. As noted, technology itself is not teaching a course, but teachers' mastery of the course's content, along with their pedagogy and their way of creatively teaching content is what can make a course a successful experience for students. In addition, Kang and Li (2010) highlighted the fact that it is difficult for students to be in contact with native speakers of a language, and that teachers can help students use technology to meet and interact with natives outside the classroom. An effective teacher would thus be able to flexibly navigate the space defined by knowledge of technology, pedagogy, and content areas and the complex interaction among them in specific contexts (AACTE, 2008) while integrating standards for language and for 21st century skills.

However, for such model of integration to be successful and to provide students with an immersive experience that will positively translate to their personal, academic and professional lives, teachers need to be adequately prepared to combine multiple approaches to teaching Spanish or foreign languages in general. Moser and Ivy (2013) demonstrated that indeed, few of their teacher participants had had formal courses specific to the integration of technology in the World Language classroom, and that many were unaware of standards in their field. They therefore suggested that professional development or teacher preparation could fill those gaps. In this next section, we explore the particular case of a Spanish hybrid program in the United States that has integrated traditional teaching with an online language lab. We report accounts shared by instructors and students about their experiences in the hybrid program, along with the benefits and challenges that they emerged from these experiences, before inferring recommendations for teacher training based on the lessons learned from this investigation.

THE EXAMPLE OF A HYBRID SPANISH COURSE

An example of the integration of technology in language learning is a Spanish language program at a small Northwestern college, which has incorporated an online component to its Beginner (Spanish I and Spanish II) and Intermediate (Spanish III and Spanish IV) Spanish courses. These courses follow the model of a flipped classroom, where students read the materials and perform online activities at home, and then meet face-to-face with their instructor twice a week for an hour and 40 minutes. The language textbooks used in said Spanish language courses, *Panorama* (2013) in the introductory level, and *Anda* (2013) in the intermediate level, come with an online package, which is a complementary online lab with resources for each traditional classroom meetings. Both the textbooks and the online component have as their primary purpose to foster communication, cultural knowledge, critical thinking skills and strategies for learning; and were designed in accordance with the ACTFL "5C's." These standards guide both the course design as well as instructors' focal pedagogy in this hybrid course, and each chapter identifies for the teacher which of the 5 C's are addressed. Thoms (2011) stated that while ongoing research continues to shed light on how hybrid foreign language courses affect students' linguistic development, little research has been done to look at how students and instructors perceive their learning and teaching experiences in a hybrid-learning context. Consequently, we conducted surveys with instructors and gathered evidence from student course evaluations to understand their experiences in the hybrid course. After describing the hybrid course components, we then discuss their views of the program, and point out the benefits and challenges that students and instructors identified regarding their participation in Spanish hybrid learning.

Course Material

Since traditional classrooms present time restriction for teachers, the online lab aims to provide students with an opportunity to continue using Spanish outside the classroom. For this, the online lab supplies:

- Readiness checks for each chapters
- Practice activities including flashcards, exercises and games
- Practice tests and oral practice exercises
- Student resources including a pronunciation guide, media files, videos and web links, announcements, discussion forums, and a calendar providing deadlines
- A summary of students' progress
- A full electronic textbook with the ability to do exercises, highlight, and add notes.

The homework, which is assigned by the instructor, has to be done in the online lab. When students log in to the online lab, they automatically see which activities have been assigned and when they are due. Some of these activities are due the day before the material that the activities cover is taught, which prepares students to understand the upcoming chapter of the textbook, and therefore permits the instructors to not spend time explaining the material from scratch, but instead clarify students' doubts. In addition, it encourages students for a self-exploration of language uses at their own pace. Other activities, on the other hand, help students review the material before a chapter's test. In order for students to get enough practice, each homework is allowed to be submitted three times, and the last attempt is the one that counts toward their grade. Activities that are not assigned can be given as additional practice.

Besides these activities, the online labs offer the opportunity for students to create a blog, which according to Gedera (2012) increases the potential for student interaction. In fact, Johnson and Johnson (2009) showed that collaborative and cooperative-learning methods can improve students' time on tasks and motivation to learn, and that learning is more effective when it is a social activity (Domalewska, 2014). The blog-based activities are course-related information in the form of reflective journals, stories, or discussion topics. Students can also peer-review and comment on other students' work, and collectively prepare written assignments or projects. Furthermore, the online lab comes with an online-chat tool that can be used by students to communicate with their instructor and classmates who are online at the same time. The blog-based activities and online chat thus allow for collaboration to take place not only inside the classroom, but also outside the classroom. Students can therefore improve their Spanish skills thanks to the connectivity and their constant interaction with culture through authentic media.

Nevertheless, while students have the freedom to explore materials on their own, the instructor's role is not diminished. On the contrary, teaching in a hybrid environment requires teachers to adapt to new challenges while maintaining their teaching creativity and prepare to interact with students in innovative ways. For teachers, the online component offers general resources, including:

- A user guide with a philosophy of the textbook
- Teaching tips, sample syllabi, lesson plans and grading rubrics
- Cultural background notes
- A gradebook with an overview of students' assignments completion and notifications of assignments that need grading
- PowerPoint presentations and testing materials
- A full electronic textbook with the ability to add notes
- The ability to assign, un-assign, manipulate, or add exercises, and the ability to send emails to the entire class and/or post announcements.

Furthermore, most of the activities are graded by the online lab system, therefore allowing the instructor to spend less time grading the homework and to spend more time on meaningful interactions with students and on the creation of relevant activities for class.

The courses thus incorporate the use of technology with students' 21st century skills through the use of culturally relevant information in the form of media and authentic documents. The hybrid class could be considered, in a way, a microcosm that mimics students' personal lives and familiarity with digital forms of communication. The time spent in the classroom through face-to-face learning, in addition to online independent learning and collaborations with the instructor and classmates, give students the opportunity to practice their language skills in real contexts. Indeed, by having a constant and continuous access to Spanish resources, and by giving students the opportunity to merge their personal use of technology with academic goals, the online tools in turn influence their use of newly-acquired skills in their digital practices. Before examining instructors' insights into the course, we look at how students rated their experiences in the hybrid program.

Student Perspectives

We analyzed students' evaluation of their hybrid courses at the end of the academic year 2014-2015 for the 97 students enrolled in the Beginning I, Beginning II, Intermediate I, and Intermediate II Spanish language. All respondents were undergraduate students enrolled in the course to fulfill their majors' language requirement. Given the scope of this chapter, we focused on items directly related to their evaluation of the hybrid program per se. When asked to evaluate the hybrid course, (i.e., "Overall I rate this hybrid course") students responded on a five-point scale (i.e., 1= very poor, 5= excellent). Students' rating of the Beginning Spanish I (n=25) course was 4.4; rating of the Beginning Spanish II (n=23) class was 4.65, the Intermediate Spanish I (n=24) obtained an average rating of 4.64 and the Intermediate Spanish II (n=25) was 4.5. In addition, students shared their thoughts about the course by answering an open-ended question asking them to discuss their experience in the hybrid class. Their responses expressed the benefits as well as the challenges that they faced in relation to the hybrid environment during the semester.

Benefits

Many of the students reported a positive experience with the course. One student expressed that "the course offers a valuable way to learn further technical skills in the Spanish language." Students agreed that the online activities in particular offered opportunities to interact with course material and resources, thus leading to greater engagement and enhanced opportunities for learning Spanish. For instance, one student explicitly said that "the most valuable element of the course was the online lab activities," while another added that "the online assignments help the student learn the language and culture behind it."

In addition to finding the online lab valuable for learning the language, students also appreciated the online environment for practical reasons. For example, they liked to practice homework online, and found that "the most valuable element was having the homework be the lesson that we were going to learn the next day, so just in case I had questions I could ask in class and not be lost." Students also liked the availability of a variety of organizational and learning tools online. One student shared that "the most valuable elements were the online grammar resources," while one said that "the online lab was very helpful for practice and extra help if you needed," and another one agreed that "I loved the online activities, and that they showed the due date and the grades."

Furthermore, students seemed to value the availability of online resources for in-class classes. One of them expressed that "the online activities helped me the most to prepare me for upcoming class work." Having access to online resources at all times provided them with a repository of available knowledge to use, to either prepare for class or to later test their own knowledge, as expressed by this student who said that "the online work really did test my knowledge on the chapters we were learning." Overall, students communicated that the hybrid system was beneficial to them as it presented them with information in multiple ways and allowed more flexibility in a constantly available learning environment.

Challenges

Nonetheless, some students also recalled challenging instances in the hybrid course. Some complained about encountering technical issues with the online lab, which impeded their overall learning experience. Generally, most negative experiences with the course were related to preview activities that were assigned as online homework before starting a lesson on a new concept or topic. One student admitted that "the preview activities were sometimes too advanced since we didn't learn it yet. I didn't always understand how the book explained things."

Many students would have preferred to see the material in class before being required to complete online assignments. Indeed, some students stated that "it was hard to do the online activities when we hadn't learned the material yet. The online activities make more sense after going over the material in class first," or that "I liked the online assignments but I wish we did them after we already learned the material. It helped having preview materials but I didn't like being graded on something I hadn't learned yet." Furthermore, as one other student described: "it's pretty hard to do the online homework before we have the material on class. I understand the idea, but because it's another language, it's harder." Students' experiences in the course are important to consider in light of teachers' role in hybrid contexts and their views of these pedagogical issues. We address these issues in the following section by looking at instructors' experiences with teaching the hybrid course.

Instructor Perspectives

We asked instructors to share their views on the benefits and challenges that a hybrid system presented for them. A survey was given as part of an end-of-the-semester evaluation to the four Spanish language instructors who had taught in the hybrid language system. Each instructor was teaching a different Spanish language level at the time of the survey: Beginning I, Beginning II, Intermediate I, or Intermediate II. Instructors were asked to answer a series of open-ended questions about their experiences teaching in the hybrid program. The four instructors were divided into two categories based on their teaching experience in general, and with a hybrid system in particular. The two categories were divided into experienced, and novice. Two instructors fit into the first category, and were teaching the intermediate courses. One of the four instructors had taught Spanish courses for seven years, of which she had used the hybrid system for five years. The second instructor had spent ten years teaching Spanish, and nine years with a hybrid program. The two other teachers were considered novices and taught the beginning level courses. Before teaching in her current program, one instructor had only taught occasionally, and had never used the hybrid system before. The other instructor was in her second year of teaching overall, both years being with the hybrid program.

A line-by-line analysis of their narratives was performed using the qualitative software Nvivo. A content analysis helped generate an initial list of 22 codes, which were merged into four overarching categories: (i) affordances of the hybrid environment, (ii) pedagogical advantages of the hybrid environment, (ii) perceived student experience, and (iv) challenges of the hybrid environment.

When asked about their general impression about the use of a hybrid system in a foreign language course, instructors shared many positive impressions. They felt that the hybrid method helped them reach more students through a variety of learning styles. They also argued that the online language lab was a useful tool for students as well as for themselves because the online components allowed for additional preparation time of materials and the creation of supplementary in-class resources. Majority of instructors also indicated their preference for a hybrid course over a traditional course because of its combination of traditional teaching methods and web-based teaching. The instructors explained that the online lab was a complement that reinforced language learning, while the traditional system helped students to interact with their peers and with the instructor. They felt confident that the hybrid method helped them reach many students thanks to the multiple learning options that the system affords.

Affordances of the Hybrid Learning Environment

Instructors agreed that a hybrid course could combine the advantages of web-based learning with the benefits of a traditional classroom. As one of the novice teachers highlighted:

As an instructor I feel the hybrid approach provides more opportunities to use class time to engage students with the language in ways that reflect their interests and ability levels. The hybrid approach enhances and enriches the traditional classroom. Through the use of preview activities on the web site students are exposed to vocabulary and new language structures and given the opportunity to practice them in a variety of formats with immediate feedback. This affords me the opportunity to use valuable class time for clarification and enrichment, for student-centered communication activities that elicit the production of the target structures and vocabulary.

The benefit that instructors saw was that the hybrid system provided opportunities for practicing the language outside of class periods, and that the hybrid tools could serve this function for the days when they did not meet with their students in the classroom. For, instance, the other novice teacher said that:

As an instructor, the hybrid system provides opportunities for course reinforcement outside of our in-class meetings. For the levels that I normally teach, I am a firm believer that language acquisition can only be achieved through daily interaction and engagement. Our hybrid tools can be used to serve this function for the days that we do not meet as a group.

Similarly, some of the instructors felt that the hybrid course helped them reach students through practice outside of class so that they could focus on other concepts during class time. A novice instructor described how, for her:

I prefer the hybrid system. I feel that students actually learn more as we can cover more material and also "practice" and "review" it. The hybrid system provides a framework that promotes independent learning to the degree that is expected of college students and necessary for them to really internalize the material. I feel that I am able to use classroom time to create an interesting, engaging learning experience that maximizes opportunities for interaction and communication in the target language.

Through the use of activities on the web site, students are exposed to vocabulary and new language structures and are given the opportunity to practice them in a variety of formats with immediate feedback. This enables the instructors to have the opportunity to use valuable class time for clarification and enrichment, and for student-centered communication activities that elicit the production of targeted structures and vocabulary. When asked which method he preferred, this experienced instructor explained that "I like both. The hybrid system is just a complement to reinforce the language while the traditional system helps my students to interact with their peers and the instructor." It is indeed thanks to the affordances of the hybrid system that instructors are able to create a stronger community within the classroom by having the opportunity to focus on students instead of aspects of the material that students can work on independently online. The other experienced instructor neatly summarized the complementarity of the hybrid method saying that "it [the online lab] takes the core of what I do in the classroom and expands it outwards in multiple directions."

Pedagogical Advantages

Not only did instructors perceive the hybrid system in a positive light in terms of learning environment, but they also expressed that it allowed them to focus on pedagogical matters such as class preparation or teaching resources. In one case, a novice instructor expressed that "generally speaking, I do like the hybrid approach. As an instructor, I feel that it gives me a much more varied methodology than textbooks alone." One of the experienced teachers also agreed that "I value very much all the materials and teachers' resources." The online resources can indeed free time for teachers during class time because students have access to material at any time. As the other novice instructor put it, "I love the fact that they [students] can reinforce my classroom teaching with the online tutorials."

The supplement that students receive online also allows instructors to adapt their teaching. In one instance, an experienced instructor shared that "I enjoy teaching my courses in this format. It allows for additional preparation time of materials and creation of additional in-class resources." That is, the online component does not stand alone, but is integrated with teachers' pedagogical intentions. The online component of the course can therefore be seen as an extension of the instructor's work, which in turn also helps them to alter their pedagogical approaches. For example, this novice instructor commented on the fact that "I am also able to review the on-line grade book prior to class so I can tailor classroom instruction based on student performance." Being able to understand students' performance through the online tools can benefit teachers in the sense that they can modify their lessons based on students' needs.

Perceived Student Experience

As a matter of fact, one of the main features of the hybrid program is that it allows teachers to observe students' comprehension and struggles. Surveyed instructors attributed many benefits to the online lab in how they perceived their students' experience of the course. Availability of class content is a major advantage, as one experienced instructor highlighted: "my students are able to learn, review, and practice the Spanish language anytime and anywhere. They can always login to the online lab and follow their own progress and be part of their own learning." Such individualization of learning is favorable to learning, according to this experienced instructor who articulated that:

The hybrid system allows the student additional practice, lab capabilities and other learning resources that they can access at their own pace. It provides them additional time to work on materials, which often leads to additional in-class questions, and further explanations and discussions.

In a similar vein, the advantages of accessibility to knowledge through technology was alluded by the following novice instructor, who expressed that:

It is wonderful to have the textbook come to life in the classroom. I continually tell the students how lucky they are to have the language lab, the textbook, videos, dictionaries, flash cards, cultural films and multiple reading options available all in one place, from their laptop or mobile device!

In addition, technology in the hybrid language course could also benefit students' different learning styles. For one novice instructor,

With this array of linguistic options, they [students] can do quick bursts of studying when the opportunity arises, whether that takes the form of a "Flash Cultura" or a practice grammar exercise. For some people those frequent dips into the language work better than long sessions in the library.

Furthermore, the online lab enables students to feel comfortable with their learning process, something that in the traditional classroom might not be possible. Case in point, this novice teacher pointed out that "another bonus is that students who are embarrassed to speak up in class can listen and do guided practice of their oral skills online on their own." Ultimately, instructors who were surveyed felt that the hybrid system worked well for students because of the availability of its content and the variety in language practices that students could experience to learn the language. One experienced instructor concluded his views of the hybrid system by affirming that "my students do better on their exams because they have practiced a lot by doing the assignments; therefore, they feel comfortable speaking the language during class time." In light of these positive benefits of the hybrid system for teaching and learning, it is also important to mention some of the challenges and limitations that instructors observed.

Challenges

Most of the instructors agreed that the hybrid system, and particularly the activities that were due the day before the material was covered in class, presented some difficulties for students. One of the experienced instructor admitted that "I find many students get frustrated with getting low scores on our current preview activities," while another novice shared that "many students have expressed their total exasperation with the preview activities (several have spoken of feeling 'overwhelmed') and it is clear to me that they would prefer to have homework based on concepts they have just been taught." These statements align with some of the comments that students expressed in their own survey. Instructors opined that for beginner students who are trying to absorb a lot of new material, it can be frustrating to not have the opportunity to consolidate what they have just learned in class and instead have to move on to the next set of concepts before completely assimilating the previous ones. Some instructors have noticed students' frustration, as the material gets more complex over the semester.

Furthermore, a novice instructor conveyed that not all students in her class used the online resources as intended. She shared that:

Unfortunately, I don't believe many of them take full advantage of the online material, other than doing the basics required of them. For example, when I recommended watching the online tutorials to reinforce at home the grammar concepts we were covering in class, I realized that many of the students did not know that the tutorials were there, and in one class only one student was actually watching them.

While this struggle might be specific to this novice instructor's class, it raises the issue of the role of the teacher in instructing students on how to take advantage of the available resources online while continuing to teach during the face-to-face periods. In one case, actually, one novice teacher also reflected on some of the challenges that the system was creating for her. She observed that "overall I really like the hybrid system. However, I will admit that, given the pace of the syllabus and what I have to cover in any given day, I rely mostly on the textbook/blackboard/group activities and handouts than online material in the classroom." Taken together, instructors' perspective on the hybrid program reveal important facets of teaching and learning a foreign language in a hybrid environment.

Overall, instructors perceived many benefits for teaching through the hybrid system. First, the Spanish language can be with them at all times, it is portable and easily accessible. Second, the hybrid system provides a framework that promotes independent learning to a degree that is expected of college students and that is necessary for them to internalize the material on their own. Third, the hybrid system allows students to have additional practice, and to access other learning resources that they can process at their own pace. It also provides them with additional time to work on assessments, which often leads to in-class questions, and further explanations and discussions of the reviewed concepts. Fourth, the online tutorials can reinforce classroom teaching as the animated online tutorial avatar gives a different and sometimes more light-hearted presentation of the material through visual reminders of concepts. Fifth, the automatic grading of homework makes it possible for students to practice and get immediate feedback to support their mastery of the concepts. As one novice instructor put it: "I can't imagine how we could accomplish that in a traditional format in which students submit homework for manual grading and there is a gap in feedback." Sixth and last, students who might not be comfortable speaking up in foreign language classroom can follow guided practices of their oral skills online on their own.

What the surveys conveyed was a sense of usefulness of the hybrid program for teachers to focus on students' learning needs, while highlighting the importance of the role of the teacher in guiding and monitoring students' progress. Lastly, it is important to note that the hybrid system does not minimize teachers' instructional practices. On the contrary, it asks them to continually adapt and find ways to help students learn the language, all the while letting them evolve at their own pace. One experienced instructor concluded that "for me, a combination of 'old school' teaching methods and web-based learning is the optimal approach, and I feel confident the resulting hybrid product helps us reach many more students with their myriad learning styles than one methodology or the other on its own." As a result, the upcoming section is a discussion of the lessons learned from instructors' experiences in the course, supplemented by an administrative perspective on the hybrid program. We explore how these lessons can be used to shape recommendations to guide the preparation of teachers who might teach in hybrid courses. These lessons learned, along with their subsequent recommendations, illustrate the essential role that technology integration plays in students' understanding of language, culture, and 21st century skills simultaneously.

LESSONS LEARNED: RECOMMENDATIONS FOR PREPARING FOREIGN LANGUAGE EDUCATORS

The observations presented in this chapter are by no means generalizable to the larger population of foreign language teachers and programs. Our sample represented a specific case in a higher education context in the United States that was limited in scope and size. Altogether, the experiences shared by

Teaching Foreign Languages in the Twenty-First Century

instructors and students in the present case can help understand the assets as well as the drawbacks that some instructors may face when teaching hybrid languages classes. Given the increasing presence of online and hybrid environments in language learning (Kessler, 2009), understanding these experiences can help current and future teachers or administrators be prepared to teach in an era of technology, whether they will teach solely online, in hybrid contexts, or simply if they wish to integrate technology in traditional language classrooms.

Here, we propose a set of recommendations for educators (i.e., instructors or administrators) who aim to incorporate technology in foreign language teaching. These recommendations emerged from the experiences shared by the instructors and the students in the Spanish hybrid program, in addition to an administrative perspective on national standards and TPACK. In order to obtain an administrative perspective regarding the hybrid courses, the program director was interviewed about his perceptions and experiences with the classes. The program director, a Ph.D. in Spanish linguistics, had taught Spanish language classes for ten years, including four with the specific hybrid program at his institution.

1. Define Technological Needs

Whether an instructor decides to integrate technology in her teaching or an administrator thinks about implementing online or hybrid classes in her institution, it is important to clarify the rationale for using technology in the classroom (Kitade, 2015). When asked about his institution's choice to implement the hybrid course in Spanish, the program director of the courses described in this chapter explained that it had become a necessity in the 21st century. He explained how:

Our Spanish language program had to be updated. In language courses, technology has become a complementary tool and resource to real-life learning. Now, more and more language course books come with a convenient and effective online supplement that introduces new and innovative ways to learn Spanish. Unfortunately, in previous traditional language courses, students were not exposed to the language long enough since they only met their instructors face-to-face twice a week for a short amount of time. So our students could not practice, and retain the material they learned in the classroom. With the online lab, our students have the opportunity to continue using Spanish anytime they want without the physical presence of instructors.

Echoing the research literature on the growing presence of online labs for language learning, the program director understood that in order to stay competitive and to adapt to students' needs, hybrid programs could provide the right balance between traditional face-to-face interactions with an instructor and current technological communication for learning. In a similar fashion, he acknowledged that the course also had to reflect students' use of technology on a daily basis in order to encourage their language acquisition outside the classroom. He further observed that "practicing Spanish in the hybrid course is a transition between learning languages at school in the traditional system and learning in authentic settings during students' personal time. It allows them to see the link between what they do at school and what they can do at home on their own."

McKeeman and Oviedo (2015) concurred that "blending communication within the context of culture via technology paves the path for the development of students' 21st century skills" (p. 106). For that purpose, they designed a technology evaluation rubric for cultural competence for teachers to help them assess whether technology can support learning outcomes as well as students' demonstration of cultural competences. Their rubric, Figure 2, can be taken as a first step to evaluate whether using technology would benefit students' learning.

The hybrid courses that we described in this chapter, for instance, would fall into the category of *highly supportive* level of classroom technology. That is, technology allows the integration of culture in the course with an authentic cultural perspective involving participants' interaction and timely feedback. Again, language instructors and administrators must keep in mind that technology is neither a replacement for a live teacher nor is the focus of the class, but is instead an extra tool aiming to reinforce language teaching and learning. Instructors should therefore first define their lesson objectives, and then select an appropriate technology to fulfill their pedagogical purposes, as indicated in the aforementioned rubric for technology evaluation.

Figure 2. Technology Evaluation Rubric
Source: McKeeman and Oviedo (2015)

		Highly supportive	Moderately supportive	Unsupported
Part 1	Products	Technology allows cultural products to be integrated, embedded and/or highlighted. Technology allows participants to interact with and/or annotate the cultural product.	Technology offers participants the ability to observe and/or analyze cultural products.	Cultural products cannot be addressed.
	Practices	Technology allows participants to participate within cultural practices.	Technology offers participants the ability to observe and/or analyze cultural practices.	Cultural practices cannot be addressed.
	Perspectives	Technology allows integration of diverse and authentic cultural perspectives. Participants can interact with these perspectives, and/or contribute to them.	Technology offers participants the ability to observe and/or analyze the different cultural perspectives.	Technology only allows for a singular perspective to be offered. Cultural perspectives are discussed but not offered.
Part 2	Authenticity	Technology encourages/ supports the integration of resources that are culturally authentic (Resources that are made by native speakers, for native speakers)	Potential exists for the integration of culturally authentic resources. Technology is used either by or for native speakers—semi-authentic.	Cultural resources are informative, but not authentic.
	Feedback	Technology offers participants timely feedback. There is ease of use when giving or receiving feedback.	Technology offers limited opportunities to provide or receive feedback.	The opportunity to give or receive feedback is unavailable.
	Language/ Culture Connection	Technology encourages/ supports language learning through cultural competency.	There is limited connection between communicative competence and cultural competence.	Cultural competence is isolated from further language learning.

Technology Evaluation Rubric for Cultural Competence (Products, Practices, & Perspectives) (TERCC-P[3])

2. Be Familiar with Standards

Technology and foreign language standards can provide teachers and administrators with an initial set of guidelines for blending technology and language learning. The International Society for Technology in Education (ISTE), the International Technology and Engineering Educators Association (ITEEA), the United Nations Educational, Scientific and Cultural Organization (UNESCO) as well as the Organization for Economic Cooperation and Development (OECD) each provides standards in technology for teachers. Additionally, each country possesses its own set of standards to be observed in terms of technology standards as well as foreign language standards.

For instance, in addition to adapting to 21st century technology use, the hybrid courses described in this chapter are also aligned with national standards in foreign language learning. When asked how these standards played out in the course design and structure, the program director answered that:

Every Spanish instructor in our program knows that the overarching goal of our program is to be able to interact in Spanish (Speaking, Listening, Reading, Writing) and to work towards the corresponding level of each course according to the ACTFL guidelines. Furthermore, our courses are designed based on the 5 Cs of ACTFL: Communication, Cultures, Connections, Comparisons and Communities. These standards are therefore present at different levels of instruction: in the overarching structure of the hybrid system, in the textbooks—which are designed based on ACTFL's standards—and also in the way instructors teach the course on an individual basis.

We highly encourage current and future instructors to familiarize themselves with standards relevant to their field in order to become informed educators in the 21st century. It is also important that instructors look at specific standards before deciding what kind of activities they will be implementing to help students learn the language and explore its culture under all its digital forms. These standards can be used as guidelines, as more and more language courses shift towards a blend of face-to-face and online instruction where many teachers find themselves in unfamiliar territories.

3. Provide Technical Guidance

While some teachers have worked for years developing strategies and techniques for the traditional classroom, many may have little experience as either a student or an instructor of online environments. It is also common among teachers to say that they do not have time for learning how to use technology or to implement technology into the classroom, and to ask themselves why they should change and why they should put the energy into something novel (Ertmer et al., 2012). However, we live in a digital era, which means that becoming a skilled language teacher in the 21st century involves mastering technology and its corresponding competencies for the sake of students' skill development. Accordingly, it has become increasingly necessary for teachers to provide similar support to their students. For instance, one of the surveyed instructors in the hybrid program expressed that "I feel that it would be really worthwhile to spend at least part of the first class of the semester going over the online content (maybe including new teachers) so that everyone understands just how much it can offer them—other than just doing the homework."

Speaking of instructor training, the program director explained how the latter were prepared to teach the hybrid course. He explained that

To help language instructors make the transition to hybrid teaching, our Spanish language program offers language instructors a professional development workshop. The purpose of this workshop is to guide the instructors to get ready to teach courses that are partially online and partially face-to-face. They have to learn how to successfully manage online interactions and to incorporate the assessment available on the online lab into the classroom. Our language instructors, however, do not need to learn how to configure the online homework and gradebook, since as the Spanish program coordinator I take care of that. I am also available during the semester to answer their questions, concerns, or issues.

In their study of hybrid French and Spanish courses, Chenoweth et al. (2013) also found through their qualitative data that students needed guidance from their instructors and that both students and instructors could benefit from continuing technical support.

Fortunately, there are many ways through which instructors can become familiar with the use of technology in a language class. First, both preservice and inservice teachers can take methodology courses or professional development workshops that prepare teachers on how to integrate technology in their curriculum. These courses develop preservice and inservice teachers' skills in using the tools of international communications for today's global instructors, and teachers can learn to use these tools to create material through projects directly related to the target language. Some examples of the technology can include: presentation software, Web-based resource, real-time communication (voice and video conferencing), apps, or authentic media, to name a few. ACTFL has a resourceful page on their website called "Tech Watch," that can help educators keep track of new technology tools for teaching foreign languages.

4. Emphasize Teachers' TPACK

Integrating technology, with pedagogy and content knowledge emphasizes the role that teachers play in teaching foreign language in an era of digital and hybrid learning environments. Teaching with and through technology is complex and often ill-structured, as Koehler and Mishra (2009) underlined, stating that "understanding approaches to successful technology integration requires educators to develop new ways of comprehending and accommodating this complexity" (p. 62). As the hybrid program director explained in his interview, this implies that "instructors should not spend too much time explaining the material, but rather clarify the more difficult aspects and answer students' questions." As such, the program director agreed that hybrid courses created a shift in instructors' role, which merged their technological, pedagogical, content knowledge in novel ways.

Some of the news ways in which teaching has evolved was expressed by some of the hybrid instructors. One of them explained how, compared to traditional courses, "a whole world of Spanish can be with them 24/7, totally portable and easily accessed." This accessibility, representative of 21st century teaching and learning, is one of the examples of adaptive instruction that instructors have to face. Unlike past centuries, teachers do not hold knowledge anymore. Information is available at all times, and teachers need to readjust their role to focus on student learning. However, this online presence of information should be seen as supplemental rather than an impediment to teaching. For example, another instructor described how "I sometimes refer back to one of these cartoon-type online tutorials and replay it in class to refresh their memories on something we did a while ago." The use of technology, in that case, is merged with the teacher's pedagogical knowledge through the content of the course. We strongly encourage educators to view hybrid environments as an opportunity to integrate technology, content, and pedagogy in innovative ways, all the while encouraging student learning, as this hybrid instructor points out: "I strongly encourage my students to maximize all the online possibilities (which I would have loved to have had at their age) and push them to test their knowledge."

4. Build Communities

Building communities of practice is central to teaching and learning foreign languages, and are important elements of connectivity for both instructors and students. Communities of practice are "groups of people who share a concern, a set of problems, or a passion about a topic, and who deepen their knowledge and expertise by interacting on an ongoing basis" (Wenger et al., 2002). Communities of practice provide a model for connecting people in the spirit of learning, knowledge sharing, and collaboration as well as individual, group, and organizational development. According to Cambridge, Kaplan, and Suter (2005), communities of practice are important because they connect individuals with shared interests; provide a context for communication and a platform to share information and build understanding; support interactivity between people; engage individuals to learn through mentoring; provide people with best practices in their field; and foster collaborations that adapt to changing needs and technologies.

Instructors are responsible for creating a community of practice within their own classroom setting, as well as for connecting with communities of professionals in their field. One way to participate in a community of practice at the professional level is to locate other educators who are interested in incorporating technology in the language classroom or are already using it as a pedagogical tool. While the online lab mentioned in the hybrid Spanish course already provides community discussion forums for instructors to exchange best practices, ideas, syllabi and course materials with other educators around the country, social media such as Facebook, Twitter, blogs, or forums can also be set up to create informal groups for language instructors or to locate existing groups. Instructors may then sign up for said groups and develop individual relationships with others in their community. These communities not only can build a sense of belonging for teachers and students, but they also reinforce the idea that teaching and learning foreign languages helps build intercultural dialogues. As one of the hybrid instructors concluded, "after all, learning a language is for building a community."

CONCLUDING REMARKS

In this chapter, we looked at various perspectives and experiences in a hybrid Spanish course. Altogether, the viewpoints expressed by instructors and students reflected on the benefits and challenges of said hybrid program. While benefits ranged from the availability of a variety of learning tools and resources online to pedagogical advantages such as practice time and teaching flexibility, some challenges included instructors' lack of agency over homework material and student assimilation of novel concepts. Combining these experiences with the course administrator's experience with the program, and with national standards and current research literature in the field of educational technology, we then proceeded to providing recommendations for the preparation of future Spanish educators, particularly those teaching in hybrid or flipped environments.

In closing, it is essential for teachers to keep in mind that technology integration, along with foreign language and technology standards and 21st century skills, aim to benefit student learning. Foreign language teachers of this century need to be prepared to facilitate not only student learning but also student independent learning. By teaching students autonomy through technology integration in the classroom, teachers will help them with their own learning processes when navigating the Internet on their own (Kessler, 2009). Additionally, becoming familiar with using a foreign language in both a physical and digital environment will help them feel comfortable when communication with native speakers in person or interacting with them in digital spaces. They will be able to "practice" culture and language instantly and use the knowledge that was modeled and acquired in class into the "real" world (Evans & Gunn, 2011; Kessler, 2013). And what the "real" world is currently reflecting is a growing presence of the Spanish language online. Spanish is indeed the third most used language on the Internet as of June 2015, ranked after English and Chinese (Miniwatts, 2015). It is one of the top languages that are used in 2% of the one million most visited webpages online in 2015 (W3Techs, 2015). By fostering a student-centered approach to teaching and learning, foreign language instructors therefore play a crucial role in helping students understand the cultural underpinning of the messages that they might come across online, which in turn will foster cultural understanding and dialogue, one of the main missions of the ACTFL, and of 21st century education in general.

REFERENCES

W3Techs. (2015). Usage of content languages for websites. Retrieved from: http://w3techs.com/technologies/overview/content_language/all

American Council on the Teaching of Foreign Languages (ACTFL). (2013). *Program Standards for the Preparation of Foreign Language Teachers*. Retrieved from: http://www.actfl.org/sites/default/files/pdfs/ACTFL-Standards20Aug2013.pdf

American Council on the Teaching of Foreign Languages (ACTFL). (2015). *National standards for foreign language education*. Retrieved from: http://www.actfl.org/sites/default/files/pdfs/WorldReadinessStandardsforLearningLangu ges.pdf

Bell, T. R. (2015). The flipped German classroom. In A. Moeller (Ed.), *Learn languages, explore cultures, transform lives*. Richmond, VA: Terry.

Bergmann, J., & Sams, A. (2012). *Flip your classroom: Reach every student in every class every day*. International Society for Technology in Education. Retrieved from: https://www.iste.org/resources/product?ID=2285

Blanco, J., & Redwine Donley, P. (Eds.). (2013). *Panorama* (4th ed.). Vista Higher Learning.

Cambridge, D., Kaplan, S., & Suter, V. (2005). Community of practice design guide: A step-by-step guide for designing & cultivating communities of practice in higher education. Retrieved from: http://net.educause.edu/ir/library/pdf/nli0531.pdf

Chenoweth, N., Ushida, E., & Murday, K. (2013). Student learning in hybrid French and Spanish courses: An overview of language online. *CALICO*, *24*(1), 115–146.

Domalewska, D. (2014). Technology-supported classroom for collaborative learning: Blogging in the foreign language classroom. *International Journal of Education and Development using Information and Communication Technology 10* (4), 21-30.

Ertmer, P. A., Ottenbreit-Leftwich, A. T., Sadik, O., Sendurur, E., & Sendurur, P. (2012). Teacher beliefs and technology integration practices: A critical relationship. *Computers & Education*, *59*(2), 423–435. doi:10.1016/j.compedu.2012.02.001

Evans, L. S., & Gunn, A. A. (2011). It's not just the language: Culture as an essential component in preservice teacher education. *Journal of Multiculturalism in Education*, *7*(1), 1–30.

Garrison, D. R., & Kanuka, H. (2004). Blended learning: Uncovering its transformative potential in higher education. *The Internet and Higher Education*, *7*(2), 95–105. doi:10.1016/j.iheduc.2004.02.001

Gedera, D. (2012). The dynamics of blog peer feedback in ESL classroom. *Teaching English with technology, 12*(4), 16-30.

Goertler, S. (2012). Students' readiness for and attitudes toward hybrid foreign language instruction: Multiple perspectives. *CALICO Journal*, *29*(2), 297–320. doi:10.11139/cj.29.2.297-320

Guidry, K. R., Cubillos, J., & Pusecker, K. (2013). The connection between self-regulated learning and student success in a hybrid course. Paper presented at the Association for Institutional Research Annual Forum Long Beach, California. Retrieved from: http://www.mistakengoal.com/docs/Self-regulated_learning_hybrid_course.pdf

Heining-Boynton, A. L., LeLoup, J. W., & Cowell, G. S. (2013). *Anda! Curso intermedio*. Pearson.

Hill, P. (2014). Online educational delivery models: A descriptive view. Retrieved from: http://er.dut.ac.za/bitstream/handle/123456789/56/Hill_2012_Online_Educational_Delivery_Models.pdf?sequence=1&isAllowed=y

International Society for Technology in Education (ISTE). (2015). *Standards for teachers*. Retrieved from: http://www.iste.org/standards/ISTE-standards/standards-for-teachers

Johnson, D. W., & Johnson, R. T. (2009). An educational psychology success story: Social interdependence theory and cooperative learning. *The Journal of Educational Research*, *38*(5), 365–379.

Kang, J., Ni, X., & Li, G. (2010). Preparing foreign language teachers to implement a technology-rich curriculum. In D. Gibson & B. Dodge (Eds.), *Proceedings of Society for Information Technology & Teacher Education International Conference 2010* (pp. 3876-3879). Chesapeake, VA: Association for the Advancement of Computing in Education.

Kessler, G. (2009). Integrating technology in the foreign language classroom. In K. Cennamo (Ed.), S. Ross, J. D., & Ertmer, P. A. (Eds.), *Technology Integration for Meaningful Classroom Use: A Standards-Based Approach* (pp. 351–367). China: Wadsworth.

Kessler, G. (2013). Collaborative language learning in co-constructed participatory culture. *CALICO Journal*, *30*(3), 307–322. doi:10.11139/cj.30.3.307-322

Kitade, K. (2015). Second language teacher development through CALL practice: The emergence of teachers' agency. *CALICO Journal*, *32*(3), 396–425.

Koehler, M. J., & Mishra, P. (2009). What is technological pedagogical content knowledge? *Contemporary Issues in Technology & Teacher Education*, *9*(1), 60–70.

Koehler, M. J., Mishra, P., & Cain, W. (2013). What is technological pedagogical content (TPACK)? *Journal of Education*, *193*(3), 13–19.

Lenhart, A. (2015). Teens, social media and technology overview 2015. Washington, DC: Pew Research Center; Retrieved from http://www.pewinternet.org/files/2015/04/PI_TeensandTech_Update2015_0409151.pdf

Lopez, M. H., & Gonzalez-Barrera, A. (2013). What is the future of Spanish in the United States? Retrieved from: http://www.pewresearch.org/fact-tank/2013/09/05/what-is-the-future-of-spanish-in-the-united-states/

Luke, C. L., & Britten, J. S. (2013). The expanding role of technology in foreign language teacher education programs. *CALICO*, *24*(2), 253–268.

McGrail, E. (2007). Laptop technology and pedagogy in the English language arts classroom. *Journal of Technology and Teacher Education*, *15*(1), 59–85.

McKeeman, L., & Oviedo, B. (2015). 21st century world language classrooms: Technology to support cultural competence. *Learn Language, Explore Cultures, Transform Lives*. Retrieved from: http://www.csctfl.org/documents/2015Report/Chapter%206.pdf

Miniwatts Marketing Group. (2015). Internet world stats. Retrieved from: http://www.internetworldstats.com/stats7.htm

Mishra, P., & Koehler, M. J. (2006). Technological pedagogical content knowledge: A framework for teacher knowledge. *Teachers College Record*, *108*(6), 1017–1054. doi:10.1111/j.1467-9620.2006.00684.x

Mishra, P., & Koehler, M. J. (2009). Too cool for school? No way! Using the TPACK framework: You can have your hot tools and teach with them, too. *Learning and Leading with Technology*, *36*(7), 14–18.

Moser, K., & Ivy, J. (2013). World language teachers: Self-perceptions of their TPACK. *Modern Journal of Language Teaching Methods*, *3*(2), 167–190.

Muldrow, K. (2013). A new approach to language instruction: Flipping the classroom. *Language and Education*, *8*, 28–31.

Olapiriyakul, K., & Scher, J. M. (2006). A guide to establishing hybrid learning courses: Employing information technology to create a new learning experience, and a case study. *The Internet and Higher Education*, *9*(4), 287–301. doi:10.1016/j.iheduc.2006.08.001

Partnership for Century (P21). (2011). *21st Century Skills Map*. Retrieved from: https://www.actfl.org/sites/default/files/pdfs/21stCenturySkillsMap/p21_worldlanguage map.pdf

Theisen, T. (2013). What are the possibilities for "student voice" in the 21st century? *Language and Education*, *8*(4), 7.

Thoms, J. (2011). Hybrid language and learning: Assessing pedagogical and curricular issues. In C. Wilkerson & P. Swanson (Eds.), *Dimension* (pp. 21–34). Valdosta, GA: SCOLT Publications.

United Nations Educational, Scientific and Cultural Organization (UNESCO). (2009). *World Report on Investing in Cultural Diversity and Intercultural Dialogue*. Retrieved from http://unesdoc.unesco.org/images/0018/001852/185202e.pdf

Van Olphen, M. (2008, March). World language teacher education and educational technology: A look into CK, PCK, and TPCK. In *annual meeting of the American Educational Research Association. NY*.

Wenger, E., & McDermott, R. Snyder, & William M. (2002). Cultivating communities of practice. Cambridge, MA: Harvard University Press.

Winke, P., & Goertler, S. (2013). Did we forget someone? Students' computer access and literacy for CALL. *CALICO, 25*(3), 482–509.

Zhao, Y. (2003). Recent developments in technology and language learning: A literature review and meta-analysis. *CALICO, 21*(1), 7–27.

Chapter 7
Implementing a Flipped Classroom in Teaching Second Language Pronunciation:
Challenges, Solutions, and Expectations

Kazuhiro Yonemoto
Tokyo Medical and Dental University, Japan

Asami Tsuda
Columbia University, USA

Hisako Hayashi
Carleton University, Canada

ABSTRACT

While the philosophy of flipped classroom has recently been drawing much attention of second language teachers, integrating technology into pedagogy is often an issue. This is also the case in pronunciation teaching. Second language pronunciation teaching has been largely dependent on teachers' intuition and beliefs, realized by repetition. Although recent technology developments in the field of linguistics, namely ultrasound imaging, enable visualization of movement and motion inside the mouth, it has not yet been widely used in second language education. In this chapter, taking a self-learning website for Japanese language pronunciation, the authors explore what makes teachers stay away from technology integration into language learning and how this barrier can be overcome to implement a flipped classroom. Specifically, the authors address the importance of taking initiative in planning how technology can be integrated into pedagogy while closely collaborating with and involving other fields of study, like linguistics, as well as information technology.

DOI: 10.4018/978-1-5225-0483-2.ch007

INTRODUCTION

Recently, a pedagogical approach called "flipped learning" or "flipped classroom" is drawing language teachers' attention. In a flipped classroom, class hours are used for more engaging, interactive, and creative activities, while direct instruction, such as teaching the proper use of grammar, is accomplished through online video lectures outside the classroom. By implementing a flipped classroom, teachers can tailor their instruction to meet a variety of students' interests, adjust the speed and level of difficulty, and, consequently, enhance students' motivation and learning effectiveness. Furthermore, this approach calls for and actively promotes a shift from transmission of knowledge to creation of knowledge (Bergmann & Sams, 2012).

In most cases of flipped classroom, learning outside the classroom can be accomplished by utilizing information technology such as through online streaming websites (e.g., YouTube) and online learning websites (e.g., moodle). However, integrating technology into pedagogy is often an issue. What kind of material should be prepared? What kind of tools should be used? How can these tools be created and by whom? How long does it take to prepare all materials? How can they be combined with learning inside the classroom? Such questions seem to keep teachers away from and make them think twice before implementing a flipped classroom. This is also the case in second language education.

In this chapter, we focus on pronunciation teaching and learning to discuss flipped classroom in second language education. Although many learners cite pronunciation as one of their priorities in second language learning (Toda, 2008), pronunciation instruction remains a less explored area in terms of technology integration. Ultrasound imaging, a recent technological development in the field of linguistics, specifically speaking, enables teachers to provide effective ways of teaching Japanese pronunciation through flipped learning and teaching. With this technology, we have developed a pronunciation self-learning website and implemented it in Japanese as a Foreign Language courses at a university in western Canada. In what follows, we first review the current issues in pronunciation instruction and flipped classroom in the field of second language education. Then, we describe a flipped classroom project we conducted, including the construction of a pronunciation self-learning website. Based on a case study, we then explore the advantages of utilizing a flipped classroom in pronunciation teaching and discuss how challenges to the implementation of a flipped classroom can be possibly overcome. Specifically, the study aimed to address two research questions:

1. How do teachers and students perceive the teaching and learning of pronunciation through a flipped classroom in a university-based Japanese as a Foreign Language program?
2. How can teachers overcome the difficulties of implementing a flipped classroom for teaching Japanese pronunciation?

BACKGROUND

Challenges in Pronunciation Teaching and Learning

Recent research has emphasized the meaningfulness of the target language in pronunciation teaching and learning. It helps to develop a strong sense of belonging in the target language community situated in a globalized world (Derwing & Munro, 2009). In the context of Japanese pronunciation teaching, some researchers argue the need for effective instruction in pronunciation in the classroom as well as outside the classroom (e.g., Shibata & Matsuzaki, 2012; Toda, 2009). According to Shibata and Matsuzaki (2012), accurate intonation, accent, and rhythm in oral communication provide better understandings of sociolinguistic and psychological connotations as well as clear syntax and sentence structures among interlocutors to carry on a smoother conversation.

Successful teaching and learning of pronunciations is challenging. Previous studies demonstrated three main concerns regarding Japanese instructors' attitudes toward pronunciation teaching: lack of pedagogical approach, lack of resources, and classroom limitations (Ogawara & Kono, 2002; Urakami, 2004; Yonemoto, Noguchi, Hayashi, Tsuda, & Yamane, 2014). Ogawara and Kono (2002), for example, reported instructors' insecure feelings towards their pedagogical approach due to insufficient knowledge of Japanese phonetics and phonology. In other words, the challenge to their teaching of Japanese pronunciation was not because of their lack of professional attitude and skills but due to the existence of wide variations in Japanese intonation. Besides, instructors' goals tend to be unclear on how much and how well students need to acquire pronunciation skills in order to sound appropriate in diverse social settings (Hirano, 2014). In addition, instructors cannot see the inside of each student's mouth to check the movement of the tongue and suggest how to improve pronunciation. All these seem to explain why instructors find it difficult to teach pronunciation in a classroom setting (Matsuzaki, 2012; Minematsu, Nakagawa & Tagawa, 2012).

Another challenge has to do with the lack of resources about teaching pronunciation. According to Urakami (2004), there are only a few textbooks that explain the various patterns and combinations of intonation and accent from language education or linguistic perspectives. Outlining details about pronunciation is a challenging task, as Hirano (2014) argues. While most Japanese textbooks on the market include a section on pronunciation at the beginning, explaining how each character should be pronounced, many do not have cross-sectional illustrations of the face to show how a pronunciation should be appropriately articulated. Also, in Japanese second language education, most teacher's manuals devote little space to methods of teaching pronunciation. Therefore, pronunciation instruction is largely left to the individual instructor's discretion.

Lastly, apart from pedagogical concerns, classroom limitations also challenge the instructors and students due to large classroom sizes, diverse linguistic demographics of student bodies, and time restriction (Yonemoto *et al.*, 2014). For example, a student's first language significantly affects his or her target language pronunciation, which, needless to say, varies from language to language. As 40.3% of the population in a metropolitan city on the West Coast of Canada speak nonofficial languages as mother tongues (Statistics Canada, 2011), despite the language of instruction at the university being English, many languages are spoken by students in one classroom. In this sense, teachers need to consider accessibility of pronunciation instruction; that is, how instruction can be easily accessible to students who have a diverse linguistic background. As such, challenges in pronunciation learning differ substantially between individuals, which call for differentiated instruction. Moreover, pronunciation learning is a time consuming task and difficult to be achieved by oneself unlike grammar or vocabulary. It needs constant practice and feedback from others. However, in reality, it is impossible for individual instructors to monitor and facilitate all these activities.

In order to investigate pedagogical and methodological challenges in teaching Japanese pronunciation, learner perspectives also should be taken into consideration. Sometimes, learners tend to believe that native speakers such as instructors and friends from Japan are ideal people to learn from; and that they cannot practice pronunciation by themselves or with their peers, as they cannot find pronunciation errors (Nakamura, 2007). Other times, learners may feel that accuracy of pronunciation is not important as long as the message is intelligible. Due to the challenges concerning pronunciation teaching, teachers may not be unable to convey the importance of pronunciation to the students, and, consequently, such erroneous beliefs are reinforced and students become more passive about improving pronunciation.

Flipped Classroom

The word "flip" in flipped classroom typically leads to a misunderstanding: teaching that traditionally has been done inside and outside the classroom can be simply switched. As we can see in Fukada's statement (2014) that a "flipped classroom cannot be used in language classes" (p.23; the authors' translation), many tend to think that grammar explanation and exercise would be switched with homework. And it is understandable that teachers may think flipped classroom cannot function well in language education if that were really the case. With such misinterpretation of flipped classroom in language educational field, there might not be much pedagogical implementation even if technological materials and instructions are created.

According to Bergmann and Sams (2012), flipped classroom is a way to provide a space for knowledge creation rather than to transmit knowledge. It is "a pedagogical approach in which direct instruction moves from the group learning space to the individual learning space, and the resulting group space is transformed into a dynamic, interactive learning environment where the educator guides students as they apply concepts and engage creativity in the subject matter" (Flipped Learning Network, n.d.). The focus of flipped teaching is not simply on how to teach by integrating media-supported study; rather, it is on how to engage students in active learning. Therefore, it cannot be considered a flipped classroom if teachers simply switch activities performed outside and inside the classroom.

Flipped Classrooms for Second Language Education

There are many ways a flipped classroom can be applied in second language education. To use the teaching of grammar as example, in a traditional language classroom, teachers typically first introduce the target grammar in the context where it is used and explain how it functions grammatically; and then repetitive exercises such as drills follow. Consequently, only little time is saved for conversational activities and other group activities to promote communicative use of the target language. On the other hand, by implementing a flipped classroom into language teaching and learning, teachers can let students prepare for in-class learning by studying grammar with videos or PowerPoint slides outside of the classroom (Muldrow, 2013; Tanno, 2013). Vocabulary learning can also be aided with technology outside the classroom. Because students can become somewhat familiar with vocabulary before attending the class, they can concentrate more on in-class activities. Quizzes can also be done outside the classroom. Overall, the content that can be moved to outside the classroom depends on the needs and demands in each context. Teachers can use flipped classroom only for a specific function or make the entire curriculum with it.

In spite of the diversity of choices, implementing flipped learning is not easy to language teachers. The need for considering how learning outside the classroom can be designed and delivered often makes teachers stay away from adopting flipped learning (Bergmann & Sams, 2012; Tanno, 2013). While there have been an increasing number of tools such as Camtasia Studio and Snagit that support material development, and more and more learning resources have been available online for free, finding the appropriate resources and arranging them along with the course contents appear to be troublesome to teachers, especially when a flipped classroom is first implemented in a course. In addition, time issues that occur on the teachers' side are also the case with students, as sometimes they need to study more outside the classroom than previously (Tanno, 2013).

The challenge to implementing to flipped teaching can also be understood from the perspective of students, as they may be confused about a flipped classroom. Tanno (2013) used a flipped classroom in a beginner's Japanese course at a public university in the United States. He found that students typically hesitated about their role as active learners, or in other words, taking initiative to learn on their own, which was especially difficult for those who were used to the traditional teacher-learner relationship. In view of this, Tanno (2013) pointed out the importance of teachers to provide their students with a better understanding of the concept of a flipped classroom.

METHODOLOGY

This case study took place in a Japanese as a foreign language course at a public university in western Canada. As with other universities in Canada, due to the large number of students in one class (25–30 per class) and the amount of materials that have to be covered in limited class time, teachers cannot devote enough time to teach pronunciation in the classroom. Consequently, even though pronunciation is assessed as an integral component of learning, it is not explicitly and formally taught in the courses. Typically, pronunciation is introduced at the beginning of an elementary course in which the teacher explains how to produce each sound with cross-sectional illustrations of the face and has students repeat after him/her for practice. However, after the elementary stage of learning, pronunciation is no longer given adequate attention.

Collaborative Work: Material Development and Project Management

As many previous studies indicated, in this project, one of the most challenging parts in implementing a flipped classroom was developing online learning materials. We used various technologies in our courses, such as WebCT, Blackboard, Facebook and so on. However, oftentimes, we did not have a clear idea or reason why we needed to use a certain tool or whether it really could not be replaced by other tools. Basically, we simply used the tools with which we were already familiar. Even if there was a tool that seemed useful, if it seemed difficult to handle, we tended to be reluctant to use it. As for the pronunciation teaching, we did not find any technology that seemed helpful or effective for us. What saved us from this qualm was collaboration with experts in other disciplines.

In our project, we as Japanese instructors who shared teaching philosophy decided to work together. Collaborating with colleagues who teach the same level of Japanese courses and share the similar pedagogical beliefs were a crucial element in setting up the project. The common goal of this project among us was for professional development as well as producing publically accessible comprehensive on-line teaching materials. We then sought for collaborators to work with from different disciplines to discuss further levels of the contents of learning, material resources, instructional structure, pedagogical approach, the selections of technological devices to build the foundation of the teaching materials.

Moreover, by involving more people, it could be ascertained whether the materials were effective and whether there was a better way to teach. While developing the website, sometimes one teacher pointed out the problems that other teachers did not notice, as shown in the following excepts of our reflective notes.

Implementing a Flipped Classroom in Teaching Second Language Pronunciation

やっぱり二人*(other authors)*やA*(linguistic expert)*と色々な話をしてると学ぶことが多い。

All in all, I learnt a lot through discussion with the two (other authors) and A (linguistic expert). (Reflective notes; October 2, 2013)

私はどっちかというと*classroom implementation*とか実際の教え方とか、そういうものを考えるのは好きだし得意だけど今でも*Theory*とかリサーチに関しては二人*(other authors)*に頼り切ってるし。

I rather prefer to and am comfortable with thinking about classroom implementation, actual pedagogy, and etc. But still now I completely rely on the two (other authors) regarding theory and research. (Reflective notes; June 25, 2014)

While our strengths are knowledge of pedagogy and phonology, we needed several different specialists in the field of linguistics, information technology, and instructional design, who can also facilitate the project in a timely manner. Several specialists in the Department of Linguistics, whose expertise is in ultrasound imaging and its application to language acquisition, joined the project. While we, Japanese language teachers, provided the information about the issues that Japanese language learners face and the ideas about what kind of exercises can be thought of, these linguistics experts focused on how these issues can be solved and how these ideas can be realized by using the technology, mainly ultrasound imaging, and the findings in the field of linguistics.

With the project funding from the Center for Teaching, Learning and Technology (CTLT), instructional designers, and technological specialists could support the project. CTLT is an institution that supports facilitation and enhancement of quality in university teaching and learning. The instructional designer oversaw the whole project, kept us on the right track, and advised us in terms of how to work collaboratively with other experts by providing workshop for facilitating project trajectory, especially in implementing the website into a course and evaluating its effectiveness. The information technology staff map out our pedagogical path for students to learn pronunciation by organizing the website to make it accessible. All in all, considering the quality of the materials and the time and energy each person can devote to the project, collaboration is a key in successfully developing the materials used in a flipped classroom.

Such collaboration brought to language instructors the opportunity to learn about pronunciation and revisit the way it is taught. As pointed out in the previous research, teachers tend to avoid pronunciation teaching due to lack of knowledge or teaching materials (Ogawara & Kono, 2002; Urakami, 2004; Yonemoto, Noguchi, Hayashi, Tsuda, & Yamane, 2014). This fact reinforces their lack of confidence. In order to fill in this gap, we sought collaboration with experts in this project. However, this does not mean that we could leave everything to them. Through this project, we could learn more about pronunciation from these experts as well as other language teachers. Also, when writing a script, we sometimes needed to read previous studies or teaching manuals.

Besides, we could learn the technology used in developing video materials. In this project, research assistants created most video materials based on the script we wrote. However, we teachers also had a chance to learn how to make a video clip using the same software, which made us realize its simplicity. Although we tended to reject such technology out of hand, working as a team provided a chance to learn

Figure 1. Handout used for pronunciation practice

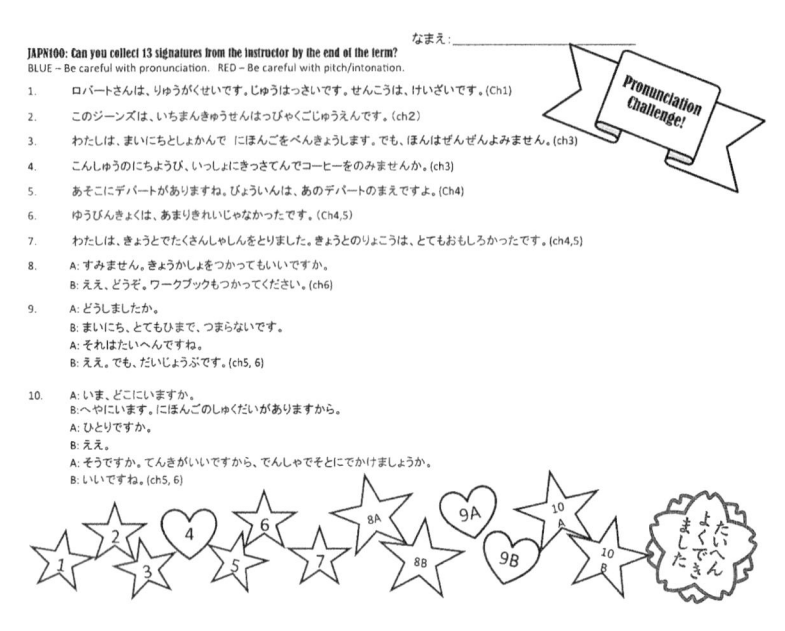

things that might not have been learned otherwise. This was the same for ultrasound imaging technology. Through this project, we came to realize the various tools that assist in learning a language.

Development of the Flipped Classroom Project

For the purpose of improving the aforementioned situation, we aimed to enhance learners' pronunciation through this flipped classroom project that was developed with the following steps: 1) We selected challenging sounds, pitches, and intonations from the textbook and made several sentences and dialogues (Figure 1); 2) recorded each sentence and dialogue and uploaded them to the course website; 3) asked students to listen to the recordings and practice by themselves outside class; and 4) asked students to test themselves face-to-face with us when they thought they could correctly pronounce each sentence and dialogue.

We started our project in collaboration with professionals in the field of linguistics. Later on, this developed into an inter-departmental project between the Department of Asian Studies and Department of Linguistics, with support from the Center for Teaching, Learning and Technology. The project team was eventually comprised of four Japanese language teachers, six linguists, one instructional designer, two technical leads and six research assistants. An outcome of the interdepartmental collaboration was the use of "ultrasound imaging technology." By using ultrasound images, the movement inside the mouth can be more easily and clearly observed than by simple drawing. In this way, students can observe and learn how native speakers move their tongues. Teachers can also save time and effort in explaining how to pronounce each sound or how to correct a student's mispronunciations.

The effectiveness of utilizing ultrasound images in teaching and improving pronunciation has already been confirmed in English language education (Gick, Bernhardt, Bacsfalvi, Wilson, Hansen Edwards, & Zampini, 2008) and French language education (Pillot-Loiseau, Antolík, & Kamiyama, 2003). After verifying its usefulness in a pilot study with two Korean students learning Japanese, we decided to de-

Figure 2. Examples of tutorials and exercises

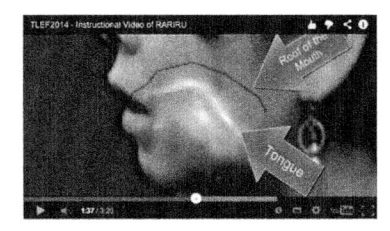

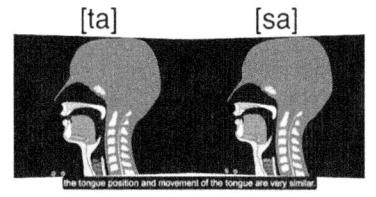

velop an online self-learning website, incorporating ultrasound images as well as other developments in the field of linguistics.

The self-learning website "eNunciate!" is roughly divided into two parts: 1) general introduction to Japanese phonetics and phonology and 2) exercises including self-check quizzes. In the second part, challenging sounds for speakers of different first languages—including English, Chinese, and Korean—are identified based on teachers' reports and linguists' expertise. For each sound, two sets of video materials have been created: tutorials and exercises. Upon understanding the features of each sound, students can proceed to the various exercises on the target sound.

Besides ensuring ease of navigation within the website, in the initial development phase, our priority has been to understand how ultrasound images can be effectively used for learning each sound. Raw ultrasound images are difficult for students to interpret, as they are in black and white. Furthermore, these images cannot show the difference between aspirated and nonaspirated sounds. To overcome these difficulties in raw ultrasound images, technologies used in linguistics—not only ultrasound images but also animations created from the ultrasound images (Figure 2)—were used in the development of the video materials. Considering accessibility, we uploaded all video materials on YouTube and embedded them on eNunciate! In addition, we have provided captions with all videos. In regard to the tutorial and exercise videos, we developed these resources to be as concise and interactive as possible. The website also features a series of quizzes to incrementally test comprehension. Although the construction is ongoing, the website is already open to public (http://enunciate.arts.ubc.ca).

Implementation into the Course

The website and the tutorials were introduced to the students of a second-year Japanese course. At the beginning of the semester, a ten minute in-class activity for the purpose of motivating and facilitating learning outside of class was held before introducing the website. In this activity, the students reflected upon their own foreign language learning experiences, especially pronunciation learning. For instance, the instructor asked such questions as what is important for making a conversation go smoothly and comfortably, what is difficult in learning a foreign language, what is challenging in learning pronunciation, why learning pronunciation is difficult, etc.

Then, the instructor introduced the website to the students, briefly explaining the structure and how to use it such as watching the videos repeatedly until they could satisfactorily pronounce each sound. In order to show students that learning that occurs outside of the classroom affects their performance in class, the instructor asked the students to watch the video on the target sound at home as a preparation for the in-class activity in the following class.

Figure 3. Cycle of learning

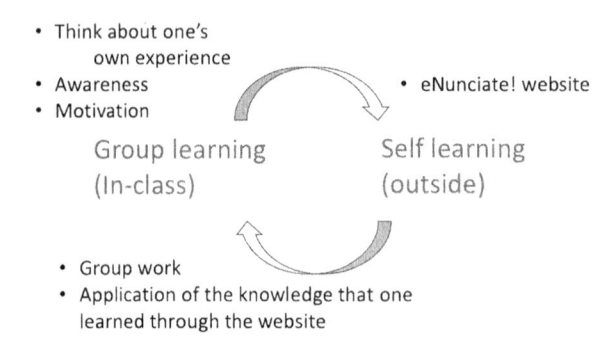

- Think about one's own experience
- Awareness
- Motivation

Group learning (In-class)

- eNunciate! website

Self learning (outside)

- Group work
- Application of the knowledge that one learned through the website

As a follow-up activity in the following class, students participated in another ten-minute small group activity where they had to check their peers' pronunciation (peer-review) and explain to each other how to pronounce challenging sounds by using what they learned from the tutorials, such as the position and movement of the tongue and key linguistic terminologies. The students were engaged in this cycle of learning as a part of the course. (Figure 3).

In this case study, only a few videos targeting native English speakers were chosen. Each video is less than five minutes long so that the students would not be overwhelmed and feel that flipped classroom add extra workload for them. In-class activity was also designed to be completed in short period of time to avoid sacrificing time for other parts of language instructions such as grammar explanation and conversational practice, etc. At the university where this study took place, 50-minute class is held four times a week. This pronunciation activity took up only 10 minutes in each week.

Data Collection

A qualitative case study was conducted to understand the implementation of the flipped classroom and the effectiveness of flipped learning of pronunciation. The data sources included: 1) a series of class observations, 2) informal semi-structured interviews with the course instructors, 3) a questionnaire survey with the students, and 4) reflective notes of the authors during the project. In the interviews with the course instructors, which were held immediately after the class observation, we asked how the instructors perceived students' attitude toward pronunciation learning through flipped classroom. The observations and interviews were conducted ten times in total.

The questionnaire survey with 17 students was conducted at the end of the project. It explored how they perceived learning pronunciation outside the classroom, the way the online materials were integrated into in-class activity, and collaborative activity with their peers. This questionnaire was anonymous and consisted of open-ended questions only. Lastly, the authors kept reflective notes while developing the website and observing the implementation into the course.

Data Analysis

We started the data analysis process by transcribing the recorded data collected during the interviews with the instructors. After transcribing all the data, we began to read through the transcriptions, field notes, survey results, and reflective notes, marking the passages that raised issues regarding the research

Implementing a Flipped Classroom in Teaching Second Language Pronunciation

questions. In order to describe what successes and challenges teachers found in teaching pronunciation through flipped learning, these passages were coded, categorized, and triangulated for emerging themes. To increase the validity of the findings, while discussing with the course instructors about the draft of this paper, a member check was carried out by the authors.

FINDINGS

To reiterate, this case study aimed to examine how teachers and students perceived the teaching and learning of pronunciation through the flipped classroom we development, and how teachers can overcome the difficulties of implementing a flipped classroom for teaching Japanese pronunciation.

To answer these two research questions, in what follows, we present the findings from two perspectives: teachers' and students perceptions of flipped classroom on pronunciation, and ways of implementations.

Advantages in Pronunciation Education: From Teachers' Point of View

Without any reliable guidelines, teachers lacked confidence in their ability to give effective response to students' pronunciation mistakes. The introduction of the video tutorial allowed them to give instruction in accordance with the video, such as in terms of the position of the tongue, and therefore enabled a systematic instruction as well as increased confidence in the teachers. Furthermore, while incorporating technology into teaching can be intimidating for unaccustomed teachers, eNunciate! requires not much more than simply referring students to the website. Thus one teacher expressed the following:

With technology I need to first learn how to use it and that can be overwhelming, but with this material it was easy because I only needed to show the video.

テクノロジーって、まずは自分が慣れるのに大変だったりするので、尻込みしがちなものも多いけど...これはビデオを見せるだけなので、教師にとっても楽だった。*(Reflective notes; February 18, 2015)*

This fact also applies to the exercises including self-check quizzes. One of the issues in pronunciation instruction is that instruction method has not been clearly introduced into the field. Since the website provided the materials for this purpose, the instructors did not need to worry about how they could teach the pronunciation itself. Therefore, our website helps overcome the lack of confidence in teaching pronunciation by enabling effective and systematic instruction, and by making it easy for the technologically hesitant teachers.

The other constraint in pronunciation education is the number of students and the limited time that can be used in class. Since these conditions are difficult to change, we focused on how to deal with this situation by utilizing the website in this project. This appeared to satisfy the instructors' needs for pronunciation education. By providing the tutorial and exercise videos that can be accessed outside the classroom, the instructors could spend less time to check each student's pronunciation in class. This is not only because the students could practice more outside the classroom, but also they learned the ways to teach themselves and also their classmates about how to correctly pronounce the sounds. More importantly, what intrigued us was its effectiveness in improving pronunciation, which is described in the next section.

Effectiveness of the Flipped Classroom Approach: From Students' Reaction

The students have also positively accepted the implementation. Prior to this approach, most students relied on traditional aural and oral learning methods, such as listening to audio and repeating words until mastering pronunciation. However, ultrasound images of movement appealed to the students' visual aspect of learning, and the instructional and practice video clips encouraged students to pay more attention to their own pronunciation. As a consequence, students gradually became more aware of their own pronunciation-acquiring processes. Among others, as seen in the following excerpts from the questionnaire survey, it is highly valued that we provided resources available outside the classroom. When it comes to learning pronunciation, unlike vocabulary and grammar, it is typically difficult for learners, by themselves, to check if their pronunciation is correct or not. However, using this website enables them to learn and practice pronunciation outside the classroom.

By providing resources for learning pronunciation outside of the classroom, it really helps the students to learn Japanese and work towards fluency.

Can always go back to it, whereas in class, we would only be able to see it once.

Students also appreciated the way we connected the website with in-class learning, as can be seen from the following survey responses. They liked the in-class activities in that they could be aware of their own pronunciation and receive instant feedback when practicing with others.

Pronunciation needs lots of independent practice, and it's easy to think your pronunciation is good when everyone is talking/pronouncing at the same time.

We are able to get instant feedback from other classmates and ensure that our pronunciation is correct.

It was good to receive pronunciation feedback from the instructor during in-class activities.

In addition, regarding the connection with the learning outside the classroom, they mentioned that, through the in-class activities, they could review, confirm, practice, and consolidate what they have learned outside the classroom.

It was good way to review what we did at home together.

It was good reinforcement and allowed processing of the materials learned outside of class, so that there was no feeling of having learned in isolation of the rest of the course.

Sounds good, reiterates material, which helps with clarification.

Overall, students were satisfied both with the new pronunciation learning style and learning outcome. They also expressed that the knowledge and technique they learned in this class for practicing pronunciation can be transferred to other foreign languages. It was very rewarding for us that students acquired a translatable skill through our project.

Challenges and Possible Solutions: The Way of Implementation

In this project, the flipped classroom we implemented was positively accepted. Having said that, according to the student feedback, the way we implemented the flipped classroom needs to be improved, especially in regards to how to do the in-class activities and how these activities are integrated in the curriculum. One of the features of this website is that specific tutorials and practices have been developed for speakers of different first languages. These tutorials, which explain common pronunciation issues stemming from students' first language phonology, allow students to efficiently improve their pronunciation. Regarding this, one student noted:

It felt like, since I was the only person with English as my first language, people were almost expecting my pronunciation to be the worst.

Since we only went through these tutorials targeting native English speakers in this study, that particular student was given more attention during in-class activity, which made him/her feel uncomfortable. One solution for this is that we can practice the challenging sounds of the two different languages at the same time. By doing so, giving certain groups of students unnecessary attention can be avoided.

Moreover, when including activities such as peer feedback, it is important for teachers to create a safe learning environment where students can collaborate more than they compete. It is also essential for each student to understand why he or she is learning a certain skill and why it is important. This will help students who are used to the traditional teacher-learner relationship in order to understand what the teacher is aiming at in implementing a flipped classroom.

Another issue students raised is about how this flipped classroom is to be integrated into the curriculum. In our project, the flipped classroom was integrated as a part of the course. That is, while we taught the overall course in the same way as before, flipped learning was integrated only for pronunciation learning. Thus, for some students, only this "flipped learning" part stood out in the course.

I think it works fine but feels like a different module entirely. For example, we learn grammar etc. in class, and then practice pronunciation as a separate topic.

This issue is somewhat peculiar to this project, as this project was specifically about pronunciation. However, it might be possible to relate pronunciation learning with other contents such as vocabulary and grammar. For example, we can use new vocabulary in pronunciation practice. There is no fixed way to implement a flipped classroom. Therefore, it is the teacher's responsibility to consider how it can be used to maximize students' learning.

Based on the students' comments, it seems that the students simply liked having more opportunities and resources to practice pronunciation. However, the implementation is the very part that we carefully considered and planned to optimize in a flipped classroom. This is because we found this step the most difficult and important in the success of a flipped classroom.

During the initiation process, the instructor raised the students' awareness of the importance of pronunciation as well as the effectiveness of the website. We found this process particularly important, as some students were not motivated toward pronunciation learning. Simply assigning the practices on the website as homework might have ended with some students not doing them or just watching the videos. However, by motivating them through in-class activities, they understood why they needed to practice. In other words, learning outside the classroom became more meaningful.

In the classroom, we also asked students several questions on the content they had learned through the website. This was to make students aware that their learning outside the classroom would have an impact on their performance in the classroom in many ways. Some students seemed to attribute their failure to the lack of ability or aptitude, especially when it came to pronunciation. However, explicitly showing the connection between learning inside and outside the classroom appeared to have encourage them to engage learning outside the classroom. In this respect, in a flipped classroom, teachers need to coordinate and facilitate learning, thus aiming at constructing a circle of learning. That is, learning inside the classroom leads to motivated and meaningful learning outside the classroom, which in turn brings back active and full participation into the classroom, and so on. By doing so, we can guide students to autonomously learn and practice, especially outside the classroom.

When it comes to a flipped classroom, the focus tends to be on what kind of activities we include inside the classroom and what kind of materials or tools we use outside the classroom. Since preparing the materials and activities is typically time consuming and energy draining for teachers, it might be natural that these parts are given more attention. Moreover, meaningful activities and effective materials can enhance students' learning. However, our implementation indicates that we teachers need to discuss and share ideas on how we can better connect the learning inside and outside of the classroom.

FUTURE DIRECTIONS

One of the significant factors that make teachers stay away from implementing flipped classrooms is, as previously noted, whether they can provide the appropriate resources for learners outside the classroom. Collaboration with other teachers and experts is, thus, one solution. In our case, we could closely collaborate not only with other language teachers but also linguists and instructional designers for the purpose of the improvement of pronunciation education.

Considering that both material development and implementation are important in a flipped classroom, exchanging information and sharing ideas with teachers in other languages can be useful as well. For most teachers, it might be a common interest in how teachers can encourage learners to learn outside the classroom. In this respect, for the purpose of advancing a flipped classroom in language education, conversation across languages is called for.

At last, as for the website we developed, we are currently working on creating the materials that can be used for in-class activities. Thus, when other teachers are going to use our website, they can easily implement a flipped classroom in their course by just using or slightly adjusting these materials. As such, although developing the materials from scratch requires enormous effort, if more information and materials are shared in the future, teachers can devote their time and energy in a more meaningful way with their students.

CONCLUSION

In this chapter, we explored how we improved pronunciation teaching and overcame the problem of technology integration into language teaching through a case study on the flipped classroom we developed for teaching university students pronunciation in Japanese as a Foreign Language. By collaborating with experts in linguistics and other areas, we Japanese instructors overcame our intimidation towards technology integration. The self-learning website we development, in particular, successfully addressed three issues in pronunciation teaching: lack of pedagogical approach, lack of resource, and limitation of time.

Thanks to the development of information technology, expanding opportunities and resources are becoming readily available outside the classroom. However, we cannot forget the importance of the teacher's role in flipped classroom. When implementing flipped classroom, teachers need to consider how learning outside and inside the classroom can be better connected so that the students can see what we are trying to achieve through this approach. Only with technology and proper facilitation can we successfully implement the flipped classroom.

REFERENCES

Bergmann, J., & Sams, A. (2012). *Flip your classroom: Reach every student in every class every day*. Eugene, OR: International Society for Technology in Education.

Derwing, T. M., & Munro, M. J. (2009). Putting accent in its place: Rethinking obstacles to communication. *Language Teaching*, *42*(04), 276–490. doi:10.1017/S026144480800551X

Flipped Learning Network. (n.d.). Retrieved from http://flippedlearning.org

Gick, B., Bernhardt, B., Bacsfalvi, P., Wilson, I., Hansen Edwards, J. G., & Zampini, M. L. (2008). Ultrasound imaging applications in second language acquisition. In J. G. Hansen Edwards & M. L. Zampini (Eds.), Phonology and second language acquisition (pp. 315-328). Philadelphia, PA: John Benjamins. doi:10.1075/sibil.36.15gic

Hirano, H. (2014). *"Soogoo Nihongo" no jugyoo de okonau zero shokyuu kara no onsee kyooiku no jissen: Akusento, intoneeshon no shizensei wo juushishita shikakuka hojo kyoozai no shiyoo* [Practice of Japanese prosody education for beginners in an integrated Japanese course: Use of visualized Japanese accent and intonation learning material]. Retrieved from http://www.ninjal.ac.jp/publication/papers/07/pdf/NINJAL-Papers0703.pdf

Matsuzaki, H. (2012). Onsee ninshiki gijutsu wo mochiita nihongo inritsu renshuuyoo sofuto no kaihatsu [The Development of Software to Study Japanese Prosody Using an Automatic Speech Recognition System]. *Bungee Gengo Kenkyuu: Gengo Hen* [Studies in language and literature. Language], *61*, 177-190.

Minematsu, N., Nakagawa, C., & Tagawa, Y. (2012). Kooritsutekina nihongo inritsu kyooiku no jitsugen ni muketa infurasutorakucha no koochiku: akusento no koopasu bunseki + onrain akusento jiten no koochiku + inritsu kyooiku jissen [Development of the infrastructure to implement an effective and efficient methodology of teaching/learning Japanese prosody: Corpus-based analysis of word accents, development of an on-line accent dictionary, and practical methodology of prosody education]. In *Proceedings of the 9th International Symposium for Japanese Language Education and Japanese Studies*. Retrieved from http://www.japanese-edu.org.hk/sympo/upload/manuscript/20121015080146.pdf

Muldrow, K. (2013). A new approach to language instruction: Flipping the classroom. *Language and Education*, *8*, 28–31.

Nakamura, N. (2007). Hatsukon kurasu jugyou houkoku [The report from the pronunciation class]. Tokyo Gaikokugo Daigaku ryuugakusei nihongo kyooiku sentaa ronshuu [Collection of theses from Japanese Education Center, Tokyo University of Foreign Studies], 33(1), 179-189.

Ogawara, Y., & Kono, T. (2002). Kyooshi no onsee kyooikukan to shidoo no jissai [The influence of teachers' beliefs toward pronunciation teaching on their teaching practices]. *Nihongo kyooiku hoohoo kenkyuukaishi* [Journal of Japanese Language Education Methods], *9*(1), 28-29.

Pillot-Loiseau, C., Antolík, T. K., & Kamiyama, T. (2013). Contribution of ultrasound visualisation to improving the production of the French/y/-/u/contrast by four Japanese learners. In *Proceedings of Phonetics, phonology, languages in contact: Varieties, multilingualism, second language learning* (pp. 86–89). Paris: Fance.

Shibata, T., & Matsuzaki, H. (2012). Onsee to shuutoku: Sooron. [Phonology and acquisition] In K. Hatasa, Y. Hatasa, M. Kudara, & T. Shimizu (Eds.), *Daini gengo shuutoku to gengo kyooiku* [Second language acquisition and language education] (pp. 196–213). Tokyo, Japan: Kurosio Publishers.

Statistics Canada. (2011). *Focus on Geography Series, 2011 Census: Census metropolitan area of Vancouver, British Columbia*. Retrieved from http://www12.statcan.gc.ca/census-recensement/2011/as-sa/fogs-spg/Facts-cma-eng.cfm?LANG=Eng&GK=CMA&GC=933

Tanno, K. (2013). A case study of implementing flipped-teaching in a beginning Japanese course. *Proceedings of the 20th Princeton Japanese Pedagogy Forum*.

Toda, T. (2008). *Nihongo Kyooiku to Onsee* [Japanese Language Education and Phonology]. Tokyo: Kurosio.

Toda, T. (2009). Nihongo kyooiku ni okeru gakushuusha onsee no kenkyuu to onsee kyooiku jissen[Learners' pronunciation and practices of pronunciation education in the field of Japanese language education]. *Nihongo Kyooiku*, *143*, 47–57.

Urakami, F. (2004). Nihongo kyooiku ni okeru onsee shidoo[Speech sound in teaching foreign languages]. *Chuugoku Gakuen Kiyoo*, *3*, 27–34.

Yonemoto, K., Noguchi, M., Hayashi, H., Tsuda, A., & Yamane, N. (2014). Chooompa eezoo wo ooyooshita nihongo hatsuon shidoo no kanoosee [Ultrasound application to the empowerment of pronunciation teaching and learning]. In *Proceedings of Annual Conference of the Canadian Association for Japanese Language Education* (pp. 248-257). Retrieved from http://www.cajle.info/wp-content/uploads/2014/09/Yonemoto_CAJLE2014_Proceedings_248-257.pdf

KEY TERMS AND DEFINITIONS

Blended Learning: A pedagogical approach that integrates face-to-face teaching and media-supported study such as through online movies and newspapers.

Cycle of Learning: A meaningful and constructive connection between learning inside and outside the classroom.

Flipped Classroom: A pedagogical approach where class hours can be used for more engaging, interactive, and creative activities by doing direct instruction such as grammar explanation outside the classroom through online materials, etc. A flipped classroom is considered a form of blended learning.

Ultrasound Images: Images created by sending ultrasound waves into an object and analyzing the waves reflected from it. Unlike an x-ray, it is considered safe, as there is no radiation involved.

Chapter 8
Divergent Teacher Viewpoints of Technology Integration in the Language Classroom

Andy D. Halvorsen
University of Oregon, USA

ABSTRACT

This chapter presents a qualitative analysis of the beliefs and practices of three language teachers in Thailand vis-à-vis their integration of technology in the classroom as well as their views regarding social networking site participation as a facilitative tool for instruction. The study brings together research on the identity development work of teachers and Computer Assisted Language Learning (CALL). Through the analysis of extensive teacher interview data and classroom observations, the study demonstrates how these teachers self-identify as users of technology, and how this sense of self interacts with and shapes various aspects of their teaching practice. The three teachers in this study represent a range of divergent viewpoints related to technology use and integration in the classroom, and the analysis of these viewpoints helps to illustrate the specific factors underlying how and why they choose to make pedagogic use of technology.

INTRODUCTION

With the ever increasing potential for integration of technology into the language classroom, teachers are confronted with a range of diverse issues for consideration. These include articulating their own personal and professional stances with respect to educational technology, modifying and adapting their pedagogy to incorporate various technologies, and deciding how best to meet the 21st century needs of today's students. The paths that teachers take as they work through these issues are mediated through the sociocultural contexts that they live and work in, as well as their own personal experiences with technology. One of the primary technological tools being considered by educators today is the use of Social Networking Sites (SNSs) for language learning and instruction. Many teachers and researchers are wondering whether or not there is a viable way to harness the obvious interest in sites like Twitter and

DOI: 10.4018/978-1-5225-0483-2.ch008

Divergent Teacher Viewpoints of Technology Integration in the Language Classroom

Facebook (FB), and to transform this interest into meaningful ways to improve language skills (Blattner & Lomicka, 2012; boyd, 2006; Halvorsen, 2014; Mills, 2011; Reinhardt & Zander, 2011).

One way to begin to analyze some of these challenges is to look in detail at the diverse approaches that teachers are taking today. The present study is an attempt to do precisely this. Through a detailed qualitative analysis of the lives and teaching practices of three high school teachers in Thailand, the study begins to shed some light on the complex interplay between how teachers self identify as users of technology, and how they build and shape classroom practices vis-à-vis educational technology.

THEORETICAL PERSPECTIVES

This study is informed primarily through two key theoretical orientations. The first of these is identity construction in the classroom and in particular our current understanding of language teacher self-identification as it relates to and informs teaching practice. Secondly, this study draws on theoretical work from Computer Assisted Language Learning (CALL) as it analyzes SNS use by teachers both in their personal and professional lives. The interplay between these two theoretical perspectives creates the primary analytic framework for the presentation of findings in this study.

Language Teacher Self-Identification and Language Teaching Practice

Identity as a construct is not a new area of social inquiry, though within the field of language education, studies have only begun to emerge within approximately the last 20-30 years. Norton (1997) is among the earliest and best known studies of language learner identity, looking at the various roles that are taken up by immigrant women in Canada. In terms of language teacher identity, much work has targeted the distinction between native and non-native speaking teachers, and their respective senses of themselves as valued members of the teaching community. Martel and Wang (2014) reviewed research on language teacher identity and identified several primary findings from the research. First, they point out that identities are shaped through social context and interaction with others. Second, research has highlighted the mutually constitutive relationship between teacher identity and classroom practice. Also, they state that "teachers' views of themselves as cultural beings bear upon their cultural teaching practices" (p. 293), suggesting that how teachers choose to position themselves within various sociocultural contexts impacts their teaching practice.

Morgan (2004), using primarily a poststructuralist framework, points out that identity itself, much like teaching practice, has inherent fluidity. A teacher's sense of self shifts through time, as they come into contact with differing social and cultural influences and develop new approaches and pedagogic skill sets. Identity and teaching practice both constitute and are constituted by one another. As one begins to change, so too will the other. Morgan used the phrase "identity as pedagogy" to highlight this fluidity, and also to better express the notion that identities are not fixed constructs but are in fact performative in nature, both in the classroom and in daily interactions with others.

One of the primary gaps in the research into teacher identity is specific to technology and its use by teachers in personal and professional contexts. In one study, Trent and Shroff (2013) looked at preservice teachers in Hong Kong and discussed how teacher identities were shaped partly through their participation in the development of their personal e-Teacher portfolios. The portfolio development process interacted with their teaching practicum experience to inform their sense of themselves as current and future

131

teachers. Beyond this, little empirical research currently exists that specifically targets the relationship between teacher identity and technology use.

Social Networking Site Use in Language Instruction

The skills needed for full participation in 21st culture are ever evolving, but one clear trend is the emergence of Web 2.0 tools for both personal and professional interaction. Conole and Alevizou (2010) define Web 2.0 as "a wide set of functional characteristics [that] not only point to increased opportunities for publication, but also encourage and are supportive of user participation" (p. 9). Online platforms available under Web 1.0 were characterized by high barriers to participation and content that was delivered primarily top-down, in one way channels (Stevenson & Liu, 2010). With Web 2.0 however, the trend is toward active user participation and content generation that happens at the individual level and is shared through social networks (Wang & Vasquez, 2012). Jenkins (2008) has termed this emergent Web 2.0 culture as a "participatory culture," which he defines as a culture which "offers low barriers to artistic expression… strong support for creating and sharing…[and] is also one in which participants believe their contributions matter" (p. 3).

SNSs like FB and Twitter are some of the most obvious current manifestation of Web 2.0 tools and our current participatory culture. And, from within the context of education, it would seem that SNSs in particular have the power to encourage genuine learner autonomy and engagement (Halvorsen, 2014). Conole and Alevizou (2010) write,

There seems to be a tantalizing alignment between the affordances of digitally networked media (the focus on the user-generated content, the emphasis on communication and collective collaboration) and the fundamentals of what is perceived to be good pedagogy (socio-constructivist approaches, personalized and experiential learning). (p. 10)

At its core, a SNS is a tool that provides three key components. First, SNSs allow users to create profiles that may either be public or semi-public. Second, these sites allow for users to identify and maintain lists of affiliated users, and finally, users are able to view and interact with content shared by others users (boyd and Ellison, 2007). As mentioned, FB and Twitter are two of the most representative SNSs today, and both embody these three characteristics. The ubiquity of these sites in the lives of users worldwide has increased dramatically in recent years. At present, there are over 1.1 billion monthly active users of FB ("Facebook," 2015) and Twitter is averaging over 500 million tweets per day ("Twitter," 2015). Despite the acceptance that SNSs have found a tools for both personal and professional networking and collaboration, there remains relatively little data on the relationship between SNS participation and language learning and development.

Blatner and Lomicka (2012) looked at FB usage in an undergraduate French course in a U.S. classroom. They reported positive outcomes in terms of student perceptions of integrating FB into the course. They also found that FB usage heightened the authenticity of the language exchange in the classroom. Mills (2011) used situated learning theory to frame a study of FB usage by French learners. The study by Mills found a high degree of mutual engagement during the project and found that participants were able explore and develop their sense of identity in a second language. It is important to note that almost no empirical work has been done looking at pedagogic use of social networking sites, or teachers' perspectives on the use of the sites in the classroom. Reinhardt and Zander (2011) looked at the use of FB

Divergent Teacher Viewpoints of Technology Integration in the Language Classroom

by 11 students in an intensive English program in a US university. Their study showed evidence of resistance to a pedagogic use of FB by some students. They frame student resistance through their analysis of divergent discourses around SNS use and language learning, suggesting that students were somewhat uncomfortable with FB as a specific learning tool because it did not conform to their preconceived notion of what university-level, academic study of language should feel like.

THE PRESENT STUDY

The range of studies discussed above is limited both in its breadth and depth, and clearly much work remains to be done. The present study fits well within this limited body of research. This study uses theoretical perspectives of language teacher self-identification and SNS participation to frame a qualitative analysis of the lives and teaching practices of three high school teachers in Thailand. Specifically, the study analyzes the relationship between how teachers self-identify as users of technology and how this self-identification impacts and is actualized through classroom teaching practice. The qualitative study brings together extensive interview and classroom observation data to target two primary research questions.

1. How do these three teachers self identify as users of technology, and what is the interplay between this self-identification and their classroom practices?
2. What issues relate to the teachers' beliefs about social networking site use as a tool for foreign language learning?

CONTEXT

The study was conducted in a mid-sized Thai city approximately 100 kilometers outside of the capital of Bangkok. In Thailand, the K-12 educational system is divided into the "prathom" level comprising grades K-6, and the "mathayom" level, comprising grades 7-12. The present study was conducted entirely in a mathayom school which housed approximately 160 students in each grade level. The school drew students from both the city and the surrounding countryside, so students in this school were mixed in terms of their urban and rural backgrounds. Similarly, there existed within the school a high level of socioeconomic diversity, and this diversity corresponded roughly to the urban and rural divide, with students from the city generally coming from more affluent families.

The school offered foreign language options of Chinese, English, French, and German. English is a required and core component of their curriculum, whereas other languages may be taken as elective options. Each foreign language class has a single instructor working with between 25 and 40 students. Foreign language teachers at the school all have completed 4-year university degrees in education, with special emphases on their chosen languages. During the time of the study, the school also hosted two native-speaking Japanese teacher, two native-speaking Chinese teachers, and one native-speaking English teacher.

The foreign language curriculum for the school was controlled by school administrators, and was designed to meet standards set at the national level. Teachers had relative freedom in their methodological choices, though the content was primarily prescribed to them in a top-down manner. The primary pedagogic approach to foreign language instruction would be considered "traditional," with a strong emphasis on didactic, teacher-fronted explanations of target language grammatical patterns and vocabulary. National standards called for Communicative Language Teaching (CLT) and also emphasized the integration of language skills, though in daily practice, teachers often de-emphasized genuine communication in the target language or any form of oral language production.

Each classroom was equipped with a teacher-controlled PC that connected to 3-4 monitors placed around the room. Teachers were able to show PowerPoint and display other PC applications, but there was only limited and unreliable Internet connectivity in the classroom.

METHODS

The data presented here constitutes a subset of a broader, mixed-methods study conducted in Thailand. For a 3-month period, I collected qualitative and quantitative data from Thai students and teachers of English. The study was intended to examine the patterns of social networking site participation of both groups, and the extent to which the use of social networking sites like FB may have a facilitative role in foreign language learning and development.

For the purposes of the present study, I am targeting the qualitative components of the data collected from teachers only. During the course of this study, I was able to look carefully at the teaching practices of three high school instructors. I observed their classroom teaching repeatedly, and I conducted several hours of face-to-face interviews with each of the teachers. Specific details of data collection and analysis procedures are presented below.

This study uses a primarily constructivist framework for the conceptualization of knowledge and truth (Mertens, 2010). Given the overall goals of understanding both how teachers self-identify as users of technology and how they view SNSs as potential tools for foreign language learning, it is necessary to fully understand the personal experiences and realities of the teachers. In constructivist interpretations, realities are multiple, often conflicting, and mediated through diverse ways of experiencing the world.

DATA COLLECTION

Data collection for the present study took place over a 3-month period, and it involved two primary components: classroom observations of teachers, and face-to-face teacher interviews. Both of these were conducted by the researcher himself, and often with the help of a trained research assistant and native speaker of Thai.

Interviews with the teachers were extensive and ongoing throughout the data collection period. The majority of the interviews were conducted in a large, shared office either during lunch or shortly after school. On rare occasions, interviews took place in an empty classroom at the school. All interviews were audio recorded and transcribed. Interviews were partially structured based of formal interview protocols, but they were also allowed to move in diverse directions based on teacher responses and the general flow of conversation. A sample interview protocol from interview #1 is included as Appendix A. I conducted interviews in English, and all three teachers had a level of English proficiency that made this possible. The research assistant conducted her interviews in Thai, then simultaneously translated them during the transcription process. A complete summary of interview data collection is provided in Table 1 below.

Divergent Teacher Viewpoints of Technology Integration in the Language Classroom

Table 1. Data collection from interviews

	Bee	Yingluck	Dang
1st interview (Week 1-3)	25 min	35 min	30 min
2nd interview (Week 4-6)	45 min	20 min	35 min
3rd interview (Week 7-8)	35 min	25 min	25 min
4th interview (Week 9)	50 min	30 min	---
Group interview #1 (Week 10)	55 min	55 min	55 min
Group interview #2 (Week 12)	45 min	45 min	45 min
Total interview time	4.1 hours	3.3 hours	3 hours

As can be seen in Table 1, total interviews were conducted on roughly a bi-weekly basis, with some variation. During the last weeks of the study, all three teachers participated in two group interviews.

Classroom observations happened on a similar timeline, with observations of each teacher happening almost every other week. Yingluck and Bee were both observed five times, and Dang was observed four times. Of the 14 total observations, the research assistant conducted six, and I conducted eight. Classroom observations were done in their grade 10 English courses, and were done after establishing consent from both classroom teachers and relevant school administrators. For each observation, note-taking was conducted in both structured and open formats. The structured portion of the observations followed the protocol attached in Appendix B, and included classroom configuration information, a technology inventory, number of students, and detailed notational timeline. Open-format observational notes included any additional thoughts, details, or concerns that developed during the course of the observation.

DATA ANALYSIS

The qualitative techniques used to analyze interview and observational data from this study have their roots in grounded theory and the constant comparative method (Corbin & Strauss, 2008). The heart of grounded theory is the view that the extraction of meaning from data is an emergent, analytic process without pre-determined biases related to a study's theoretical orientation. Interpretations are allowed to emerge from the data itself. When patterns begin to develop, these patterns are systematically checked against new and incoming data, and confirmed, refined, or rejected depending on available information. In these ways, broader themes are allowed to develop from the data, and these themes undergo the constant process of refinement throughout the analysis.

The data analysis of teacher interviews began with the general reading and rereading of transcripted data. Following this, I began the process of data coding by tagging portions of interview transcripts with specific codes. Consistent with grounded theory, these codes developed from the data itself, and were constantly refined as the process continued. In the end, I utilized a series of 19 codes to begin analyzing

Table 2. Final code groups from teacher interviews

Thematic code groups	Interpretation	Sample
Personal Facebook use (PFU)	FB likes and dislikes, daily use of FB, how FB is accessed, friend # and type	I don't use often FB. Really I don't like to use it. – Dang (PFU)
Instructional Facebook use (IFU)	Challenges, advantages, evidence of engagement, evidence of learning	I write in English on FB so they can read. – Bee (IFU)
Cultural context (CC)	Thai language, Thai viewpoints, Asian educational models	This sometimes not in the Thai news so I like it. – Yingluck (CC)
Institutional context (IC)	Administrative constraints and challenges, Thai schools, diverse students, technology literacy	No phones! Our director would be…not happy with this. – Yingluck (IC)
Identity development (ID)	Personal views of self, changing views of self, views on personal privacy	When I was in high school I was not so good at English, but I loved English and really tried. – Dang (ID)

interview data. Once I had a substantial series of codes in place for the interpretation of interview data, I then began to thematically link codes into broader groups. These final coding groups are summarized in the table 2 below.

For classroom observations, raw data derived from structured teacher observation protocols were entered directly into a database for comparative analyses. The timelines of activities for each class, along with the unstructured observational notes, were coded and analyzed in a process similar to that described above for teacher interview data.

Once coded and analyzed separately, the teacher interview and classroom observation data were brought together for reinterpretation and collective analysis. Emergent themes from each data source were set side-by-side with one another. All findings presented later in this chapter are the result of this side-by-side analytic format, rooted in the constant comparative method. Findings are based on the triangulation of data from two distinct sources.

PARTICIPANTS

As mentioned, three teachers took part in this study. The teachers represent continua of language teaching experience, technology literacy, and English proficiency. All three of the teachers are female. This is consistent with the general demographics of the school where only one of the 19 teachers involved in language teaching was male. The teachers are all native speakers of Thai with at least the equivalent of a Bachelor's degree in education. The following section provides some further detail about each teacher. All names used in this study are pseudonyms.

- **Teacher 1:** Yingluck is a 41 year-old Thai woman with 15 years of experience as an English teacher. Her English proficiency is advanced, and she has completed some post-graduate training and study in the United States. Yingluck does not consider herself to be technologically adept, but she tends to make use of the classroom computer and projector quite frequently in her lessons. She is a active user of social media, and makes frequent posts to FB. She has numerous friends abroad, and often uses English on FB as a communicative tool. She has never considered or attempted the

integration of SNSs into her teaching practice, but she is not opposed to the idea. She consciously avoids friending students on FB or involving herself in the digital lives of her students.
- **Teacher 2:** Dang is a 38 year-old Thai woman with 12 years of English teaching experience. Her English proficiency is intermediate. Dang is generally resistant to the use of computers in the classroom, and will rely on the blackboard whenever possible. She often struggles when attempting to make use of classroom technology, and frequently abandons efforts midway through to resort to the blackboard. She is a passive and infrequent user of FB, and she is strongly opposed to the use of SNSs for pedagogical purposes.
- **Teacher 3:** Bee is a 25 year-old Thai woman with 3 years of English teaching experience. Her English is at an intermediate level. Bee considers herself technologically skilled, and is particularly proud of classroom teaching practices that integrate technology. She is quite vocal at the school about the need for Internet connections in the classroom. Bee is a frequent and heavy user of FB, and also uses Instagram and Twitter as well. She has actively embraced FB as a tool for English language learning, both in her personal life and in her teaching practices. Bee sends friend requests to many students, and she encourages them to follow her activities and posts on various social networking sites. She rarely makes use of English on these sites for authentic communication, as most of her social network is based in Thailand, though she does use English with students quite often for pedagogic purposes.

These three participants were deliberately and consciously selected to represent a range of experiences and viewpoints related to technology literacy and technology integration in the classroom. The selection process also involved considerations of teachers' willingness to participate in the study and their self-estimated time available for participation.

RESULTS

Results from the present study have been divided into four categories. Within each of these categories, data from classroom observations and teacher interviews are presented alongside one another wherever possible to give the most complete picture available.

Six Hours a Day or Twice a Week?: Personal Use of SNSs by Teachers

Data regarding how each of these teachers make use of SNSs in their daily lives comes primarily from face-to-face interviews with the teachers. In Bee's case however, because she tended to blur the line between the personal and pedagogic use of SNSs, there is also limited classroom observation data to discuss as well.

Overall, Dang was the most reluctant and infrequent user of SNSs. She was 38 years old, married, and had two children under the age of 10. Dang was disconnected from her family, most of whom lived over 100 miles away in Bangkok, and her only real motivation to involve herself in social networking was to stay connected with her family. In this first interview excerpt, she explains that she did use FB to view content shared by family members, but she was almost entirely a passive user of the site, and she rarely posted content of her own.

Interview excerpt 1

Interviewer: *Can you describe how you use FB and what you use it for?*

Dang: *I don't use often FB. Really I don't like to use it. My sisters in Bangkok say me I should be on it more, but I don't like it.*

Interviewer: *How often do you check FB?*

Dang: *I check some when my sister tells me she made a picture or video of her daughter. She is very cute! Maybe this is 2-3 times per week I look at it.*

Interviewer: *Do you just look at other people's posts, or do you post information yourself?*

Dang: *I really don't like it [posting on her own]. I don't really know how and it takes a long time. I am a teacher you know. This is very busy for me. At home it is always my kids since my husband is at work. When my sister comes she try to explain me about FB, but it is not so important in my life. I talk to my family on the phone and text with pictures, and we visit a lot. This is good for me. I did not have this [FB] like all kids now when I was student, so it is much for me to learn at my age.*

A couple of interesting themes emerge from this excerpt with Dang. Firstly, she view FB usage as related to time management. She references her busy life as a teacher an mother, and mentions not having time to participate in the site. She doesn't tend to post content of her own, even though family members wish she would, out of concerns over her technology literacy and limited time. Secondly, she does not appear to view FB as a pragmatic tool in her life. She sees the site as a way to share pictures and videos, but also points out that she is perfectly happy to do this via text message or in face-to-face communication. In Dang's view, FB or other SNSs are not tools worthy of her limited time, because she does not see a meaningful purpose in participating on these sites.

Here it is possible to contrast Dang's views related to the pragmatic use of SNSs with those of Yingluck. Her social and academic background are quite different from that of Dang. Yingluck is 41 years old and single. She has travelled abroad extensively, and she spent most of two years as a graduate student in the United States. Yingluck actively uses both FB and Instagram, and by her own estimation spends about an hour a day on these two sites. In the following excerpt, Yingluck explains how valuable she finds these sites for keeping up with her extensive social network abroad.

Interview excerpt 2

Interviewer: *Can you explain how you use SNSs and what you use them for?*

Yingluck: *Sure! FB is the most useful by me, but I use Instagram to share pictures of Thailand and see pictures from friends too.*

Interviewer: *How do you use FB exactly? Do you just read, or do you post as well?*

Yingluck: *Oh, I do lots of both. I really like the site because it is so easy to keep in contact with friends in other countries. I also see lots of news stories and other information people share. This sometimes not in the Thai news so I like it.*

Interviewer: *How did you stay in touch with friends abroad before FB?*

Yingluck: *I didn't! This is why it is so good. It's interesting now because friends I met in the US before FB, like in 2003, I lost them. But then with FB we find each other again and it is so surprising to see their kids and new jobs. I am very happy for this.*

In contrast to Dang, Yingluck has integrated SNSs into her daily life because she has found a clear, pragmatic use for them. They allow her to stay in constant contact with friends in other parts of the world.

Divergent Teacher Viewpoints of Technology Integration in the Language Classroom

She has moved beyond any frustration with the technological tools themselves, and fully invested herself in social participation online. She also references the ability to gain access to news and information that might not be available to her in Thailand. In this sense, she seems to value the sites not just for their social component, but also for the access they provide to diverse sources of information.

Interestingly, Yingluck seems to make relatively little use of FB or other sites to keep track of friends and family in her immediate community. When I asked about this in excerpt 3, she responded with not really understanding what the purpose would be, since she has face-to-face communication options for friends and family locally.

Interview excerpt 3

Interviewer: *What about friends, teachers, and family around here? Do you have them on FB or Instagram?*

Yingluck: *Not really much since I see them a lot. I know my students do this. They are friends [on FB] with everybody. Like with Jay [a colleague], we work in the same office all day. We both use FB, but why do we need to be friends on FB since I see her all day? I guess with my family in Chiang Mai I am on FB some, but they are very far and I don't see them much.*

In keeping with Yingluck's pragmatic views about FB usage, she highlights that she is able to see and interact with friends on colleagues on a daily basis. However, as she points out, it does set her in contrast to her students' behaviors with respect to FB usage. They tend to have extensive friend networks from within their local community and school. This is also the case for Bee, by far the most active user of SNSs amongst the three teachers in this study.

Bee says that she spends "a lot of my day, when I am not busy" on SNSs. She actively uses FB, Instagram, and Twitter, as well as a variety of other collaborative, group messaging chat applications. For Bee, SNSs have gone beyond pragmatic tools for communication, and instead have become fully integrated components of her life. Unlike Yingluck, Bee's online and face-to-face social networks run entirely together. This extends as well to her interactions with students at the school. On FB, Bee has friended the majority of her students, and she does not hesitate to participate in their daily interactions. Bee explains the extent of her SNSs site use, as well her views about interacting with students, in the following excerpt.

Interview excerpt 4

Interviewer: *Can you say how you use SNSs and what you use them for?*
Bee: *Yes, I use sites like FB and Twitter a lot. I use everyday.*
Interviewer: *How much time per day do you spend on social networking online?*
Bee: *I don't know. I am on a lot of my day, when I am not busy. All day maybe 6-7 hours.*
Interviewer: *What are you mostly doing during that time? For example on FB, do you mostly read, or mostly write posts of your own?*
Bee: *I do a lot of both of these, but maybe I do chat most. I use the chat on FB a lot. I guess I don't write a lot of status [updates] but of course there are lots of pictures and videos I share. Since I am a teacher all day, I like to have some pictures and funny videos of students doing things.*
Interviewer*: Can you describe who your friends are on FB?*
Bee: *Well, most of my students are, and my family here and in Bangkok. All my classmates from school, and my friends at this school too. And you! I'm friends with anybody who wants to.*

Interviewer: *Some teachers might choose not to be friends with all their students on FB. Why do you do this?*

Bee: *It just like I want to have all the people be friends, and I don't mind if they are students or not. We are still friends. And they like it and FB is funny for them. I think they are happy to have me there. Really I get to know them a lot better, like what they do and music and hobbies and that. This is helpful for the teacher.*

During one classroom observation, the research assistant for this study observed Bee showing students a variety of funny pictures on FB in the minutes before class. She had these on the classroom computer, and they were projected for the whole class to see. They were pictures she had taken of students from the day before, and many were asking to see them and show them to the rest of the class. Generally, Bee makes no distinction between her face-to-face and her online social community. They are one group to her, and her interactions range fluidly back and forth between the two.

Thus the three teachers can be seen to hold very different views about their personal use of SNSs. Dang is primarily a frustrated and infrequent user, and she only makes use of FB. She does not see any advantage to FB, given that she relies primarily on face-to-face connections for her social interactions. Yingluck is somewhat different in that her social network is global, and she is geographically cut-off from many of her friends. For this reason, she has found a pragmatic value in SNSs as a way to bridge the geographic gaps and maintain a sense of connectedness to her community. Finally, Bee brings her face-to-face and online networks together. She does not have the pragmatic need to stay in touch with friends in other countries as does Yingluck, but Bee does clearly feel that the online component of her social interactions enriches and strengthens friendships at the local level.

Divergent Views: Pedagogic Use of Technology by Teachers

During both individual and group interviews, the teachers were asked about their current teaching practices related to technology use in the classroom. We also specifically addressed the pedagogic use of SNSs for language learning and development. Of the three teachers, Dang was generally the most resistant to technology use in the classroom. In fact, she specifically stated that she preferred to avoid, "all the confusing things and buttons that need to be done rightly." This sentiment aligned well with the classroom observation data from Dang's classes. During over three hours of classroom observations, Dang only made use of the computer and projector in class two times. On both occasions she used the computer to show the same prepared PowerPoint presentation, which lasted about four minutes each. Other than this, all instruction was done with the blackboard and chalk.

Yingluck's classroom was quite different from Dang's. Yingluck actively embraced technology in the classroom, and in each of the five lessons we observed with her, she made use of the computer and projector for at least part of the class time. Her primary application of choice was PowerPoint. During 4.5 hours of observations in Yingluck's classroom, she was actively engaged in PowerPoint presentations for approximately 75 minutes. She also occasionally used a blank MS Word document as a substitute for the blackboard. In one instance when Internet was working in the classroom, she also searched for, found, and played a 3 minute video from YouTube. In the following excerpt from our interview, Yingluck explains that her general view about the use of technology in the classroom is in a state of transition.

Divergent Teacher Viewpoints of Technology Integration in the Language Classroom

Interview excerpt 5
Interviewer: *Today I watched you use the computer a lot in class. How do you generally feel about the use of technology in the classroom?*
Yingluck: *I'm learning it. It is good. I know it is. The Power Points are fun for the students and they make class more happy. I like to add in the pictures to help them understand vocabulary. I know the computer can help in class. It really is convenient, but not how I remember school, so I try to adjust.*
Interviewer: *What other tools or applications have you used in class besides PowerPoint? Have you tried anything with FB or letting students use phones in class?*
Yingluck: *No phones! Our director would be…not happy with this. Besides, they would not be able to focus on the lesson and would just chat on FB. I like to show videos from the Internet, but you know our Internet is bad here and seldom works, so I can't rely on it.*

Generally Yingluck is not opposed to technology in the classroom, nor does she fear it, but she does recognize what she perceives to be both institutional and pedagogic constraints. Though most all students have smartphones with them at school, she points out that the director would certainly not approve of their use in class. Significantly though, she also says that their use in class would likely be disruptive to the educational process. She'd like to make more use of video in the classroom, but she also feels limited by the school's poor Internet access.

In contrast to her colleagues, Bee's use of technology for pedagogic purposes, and in particular her use of FB with her students, was substantially more robust and intentional on her part. In my general conversations with Bee, I knew her to be a strong advocate for the use of technology in the classroom, and I also knew her to be frequently frustrated by the poor Internet access at the school. During classroom observations, Bee was seen to rely on technology to a certain extent for her lessons. She was particularly fond of typing as opposed to writing on a board, and she almost always used her computer terminal as a blackboard substitute. She encouraged her students to do this as well, and in each of five observations with Bee, we watched her having students typing out responses on her computer terminal during class.

Bee always knew when the Internet was and was not working at the school, and she always had elements of her lesson plans that relied on websites. She often used online content as a proxy for grammatical instruction, showing websites with clear grammatical instructions for example, as opposed to presenting the grammar deductively to the students. Because of her frequent dependence on websites for class content however, the infrequent Internet connectivity was a constant source of struggle for her. During observations of Bee's classes, we often heard her saying, in Thai, "Well, unfortunately it looks like the Internet is down AGAIN today" or something quite similar to this. Though often frustrated, Bee was clearly a supporter of educational technology in general, and SNS use in particular. In the following excerpt, Bee was explaining what she tells students when they come to her for help, asking for resources or tools to learn English faster.

Interview excerpt 6
Interviewer: *So, what do you say to students when they ask you this?*
Bee: *I usually say to them about FB. I write in English on FB so they can read. They also see celebrities and music and watch videos, whatever they want. They maybe read and write English everyday when they want.*
Interviewer: *But how do they know where to look to find English?*

Bee: *I show. Or they talk to friends and see [music, videos, etc.] on friends' FB. Everything is shared on FB, so it is easy to see what your friends do and learn like that.*

From this, we can see that Bee views FB itself as a repository for authentic language in use. However, Bee went even beyond suggesting that students use FB as a resource. In fact, she actively used FB as a type Learning Management System (LMS) for her courses.

Many universities and high schools around the world are now making use of integrated LMS tools such as Moodle or Blackboard to support face-to-face courses. LMS tools often include enrollment management, document organization and storage, and options for peer-to-peer interaction. The use of LMSs in education has yet to catch on in Thailand however, and there are a couple of reasons for this. Firstly, Thailand is still a developing country with a developing country's online infrastructure. Outside the capital of Bangkok, connectivity is unreliable. Also, Thailand is still quite traditional in its adherence to paper-based educational administration and delivery.

Though many Thai teachers are comfortable with the system as is, some advocates for educational technology use such as Bee are starting to look for options. One of the great challenges faced by teachers in a paper-based system is the large amount of time spent tracking students, managing enrollments, and marking assignments. It all must be accounted for physically. In Bee's case for example, she teaches English to all grade 10 and 11 students on a rotating basis. This means she tracks the work of over 200 students. The time consuming nature of tracking the progress of this many students means that individual students get little to no personal feedback. Evidence of this can clearly be seen in the homework practices of many students where copying from one-another and general poor attention to detail is often the norm. Administrative concerns and general institutional traditions of course prevent teachers from making large scale changes, but Bee has found that FB offers her some support.

In Bee's courses, she was making use of the FB "groups" feature, and setting up separate groups for some courses. This controlled privacy and limited access to only enrolled students. During this study, Bee was only beginning to experiment with this pedagogic approach, but she very positive about its potential. In this excerpt, Bee talks about how groups are set up and how she takes advantage of them.

Interview excerpt 7
Interviewer: *So you have groups set up [on FB] for all of your classes, or just some?*
Bee: *Just two right now, but next semester I use all my classes.*
Interviewer: *How do the students get into the group?*
Bee: *In class I tell them. Then they go home and ask on FB to join and get notice on FB and add them if they are in the class.*
Interviewer: *What are assignments that you give on FB?*
Bee: *I have to give regular journal writing assignments to the students, but on FB I ask them to do others.*
Interviewer: *Like what?*
Bee: *We study grammar so I found a website for the grammar and I asked students to see it and practice through FB link. And in class we learned about airplane travel but no students go on airplanes so I showed a YouTube video on FB and told them to watch and ask questions.*
Interviewer: *But the students don't have to these things, right? They are just extra help for them and not actual assignments where you grade them, is that right?*
Bee: *Yes, I want to give assignments and grade them as comments on FB, but the school says we must have the writing journal work only for the assignments.*

Bee's innovation and creativity as an educator are clear, but so too is her frustration with the traditional structure of the system she is working under. Overall it is Bee who is clearly pushing the boundary in terms of what is possible in her educational context.

Orientation toward the Future or Orientation toward the Past?

One clear point of differentiation amongst the teachers, particularly between Bee and Dang, was the general orientation of perspectives between the future and the past. In interviews with Dang, a common theme was her perception of steadily declining student skills, the general decrease in the quality of their work, and the lessening of respect that students show toward teachers. These were points that Dang often made in class, generally in reference to problems or poor performance from her students. On one occasion, when students were not quieting down as quickly as she would have liked, the research assistant noted that Dang said "When I was a student, we never behaved in this way. What is happening to all of you?" During another observation, notes from the class show Dang spending a total of 7 minutes of class time lecturing students on the poor quality of their work and their general decline in work ethic.

Similarly, during our interviews with Dang, this topic came up repeatedly. On one occasion I asked her to talk generally about how her class had gone on that day. She responded by comparing students today to those of the past.

Interview excerpt 8
Interviewer: *What did you think of the class today? How did it go?*
Dang: *They make me very tired. Their attitude is so poor in class. They are much less respectful now. When I was a student, we sat quietly and respected the teacher and listened. My students now don't be quiet. They don't sometimes even know what is happening in class!*
Interviewer: *How about their homework and skills like reading and writing in English?*
Dang: *When I was in high school I was not so good at English, but I loved English and really tried. I remember so many hours using dictionaries and translating everything. I think none of my student do this now. They spend their free time on their phones instead of practice and study.*

During another interview, the research assistant asked Dang what kinds of skills she felt students needed to be successful in the future. For Dang, the answer was to more clearly emulate behaviors and attitudes from the past.

Interview excerpt 9
Interviewer: *So what do you think these students need to be successful after graduation from high school? What skills are important for them?*
Dang: *Certainly English is important, but they are learning and studying so little. They really need to learn to study harder and work more. When I was a student we spent many hours everyday doing homework. I think many of these students have lazy attitudes about school work and study. If they will be successful in the future, they need to learn to study more and work harder. I have never seen students that read and write so badly. Even in Thai they cannot read or write. All the time they are on their phones chatting, but they need to improve their language skills and study more!*

Clearly for Dang, the students of today do not live up to the standard of students from previous generations, and she connects technology in general and mobile phone use specifically to the general decline in their skills.

Bee's views seem almost the opposite to those of Dang. Bee has a general vision for her students that is very much oriented toward future success. She consciously does not want to replicate educational approaches of the past, and in fact she struggles with this view on an almost daily basis through resistance from colleagues and administrators. Repeated observations of Bee's classes showed that she often framed questions of "why this is important" with references to the students' future lives and careers. For example, during her introduction to a textbook unit on "Travel & Tourism," she rhetorically asked her students, "Why should we be studying this, what do you think?" In an answer to her own question, she explained how many foreigners come to Thailand for travel, and how they spend lots of money while they are in Thailand. She asked her students, "Wouldn't you like to be a part of this? Wouldn't you like to earn money in this industry and work with foreigners?" This manner of justifying the study of topics and materials with references to the students' futures was very common for Bee, and something we observed often in her instruction.

During her recent teacher training course, Bee had encountered the notion of "21st century skills," and she often brought up this term in our interview discussions. In the previous excerpt, we asked Dang what she felt students needed to succeed after graduation. The same question asked of Bee elicited a very different response. Bee spoke specifically about 21st century skills and the need for students to break away from traditions.

Interview excerpt 10
Interviewer: *What tools or skills do you think these students need to succeed after high school?*
Bee: *I think the most important are the 21st century skills like collaboration, cooperation, and having literacy about technology. If they want to get good jobs, they need to have these things and not have fear about being different and creative.*
Interviewer: *Do you think schools in Thailand are helping with the development of these skills?*
Bee: *Uh, no, not really at all. Like here, we don't have any courses that help students with technology. Our computer lab doesn't work at all. All our students have phones, but we don't let them use for practice and communication. Our classes have lots of lecturing and practice and drills, but not students doing work together or in teams like they need to practice.*

Bee seems mostly concerned that the school is not doing the most that it can to help students succeed. It is not helping them build technology literacy, and it is not sufficiently targeting 21st century skills. Interestingly, unlike Dang, Bee does not see students' skills in decline at all, she just views them as disconnected from much of the traditional focus of education. When the research assistant asked Bee about her views contrasting students of the past with now, she took a mostly positive tone.

Interview excerpt 11
Bee: *I think that students today have great opportunities that I did not have even 10 years ago. They all have phones and they can look up anything at anytime. They are on FB all day, so they are constantly reading and writing. And if they want to find English for study or listening, it is so easy now – just with YouTube or something like it.*

Divergent Teacher Viewpoints of Technology Integration in the Language Classroom

Overall, Dang and Bee appear to be framing educational change in very different ways. Dang's primary mindset is one of deficit and decline. She looks at student skills and attitudes today in contrast to the past, and finds them lacking. Bee on the other hand, looks mostly toward the future, and encourages her students to do the same. She is challenged by the school's inability to fully target 21st century skills, but nevertheless she continues to push her own pedagogy in this direction.

Concerns with Student Engagement

A final theme that emerged through analysis of both observational data and teacher interviews was student engagement. Yingluck stated often that student engagement was her primary concern. She was often frustrated by curricula and materials that were selected for her, and she struggled to find ways to make her classes engaging for students. Classroom observations suggest that Yingluck, more so than either Dang or Bee, made frequent use of group work and peer-to-peer interactions in her teaching. In one observation of a 45-minute lesson, Yingluck had students working collaboratively in groups for over 30 minutes. This is quite unusual in the context of a Thai high school, where instruction tends to be much more teacher-fronted.

The research assistant asked Yingluck about her approach to collaboration and she framed her response in terms of student engagement. Specifically, she talked about the value of groups in keeping students motivated, interested in the lesson, and having fun.

Interview excerpt 12
Yingluck: *I just can't look at my students and see them bored. I always want them to be engaged. I want them having fun while learning. This is why we spend a lot of time in groups. If I just lecture to them they get bored easily. I think students now have shorter attention spans and it is not easy to keep them engaged, but they are used to being social, so I think groups work really well.*

Perhaps not surprising, Bee also tends to foreground student engagement in her instruction. In Bee's case, she feels that technology is the main solution to limited student engagement, but she struggles with the poor access in the classroom. Unlike Yingluck, Bee does not seem to see other alternatives for increasing student interest and engagement. Classroom observations of Bee's classes show frequent teacher use of technology via the classroom computer, and limited use of group and pair work. Her primary model of interaction was teacher to student. In two of the five observations of Bee's classes, she did not break into groups or pairs at all, and stayed with a teacher fronted model for the entirety of each 45 minute session.

The primary response to student engagement with Bee was one of frustration. When asked about keeping the students interested and engaged in the classroom, she focused on challenges rather than solutions.

Interview excerpt 13
Bee: *I know that sometimes they are not interested. Sometimes me too! I am not interested! The book is quite boring, right? And we have to cover this grammar and vocabulary and each week it is all prepared for us. If we had better internet I could make the lesson more interesting, but then the director tells me to get back to the book. Even if they could use their phones they would be happy to learn like this with technology, but no phones allowed in class. I have to keep with the books.*

Bee's frustration around student engagement contrasts strongly with Yingluck's successes in making use of group work in the classroom. Neither are entirely happy with the top-down model of assigning texts and topics to be covered, but Yingluck has found methods that she is comfortable with, whereas Bee remains frustrated that she is not able to make greater use of technology.

Dang takes a much more traditional view of student engagement in the classroom. For her, this should not necessarily be the teacher's primary responsibility. Dang understands instruction as largely the delivery of content to the students. She recognizes that content should be delivered in a professional way, and in a way that is comprehensible to the students, but she views the classes level of interest in that material as secondary and as the responsibility of the student. The following interview excerpt gives some insight into Dang's views about student engagement.

Interview excerpt 14
Interviewer: *What do you do when students seem not interested in class or not engaged in the topic?*
Dang: *Yes, I often have students not listening in class. They are looking out the window or starting to get tired. Sometimes I feel bad for them. I know they are tired and maybe the book is not so interesting. It is hard to focus when you are like this in the hot room.*
Interviewer: *So how do you help them be more engaged?*
Dang: *I just remind them that they need to focus and work hard. They have to keep listening. I talk to them with sympathy and try not to get frustrated and I tell them I remember what it was like. But they have tests to take soon and they need to focus.*

Dang tends to equate student engagement with "focus," and this is the responsibility of the listener. She recognizes that the content may at times be less than interesting, but in Dang's view, these occasions require increased focus on the part of the student.

All three teachers then, take very different approaches with respect to student engagement. Yingluck is pragmatic and utilizes pair and group work extensively in her instruction. Bee feels that technology is the solution, but remains frustrated by her inability to fully integrate technology into her classes. Dang places the primary burden of student engagement onto the learners themselves, equating engagement with mental focus on the lesson and on the material.

DISCUSSION AND IMPLICATIONS

This study looks at now three Thai teachers of English make use of technology, and in particular how they utilize SNSs, both in their personal lives and their professional practices. Because this study offers a detailed case analysis of the views of three instructors, it was not designed to provide broad generalizations from its findings. Instead, the study offers the chance to look deeply into the lives and teaching experiences of these three instructors, and to broaden our general understanding of the interplay between a range of diverse factors impacting technology integration and use.

Returning now to research discussed previously in this chapter, though learner engagement was not a primary theoretical framework for the study, it was addressed explicitly in Mills (2011). In her framing of classroom use of FB through situated learning theory, she found high levels of mutual engagement in her study's participants. Generally, this would seem to align in part with Bee's view that technology integration and SNS use in the classroom may be one way to increase engagement. Frustratingly for Bee however, she continued to encounter sociocultural and institutional constraints that prevented her from integrating technology into her pedagogy in a way that she would have liked.

Interestingly, the components of mutual engagement that Mills (2011) found most salient, including collaboration and problem solving, were exactly those that Yingluck targeted in her own efforts to maintain and increase student engagement in the classroom. In the study from Mills, she stated that her FB project allowed learners to "reconfigure standard communication patterns and transform relationships with people" (p. 364), thus increasing student engagement. Within the context of a Thai high school classroom, the standard communication pattern is didactic and teacher fronted. By reconfiguring this through group and pair work, Yingluck found a viable way of working toward greater student engagement that was not dependent on technology alone.

Bee's continued emphasis on 21st century skills development and technology integration in the classroom stems, at least in part, from her personal and active participation in what Jenkins (2008) refers to as a participatory culture. Web 2.0 tools like SNSs facilitate a flattening of models of information transmission. SNS participation deemphasizes a traditional media approach, with a top-down transmission of knowledge from source to reader. Instead, they allow for real-time, peer-to-peer sharing of information, and genuine authorship of content in authentic settings. These participatory cultures likely encourages and supports student engagement and autonomy in the learning process (Conole and Alevizou, 2010;; Halvorsen, 2014; Jenkins, 2008; Zourou, 2012). Because Bee lives fully in this world, and because she is able to see its perceived advantages, she clearly wants the same for her students.

Dang's interactions with online and participatory cultures have been quite different, and primarily for this reason, she has substantially different viewpoints about technology and its role in the classroom. For Dang, tools like SNSs constrain, rather than afford, student learning. She views them as distractions in the lives of her students that keep them from adopting better study habits.

From interview data it is clear that all three teachers self-identify quite differently as users of technology. Bee is an avid and frequent user of many technology tools, including a variety of SNSs, whereas Dang is much more concerned with face-to-face social interaction and is only a reluctant and infrequent user of technology. Yingluck is somewhere in between. She recognizes the value of technological tools like FB to maintain her own social network, and views her use of these tools through a utilitarian and pragmatic framework.

The differing ways that these teachers self identify as users of technology seem to translate clearly into differences in their classroom practices vis-à-vis technology integration. In their review of studies Martel and Wang (2014) noted a theme suggesting that teacher self-identity and teaching practice mutually influenced one another. Morgan (2004) referred to the notion of "identity as pedagogy" in his poststructural interpretation of teachers' performative identities in the classroom.

Bee clearly views herself as someone who has actively integrated technology and SNS participation into her life. She has also positioned herself within the school as an outspoken advocate for greater technological access, and as a critic of institutional policies she views as limiting. These roles that Bee has taken on are core components of her identity, and they clearly manifest themselves in her classroom practices that foreground technological integration. A large part of Bee's culture is her online presence. She see both social and professional value in participation within this culture, and she wants her students to have the 21st century skills necessary to participate as well.

In contrast to Bee, Yingluck's interest in SNS site participation has not translated into clear classroom practices. Yingluck uses FB and other sites to interact in English with friends living abroad. These relationships she has formed are a key part of her identity. However, in Yingluck's case, she has not made the connection to fostering a 21st century skill set for her students. She views her need to use SNSs simply as a product of her particular sociocultural context. For her students, many of whom have never been abroad and do not have social networks similar to Yingluck's she does not see the need to encourage their participation.

Finally, Dang has come to represent herself as someone for whom FB use is primarily a frustration, and she speaks out strongly against its use by students. Dang aligns herself with cultural and educational practices of the past, and sees the present deviation from those practices as problematic for the educational development of her students. She makes limited use of technology in the classroom both because the technologies are not a part of her personal, daily life, and because she does not see value in them, but rather sees disruption.

In response to the final research question, from data presented in this study, we can see that there are three primary factors impacting the teachers views about SNS site use of for foreign language learning. The first of these is clearly the institutional constraints and desire of administrators to adhere to traditional educational approaches. Despite Bee's efforts to make use of FB as a functional LMS for her courses and to give actual assignments through the site, she was blocked from so doing so through the institution. A second factor is the broad views that each of these teachers hold about education in general. The clearest distinction here is between Bee, who sees her job at least in part as to prepare students for success through the development of 21st century skills, and Dang, who sees her role as to transmit knowledge to students in the same manner that she experienced her own education. Finally, each teacher has varied personal experiences with SNS participation, and these experiences also shape their views about how well SNSs might be used as educational tools.

CONCLUSION

This study, though limited in scope and complexity, offers a brief snapshot of how three teachers are making use of educational technology in their pedagogic approaches, and how the decisions they make are influenced by their self-defined identities as users of technology.

From within a social constructivist framework, SNSs appear to be a strong candidate for increasing language learning potential. They offer easy interaction with authentic content, and they foreground an emphasis on connectivity with others and engaging interactions. SNSs like FB are, quite literally, a socially constructed space. They would not exist without users forming and reforming their constant connections with one another. Future research into the use of SNSs for language learning and development will hopefully further develop our understanding of how participation in these sites may complement more traditional forms of face-to-face classroom instruction.

REFERENCES

Blattner, G., & Lomicka, R. (2012). Facebook-ing and the Social Generation: A new era of language learning. *ALSIC, 15*(1), 1–25.

boyd, d., & Ellison, N. (2007). Social networking sites: definition, history, and scholarship. *Journal of Computer Mediated Communication, 13*(1). Retrieved from http://jcmc.indiana.edu/vol13/issue1/boyd.ellison.html

Conole, G., & Alevizou, P. (2010). *A literature review of these of Web 2.0 tools in higher education*. Milton Keynes, UK: Open University.

Corbin, J., & Strauss, A. (2008). *Basics of Qualitative Research: Techniques and Procedures for Developing Grounded Theory* (3rd ed.). Thousand Oaks, CA: Sage.

Facebook. (2015, May 5). In *Wikipedia, the free encyclopedia*. Retrieved from http://en.wikipedia.org/wiki/Facebook

Halvorsen, A. (2014). *Facebook usage in Thailand: The plurilingual competencies of Thai high school students and teachers* (Doctoral Dissertation). Retrieved from http://hdl.handle.net/2142/49516

Jenkins, H. (2008). *Confronting the challenges of participatory culture: Media education for the 21st century (John D. and Catherine T. MacArthur Foundation Reports on Digital Media and Learning)*. Chicago, IL: MacArthur Foundation.

Martel, J., & Wang, A. (2014). Language teacher identity. In M. Bigelow & J. Ennser-Kananen (Eds.), *The Routledge Handbook of Educational Linguistics*. New York: Routledge.

Mertens, D. M. (2010). *Research and evaluation in education and psychology* (3rd ed.). Thousand Oaks, CA: Sage.

Mills, N. (2011). Situated learning through social networking communities: The development of joint enterprise, mutual engagement, and shared repertoire. *CALICO Journal, 28*(2), 345–368. doi:10.11139/cj.28.2.345-368

Morgan, B. (2004). Teacher identity as pedagogy: Towards a field-internal conceptualization in bilingual and second language education. *Bilingual Education and Bilingualism, 7*(2-3), 172-188.

Norton, B. (1990). Language, identity, and the ownership of English. *TESOL Quarterly, 31*(3), 409–429. doi:10.2307/3587831

O'Reilly, T. (2005). *What is Web 2.0?* Retrieved from http://www.oreilly.com/go/web2

Reinhardt, J., & Zander, V. (2011). Social networking in an intensive English program classroom: A language socialization perspective. *CALICO Journal, 28*(2), 326–344. doi:10.11139/cj.28.2.326-344

Stevenson, M., & Liu, M. (2010). Learning a language with Web 2.0: Exploring the use of social networking features of foreign language learning websites. *CALICO Journal, 27*(2), 233–259. doi:10.11139/cj.27.2.233-259

Trent, J., & Shroff, R. H. (2013). Technology, identity, and community: The role of electronic teaching portfolios in becoming a teacher. *Technology, Pedagogy and Education, 22*(1), 3–20. doi:10.1080/1475939X.2012.720416

Twitter. (2015, May 8). In *Wikipedia, the free encyclopedia*. Retrieved from http://en.wikipedia.org/wiki/Twitter

Wang, S., & Vasquez, C. (2012). Web 2.0 and second language learning: What does the research tell us? *CALICO, 29*(3), 412–430. doi:10.11139/cj.29.3.412-430

KEY TERMS AND DEFINITIONS

Computer Assisted Language Learning (CALL): A field of academic study that specifically looks at how the use of computers and other forms of technology impact language learning.

Engagement: In education, the term refers to the extent to which learners are fully involved in the learning process and motivated to participate.

Facebook (FB): This site is currently the largest and most widely used SNS across the globe. FB allows users to view one another's personal profiles and easily share content.

Identity: Identity is a person's sense of self and understanding of who they are in the world. Identity is shaped and formed through social interaction with others.

Learning Management System (LMS): An LMS is an online platform that allows a teacher to integrate several educational tools such as enrollment, assessment, and class discussions.

Pedagogy: This term refers to the act and process of teaching.

Social Networking Sites (SNSs): Online sites that allow participants to create personal profiles and engage with one another through profile viewing.

Technology: Technology can mean different things in different contexts, but in this chapter it refers to the various digital tools teachers may choose to use in the classroom.

APPENDIX 1: TEACHER INTERVIEW PROTOCOL 1

1. Introductions and general greetings
2. Language teaching background and experience
   - How long have you been an English teacher?
   - How long have you worked at this school?
   - Can you tell me about the specific classes you teach here?
   - Why did you decide to become a language teacher?
3. General views about language teaching
   - How successful do you think the classes are here in teaching students to use English?
   - What do you think this school could do to help students learn English better?
   - What do you think teachers and students need to do help make English learning better at this school?
4. General views about technology use the classroom
   - How do you feel about using technology in the language classroom?
   - What are some ways you use technology in your teaching?

*Note – this theme is discussed in more detail during the second phase of the interviews

APPENDIX 2: CLASSROOM OBSERVATION TOOL

Classroom and teacher _____
Date and time_____
\# of students present _____
Technology tools available for use _____
Classroom configuration (diagram of student seating, teacher position, computer, and screens)

Detailed notes on classroom activities

Time	Describe activity	Describe technology use

*multiple pages used as needed

Section 3
Technology in Language Teacher Preparation and Learning

Chapter 9
Learning to Teach for Next-Generation Education:
A Careful Blend of Action and Reflection

Muriel M. Grosbois
Université Paris – Sorbonne, France

Cédric G. Sarré
Université Paris – Sorbonne, France

ABSTRACT

This chapter examines how pre-service teachers specializing in English Language Teaching (ELT) in secondary schools can learn to teach for Next-Generation Education by developing professional skills that are in line with today and tomorrow's technology-mediated environments. To face this challenge, some specific CALL-based ELT training combining action and reflection has recently been introduced in the Education Department at Paris-Sorbonne University. In order to examine the specific CALL-based ELT training offered in light of the set objective, its theoretical underpinnings will first be considered. The design and content of a CALL-based ELT course and of an online tutoring module will then be studied. The pre-service teachers' perception of this CALL-based ELT training will then be explored through the results of online surveys. Conclusions will be drawn from these results and future directions will be outlined.

INTRODUCTION

This chapter sets out to examine how pre-service teachers can learn to teach for next-generation education. The position favored here is one that implies probing into the use of technology for learning and teaching, given that Information and Communication Technology (ICT) has permeated society widely. In fact, the central question today is no longer whether technology should be used or not in education, but rather how to use it effectively (Bertin & Sarré, 2014). This is why further knowledge is needed about the technology training that should be provided to pre-service teachers.

DOI: 10.4018/978-1-5225-0483-2.ch009

More precisely, this chapter sets out to study how pre-service second language (L2) teachers are prepared to use ICT. It analyzes in particular how pre-service teachers specializing in English Language Teaching (ELT) in secondary education in France, can develop professional skills in a technology-mediated environment, by combining action and reflection. As in many other countries, ICT is now part of the set of core skills that every teacher is expected to develop in France. This is specified in the new list of professional key skills for teachers and educational staff issued in 2013 by the French Ministry for Education (Bulletin Officiel de l'Éducation Nationale, 2013). Therefore, as pre-service teachers enroll in a Master's program to become fully qualified teachers of English, the objective is not only to enhance their specialist knowledge of English, but also to develop their professional skills, including CALL-related ones. To face this challenge, some specific CALL-based ELT training has recently been introduced in the Education Department at Paris-Sorbonne University. This specific training is part of the two-year Master's program during which pre-service teachers follow lectures at university (during Year 1 and Year 2) and carry out several placements in secondary schools (for the most part in Year 2). It consists of a CALL-based ELT course, which every pre-service teacher is required to take. Moreover, at the same time as the CALL-based ELT course was implemented, our university set up a new language center named SIAL (*Service Interuniversitaire d'Apprentissage des Langues*). The SIAL is meant to provide language modules to undergraduate students who specialize in disciplines other than languages. The first module offered to SIAL students was an English as a Foreign Language (EFL) module delivered in blended format (B1 level). When studying on the Virtual Learning Environment (VLE), SIAL learners benefit from the mediation of online tutors. This innovative online EFL module was viewed as an extra opportunity to turn pre-service teachers into agents of change for L2 learning and teaching. Therefore, pre-service teachers, though trained for Secondary Education, had the opportunity to teach for the online SIAL course as tutors in their second year in the Master's program, on a voluntary basis. This experience was considered as extra practicum for them since L2 online tutoring is likely to be useful when teaching at secondary school level as well. Consequently, pre-service teachers were introduced to L2 learning and teaching with the use of technology thanks to the CALL-based ELT course, centered on Secondary Education, and to the extra training some of them received to teach a university-based online course for SIAL students. This extra training experience, however, was not a mandated component for all pre-service teachers in the Master's program, unlike the CALL-based ELT course, but rather an elective module of the program.

In order to examine the specific CALL-based ELT training offered in light of the set objective, the theoretical underpinnings will first be considered. The design and content of the CALL-based ELT course and of the online tutoring elective module will then be studied. Finally, the pre-service teachers' perception of this specific CALL-based ELT training will be explored through the results of online surveys. Conclusions will be drawn from these results and future directions will be outlined.

LITERATURE REVIEW

Given the scope of the present study, it is necessary to first consider what research indicates regarding ICT integration in the secondary classroom, as well as regarding pre-service teacher ICT training. It will then be useful to complement these research findings with CALL-related ones.

ICT Integration in Secondary Education

Despite institutional and governmental incentives, technology still tends to be under-utilized in education (Hew & Brush 2007, Guichon 2012), mainly due to a number of barriers, whether external to the teacher (access, support, etc.) or internal (confidence and beliefs) (Ertmer et al. 2012). According to Hew and Brush (2007), one of the most common reasons why teachers do not use technology for instructional purposes is their lack of specific knowledge and skills.

It has also been noted that when technology is used in secondary education, it does not systematically induce a change in teaching styles, as most of the uses of technology observed and reported on in the literature still correspond to "low-level" teacher-centered practices (Becker 1994, Ertmer 2005). At the other end of the scale, high-level uses of technology are generally associated with constructivist student-centered practices (Becker 1994) and correspond to the best practices advocated by researchers. However, low-level uses precede high-level uses according to Ertmer (2005), since "increased or prolonged technology use will actually prompt teachers to change their practices toward more constructivist approaches" (p.27). In other words, prolonged low-level uses help teachers gain enough technological expertise to then modify their pedagogical practices.

Unsurprisingly, some teachers consider themselves unfamiliar, not only with the technological aspect, but also with the pedagogy of using technology (Hew & Brush 2007). In addition, teacher attitudes and beliefs towards technology can be another barrier to technology integration (Ertmer 2005, Ertmer et al. 2012). In that respect, Ertmer (2005, p. 32) advocates the implementation of three strategies to promote change in teachers' beliefs about technology: (1) personal experiences, starting with simple uses of technology to help teachers achieve current goals more effectively and thus initiate the adoption process, (2) vicarious experiences, observing others (their peers) use technology in their classrooms for information and motivation purposes, (3) social-cultural influences, as teachers' beliefs are shaped through their interactions with others, and colleagues in particular, through professional networks for example. These strategies could obviously be part of teacher education programs. Hence the fact that pre-service and in-service ICT training seems essential.

Indeed, among the strategies identified to overcome the previously mentioned barriers to technology integration, Hew and Brush (2007) explain that providing professional development can influence teachers' attitudes and beliefs towards technology, and can provide them with the knowledge and skills to employ technology in their classrooms. Furthermore, research on effective professional development for teachers highlights the importance of "hands on" experience during training, as well as the necessity to articulate the training and the professional contexts. As stated by Hew and Brush (2007), "A review of relevant literature shows that effective professional development related to technology integration: (a) focuses on content (e.g., technology knowledge and skills, technology-supported pedagogy knowledge and skills, and technology-related classroom management knowledge and skills), (b) gives teachers opportunities for "hands-on" work, and (c) is highly consistent with teachers' needs" (p. 238). Effective professional development should then provide teachers with opportunities for active and situated learning.

However, research also highlights a gap between pre-service training programs and teachers' needs. In that respect, Ottenbreit-Leftwich et al. (2012), who compare the technology topics offered in pre-service education with what teachers actually consider to be useful for their teaching practices, uncover similarities as well as differences. Among the differences, they identify the widest disparity in the development of higher-order thinking skills: "Seventy percent of teachers reported that they used technology to support the facilitation of higher-order thinking skills during a typical week, while only 37% of teacher educators reported that they included this topic in their programs" (Ottenbreit-Leftwich et al., 2012, p. 410). They add that the use of Web 2.0 technologies to support student collaboration and the use of technologies to support project-based learning are key to facilitate the development of higher-thinking skills. Tondeur et al. (2012) also insist on the value of authentic technology experiences, the part played by collaboration with peers, and the importance of teacher educators as role models. They consider such critical factors as interrelated and interacting with other elements within and between institutions.

ICT Integration in Secondary Language Teacher Education

Unsurprisingly, research in the field of CALL-based ELT emphasizes key points that are similar to the ones highlighted by research findings regarding ICT integration in the secondary classroom and pre-service teacher ICT training. Thus, successful technology integration in the language classroom, according to Guichon and Hauck (2011), implies acquiring a repertoire of techno-pedagogical competences, namely the capacity to assess the potential and limits of technologies for language and culture learning; the capacity to carry out a needs analysis to introduce adequate technologies at appropriate moments in a pedagogical sequence; the capacity to handle basic tools and applications, and to solve simple technical problems; the capacity to design appropriate tasks; the capacity to design for interactions within and outside the classroom in view of the technologies' affordances; the capacity to rethink the contract with learners and colleagues; the capacity to manage time and optimize the integration of technologies.

Language teachers' professional development is also viewed as a continuous process of action and reflection by Müller-Hartmann (2012). This is similar to Hoven's "experiential modelling approach", which aims to "immerse students in the use of the technologies while at the same time providing them with the freedom and framework within which to experience the practical application of the theory in their own learning" (Hoven, 2007, p. 137). This means that pre-service teachers get to model and experience the tools and processes they are likely to use once they are fully qualified teachers. Whyte (2014) also considers that offering ICT training to pre-service language teachers consists in bridging gaps between their experience and their needs as future language teachers. Through a review of the literature on ICT integration in ELT, she claims that (1) teachers need to develop specific techno-pedagogical skills, (2) attention should be paid to teachers' knowledge of and attitudes towards second language learning and teaching, (3) the integration of ICT in ELT requires long-term support. In other words, courses should include a didactic dimension (theory of L2 learning and teaching and of ICT integration), a techno-pedagogical dimension (technical knowledge of tools and their pedagogical affordances), and specific support in the classroom.

As regards L2 online tutoring in particular, research has also prompted the need for new teaching approaches and skills that are different from face-to-face ones, as explained by Compton (2009) and Hampel and Stickler (2005). In fact, tutor mediation and feedback remain central to L2 learning in online settings, but they can take various forms (Sarré 2013). Hampel and Stickler (2005) put forward a pyramid composed of seven sets of skills: (1) technological skills ("basic ICT competence") at the base of the pyramid, followed by (2) more complex technical skills to use specific software applications, (3) the ability to understand the affordances and constraints of the specific software applications, (4) "online socialization" skills, (6) "creativity and choice" in the selection and design of the materials used, in designing online activities for communication purposes, in finding new uses of online tools, and finally (7) the ability to develop a personal teaching style, probably different from the face-to-face teaching style. More simply, Guichon posits that an online tutor's main competence is "a competence of regulation" defined as a "set of actions and utterances deployed by a language teacher to create and maintain optimal conditions in a learning situation in order to provide opportunities to get learners to develop language skills" (Guichon, 2009, p. 169). He identifies three categories of regulation competencies that online language tutors should master: socio-affective regulation (establishing a relationship with learners, building a learning community), pedagogical regulation (providing instructions and designing learning scenarios, giving positive and negative feedback, deploying strategies to facilitate L2 learning) and multimedia regulation (using appropriate communication tools, managing interactions).

RESEARCH QUESTIONS

Research thus indicates that in order to foster adoption of technology in education, pre-service training is key. It should articulate the development of specific techno-pedagogical skills, and be experience-based. Research also stresses that pre-service teacher education programs currently do not sufficiently align with what teachers actually need in their classrooms. The necessity to develop high-thinking skills through collaborative project-oriented activities, and to have teacher educators act as role models, is also emphasized.

The objective of this study is therefore to answer the two following questions:

1. How does the specific CALL-based ELT training offered to the pre-service teachers help them integrate ICT in their teaching practice?
2. What is the pre-service teachers' perception of the specific CALL-based ELT training offered to them?

RESEARCH METHODOLOGY

This paper uses a case study research design to examine pre-service L2 teachers' perception of the specific training offered to them on the integration of technology in their teaching. The purpose of the study is therefore to probe into the perceived usefulness of the CALL-based ELT training offered to pre-service L2 teachers in the Education Department at Paris-Sorbonne University.

To do so, different types of data were collected: (1) descriptions of the design and content of the two components of the specific CALL-based ELT training will first be presented, as they provide evidence of the views shared by the authors of this chapter on how technology integration in L2 teaching can be achieved from a practical point of view; (2) project reports (presenting actual CALL-based projects designed and implemented by pre-service teachers) were also collected and analyzed, and a few conclusions will be drawn from these about the extent to which they align with the main CALL-based ELT course offered; (3) quantitative and qualitative data were collected via two surveys in order to analyze whether the format and content of both components of the specific CALL-based ELT training met the future secondary school teachers' perceived needs. Indeed, this set of data made it possible to examine the gap between the pre-service teachers' prior knowledge, and the techno-pedagogical skills they acquired through participation in the training. Similarly, the link between what they studied in the program and what they managed to implement while on school placement (or what they feel comfortable implementing in their future career), was explored through the analysis of their survey responses. Quantitative data were analyzed using simple descriptive statistics, while qualitative data were analyzed through content analysis (identification and comparison of recurring key notions).

Participants

Participants were first and second year students enrolled in the Master's ELT program in the Education Department at Paris-Sorbonne University. The main objective of the program being to train future English teachers for French secondary education, all of the participants were pre-service secondary school teachers of English.

More precisely, two different groups of participants took part in the study:

- **Group 1:** 80 first year Master's students who took the CALL-based ELT course in 2013/2014 and then went on to the second year of the program in 2014/2015. These participants (1) took part in the survey on the CALL-based ELT course while in the first year of the program and (2) produced project reports while in the second year of the program.
- **Group 2:** 14 second year Master's students who were hired as online tutors in 2013/2014 (n=8) and in 2014/2015 (n=6). These participants took part in the survey on online tutoring.

Group 1 consisted of the whole cohort of Master's students, whereas Group 2 only involved some of Group 1 students, i.e. those who volunteered to tutor SIAL students online and therefore had to follow an elective module on online tutoring (in addition to taking the CALL-based ELT course).

Both Group 1 and Group 2 participants were aged between 22 and 26 and comprised a majority of female students (just under 83%). Group 1 and Group 2 participants had no formal previous experience of teaching English.

As for the teacher educators who participated in the study (n=3), both authors of this paper were in charge of providing training in the CALL-based ELT course and in the elective module on online tutoring. Another colleague provided training within the CALL-based ELT course, using the exact same curriculum and resources (see next section).

Procedure

The study procedure is summarized in Figure 1.

Figure 1. Flowchart of the study

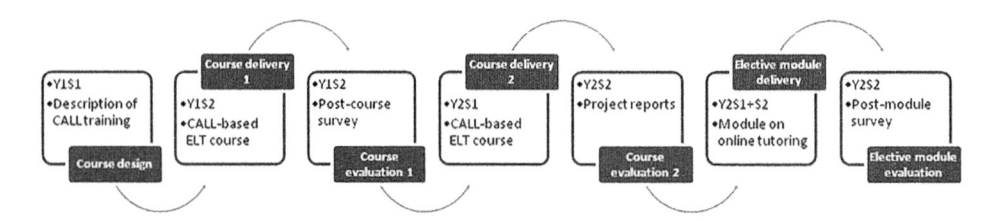

Learning to Teach for Next-Generation Education

The study was carried out over a two-year period. It comprised several phases and enabled the collection of different types of data.

Course Design was performed in the first semester of Year 1 (abbreviated as Y1S1 in Figure 1).

Course Delivery 1 occurred in the second semester of Year 1: the CALL-based ELT course on ICT integration was given to first year students.

Course Evaluation 1 was carried out in the same semester, right after the end of the course. A post-course survey was conducted and both quantitative and qualitative data were collected (survey responses).

Course Delivery 2 occurred in the first semester of Year 2: individual support was given to second year students who were asked to design a CALL-based project and to implement it while on placement in secondary schools (the project component being a course requirement of Year 2).

Course Evaluation 2 was carried out in the second semester of Year 2, at the end of the academic year, on the basis of their project reports (collected in the second semester).

Elective Module Delivery: extra training was given in the first and second semesters of Year 2 to second year students who had volunteered to become online tutors for the SIAL. This elective module on online tutoring was spread out over the academic year.

Elective Module Evaluation: a survey was also administered to those students who had followed the elective module on online tutoring (and done the 24-week online tutoring practice as part of the module).

In terms of data collection, the CALL-based ELT survey (Appendix 1) provided both quantitative and qualitative data, as some of the questions were open-ended to convey the pre-service teachers' views and suggestions on the course. Indeed, the survey consisted of 12 questions in total, seven multiple-choice and five open-ended questions. Quantitative and qualitative data about the elective module on online tutoring and the pre-service teachers' online tutoring practice for the SIAL course (field experience) were also collected via another questionnaire (Appendix 2) comprising five multiple-choice questions and four open-ended questions. Both surveys were administered online via LimeSurvey[1] (an open-source PHP web application to develop and administer online surveys), and were completed anonymously.

As previously mentioned, the specific CALL-based ELT training comprised two components: a CALL-based ELT course, which all students had to take as it was a requirement, and an elective module on online tutoring which was aimed at the students who had volunteered to become online tutors for the SIAL. The design and content of both components will now be presented, starting with the CALL-based ELT course.

DESIGN AND CONTENT OF THE CALL-BASED ELT COURSE

During the first year of the Master's program, 20 hours were devoted to this course comprising eight sessions including two for assessment. Given the limited amount of time, priorities had to be set. It was decided to lay particular emphasis on three of the competences listed by Guichon and Hauck (2011), namely the capacity to assess the potential and limits of technologies for language and culture learning, the capacity to handle basic tools and applications, and the capacity to design appropriate tasks. It was also considered important for pre-service teachers (1) to acquire the technological skills necessary to use different tools, in line with Hew and Brush (2007), (2) to reflect on the affordances and constraints of such tools in specific situations, in line with Gibson (1979), and (3) to question the extent of their integration using Puentedura's 2006 SAMR model. This model provides an ICT integration continuum comprising four degrees (Substitution-Augmentation-Modification-Redefinition) "which can serve as both a set of guidelines to question the integration of technology and a progression to follow" (Bertin & Sarré 2014, p.6). In each session, students had to engage in a hands-on approach in which various technologies were first presented to them and then experimented: sound and video capturing and editing tools (e.g., *Firefox Downloadhelper*, *Audacity*, *Windows Movie Maker*, *Photostory*), blogs, Interactive White Boards (IWB), podcasting tools (e.g., *Balibom*), collaborative writing tools (e.g. *TitanPad*) and concordancers (e.g., *Lextutor*, *Antconc*).

The use of each technology was also reflected upon for learning purposes by referring to key research findings, for example Blin and Appel (2011), Mercer (2011), Elola and Oskoz (2010), Grosbois (in press) as regards the complexity of Computer Supported Collaborative Writing (CSCW). Examples of integration of these technologies, through "vicarious experiences" via electronic means (e.g., clips from lessons and teacher interviews), were also included to each session in order to help pre-service teachers increase their "ideas about and self-efficacy beliefs for implementing technology in their classrooms" (Ertmer, 2005, p.34). Finally, pre-service teachers were asked to use lesson plans that they had either observed or implemented during their school placements and to redesign some of the tasks by integrating one or more of the technologies studied in the course. During sessions 7 and 8, they had to give an oral presentation on the redesigned tasks and analyze the way they had integrated technology, as well as the extent of the integration, so as to encourage reflective practice.

In the second year of the Master's program, pre-service teachers being on school placement on a weekly basis, they were asked to design a technology-rich project and to implement it with their pupils. This was to become their first "personal experience" of technology integration (Ertmer, 2005). During the CALL-based ELT course, they were guided in the design and setting up of their project. They were then invited to share their field experience with the group, so as to trigger discussions around the added value of technology for L2 learning and teaching and therefore benefit from the "social-cultural influences" of their peers (Ertmer, 2005). A close link was thus established between pre-service training and their classroom practices.

Despite their shared techno-pedagogical dimension, the CALL-based ELT course differed from the elective module on online tutoring which will now be presented.

DESIGN AND CONTENT OF THE ELECTIVE MODULE ON ONLINE TUTORING

Training in online tutoring being an optional component of the specific CALL-based ELT training offered only to the second-year pre-service teachers who had volunteered to become online tutors for the SIAL, it did not aim to develop a full set of skills for online language teaching as in Hampel and Stickler's (2005) or Compton's (2009) frameworks, all the more so as this additional training was very short: six hours in total. Instead, its objective was limited to providing pre-service teachers with the skills they would immediately need to be efficient online tutors in a real setting, i.e. that of an online EFL module that was already designed and implemented. Thus, this training in online tutoring focused on the different types of regulation tutors would have to provide and consisted in:

- Providing information about the four dimensions of the tutor's role: pedagogical, organizational, socio-affective and technical dimensions.
- Insisting on the pedagogical dimension with the forms and types of feedback they would be expected to give to students.

- Offering technical training on the Virtual Learning Environment.
- Providing in-depth pedagogical training in online language teaching through the analysis of the online EFL module, which had been designed previously.

The training of the online tutors actually consisted of five stages. The first stage was one Face-to-Face (F2F) session of three hours during which students were familiarized with some of the theoretical underpinnings of online language learning pedagogy: task-based language teaching, action-oriented approach, etc. The objective was to explain the way the EFL online module had been designed, and to justify the importance of feedback, in particular the fact that different types had been implemented because there is currently no consensus in the literature as to which method is the most efficient. Needless to say that the EFL online module was carefully designed as it also aimed at providing pre-service teachers with an example of good practice. This is actually in line with the usefulness of teacher educators as role models put forward by Tondeur et al. (2012).

The first phase was then followed by an early field experience as each pre-service teacher had to tutor two groups of students online over a period of 12 weeks (one semester).

At the end of the semester, another F2F training session centered on reflective analysis of the pre-service teachers' practice, in the form of retrospection. They had to select and analyze their own activity: they were asked to identify one unsuccessful experience – a problem situation/critical incident they couldn't solve by themselves – and one problem that they had faced and managed to solve. Critical analysis and collective debriefing fosters "the creation of a community of practice that favours professional development" (Guichon, 2009, p. 180). This is also in line with the importance of collaboration with peers noted by Tondeur et al. (2012) and the "social-cultural influences" mentioned by Ertmer (2005).

The last phase consisted of another field experience as the pre-service teachers had to tutor another two groups of SIAL students online during the second semester (another 12 weeks). It should be added that throughout the entire process, support was provided to tutors. Indeed, a specific forum was set up for them so that they could help each other and ask for help whenever needed, thus sustaining their collaborative work.

It should be noted that, even though these students were hired as online tutors and paid by the SIAL for this, their role as online tutors was first and foremost considered by the authors of this paper as a training activity. All in all, extra training in online tutoring therefore comprised a 6-hour module and a 24-week online tutoring practice.

RESULTS

First, as previously mentioned, project reports were collected from second year students and served as valuable tools to analyze to what extent pre-service teachers had managed to appropriate the CALL-based ELT course content described above. These projects were elaborated by pre-service teachers and carried out during their school placements. Overall, the projects pre-service teachers had designed and implemented aligned with the course content provided to them. This is unsurprising though, since projects were graded and it was therefore in the pre-service teachers' best interest to make sure that these reflected the specific training they had been offered in order to pass the course. This is the reason why it was decided that data triangulation was necessary, as it was believed that an anonymous online post-course survey would give complementary and more reliable insights in their true perception of ICT integration.

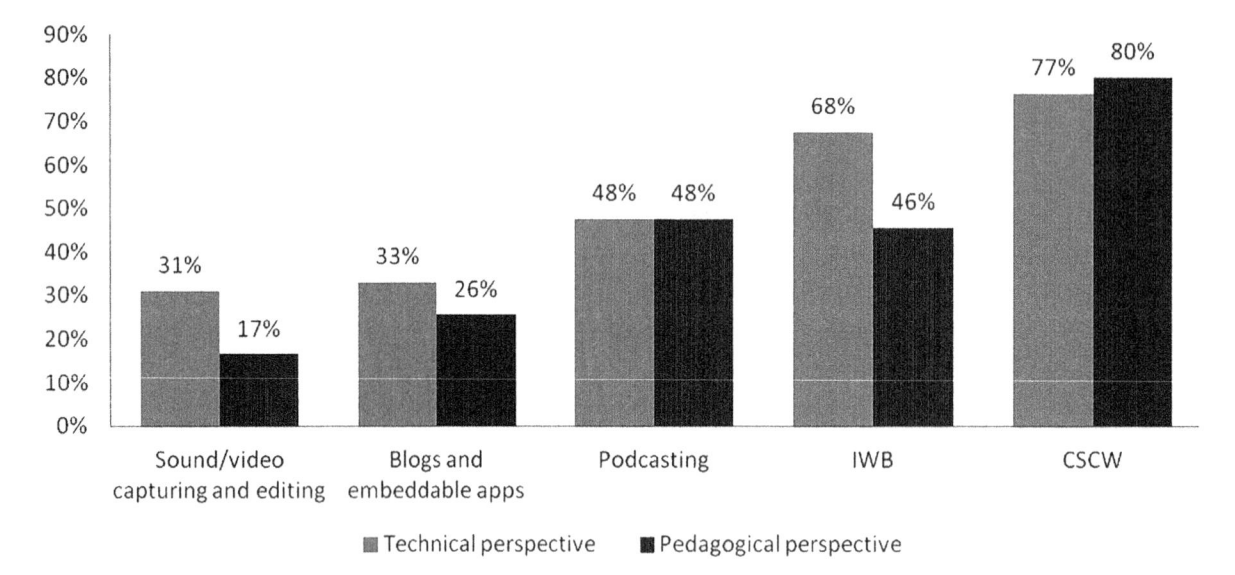

Figure 2. Technologies I could not use prior to the course

Technology	Technical perspective	Pedagogical perspective
Sound/video capturing and editing	31%	17%
Blogs and embeddable apps	33%	26%
Podcasting	48%	48%
IWB	68%	46%
CSCW	77%	80%

The data collected through the online survey was meant to analyze whether the format had met the needs of the future teachers. The survey results thus helped evaluate the CALL-based ELT course and the elective module on online tutoring in light of the set objectives, and envisage new perspectives.

Survey Results for the CALL-based ELT Course

80 pre-service teachers were considered for the study, but only 55 of them responded to the survey, (n=55), which amounts to a 69% response rate and makes the results truly representative.

First, the objective was to find out how much pre-service teachers knew about different technological tools from both a technical and pedagogical perspective, prior to the start of the course (Figure 2). This is why they were asked to identify which of the technologies they were unable to use before the course.

Interestingly, participants felt they could not use the different technologies first and foremost because of their inability to use them from a technical point of view. This can be seen in the consistently higher percentages for the "technical perspective", with the exception of CSCW. Unsurprisingly, the more uncommon and distant from their everyday practice the technology, the higher the percentages of pre-service teachers who felt unable to use them. CSCW, IWB and podcasting were thus perceived as the most challenging technologies to use, whereas blogs, sound/video capturing and editing tools were comparatively considered the easiest.

It was then necessary to know to what extent their perception of the different technologies had evolved through their participation in the CALL-based ELT course (see Figure 3), since teachers' attitudes and beliefs can influence their use of technology, as stated by Hew and Brush (2007). They were therefore asked which technologies they then felt capable of integrating in their ELT classes, and which ones they would definitely integrate in their classes.

The large majority of pre-service teachers who took part in the course felt they had developed specific skills which now enable them to integrate the different technologies in their language classes: over 90% can now integrate blogs and sound/video capturing and editing, while around 70% of them can integrate

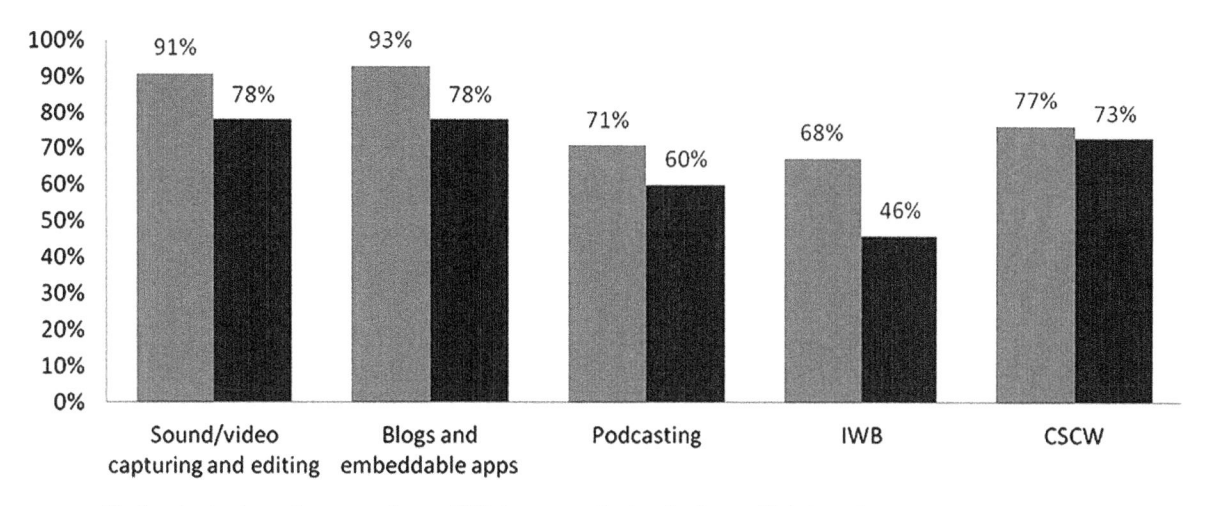

Learning to Teach for Next-Generation Education

Figure 3. Technologies I can/will integrate in my future ELT classes

Technology	Technologies I can integrate in my ELT classes	Technologies I will definitely integrate in my ELT classes
Sound/video capturing and editing	91%	78%
Blogs and embeddable apps	93%	78%
Podcasting	71%	60%
IWB	68%	46%
CSCW	77%	73%

podcasting and IWBs, and over three quarters have developed the ability to integrate CSCW. When comparing these proportions with the ones in Figure 2, it appears that the percentages of pre-service teachers who feel they cannot integrate each one of these technologies has dramatically decreased: -22% for file capturing and editing, -26% for blogs, -19% for podcasting, -36% for IWBs and -54% for CSCW. Unsurprisingly, the technologies that pre-service teachers feel confident they will definitely integrate in their classes are the ones they were the most familiar with prior to their participation in the course (file capturing and editing, and blogs). Still, it is worth noting that almost three quarters of participants (73%) will definitely integrate CSCW in their ELT classes even though around 80% of them were unable to use it before the course. As for IWBs, although just under 70% of pre-service teachers feel they can now integrate them in their language teaching, under half of them (46%) will definitely integrate them, mainly because of their technical complexity as mentioned by several participants in one of the open-ended questions.

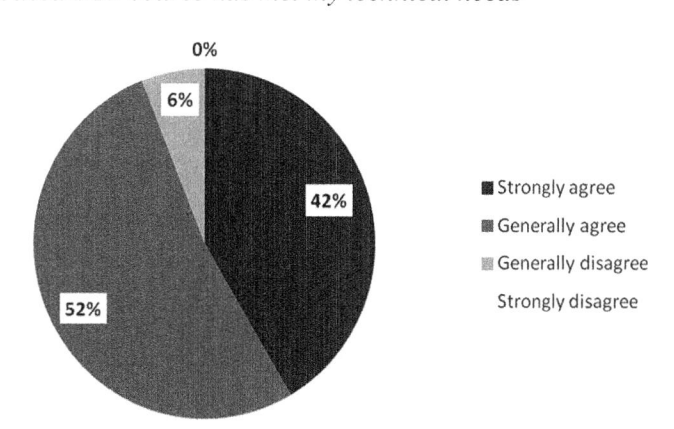

Figure 4. The CALL-based ELT course has met my technical needs

Response	Percentage
Strongly agree	42%
Generally agree	52%
Generally disagree	6%
Strongly disagree	0%

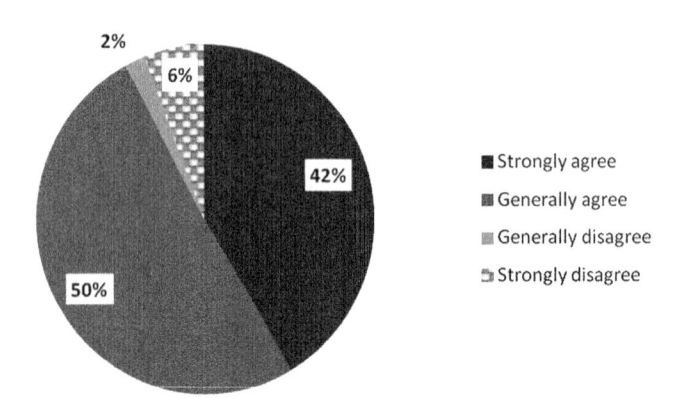

Figure 5. The CALL-based ELT course has met my pedagogical needs

- Strongly agree: 42%
- Generally agree: 50%
- Generally disagree: 6%
- Strongly disagree: 2%

In addition to this, participants were asked to give feedback on the perceived relevance of the CALL-based ELT course as regards their technical and pedagogical needs (Figures 4 and 5).

The large majority of pre-service teachers (94%) felt that the course had met their technical needs. The 6% of participants who did not feel that way might have had technical skills that were too under-developed for them to fully benefit from the course, since they were mainly the ones who asked for more technical manipulation of the tools in one of the open-ended questions. At the other end of the scale, those 6% also seem to include pre-service teachers who showed particular interest in ICT before the course, and whose technical skills were therefore possibly too advanced to learn much from a technical point of view.

As for their pedagogical needs, they seem to have been met for 92% of participants, which is a fairly similar proportion to that of the technical needs. Unsurprisingly, those whose technical needs were not met by the course felt that their pedagogical needs were not met either, as both types of needs are closely related. Besides, the open-ended question related to this Likert scale question points out that the 8% of pre-service teachers whose pedagogical needs were not met were either those who felt that they needed more concrete examples of integration in lesson plans, or those who felt that integrating such tools was not something they could do in the field because of the absence of appropriate equipment in secondary schools. Finally, participants were asked to assess the usefulness of the CALL-based ELT course in relation to their future career (Figure 6).

While over 90% of participants felt that the course was useful for their future career, only 9% felt this was not the case. This is closely related to their suggestions for adjustments made in answer to the final open-ended question:

- Increase the number of classes and reduce the length of each class.
- Include more concrete examples of technological integration in lesson plans.
- Include more technical manipulation of the tools, IWBs in particular.
- Include the step-by-step creation of an ICT-based teaching sequence together in class.

According to participants, the overall potential of the CALL-based ELT course was related to the fact that it enabled them to (1) discover new technological tools and question their pedagogical use in terms of added value, (2) gain "hands-on" experience of these tools from a technical and pedagogical

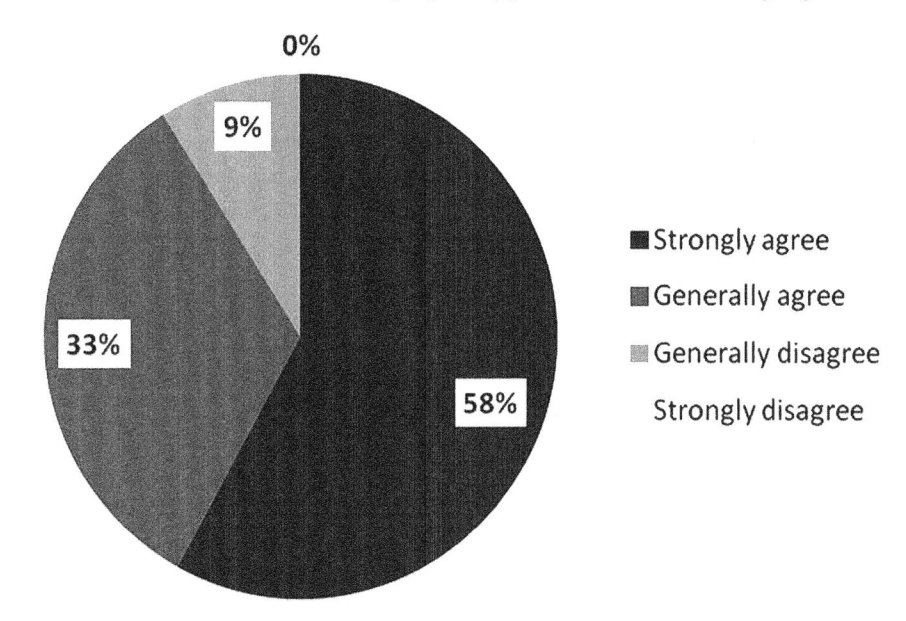

Figure 6. The CALL-based ELT course is useful for my future career as a language teacher

- Strongly agree: 58%
- Generally agree: 33%
- Generally disagree: 9%
- Strongly disagree: 0%

perspective and (3) learn about useful tips, resources and websites to facilitate the integration of ICT in language teaching.

Survey Results for the Elective Module on Online Tutoring

As mentioned previously, the participants were the eight tutors hired in 2013/2014 and the six tutors hired in 2014/2015 for the SIAL, that is a total of 14 potential respondents (figure 7). The response rate is 43%, since the answers from six tutors in total (n=6) were collected. This rather low response rate is probably due to the fact that the survey was administered at the end of the academic year, once pre-

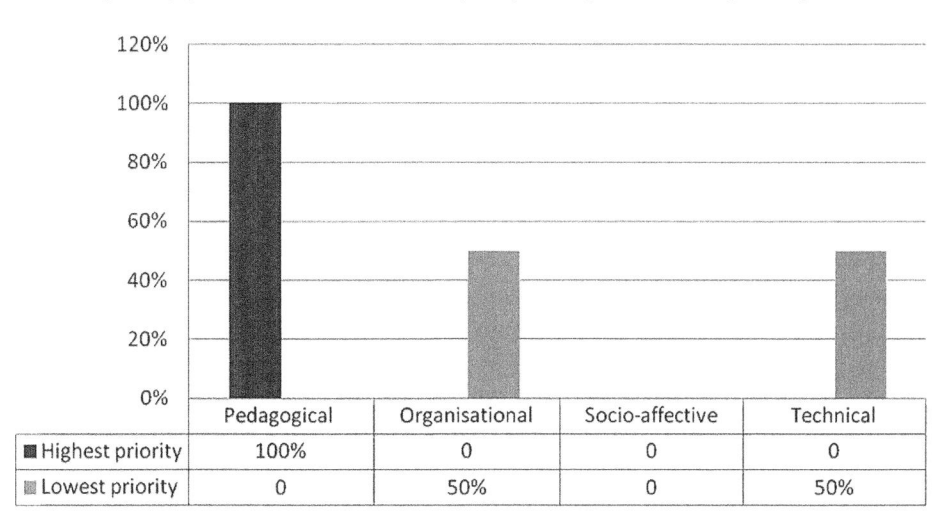

Figure 7. Which aspect of your role as a tutor did you give highest/lowest priority to?

	Pedagogical	Organisational	Socio-affective	Technical
Highest priority	100%	0	0	0
Lowest priority	0	50%	0	50%

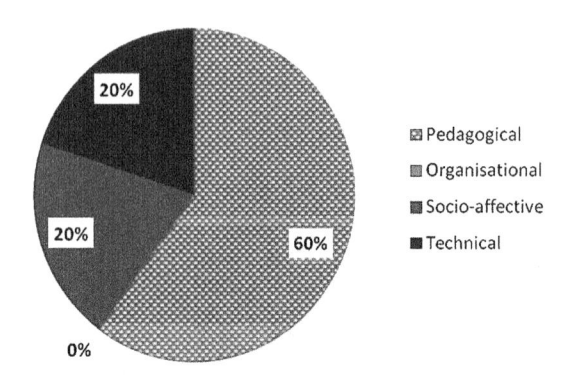

Figure 8. Which aspect of your role as a tutor do you require more training in?

[Pie chart: Pedagogical 60%, Organisational 0%, Socio-affective 20%, Technical 20%]

service teachers had completed all of their online tutoring tasks. This marked the start of their new life as fully qualified teachers, which made it very difficult to contact them to ask those who hadn't done it to take the survey (unlike first year students with the CALL-based ELT course).

If all participants felt they had given priority to the pedagogical aspect of their role as a tutor, half of them acknowledged that they had given little thought to the organizational aspect of their job, and the other half to the technical part of their role. This can be partly explained by the fact that students could get help from a specific support staff who could provide technical assistance. Therefore, tutors probably felt that this aspect of their job was being taken care of by someone else and that they did not have to give it too much thought. Interestingly, the socio-affective aspect of their role was not identified as either a high or low priority, as they probably felt that it permeated the other aspects of their job, most probably the pedagogical part of their role, which was rated as their highest priority (figure 8).

If all of the tutors (100%) thought they had been useful and helpful to their students, 84% of them required further training on different aspects of a tutor's role (Figure 8): 60% of tutors felt they needed more pedagogical training, whereas the remaining 40% required more training on the socio-affective (20%) or technical aspects (20%) of their job.

According to participants, the overall potential of the training for online tutors combined with the field experience as online tutors was related to the skills they had developed, and which enabled them to (1) use a VLE to teach online, (2) raise their awareness of the importance of corrective feedback, (3) give appropriate feedback, (4) work in a team when collaborating with other tutors and with the teachers in charge of the face-to-face classes.

DISCUSSION

The objective of this study was (1) to examine how the specific CALL-based ELT training offered to pre-service teachers helped to bridge the gap between their needs and their prior knowledge and skills, and (2) to analyze pre-service teachers' perception of this training and of ICT integration in L2 teaching.

First, it appears that, within the CALL-based ELT course, students had successfully designed and implemented projects that reflected the course content offered to them, thus showing that the training offered had helped them take the plunge and actually use technology in the classroom after giving it considerable thought. In addition, the analysis of survey responses for the CALL-based ELT course has

Learning to Teach for Next-Generation Education

yielded several interesting results. First, pre-service teachers do not know how to use ICT in the classroom simply because they are unable to use the tools from a technical point of view (as evidenced by their inability to use the tools from a technical point of view prior to the course), which is consistent with the literature (Hew & Brush 2007, Guichon 2012). Along the same lines, the technical complexity of IWBs is the main reason put forward by participants to explain why they will not be using them in their classes, even though 70% of them claim to now know how to integrate them in their teaching. Technical barriers induced by more complex technologies thus seem to override any pedagogical know-how. These specific barriers can also explain why 6% of participants felt that the training course did not meet their needs as the same 6% of participants were the ones who asked for more technical manipulation of the tools, which also suggests that teachers need to feel comfortable using the tools before they can envisage changing their pedagogical practices (as noted by Ertmer 2005). In addition, a high proportion of pre-service teachers (almost three quarters of them) claim that they will integrate CSCW in their classes, even though around 80% of them were unfamiliar with this technology before the course, as it is a less complex technical tool to use, and as it can help support their most immediate needs (writing collaboratively in this case). This tends to support Ertmer's claim that simple technologies that can support teachers' immediate needs should be introduced first, in order to help teachers gain confidence in using technology in the classroom (Ertmer, 2005, p. 36). Finally, when participants assessed the potential of the CALL-based ELT course, several points were put forward: (1) the discovery of new tools and the analysis of their pedagogical added value, (2) the hands-on approach from both a technical and pedagogical perspective and (3) the numerous tips, resources and websites. These elements tend to show that their perception of the course corresponds to what is advocated in the literature: the course seems to have combined different strategies to help them change their beliefs (Ertmer 2005, Ertmer et al. 2012) through the provision of vicarious experiences (point 1), personal experiences (point 2) and social-cultural influences (point 3, useful tips and resources being what interactions with peers and professional networks typically provide). Their perception of course content also aligns with what Hew & Brush (2007, p.238) advocate, as the participants claimed the course focused on content, provided hands-on experience, and was consistent with their needs (for a wide majority). Finally, the perceived qualities of the course also illustrate the value of authentic technology experiences advocated by Tondeur et al. (2012), and partly align with Guichon and Hauck's (2011) views on successful technology integration since the pre-service teachers mentioned they had developed their capacity to assess the potential and limits of technologies for language learning as well as the capacity to handle basic tools and applications.

Overall, these results suggest that pre-service teachers have a fairly accurate perception of the approaches adopted in the CALL-based ELT course, which is a sign of the development of their critical thinking and metacognitive skills, a necessary skill set for any reflective practitioner.

As for the analysis of survey responses related to online tutoring, it showed that pre-service teachers clearly gave priority to the pedagogical dimension of their role as online tutors but didn't really seem to consider the socio-affective dimension of a tutor's job as essential. This is in contrast with Guichon (2009) who lays as much emphasis on the pedagogical regulation of the teacher as on their socio-affective and multimedia regulation. Besides, 60% of participants felt they needed more pedagogical training, which is consistent with the literature. Indeed, teachers regularly acknowledge their lack of familiarity, not only with the technological but also with the pedagogical aspect of using technology (Hew & Brush 2007), and therefore require "ongoing technical and pedagogical support as [they] develop confidence and competence with the technological tools, as well as the new instructional strategies required to implement a different set of pedagogical beliefs" (Ertmer, 2005, p.35). This need for long-term support, which is felt beyond the end of any training course (the elective module on online tutoring in this case), is also in line with Whyte (2014).

The results of this study are, however, not generalizable because of a number of limitations. First, the sizes of samples (55 respondents for the CALL-based ELT course and six for the elective module on online tutoring) were too limited. In addition, this study is mostly based on pre-service teachers' perception of ICT integration, as they were not directly observed while implementing their CALL projects in class. This kind of observation would certainly provide better insights in how pre-service teachers view ICT integration from a practical point of view, as it could be compared with their perceptions. Finally, this study was carried out over a relatively short period of time. It would be interesting to either observe or/and survey the same teachers a couple of years on, to check whether their practices have evolved over time, in an attempt to give this study a more longitudinal dimension.

CONCLUSION

This chapter set out to investigate how secondary school pre-service teachers specializing in ELT can learn to teach for Next-Generation Education, that is to say with technology as an integral part of education. Indeed, in language education in particular, "integrated CALL" is considered to be the future of CALL (Bax 2003), the ultimate step of ICT integration on a continuum being "CALL normalization", a stage when technology becomes invisible due to its full integration into practices.

The question raised in this chapter was to know whether the specific CALL-based ELT training offered could foster change and innovation. Overall, the findings are in line with Hoven who pointed out that teachers' adoption of change and innovation are more likely "when they can see positive benefits in terms of direct relevance to their content area, usefulness from a practical task perspective, and increased effectiveness for their day-to-day classroom teaching" (2007, p.137). The specific CALL-based ELT training offered thus seems to contribute to this objective in many ways. However, it will have to be updated on a regular basis – a requirement in today's ever-changing society.

Regarding future directions, it will be worth exploring the possibility to provide a situated learning experience for online tutoring, which is in line with Slaouti and Motteram (2006) who point out that "teachers need to learn about online learning through online learning" (p. 89). This would enable online tutors to acquire professional skills using the very same technological environment they will have to use to tutor their own students online, which is likely to happen in their future career. This experience can be viewed as an extra opportunity for them to develop their skills in CALL, and to help them set up blended learning environments themselves. Besides, it is believed that another way to raise pre-service teachers' awareness of the potential of ICT integration in language education is to get them involved in research. In that respect, it should be noted that the pre-service teachers who volunteered to become online tutors for the SIAL actually also contributed to a large-scale research program. Indeed, as researchers who set up the SIAL blended learning EFL module, the authors of this chapter are very much involved in studying the type of corrective feedback (CF) which has to be implemented to promote L2 acquisition in a virtual learning environment. CF can be provided to learners in different ways (direct/explicit, indirect/implicit, focused or unfocused) and is the subject of major controversies in SLA research (Ferris, 1999; Truscott, 1996). It is therefore believed that more empirical evidence is needed to investigate the optimal conditions for effective feedback, even more so in the case of virtual learning environments, which offer new opportunities to complement current CF strategies. When they were hired as online tutors, pre-service teachers were therefore assigned a specific type of corrective feedback each. They were thus initiated to research by taking part in an experimental protocol which aims to study the impact of a particular CF on L2 acquisition in a virtual learning environment. This illustrates that the benefits of research sustaining teacher education and of research nourished by practitioners can be key to the implementation of innovative learning environments.

Finally, as noted by several researchers (Hew & Brush 2007, Ertmer et al. 2012, Guichon 2012), the lack of technology implementation in the classroom is first and foremost due to the lack of professional development for teachers. Although many English teachers in French secondary education still fail to integrate technology in their classroom practice (Guichon 2012), it is believed that pre-service training and continuing professional development are powerful ways of starting "a perfect 'technology integration' storm that continues to empower more and more teachers to use technology in ways that prepare our students for the future they will inherit" (Ertmer et al. 2012: 434). In that respect, the results of this study have several implications for the professional development of teachers. First, it illustrates the fact that one of the ways to foster change and innovation in education is to combine action and reflection sustained by research. It also tends to show that pre-service language teachers should be given the opportunity to develop different types of experience during training – personal, vicarious and socio-cultural – to help them change their beliefs about ICT integration. In this respect, pre-service teachers should be encouraged to become members of professional networks, as this is a way of integrating communities of practice that will support them throughout their careers. In addition, this study also points to the benefits of introducing pre-service teachers to technologies that can support their most immediate needs (Ertmer 2005) in order to give them time to become more confident using the technology, which should later allow them to implement higher level uses of the technology. However, in the case of pre-service teachers, there is no guarantee that they will ever receive further training on ICT integration in their career in France, so it is believed that examples of more complex technologies and higher level uses remain a necessary component of their training. Finally, this study also points to the need for ongoing support in ICT integration, which goes far beyond the very limited period of time devoted to pre-service teachers' training: continuing professional development courses are therefore essential. Given the vast array of computer-mediated learning situations in today's society – distance or blended environments, formal as well as informal or non formal settings (Sockett & Toffoli, 2012) – and the complexity attached to them, it is of the utmost importance for both pre-service and in-service teachers to experience various learning contexts themselves and to reflect upon them in terms of potential and limits. This is precisely the aim of the multifaceted CALL-based ELT training discussed in this chapter. Based on a careful blend of action and reflection, its format is likely to help teachers adapt to change, be creative and innovative, develop skills that are needed in today and tomorrow's society, and thus sustain next-generation education.

ACKNOWLEDGMENT

The authors would like to thank all the reviewers for their insightful comments on an earlier version of this chapter.

REFERENCES

Bax, S. (2003). CALL - Past, Present and Future. *System*, *31*(1), 13–28. doi:10.1016/S0346-251X(02)00071-4

Becker, H. J. (1994). How exemplary computer-using teachers differ from other teachers: Implications for realizing the potential of computers in schools. *Journal of Research on Computing in Education*, *26*(3), 291–321. doi:10.1080/08886504.1994.10782093

Bertin, J.-C., & Sarré, C. (2014). New approaches to CALL. *Arab World English Journal*, 2-8.

Bitchener, J., & Knoch, U. (2009). The relative effectiveness of different types of direct written corrective feedback. *System*, *37*(2), 322–329. doi:10.1016/j.system.2008.12.006

Blin, F., & Appel, C. (2011). Computer Supported Collaborative Writing in Practice: An Activity Theoretical Study. *CALICO Journal*, *28*(2), 473–497. doi:10.11139/cj.28.2.473-497

Compton, L. K. (2009). Preparing language teachers to teach language online: A look at skills, roles, and responsibilities. *Computer Assisted Language Learning*, *22*(1), 73–99. doi:10.1080/09588220802613831

Elola, I., & Oskoz, A. (2010). Collaborative Writing: Fostering Foreign Language and Writing Conventions Development. *Language Learning & Technology*, *14*(3), 51–71.

Ertmer, P. A. (2005). Teacher pedagogical beliefs: The final frontier in our quest for technology integration? *Educational Technology Research and Development*, *53*(4), 25–39. doi:10.1007/BF02504683

Ertmer, P. A., Ottenreit-Leftwich, A. T., Sadik, O., Sendurur, E., & Sendurur, P. (2012). Teacher beliefs and technology integration practices: A critical relationship. *Computers & Education*, *59*(2), 423–435. doi:10.1016/j.compedu.2012.02.001

Ferris, D. R. (1999). The case for grammar correction in L2 writing classes. A response to Truscott (1996). *Journal of Second Language Writing*, *8*(1), 1–10. doi:10.1016/S1060-3743(99)80110-6

Gibson, J. (1979). *The ecological approach to visual perceptions*. Boston: Houghton Mifflin.

Grosbois, M. (2014). Practicum experience in teacher education: is experience the best teacher? In J. Martínez Agudo (Ed.), *English as a foreign language teacher education: Current perspectives and challenges* (pp. 107–126). Amsterdam, New York: Editions Rodopi.

Grosbois, M. (in press). Computer supported collaborative writing and language learning. In F. Fiarr & L. Murray (Eds.), *Handbook of Language Learning and Technology*. London: Routledge.

Guichon, N. (2009). Training future language teachers to develop online tutor's competence through reflective analysis. *ReCALL*, *21*(2), 166–185. doi:10.1017/S0958344009000214

Guichon, N. (2012). *Vers l'intégration des TIC dans l'enseignement des langues*. Paris: Didier.

Guichon, N., & Hauck, M. (2011). Teacher education research in CALL and CMC: More in demand than ever. *ReCALL*, *23*(3), 187–199. doi:10.1017/S0958344011000139

Hampel, R., & Stickler, U. (2005). New skills for new classrooms: Training tutors to teach languages online. *Computer Assisted Language Learning*, *18*(4), 311–326. doi:10.1080/09588220500335455

Hew, K. F., & Brush, T. (2007). Integrating technology into K-12 teaching and learning: Current knowledge gaps and recommendations for future research. *Educational Technology Research and Development*, *55*(3), 223–252. doi:10.1007/s11423-006-9022-5

Hoven, D. (2007). The affordances of technology for student teachers to shape their teacher education experience. In M. A. Kassen, L. R. Lavine, K. Murphy-Judy, & M. Peters (Eds.), *Preparing and Developing Technology Proficient L2 Teachers* (pp. 133–163). San Marcos, TX: CALICO.

Mercer, S. (2011). Understanding learner agency as a complex dynamic system. *System*, *39*(4), 427–436. doi:10.1016/j.system.2011.08.001

Müller-Hartmann, A. (2012). The Classroom-Based Action Research Paradigm in Telecollaboration. In M. Dooly & R. O'Dowd (Eds.), *Research Methods for Online Interaction and Exchange* (pp. 156–192). Bern: Peter Lang.

Officiel de l'Éducation Nationale, B. (2013). *Référentiel des compétences professionnelles des métiers du professorat et de l'éducation.* BOEN n°30. Retrieved from http://www.education.gouv.fr/pid285/bulletin_officiel.html?cid_bo=73066

Ottenbreit-Leftwich, A. T., Brush, T. A., Strycker, J., Gronseth, S., Roman, T., Abaci, S., & Plucker, J. et al. (2012). Preparation versus practice: How do teacher education programs and practicing teachers align in their use of technology to support teaching and learning? *Computers & Education*, *59*(2), 399–411. doi:10.1016/j.compedu.2012.01.014

Puentedura, R. (2006). *Transformation, Technology and Education*. Retrieved from http://hippasus.com/resources/tte/

Sarré, C. (2013). Technology-mediated tasks in English for Specific Purposes (ESP): Design, implementation and learner perception. *International Journal of Computer-Assisted Language Learning and Teaching*, *3*(2), 1–16. doi:10.4018/ijcallt.2013040101

Slaouti, D., & Motteram, G. (2006). Reconstructing practice: Language teacher education and ICT. In P. Hubbard & M. Levy (Eds.), *Teacher Education in CALL* (pp. 80–97). Philadelphia: John Benjamins. doi:10.1075/lllt.14.09sla

Sockett, J., & Toffoli, D. (2012). Beyond learner autonomy: A dynamic systems view of the informal learning of English in virtual online communities. *ReCALL*, *24*(2), 138–151. doi:10.1017/S0958344012000031

Tondeur, J., van Braak, J., Sang, G., Voogt, J., Fisser, P., & Ottenbreit-Leftwich, A. (2012). Preparing pre-service teachers to integrate technology in education: A synthesis of qualitative evidence. *Computers & Education*, *59*(1), 134–144. doi:10.1016/j.compedu.2011.10.009

Truscott, J. (1996). The case against grammar correction in L2 writing classes. *Language Learning*, *46*(2), 327–369. doi:10.1111/j.1467-1770.1996.tb01238.x

Whyte, S. (2014). Bridging the gaps: Using social media to develop techno-pedagogical competences in pre-service language teacher education. *Recherche et pratiques pédagogiques en langues de spécialité, 33*(2), 143-169.

KEY TERMS AND DEFINITIONS

Blended Learning: It refers to an environment which combines distance online learning and face-to-face sessions. The balance between both modalities varies.

Complexity: Complexity theory refers to the numerous components of a system that constantly interact, thus generating instability. This may apply to computer-mediated language learning environments.

Engagement: It refers to the commitment of learners, teachers and/or the institution to work towards the learning objective(s).

Innovation: It cannot be reduced to integrating new digital tools in teaching but should imply reconsidering the way language is learnt (and taught) through technologies.

Online Tutor: Someone who provides online mediation (multi-faceted help) in a virtual learning environment.

Reflection: Reflective practice based on the analysis of concrete examples, sustained and mediated by research(ers) and peers (Grosbois, 2014).

Situated Learning: It refers to the contextualized, pragmatic and thus meaningful approach to learning and teaching.

ENDNOTE

[1]   http://www.limesurvey.org

APPENDIX 1: SURVEY ON THE CALL-BASED ELT COURSE

Question 1: Before the course, which of these technologies were you unfamiliar with from a technical point of view?
- sound and video editing software
- blogs
- interactive white boards
- podcasting tools
- computer-supported collaborative writing applications

Question 2: Before the course, which of these technologies were you unfamiliar with from a pedagogical point of view?
- sound and video editing software
- blogs
- interactive white boards
- podcasting tools
- computer-supported collaborative writing applications

Question 3: Which of these technologies do you now feel comfortable integrating in your teaching?
- sound and video editing software
- blogs
- interactive white boards
- podcasting tools
- computer-supported collaborative writing applications

Question 4: Which of these technologies do you think you will integrate as a priority in your teaching?
- sound and video editing software
- blogs
- interactive white boards
- podcasting tools
- computer-supported collaborative writing applications

Question 5: Explain why.

Question 6: The course has met your needs from a technical point of view.
- strongly agree
- mostly agree
- mostly disagree
- strongly disagree

Question 7: Explain why/why not.

Question 8: The course has met your needs from a pedagogical point of view.
- strongly agree
- mostly agree
- mostly disagree
- strongly disagree

Question 9: Explain why/why not.

Question 10: The course content will be useful for my future teaching career.
- strongly agree

- mostly agree
- mostly disagree
- strongly disagree

Question 11: Explain why/why not.

Question 12: What suggestions could you make to improve the course?

APPENDIX 2: SURVEY ON ONLINE TUTORING

Question 1: Which of the four aspects of an online tutor's role did you give highest priority to?
- pedagogical aspect
- organizational aspect
- socio-affective aspect
- technical aspect

Question 2: Which of the four aspects of an online tutor's role did you give lowest priority to?
- pedagogical aspect
- organizational aspect
- socio-affective aspect
- technical aspect

Question 3: Overall, do you think that more training in online tutoring is necessary?
- Yes
- No

Question 4: If so, in which of the four aspects of an online tutor's role in particular?
- pedagogical aspect
- organizational aspect
- socio-affective aspect
- technical aspect

Question 5: Overall, do you think you have been helpful and useful to your students as an online tutor?
- Yes
- No

Question 6: If not, explain why.

Question 7: To what extent is the practical experience as an online tutor you gained in semester 1 going to be useful to you in semester 2?

Question 8: To what extent is your experience as an online tutor going to be useful in your future career?

Chapter 10
Mentoring Preservice EFL Teachers for Technology Integration:
A Cloud-Based Internship Project

Mei-Hui Liu
Tunghai University, Taiwan

ABSTRACT

This chapter proposes an integrated mentoring model in the context of established and emerging Information and Communications Technology (ICT) tools to be applied into teacher professional development. Twenty preservice English as a Foreign Language (EFL) preservice teachers participating in a Cloud-based internship project were involved in a series of training activities, including virtual technology training workshops, in-class methods instruction, design and implementation of teaching projects on a Cloud platform, and subsequent face-to-face and online discussions on teaching practices. Multiple qualitative data collected offers evidence to examine the potential of employing this mentoring mechanism to make amends for what has been rarely exploited in the extant technology teacher training models in the foreign language education field. Based on the research findings, a revised mentoring model is suggested for further investigation.

INTRODUCTION

Teacher educators have advocated the preparation of prospective teachers to act as change agents for technology integration in an attempt to impact student learning outcome (Jimoyiannis, 2010; Mouza, Karchmer-Klein, Nandakumar, Ozden, & Hu, 2014; Polly, Mims, Shepherd, & Inan, 2010). Previous researchers have investigated the effects of mentoring preservice teachers' learning to teach with technology in the past decade. Most of these studies are related to the effects of coursework instruction on teacher candidates' technology professional development in the fields of educational technology, mathematics, or science (e.g., Funkhouser & Mouza, 2013; Holmes, 2009; Jang & Chen, 2010; Koh & Divaharan, 2011;

DOI: 10.4018/978-1-5225-0483-2.ch010

So & Kim, 2009). Preservice teachers in these studies were mostly involved in campus-based preparation activities in which they learned and designed potential technology infusion to simulate subject matter instruction. Yet, Niess (2011) pinpointed that the major failure for many courses to prepare teachers to teach with technology can be attributed to the emphasis on acquisition of technical skills, with less focus on how technology may interact with teaching content and content-specific pedagogy (see also Chai, Koh, Tsai, & Tan, 2011). While previous researchers vigorously examined the experience or perceptions of preservice teachers' learning to teach with technology after completing teacher preparation courses, limited studies have been conducted to explore an in-depth analysis of how preservice teachers apply the technology they have learned into real classroom practices (Young, Young, & Shaker, 2012), especially in the foreign language education field. As reiterated by researchers (e.g.,Chai, Koh, & Tsai, 2010; Pamuk, 2012), lack of pedagogical experience is the major barrier to prepare preservice teachers for technology integration.

In addition to face-to-face field-experience, with the advent of ICT applications online practicum mechanism has been promoted to offer teachers additional professional growth experiences without geographical barrier (e.g., Allaire & Laferriere, 2005; Chen & Chan, 2011; Jiyoon, 2008; Seo, Templeton, & Pellegrino, 2008). Preservice teachers with experience of technology-enabled internship implemented on the Internet could have direct access to various multimedia tools to be applied into subject teaching. Most of them were proved to have more motivation to use technology in future instructional practices. This new trend of practicum echoed Kennedy and Archambault's (2012) contention that teacher education programs need to provide coursework that includes online pedagogy curriculum as well as instructional design work in online learning environments with the aim of meeting the digitalized educational trend in the 21st century.

This chapter reports partial findings of a research project sponsored by the Ministry of Science and Technology in Taiwan. The yearlong project aimed to explore the development of preservice EFL teachers' technological pedagogical content knowledge (TPCK) when blending *TEFL Methodology Course* with a Cloud-based internship project. The focus of this chapter is to further propose an integrated mentoring model to facilitate preservice EFL teachers' technology integration after examining the effectiveness of the aforementioned internship project. In the teacher education field, conventional programs are criticized for their failure in facilitating preservice teachers' critical re-examination of the connection between the affordances of technology and their teaching practices (Chien, Chang, Yeh, & Chang, 2012; Jang, 2008). Lagging behind the general education field, foreign language teacher education also does not provide enough preparation for preservice teachers to integrate technology into their emerging teaching practices (Chen & Chan, 2011; van Olphen, 2007). This chapter hence investigates the application of an integrated mentoring program which may provide a viable context for mentoring preservice teachers' learning to teach with technology. The following research questions serve to guide this investigation.

1. How did the preservice EFL teachers learn to teach with technology in the professional development program?
2. What were the difficulties or concerns, if any, these preservice teachers encountered when they were engaged in this program?
3. What were the factors, if any, that facilitated or hindered the teacher educators' online mentoring in this program?

BACKGROUND

The current research project referred to relevant types of technology professional training in the teacher preparation literature, including 1) collaborative design-based model, 2) mentoring or coaching model, and 3) Web-based learning model. In a school of design-based research studies, preservice teachers drafted teaching projects in groups after receiving instructional modules related to technology infusion (e.g., Archambault & Barnett, 2010; Chai et al., 2011; Chien et al., 2012; Koehler, Mishra, & Yahya, 2007). This instructional approach afforded presevice teachers an opportunity to have active engagement in learning how to design specific technology application situated in the context of future classroom instruction. They were usually requested to present their design projects in class sessions, followed by peer assessment and self-reflection on their instructional plans. It was commonly found that preservice teachers' technology literacy and pedagogical knowledge would determine the success of designing technology-integrated teaching projects. In a review of earlier studies, Lawless and Pellegrino (2007) maintained that teacher candidates completing design-based tasks may build up higher confidence in integrating the task units as future teaching tools. These prospective teachers were more likely to believe that the technology-related curriculum has a positive impact on student learning achievement. Nonetheless, a lack of authentic technology experiences in classroom settings appear not to guarantee that preservice teachers' perceived competence or beliefs could be put into real classroom practices (Tondeur, van Braak, Sang, Voogt, Fisser, & Ottenbreit-Leftwich, 2012).

Another school of studies used a mentoring approach to provide preservice teachers with assistance in the context of personal relationships to meet individual needs in technology integration (e.g., Haydn & Barton, 2007; Peirson & McNeil, 2000; Smith & Robinson, 2003; Vannatta, Beyerbach, & Walsh, 2001). These studies highlighted the "role model" offered by inservice teachers and/or teacher educators who demonstrated to preservice teachers specific resources, information, or associated skills with respect to the application of technology into classroom instruction. The prospective teachers either compiled personal electronic portfolios to keep track of their learning experience or had reflections on professional learning when partaking in a collaborative learning cohort throughout a field-based experience. In general, the prevalent findings indicated the participating preservice teachers' professional growth shifting their views from a focus on what they would teach and learn about technology to an emphasis on how they could employ technology to effectively support student learning. It was further documented that some factors appeared to hinder these preservice teachers from developing, implementing, and evaluating their technology professional development. They mainly included limited face-to-face communication between mentors and mentees, insufficient rapport from mentors with heavy teaching schedules, and lack of access to technology sources and facilities in the mentoring contexts. Accordingly, it is recommended to employ online mentoring framework as an alternative to support preservice teachers' practicum in a more flexible manner in terms of meeting schedules and venues (Gentry, Denton, & Kurz, 2008; Knapczyk, Hew, & Frey, 2005).

Different from the above traditional modules, web-supported professional development mechanism has been employed to facilitate preservice teachers' learning to teach with technology in the past decade. Most of the previous research tended to offer theory- or concept-based coaching to teacher candidates. Of which, asynchronous online discussion forums were generally built up to create professional learning communities among preservice teachers or between preservice and inservice teachers to enhance existing structure for technology professional growth (e.g., Barnett, 2006; Nicholson & Bond, 2003; Sutherland, Howard, & Markauskaite, 2010). The participating student teachers discussed and reflected on what they had learned from technology training and/or methodology courses to be implemented into classroom instruction. Some empirical studies have exploited online synchronous networked tasks to re-conceptualize and foster preservice (foreign language) teachers' instructional beliefs or pedagogical skills in technology application (e.g., Develotte, Guichon, & Vincent, 2010; Lan, Chang, & Chen, 2012; Martin & Vallance, 2008; Vallance, 2007). The other studies have started to apply technology-enabled teaching projects into classroom sharing or microteaching in (foreign language) teacher preparation programs (e.g., Dooly & Masats, 2011; Lavy & Shriki, 2008; Roessingh & Chambers, 2011; Seo, Templeton, & Pellegrino, 2008). The findings of these investigations showed that the participating teacher candidates both increased their confidence or motivation in and enhanced their knowledge of infusing technology to future classroom instruction.

To date, limited empirical studies have depicted preservice teachers' technology professional growth by covering the period of authentic teaching practices, except for a few extant studies (e.g., Chen & Chan, 2011; Howard, 2002; Marshall, Petrosino, & Martin, 2010; Mouza et al., 2014; Wang, Chen, & Levy, 2010). These researchers offered web-based instruction to foster preservice teachers how to design teaching projects which were later put into practice in face-to-face field experience, except for Wang et al. (2010) providing synchronous cyber teaching practices. Among this piece of literature, only Chen and Chan (2011) and Wang et al. (2010) was related to foreign language education and the others were conducted in the science or mathematics education field. The apprentice teaching employed in these research projects had cultivated preservice teachers to change from teacher-centered to student-centered teaching philosophy in web-based learning environments. With the scaffolding offered by course instructors, the recruited preservice teachers had more chances to broaden their perception of technology integration and strengthen their competence and self-efficacy in using such an instructional module after engaging in practical teaching experience. Wang et al. (2010) further posited that the relationship between teachers and technology-mediated environment was found to influence the participating trainee teachers' emotions, feelings, and reactions during professional growth. This reveals different kinds of challenges to be investigated, in comparison to campus-based teacher education.

In a recent study, Mouza et al. (2014) juxtaposed educational technology courses, methods coursework, and field experience for presevice teacher preparation in the elementary education field. Findings indicated the improvement of teacher candidates' technology application knowledge after their teaching practices in face-to-face classroom settings. Yet, Mouza et al. echoed a challenge encountered by previous teacher training programs; that is, in face-to-face field placements preservice teachers usually had limited access to technology use and the assigned cooperating teachers tended to provide few role models with respect to the effective technology integration.

The above literature review shows why it is of significance to offer preservice teacher a chance to have online teaching practices (Kennedy & Archambaut, 2012) from which teacher candidates could have one hundred percent of opportunities to access and infuse technology into instruction. The mentoring model reported in this chapter offered Cloud-based internship experience to preservice EFL teachers, which is expected to have great potential to make amends for what has been rarely exploited in the extant technology teacher training modules in the foreign language education field.

THE MENTORING MODEL OF TECHNOLOGY INTEGRATION

The mentoring model includes four major components: 1) virtual training of a Cloud-based platform interface and multimedia functions, 2) in-class instruction of TEFL methods and project-based learning theories, 3) design and implementation of teaching projects on the Cloud platform, and 4) face-to-face and online discussions on teaching practices (see Table 1 for a summary). Each component is described as follows:

- **Technology Training:** The prospective teachers received a series of 9-hour online training workshops offered by two teacher educators to get familiar with the Cloud platform interface built by JoinNet Company (http://blog.joinnet.tw/) in Fall Semester 2013. They were introduced to technologies available for use in online practicum implemented on this learning platform which combines the major multimedia functions of Interactive White Board, sharing website sources, asynchronous and synchronous chatting rooms, and online Messenger (see Figure 1 and 2).
- **Methods Instruction:** In the same semester, these preservice teachers received in-class instruction related to TEFL teaching approaches or methods, such as grammar-translation method (GTM), audiolingual method (ALM), communicative language teaching (CLT), whole language, and multiple intelligence (MI). Also included were theories in relation to computer-assisted language learning (CALL) and project-based instruction (PBI). The course instructor (i.e., the teacher-researcher) offered role models of these methods and approaches via video-taped teaching demonstrations.

Table 1. Learning activities in the mentoring model

Components	Learning Activities
Virtual Training of Platform Interface and Multimedia Functions	Attending Workshop (1): [2 hrs] - Distance learning in language education - Basic functions of the JoinNet platform
	Attending Workshop (2): [2 hrs] - Multimedia and Interactive White Board on the platform - Observation of teaching models of technology integration (1) - Steps to set up a synchronous classroom and group discussion
	Attending Workshop (3): [2 hrs] - Application of JoinNet Messenger in online instruction - Observation of teaching models of technology integration (2) - Steps to manage and share the recorded class sessions
	Attending Workshop (4): [3 hrs] - Online simulation teaching practice and discussion
In-class Instruction of TEFL methodology	Learning language teaching approaches and methods (e.g., GTM, ALM, CLT, Whole Language, MI, CALL, and PBI.)
Design and Implementation of Teaching Projects	Designing and implementing the first teaching project with respect to color recognition in 5 weeks (3-4 hrs per week)
	Designing and implementing the second teaching project with respect to direction inquiry in 5 weeks (3-4 hrs per week)
Discussion on Teaching Practices	Reflecting on instructional practices and having online/face-to-face discussions with peers, teacher educators, and course instructor after each teaching session

- **Online Practice:** After receiving the aforementioned training, the participating preservice teachers served as free online tutors teaching English to underprivileged elementary school students living in remote areas for 10 weeks in the second semester (see a sample snapshot in Figure 3). These prospective teachers were divided into small groups (N= 4 or 5) to engage in collaborative project-based instruction (PBI) delivered online. Each group of the participating teachers taught 6-10 students 3 to 4 hours per week after school. The major goal of this online tutoring course was to teach elementary school students vocabulary in assigned instructional hours, when all the four language skills (speaking, listening, reading, and writing) were simultaneously taught in an integrated way. To meet this goal, the methodology course instructor guided these prospective teachers to design and implement two projects (i.e., color recognition and direction inquiry) which covered the online instruction of the required vocabulary. The preservice teachers in each group which was divided into two teams rotated to design online instructional materials (e.g., Powerpoint files, worksheets, and quizzes) and team teach the pre-scheduled online classes. For example, when Team A in Group 1 was in charge of the class session, Team B was assigned to complete related instructional materials after discussing with Team A members two days before the class. Team teaching was implemented by sharing the teaching equally and playing the role of co-teachers as teaching assistants. On average, the duration of respective group's online teaching were around 35 hours during 10 weeks. Depending on elementary school students' language proficiency levels, each team negotiated time allocation and finished their weekly practice within 3 hours for high-level students or up to 4 hours for low-level students in each class session. Each of them approximately taught 1.5 hours at a time. In total, individual preservice teacher's online authentic practice lasted for 7.5 to 8 hours and his/her engagement in designing instructional materials was about 10 to 12 hours in this online practicum module.
- **Reflective discussion:** Each group of preservice teachers had online and face-to-face discussion with two teacher educators and the course instructor respectively within two weeks after they

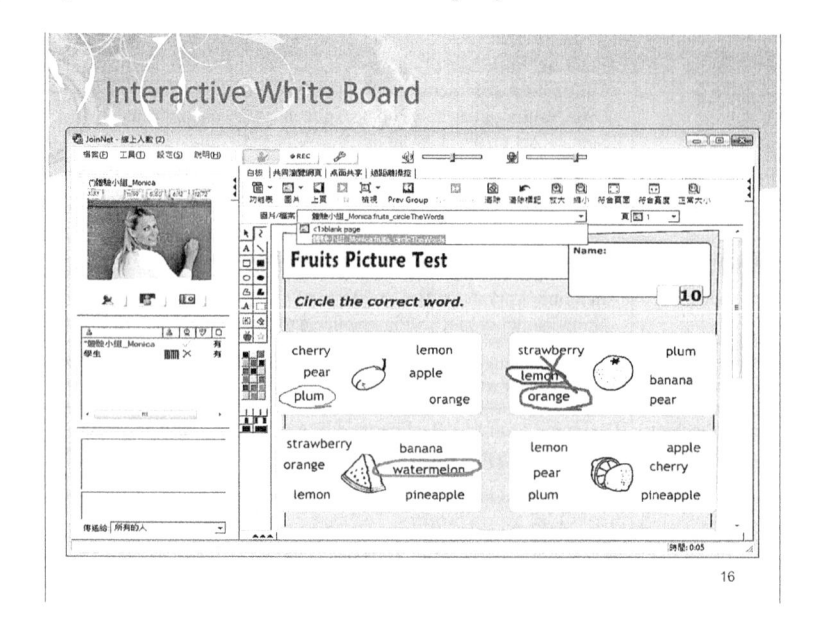

Figure 1. Interface of interactive white board on cloud platform

Mentoring Preservice EFL Teachers for Technology Integration

finished each session of online instructional practice. First, they were requested to review streaming videos and reflect on the strengths or drawbacks of teaching practices in written forms on the discussion forums. Then, based on their availability, they had synchronous oral discussion or asynchronous written discussion with peers and the teacher educators on what they had reflected, especially in terms of how technology application matched the delivery of language learning content. The teacher educators afterwards made suggestions on these preservice teachers' design of next teaching session. Finally, each group took turns to have face-to-face meetings with the course instructor to evaluate their collaborative teaching practices by referring to a set of assessment checklist and rubrics in terms of individual performance and group collaboration (see Appendix 1 and 2). They also revisited what they have learned from online discussions and drafted their teaching plan of the subsequent class session accordingly by reinforcing their strengths and avoiding potential drawbacks, if any.

METHODOLOGY

The Research Context and Participants

The mentoring model of technology integration was implemented in a 10-month internship project which was included in the teaching schedule of a yearlong *TEFL Methodology* course offered at a private university in central Taiwan. The focuses of this course in the first semester were on covering major language teaching theories, approaches, or methods, and technology application skills as well. In the second semester, student teachers were further trained how to put theories into practice by means of microteaching and practicum. The class meeting time was two hours per week in the first semester and 4 hours per week in the second semester.

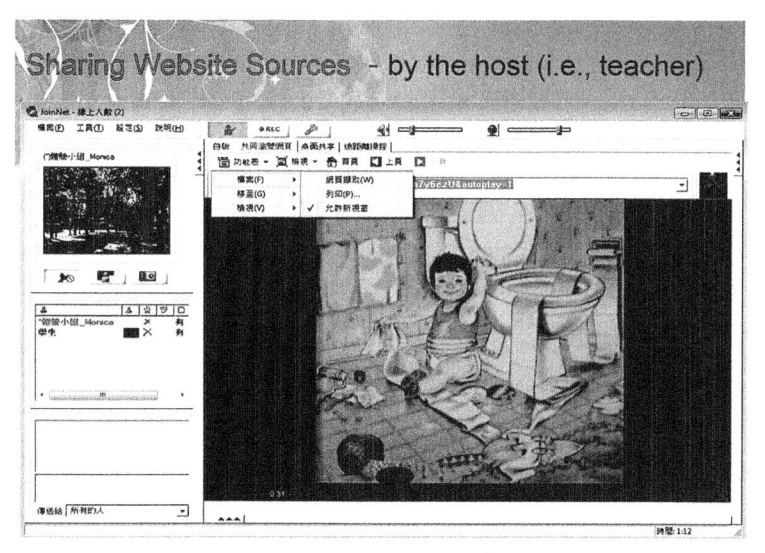

Figure 2. Sharing website sources on the cloud platform

Figure 3. Sample snapshot of online practice

The central participants included 20 undergraduate students (2 males and 18 females) registered for this elective course during the School Year 2013 (from September 2013 to June 2014). These preservice EFL students, aged from 21 to 23, were in their junior or senior year of studying at the university. Most of them were prospective English teachers taking preservice training courses while they were pursuing a B.A. degree in the meantime. They took this methodology course as a requirement to become certified English teachers in Taiwan. The others were potential English teachers aiming to teach at cram schools or private language institutes. They joined this course on account of equipping themselves with knowledge and expertise related to their career plan. More than three-fourths of these undergraduate students (N=16) had part-time jobs as English tutors before or during this study. They had ever taught English to elementary or junior high school students for 6 months up to 1.5 years (two or three times per week; 1.5 to 2 hours each time). Additionally, in their early thirties two female teacher educators with the expertise in the CALL field were invited to serve as online mentors scaffolding the participating preservice teachers' technology professional development. These two professionals are full-time staff serving at the *Association for the Advancement of Online Tutoring* (AAOT) in Taiwan (see http://www.aaot.tw/). As a charity association, the AAOT offers free technology training workshops and online practicum opportunities to college English majors who volunteer to offer online English instruction to underprivileged students. The participating mentors are both qualified technology coaches and evaluators of online instruction based on their previous face-to-face or online English instruction offered to students at elementary and junior high school levels. These two professionals' major job duties at AAOT is to train inservice and preservice teachers how to employ multimedia tools on synchronous learning platforms. They had ever supervised student teachers' online practicum at several Taiwanese universities for more than three years before partaking in the current research project.

Data and Data Analysis

To investigate the effectiveness of this mentoring model, multiple qualitative data sources collected from the preservice teachers were focus group interviews, reflection entries, and artefacts related to teaching practices. Also included were interviews conducted with online teacher educators and the present researcher's field notes. First, a focus group interview was conducted with preservice teachers of the same practicum group after each teaching project. Afterwards, the two online teacher educators were interviewed respectively to gain more insights about the process of the preservice teachers' learning to teach with technology (see sample interview questions in Appendix 3). These participants was encouraged to reveal their responses to 8 -10 questions adapted from previous studies on technology infusion or preservice English teachers' professional development (Doering, Veletsianos, Scharber, & Miller, 2009; Frey, 2008). Second, the preservice teachers were requested to complete reflection entries after they reviewed the streaming videos of their online instruction. Referring to previous related studies (Jang & Chen, 2010; Koh & Divanaran, 2011; Roessingh & Chambers, 2011), 6 guiding questions were provided to help each participant locate themselves in the context of growth, get a sense of where they have come from, and reflect on the themes and issues being investigated (see Appendix 4). Third, all the artifacts related to these preservice teachers' professional growth were collected in a private group Facebook, including electronic files of lesson plans, handouts, worksheets, and Powerpoint files…etc. Also included were the streaming videos of preservice teachers' online teaching practices automatically recorded and saved by the JoinNet data-management system. Fourth, the present researcher kept field notes based on her observation of the preservice teachers' professional development process throughout the study.

Multiple data sources collected from the participants were analyzed and compared continuously until theories or patterns emerged (Silverman, 2006). The data collected from (focus group) interviews and reflection entries were analyzed by Nvivo 8.0 for windows and open/axial coding techniques (Corbin & Strauss, 2007) to organize groups of data in particular themes or issues being investigated. Furthermore, the artifacts and field notes were outlined to offer further evidence to buttress these preservice teachers' professional learning experience. Finally, the various data sources were compared and contrasted to depict how helpful this mentoring program would prepare these teacher candidates for technology-enhanced language instruction. Also included were the challenges or difficulties these participants perceived during this professional learning process, and the factors that facilitated or hindered the online teacher educators' mentoring.

FINDINGS

The findings drawing on various data sources will reveal specific issues related to preservice EFL teachers' technology professional development in an integrated mentoring program. For clarity, the data collected from focus group interviews, individual interviews, and reflection journals will be noted as FG, IN, and RJ in this section. Additionally, the codings of FN and AF represent field notes and artifacts.

Preservice Teachers' Professional Development

Throughout this study, all the preservice teachers (N=20) highlighted their appreciation for joining each learning component of this internship project. Typically, one participant said that "We had a great opportunity to learn how to conduct online instruction, which is an alternative to the traditional face-to-face classroom instruction" (1st RJ). First of all, when participating in technology training workshops, all of them learned and employed the major functions with regard to language education on the Cloud platform. Among others, these technical skills mainly included how to "upload teaching materials to the *Interactive Whiteboard*," "make good use of *Youtube* or video-clips for students' learning," "manage students' learning flow based on a *Monitoring Pen* and *Highlighter*," and "design online assessment sheets." Both teacher educators echoed these preservice teachers' achievement in learning technology by saying, for example, "This bunch of e-generation youth were quite good at picking up what we covered in the [technology] training workshops" (1st IN).

Second, the in-class instruction of TEFL methodology fostered more than half of the participating teachers (N=11) to have more options of using different teaching approaches or methods with the technology they had learned. For example, one of them described that "It's great to have [the course instructor] tell us what kinds of [teaching] methods are more suitable for matching the technological functions we could apply on the Cloud platform" (2nd FG). Moreover, the present researcher noted,

Those who taking the teacher training program were more devoted to reviewing various methods and discussing with me about how each method could match online teaching practice. (FN- Nov. 25, 2013)

Some of the submitted lesson plans did not specify which teaching methods or approaches were more suitable for the sessions of teaching projects they designed for online practicum. (AF- Dec. 10, 2013)

The findings imply that some of these preservice teachers may need more instructional experience in order to put TEFL methodology theories into technology-based instruction.

Third, more than two-thirds of these teacher candidates (N=15) reported their confidence and attainment when it came to the design and implementation of teaching projects. One said, "I cannot overemphasize how terrific it is for us to learn the application of online platform and multimedia. This is much more interesting than just having students sit inside a classroom and learn English via textbooks, blackboard, and chalk" (1st FG). The other highlighted, "I found my students were willing to learn English when we asked them to work on interesting group work on the Internet" (1st RJ). Moreover, one of the teacher educators further stressed that "There is no doubt that most of [the preservice teachers] do make progress in conducting teaching projects. According to my observation and discussion with them on the forums, they have great potential to become professional online instructors very soon" (2nd IN). As observed by the present researcher,

Except for group 2, the other groups showed their satisfaction with the first teaching project by complimenting group members' novice and brilliant ideas regarding how to integrate specific teaching methods into online instruction. (FN- May 16, 2014)

Fourth, almost all of the preservice teachers (N=19) agreed that both face-to-face and synchronous/asynchronous online discussions benefited their improvement in teaching practices with technology. The peer review offered them frequent encouragement and suggestions on what they had delivered in each teaching session, which is "strong impulse pushing each other to move forward when encountering obstacles during our learning to teach" (2nd FG). More specifically, due to the convenience and strengths triggered by the Cloud technology, these preservice teachers could reach the teacher educators "at each other's most convenience without the barriers of geographical areas" (1st FG). Some of them chose to "leave a message inside the Messenger which could be replied a bit later when we were too busy to have a discussion at the same time" (1st FG). The others would like to "have instant synchronous discussion with the two patient [teacher educators] on the synchronous platform as there was an urgent need to deal with the teaching difficulties [they] were facing" (2nd FG).

Finally, more than four-fifths of these prospective teachers (N=17) contended that the online practicum experience would be beneficial for their future classroom instruction. All of them mainly underscored the significance of blending in-class instruction with online learning platforms for their future students. Typically, one described, "If possible, I'd like to try a blended instructional module by integrating both face-to-face and asynchronous or synchronous learning platform, just like what we are learning from this TEFL Methodology course" (2nd FG). Additionally, 13 out of these participants regarded this online practicum experience as the cornerstone of strengthening their competence in applying ICT tools into language classrooms. Two of them reiterated, "If I could manage the use of multimedia tools online, there shouldn't be any problems for me to use them in a classroom setting" (2nd FG). "The more I get used to using all the interesting tools on the JoinNet platform, the more confidence I become to serve as a high-tech English teacher in this digital education era" (2nd RJ). Furthermore, 11 of these teacher candidates stated that they could transfer the classroom management experience they had as well as the pedagogical skills they practiced online into face-to-face instruction. Take two participants' reflection as examples. "I learned how important it is to control students' noisy behavior and crazy reaction when they are playing games with peers online. I guess this is the same as what we may come across in real classroom settings" (1st FG). "I normally would use CLT [communicative language teaching] activities or the concept of MI [multiple intelligences] in the two online teaching projects. There is no doubt that I could sharpen these TEFL teaching skills and put them into my future classroom practice" (2nd RJ).

Difficulties or Concerns Encountered

Notwithstanding the aforementioned positive learning experience, around half of the participating teachers (N=9) appeared to encounter four major difficulties or concerns during this technology professional development. To begin with, most of them felt perplexed about how to integrate several language teaching approaches/methods into each session of online teaching practice. When requested to design and implement teaching projects with different themes, these trainee teachers encountered difficulties in choosing other supplementary teaching approaches or methods to match online project-based instruction at the same time. As confessed by one preservice teacher, "We have no ideas about how to apply different teaching approaches, such as *Communicative Language Teaching*, *Whole Language*, and *Project-based Instruction*, all together into our teaching practice yet" (1st FG). These trainees often revealed uncertainty when having face-to-face discussions with the *TEFL Methodology* course instructor.

From time to time, [these preservice teachers] asked me to repeat explaining which method could match their teaching sessions in a pedagogically sound way. I encouraged them to brainstorm together as a group by referring to role models they had observed in my class. (FN- December 10, 2013)

Additionally, choosing the best teaching activities or multimedia to motivate students' online learning was a great challenge to them as a novice teacher. For instance, two of them maintained that "There are heaps of stuffs in the online multimedia, so sometimes we found it difficult to decide which one would be better than the other" (2nd FG). "Our group members were usually uncertain about which teaching game students like best. For example, some were crazy about the *Explosion Game* we played last time, but the others seemed not interested in it" (1st FG). Both teacher educators commented on these trainee teachers' failure in designing several games "because the game regulations were a bit complex for elementary school students to follow" or "the design of games did not include encouraging rewards for the winning side" (2nd IN).

Furthermore, not enough training of online assessment skills made these participants solely relied on quizzes to evaluate student learning outcome. Typically, it was confessed that "As most members in my group had not taken any language assessment course, it sounds not so professional that we usually gave students quizzes to check whether they had acquired what we taught them" (1st RJ). The course instructor noted that "When asked to replace some quizzes with communication-oriented assessment techniques, some of [these preservice teachers] were not familiar with the related testing skills. So, obviously not all the groups could follow my suggestion" (FN- April 29, 2014). With a voice, one of the teacher educators added, "I know they are not ready for online assessment since most of them confessed to me that they had no related background knowledge about it" (1st IN). The other described, "They seemed not very clear about why language assessment counts a lot for students' online learning…. If they keep using quizzes, that will make students bored and even lose learning interest" (2nd IN).

Finally, online classroom management is a difficult lesson for the teacher candidates to learn in distance education. For instance, when facing students' negative learning experience, one of them stated, "I have done my best to console and encourage those students who are not able to catch up with my teaching, yet they still looked upset and timid" (2nd FG). The other also confessed "I really could not handle the chaos when those kids were going nuts with the outcome of competitive games that our group included in the teaching flow. They were too mad to settle down themselves during the class session" (1st FG). Both teacher educators highlighted this issue which was a challenging obstacle for preservice teachers to conduct successful online instruction. For example, one of them explained that "Most of [the preservice teachers] had no experience in managing students in real classroom context. So, it is out of my depth to help them manage, if not discipline, elementary school students' behaviors in distance learning" (2nd IN).

Facilitating and Hindering Factors of Mentoring

Both teacher educators reported three positive factors contributing to the success of their online mentoring experience in this research project, including 1) mentees' proficient computer literacy, 2) *TEFL Methodology* course instructor's constant collaboration, and 3) explicit assessment rubrics on mentees' teaching performance. First, the two professionals regarded these preservice teachers' basic computer skills as an essential requirement "for us to facilitate their readiness of using the platform functions and multimedia in two teaching projects" (1st IN). According to the present researcher's observation, "It's a success in this series of technology training workshops. Only two preservice teachers were a bit slow in picking up what was taught in the workshops. The others were good at learning how to manage the platform functions" (FN- November 28, 2013).

Second, two teacher educators complimented on the methodology course instructor's cooperation with them during the mentoring process. When interviewed, they kept reiterating, "It's of great importance to have your liaison between these mentees and us. This saves us a lot of efforts to communicate with them" (1st IN). "Without your support, we could not make it happen to guide the teacher candidates how to do what they have to do as an online teacher" (2nd IN).

Third, the teaching practice evaluation checklist set up by the methodology course instructor assisted these teacher educators to "check the strengths and drawbacks of each group's teaching practices with technology integration" (1st IN). One teacher educator further contended, "We prefer to rely on the checklist you designed for this online practicum. It's more objective for us to keep track of [preservice teachers'] performance in each teaching session" (2nd IN). As shown in the field notes, "The mentors usually referred to the evaluation checklist when making comments or suggestions on preservice teachers' specific teaching behavior. For example, they reminded mentees of paying attention to students' reaction or feedback to their instruction on the discussion forum tonight" (FN- June 4, 2014).

By contrast, four constraints appeared to hinder these teacher educators' technology-based mentoring from fostering these preservice teachers' online teaching practices: 1) limited number of online mentors, 2) mentees' insufficient background knowledge of elementary English education, 3) timetable clashes among mentors and mentees for synchronous discussion, and 4) introverted mentees' hesitation of joining online face-to-face discussion. The first issue was concerned with lack of manpower to supervise 20 mentees in this Cloud-based practicum. One explained why there was a need to have a cohort of 4 to 5 mentors in this program. "Sometimes it was far beyond the workload we could burden when all the five groups finished their teaching session at the same time, and we needed to have discussion with each group in two consecutive weeks" (2nd IN). The other stressed that "if we could have more colleagues to work together, we could take turns to take care of these preservice teachers' learning to teach online" (2nd IN).

Additionally, it seemed that the efficiency of mentoring was influenced by the background knowledge espoused by most mentees who had very limited experience in teaching English to elementary school students. Both teacher educators raised their concerns in sharing successful online instruction with those preservice teachers who appeared to overestimate or underestimate K-12 children's learning outcome. As one of the mentors stressed,

It is tough to explain everything clear to them if they have unclear idea about what the focus of keeping track of elementary school students' learning achievement is. They have to make themselves familiar with the teaching goals and competence indicators prescribed by our Ministry of Education. (2nd IN)

Furthermore, what made the mentors a challenge to interact with their mentees on the synchronous platform was due to the conflicts among each other's available time slots. One of the teacher educators mentioned, "Everybody is busy, so it's not always easy for us to have the same free time and gather together online" (1st IN). Except for the group reflective discussions pre-scheduled by the teacher researcher, "the participants usually had no choice but to choose asynchronous discussion, despite that most of them were planning to make good use of real-time communication between or among individuals which was feasible on this Cloud platform" (FN- May 13, 2014).

Finally, the other reason was attributed to several mentee's introverted personality causing their shyness and hesitation in oral discussion. One teacher educator expressed that "I am quite good at mentoring timid students in face-to-face settings because we could use 'spiritual' eye contacts and gestures to touch upon their heart. Yet, I found it really tough to reach this point when it's to communicate with these preservice teachers in a remote status via the computer monitor" (2nd IN). In a similar vein, the present researcher observed that "Some shy preservice teachers preferred to leave written messages on the asynchronous discussion forums. They tended to often keep quiet during the synchronous group discussion sessions" (FN- June 10, 2014).

SOLUTIONS AND RECOMMENDATIONS

The above findings provide a complex picture depicting the range of interactions among the participating preservice teachers, online teacher educators, and the present researcher within this flexible and supportive mentoring mechanism. These prospective teachers showed their motivation in applying a blended teaching module and confidence in infusing more ICT tools in their future language classroom, despite that the virtual teaching experiences promoted in the current project may not fully guarantee these prospective teachers' instructional performance in face-to-face settings. The positive evidence emerging from data sources reveals the potential of employing similar integrated models to foster preservice EFL teachers' technology professional development. Yet, solutions need to be discussed to deal with the difficulties or concerns encountered by these preservice teachers and the possible factors hindering the effectiveness of mentoring.

The present researcher would encourage adoption of the following mentoring guidelines to further enhance professional development for all preservice teachers and improve the mentoring model. First, adding online microteaching experience into traditional face-to-face teaching practices during the methodology course instruction is key to alleviate preservice teachers' perplexity and concern regarding how to integrate several language teaching approaches/methods into online instruction. To save the time for more microteaching activities, a flipped classroom approach for professional development (McDonald & Smith, 2013) may be employed in the *TEFL Methodology* course to make preservice teachers familiar with theory-related content before class and then have them concentrate on practice *per se* during meeting sessions. Also included in the flipped classroom could be an introduction to English education at different school levels, which may solve mentees' dilemma in lacking sufficient background knowledge about their target students. Second, providing more "role models" of arousing elementary school students' learning motivation (via either video-taped teaching videos or on-site demonstrations) may be attempted to help preservice teachers integrate similar teaching activities or choosing applicable multimedia online. Third, as to preservice teachers' limited knowledge of evaluating student learning outcome and disciplining student learning behavior on the Cloud platform, the future mentoring model may consider including training workshops with a specific focus on online language assessment and management skills which are different from traditional in-class modules at elementary school contexts. This in turn will equip preservice teachers with more related knowledge of instructing elementary English education. Fourth, the future researchers may recruit more teacher educators to serve as a cohort of mentors, which will reduce individual mentor's supervision workload and allocate more free meeting time slots among each other to avoid timetable clash problems. Finally, with regard to timid preservice teachers' hesitation in joining online real-time discussion, perhaps including informal face-to-face discussions among mentors and mentees would develop "closer bonds between members both within and between groups" during their professional development (Thang, Hall, Murugaiah, & Azman, 2011, p. 100).

FUTURE RESEARCH DIRECTIONS

As highlighted in the theme of this edited book, little has been documented concerning how foreign language teachers learn to teach with technology and why they succeed or fail in reaching the aim of technology integration in instructional practice. One of the determinants is available training and mentoring mechanism in which teachers could engage themselves during professional growth process.

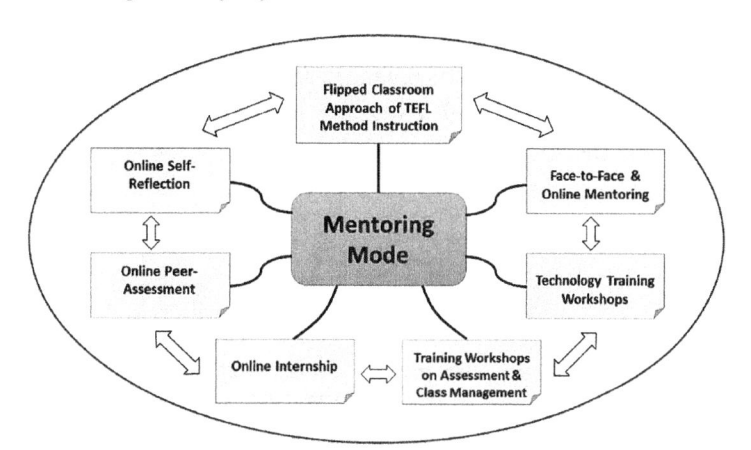

Figure 4. Proposed mentoring model for future research

Researchers contend that there is always a need to propose potential mentoring models to test, verify, and reinforce teacher candidates' technology infusion in future classroom contexts (e.g., Haydn & Barton, 2007; Pachler, Daly, & Turvey, 2010). In the future, the model of mentoring preservice EFL teachers' technology growth may become more fluid and interrelated between/among designed elements. Referring to the research findings of the present study, a viable model is further proposed to be investigated (see Figure 4). For example, the traditional in-class *TEFL Methodology* course could be taught by a flipped classroom approach. Online mentoring discussion may be incorporated with face-to-face communication or negotiation, if needed. Professional development workshops include not only technology training but also online language assessment and management skills. A cohort of professional mentors could be invited to nurture teacher candidates' knowledge construction.

CONCLUSION

This research project shows the potential of technology-based mentoring program on enhancing preservice EFL teachers' professional development. Coupled with in-class training of TEFL methodology and online instructional experience, these participants had a great chance to transfer what they had learned into Cloud-based practicum via peer review and self-reflection which are beneficial for design-based teaching practices (Chen & Chan, 2011; Koh & Divaharan, 2011). Different from the previous related literature, these teacher candidates further received the rapport and guidance from two online teacher educators without geographical barriers. The originality of keeping track of preservice teachers' technology professional learning process from course-based training to engaging in online classroom practices remains less studied in the foreign language or EFL teacher education field.

Investigation on the effectiveness of online mentoring and internship on preservice foreign language teachers' technology professional development is still in its infancy. Studies conducted with more participants and various data collection methods in different online contexts are encouraged to sketch, chart, and map a promising landscape for foreign language education in the current digital era.

ACKNOWLEDGMENT

This research was sponsored by the Ministry of Science and Technology in the Republic of China under grant number of MOST 102-2410-H-029-049. I am most grateful to anonymous reviewers and the editors for their valuable suggestions.

REFERENCES

Allaire, S., & Laferriere, T. (2005). The knowledge-building oriented virtual practicum. In C. Crawford et al. (Eds.), *Proceedings of Society for Information Technology & Teacher Education International Conference 2005* (pp. 800-804). Chesapeake, VA: AACE.

Archambault, L. M., & Barnett, J. H. (2010). Revisiting technological pedagogical content knowledge: Exploring the TPACK framework. *Computers & Education*, *55*(4), 1656–1662. doi:10.1016/j.compedu.2010.07.009

Barnett, M. (2006). Using a web-based professional development system to support preservice teachers in examining authentic classroom practice. *Journal of Technology and Teacher Education*, *14*(4), 701–729.

Chai, C. S., Koh, J. H. L., & Tsai, C. C. (2010). Facilitating preservice teachers' development of technological, pedagogical, and content knowledge (TPACK). *Journal of Educational Technology & Society*, *13*(4), 63–73.

Chai, C. S., Koh, J. H. L., Tsai, C. C., & Tan, L. L. W. (2011). Modeling primary school pre-service teachers' technological pedagogical content knowledge (TPACK) for meaningful learning with information and communication technology (ICT). *Computers & Education*, *57*(1), 1184–1193. doi:10.1016/j.compedu.2011.01.007

Chen, C. H., & Chan, L. H. (2011). Effectiveness and impact of technology-enabled project-based learning with the use of process prompts in teacher education. *Journal of Technology and Teacher Education*, *19*(2), 141–167.

Chien, Y. T., Chang, C. Y., Yeh, T. K., & Chang, K. E. (2012). Engaging pre-service science teachers to act as active designers of technology integration: A MAGDAIRE framework. *Teaching and Teacher Education*, *28*(4), 578–588. doi:10.1016/j.tate.2011.12.005

Corbin, J., & Strauss, A. (2007). *Basics of qualitative research: Techniques and procedures for developing grounded theory* (3rd ed.). Thousand Oaks, CA: Sage Publications.

Develotte, C., Guichon, N., & Vincent, C. (2010). The use of the webcam for teaching a foreign language in a desktop videoconferencing environment. *ReCALL*, *22*(3), 293–312. doi:10.1017/S0958344010000170

Doering, A., Veletsianos, G., Scharber, C., & Miller, C. (2009). Using the technological, pedagogical and content knowledge framework to design online learning environments and professional development. *Journal of Educational Computing Research*, *41*(3), 319–346. doi:10.2190/EC.41.3.d

Dooly, M., & Masats, D. (2011). Closing the loop between theory and praxis: New models in EFL teaching. *ELT Journal*, *65*(1), 42–51. doi:10.1093/elt/ccq017

Frey, T. (2008). Determining the impact of online practicum facilitation for inservice teachers. *Journal of Technology and Teacher Education, 16*(2), 181–210.

Funkhouser, B. J., & Mouza, C. (2013). Drawing on technology: An investigation of preservice teacher beliefs in the context of an introductory educational technology course. *Computers & Education, 62,* 271–285. doi:10.1016/j.compedu.2012.11.005

Gentry, L. B., Denton, C. A., & Kurz, T. (2008). Technologically-based mentoring provided to teachers: A synthesis of the literature. *Journal of Technology and Teacher Education, 16*(3), 339–373.

Haydn, T. A., & Barton, R. (2007). Common needs and different agendas: How trainee teachers make progress in their ability to use ICT in subject teaching. Some lessons from the UK. *Computers & Education, 49*(4), 1018–1036. doi:10.1016/j.compedu.2005.12.006

Holmes, K. (2009). Planning to teach with digital tools: Introducing the interactive whiteboard to pre-service secondary mathematics teachers. *Australasian Journal of Educational Technology, 25*(3), 351–365. doi:10.14742/ajet.1139

Howard, J. (2002). Technology-enhanced project-based learning in teacher education: Addressing the goals of transfer. *Journal of Technology and Teacher Education, 10*(3), 343–364.

Jang, S. J. (2008). The effects of integrating technology, observation and writing into a teacher education method course. *Computers & Education, 50*(3), 853–865. doi:10.1016/j.compedu.2006.09.002

Jang, S. J., & Chen, K. C. (2010). From PCK to TPACK: Developing a transformative model fro pre-service science teachers. *Journal of Science Education and Technology, 19*(6), 553–564. doi:10.1007/s10956-010-9222-y

Jimoyiannis, A. (2010). Designing and implementing an integrated technological science knowledge framework for science teachers professional development. *Computers & Education, 55*(3), 1259–1269. doi:10.1016/j.compedu.2010.05.022

Jiyoon, Y. (2008). Cyber practicum: A future practicum classroom. *British Journal of Educational Technology, 39*(1), 163–165.

Kennedy, K., & Archambault, L. (2012). Design and Development of Field Experiences in K-12 Online Learning Environments. *The Journal of Applied Instructional Design, 2*(1), 35–48.

Knapczyk, D. R., Hew, K. F., & Frey, T. J. (2005). Evaluation of online mentoring of practicum for limited licensed teachers. *Teacher Education and Special Education: The Journal of the Teacher Education Division of the Council for Exceptional Children, 28*(3-4), 207–220. doi:10.1177/088840640502800407

Koehler, M. J., Mishra, P., & Yahya, K. (2007). Tracing the development of teacher knowledge in a design seminar: Integrating content, pedagogy and technology. *Computers & Education, 49*(3), 740–762. doi:10.1016/j.compedu.2005.11.012

Koh, J. H. L., & Divaharan, S. (2011). Developing pre-service teachers' technology integration expertise through the TPACK-developing instructional model. *Journal of Educational Computing Research, 44*(1), 35–58. doi:10.2190/EC.44.1.c

Lan, Y. J., Chang, K. E., & Chen, N. S. (2012). CoCAR: An online synchronous training model for empowering ICT capacity of teachers of Chinese as a foreign language. *Australasian Journal of Educational Technology, 28*(6), 1020–1038. doi:10.14742/ajet.808

Lavy, I., & Shriki, A. (2008). Investigating changes in prospective teachers' views of a 'good teacher' while engaging in computerized project-based learning. *Journal of Mathematics Teacher Education, 11*(4), 259–284. doi:10.1007/s10857-008-9073-0

Lawless, K. A., & Pellegrino, J. W. (2007). Professional development in integrating technology into teaching and learning: Knowns, unknowns, and ways to pursue better questions and answers. *Review of Educational Research, 77*(4), 575–614. doi:10.3102/0034654307309921

Marshall, J. A., Petrosino, A. J., & Martin, T. (2010). Preservice teachers' conceptions and enactments of project-based instruction. *Journal of Science Education and Technology, 19*(4), 370–386. doi:10.1007/s10956-010-9206-y

Martin, S., & Vallance, M. (2008). The impact of synchronous inter-networked teacher training in Information and Communication Technology integration. *Computers & Education, 51*(1), 34–53. doi:10.1016/j.compedu.2007.04.001

McDonald, K., & Smith, C. M. (2013). The flipped classroom for professional development: Part I. Benefits and strategies. *Journal of Continuing Education in Nursing, 44*(10), 437–438. doi:10.3928/00220124-20130925-19 PMID:24098988

Mouza, C., Karchmer-Klein, R., Nandakumar, R., & Ozden, S. Y. (2014). Investigating the impact of an integrated approach to the development of preservice teachers' technological pedagogical content knowledge (TPACK). *Computers & Education, 71*, 206–221. doi:10.1016/j.compedu.2013.09.020

Nicholson, S. A., & Bond, N. (2003). Collaborative reflection and professional community building: An analysis of preservice teachers' use of an electronic discussion board. *Journal of Technology and Teacher Education, 11*(2), 259–279.

Niess, M. L. (2011). Investigating TPACK: Knowledge growth in teaching with technology. *Journal of Educational Computing Research, 44*(3), 299–317. doi:10.2190/EC.44.3.c

Pachler, N., Daly, C., & Turvey, A. (2010). Teacher professional development practices: The case of the Haringey transformation teachers programme. In J. O. Lindberg & A. D. Olofsson (Eds.), *Online learning communities and teacher professional development* (pp. 77–95). Hershey, PA: Information Science Publishing. doi:10.4018/978-1-60566-780-5.ch005

Pamuk, S. (2012). Understanding preservice teachers' technology use through TPACK framework. *Journal of Computer Assisted Learning, 28*(5), 425–439. doi:10.1111/j.1365-2729.2011.00447.x

Pierson, M. E., & McNeil, S. (2000). Preservice technology integration through collaborative action communities. *Contemporary Issues in Technology & Teacher Education, 1*(1), 189–199.

Polly, D., Mims, C., Shepherd, C. E., & Inan, F. (2010). Evidence of impact: Transforming teacher education with preparing tomorrow's teachers to teach with technology (PT3) grants. *Teaching and Teacher Education, 26*(4), 863–870. doi:10.1016/j.tate.2009.10.024

Roessingh, H., & Chambers, W. (2011). Project-based learning and pedagogy in teacher preparation: Staking out the theoretical mid-ground. *International Journal of Teaching and Learning in Higher Education*, *23*(1), 60–71.

Seo, K. K., Templeton, R., & Pellegrino, D. (2008). Creating a ripple effect: Incorporating multimedia-assisted project-based learning in teacher education. *Theory into Practice*, *47*(3), 259–265. doi:10.1080/00405840802154062

Silverman, D. (2006). *Interpreting qualitative data: Methods for analyzing talk, text, and interaction* (3rd ed.). London: SAGE Publications.

Smith, S. J., & Robinson, S. (2003). Technology integration through collaborative cohorts preparing future teachers to use technology. *Remedial and Special Education*, *24*(3), 154–160. doi:10.1177/07419325030240030401

So, H. J., & Kim, B. (2009). Learning about problem based learning: Student teachers integrating technology, pedagogy and content knowledge. *Australasian Journal of Educational Technology*, *25*(1), 101–116. doi:10.14742/ajet.1183

Sutherland, L., Howard, S., & Markauskaite, L. (2010). Professional identity creation: Examining the development of beginning preservice teachers' understanding of their work as teachers. *Teaching and Teacher Education*, *26*(3), 455–465. doi:10.1016/j.tate.2009.06.006

Thang, S. M., Hall, C., Murugaiah, P., & Azman, H. (2011). Creating and maintaining online communities of practice in Malaysian smart schools: Challenging realities. *Educational Action Research*, *19*(1), 87–105. doi:10.1080/09650792.2011.547724

Tondeur, J., van Braak, J., Sang, G., Voogt, J., Fisser, P., & Ottenbreit-Leftwich, A. (2012). Preparing pre-service teachers to integrate technology in education: A synthesis of qualitative evidence. *Computers & Education*, *59*(1), 134–144. doi:10.1016/j.compedu.2011.10.009

Vallance, M. (2007). An information and communications technology (ICT)-enabled method for collecting and collating information about pre-service teachers' pedagogical beliefs regarding the integration of ICT. *Research in Learning Technology*, *15*(1), 51–65. doi:10.1080/09687760601129851

van Olphen, M. (2007). Perspectives of foreign language preservice teachers on the use of a web-based instructional environment in a methods course. *CALICO Journal*, *25*(1), 91–109.

Vannatta, R., Beyerbach, B., & Walsh, C. (2001). From teaching technology to using technology to enhance student learning: Preservice teachers' changing perceptions of technology infusion. *Journal of Technology and Teacher Education*, *9*(1), 105–127.

Wang, Y., Chen, N. S., & Levy, M. (2010). Teacher training in a synchronous cyber face-to-face classroom: Characterizing and supporting the online teachers' learning process. *Computer Assisted Language Learning*, *23*(4), 277–293. doi:10.1080/09588221.2010.493523

Young, J. R., Young, J. L., & Shaker, Z. (2012). Describing pre-service teacher technological pedagogical content knowledge (TPACK) literature using confidence intervals. *TechTrends*, *56*(5), 25–33. doi:10.1007/s11528-012-0600-6

KEY TERMS AND DEFINITIONS

Field-Based Experience: An instructional practice that (preservice) teachers conducted in authentic contexts where they test teaching skills, strategies, or techniques.

Online Practicum: Teaching practice that (preservice) teachers experience in the Web-based context.

Peer Assessment: An alternative of traditional teacher-oriented assessment in which peers review and assess each other's performance on assigned learning tasks.

Project-Based Instruction: An authentic instructional strategy in which (preservice) teachers design and implement student-centered learning activities related to real-world application.

Role Model: A teaching practice sample demonstrating particular skills, strategies, or techniques for (preservice) teachers' reference.

Self-Reflection: An alternative of traditional teacher-oriented assessment in which learners review and reflect on their own achievement in assigned learning tasks.

Technology Infusion: An application of technology-related activities into instructional practice.

APPENDIX 1: INDIVIDUAL TEACHING PRACTICE EVALUATION CHECKLIST

I. Teaching Activities and Behaviors
- ☐ Teach vocabulary assigned to be covered
- ☐ Include warm-up activities
- ☐ Include review activities
- ☐ Include teaching activities or games
- ☐ Use classroom English
- ☐ Have interaction with students
- ☐ Keep track of student learning process
- ☐ Offer guided questions to enhance student learning
- ☐ Correct student learning mistakes
- ☐ Discipline student learning behavior

II. Technology Application
   - Interactive Whiteboard
     - ☐ Use chatting textbox
     - ☐ Use Youtube video clips
     - ☐ Use vote calculation
     - ☐ Use turn-taking functions
   - Other Multimedia
     - ☐ Use Messenger functions
     - ☐ Use remote control functions
     - ☐ Use browser-sharing interface
     - ☐ Use picture/photo-editing tools

APPENDIX 2: GROUP COLLABORATION EVALUATION RUBRICS

Period_____ Group #_____ (important)
Role A: _____ Score:_____
Role B: _____ Score:_____
Role C: _____ Score:_____
Role D: _____ Score:_____
Role E: _____ Score:_____

Directions: Place the names of the peers being evaluated at the top of this page. Place the number of points in the blanks below that best describes how you feel about a peer's participation regarding each statement. Total points and fill in scores next to names.

10 points - strongly agree

Table 2.

	(A)	(B)	(C)	(D)	(E)
1. This person worked hard during class time and outside of class time to help our group meet the group objectives.					
2. This person completed their assigned role without any prodding from their group members.					
3. This person stayed with our group and did not waste time socializing in other groups.					
4. This person worked hard at accepting other members of the group and the ideas they presented.					

8 points - very much agree
6 points - agree
4 points - somewhat agree
2 points - somewhat disagree
0 points – disagree

APPENDIX 3 SAMPLE (FOCUS GROUP) INTERVIEW QUESTIONS

I. **Focus group interview questions with preservice teachers**
   1. Overall, how do you feel about the implementation of your first/second online teaching project?
   2. What are the strengths of your first/second online teaching project? Please specify the strengths and explain the reasons.
   3. What are the drawbacks, if any, of your first/second online teaching project? Please specify the drawbacks and explain the reasons.
   4. What do you think about the content you were teaching to students on the Cloud platform?
   5. What do you think about the pedagogy you used in the first/second teaching project?
   6. What do you think about the technology you applied in the first/second teaching project?
   7. Did your group apply what you have learned from the TEFL Methodology course to the first/second teaching project? Why or why not?
   8. Did your group apply what you have learned from the AAOT training workshops to the first/second teaching project? Why or why not?
   9. What do you think about your application of ICT tools into English language education either on online instructional platform or in face-to-face instruction after completing the two teaching projects?
   10. Do you think what you have learned from these online teaching projects will benefit your future classroom instruction? Why or why not?

II. **Individual interview questions with online teacher educators**
   1. According to your observation, did the preservice teachers apply appropriate ICT tools to the first/second online teaching project?
   2. What did you usually discuss and share with the preservice teachers during their online reflection after the first/second teaching project?
   3. What are the strengths of these preservice teachers' learning to teach with technology?

4. What are the drawbacks, if any, these preservice teachers need to improve in their first/second teaching project? How could they improve it/them?
5. What made your online mentoring a successful experience?
6. What were the difficulties or concerns, if any, you encountered during the online mentoring process?
7. Overall, how would you rate the effectiveness of the online mentoring on preservice teachers' technology professional development?
8. How could we improve online mentoring for future teacher preparation program, if needed?

APPENDIX 4: REFLECTION GUIDING QUESTIONS

1. What are some salient ideas and experiences you gained from this online teaching project?
2. How do think you can use the ICT tools on the JoinNet platform for your teaching practices?
3. What is your understanding of language teaching as a result of completing this teaching project?
4. How did you select technology tools with pedagogy to afford content transformations of the topics you were teaching in this teaching project?
5. What are the difficulties you encountered when preparing and implementing this teaching project?
6. How would you apply the online teaching with technology into your future English instruction?

Chapter 11
A TL-TPACK Model on CSL Pre-Service Teachers' Competencies of Online Instruction

Hsiu-Jen Cheng
National Kaohsiung Normal University, Taiwan

ABSTRACT

This chapter aims to introduce the integration of TPACK into a Chinese pre-service teacher training program and discuss its outcomes and challenges. First, the concept of TPACK was introduced and relevant TPACK research and its constraints in the previous studies were discussed. Through the partnership between a Chinese pre-service teacher training program in Taiwan and a Chinese learning program in the States, the author developed a Teaching and Learning Model, entitled TL-TPACK model, integrating practicum, course design, advisors, peer cooperation, and reflections—five training strategies to ensure the training and learning outcome. At the end of the chapter, an empirical Chinese pre-service teacher training study applying the TL-TPACK model was conducted to investigate pre- service teachers' seven TPACK competences and Chinese learners' learning performance. Finally, research implications and suggestions for future studies were discussed.

INTRODUCTION

In the 21st century, Chinese as second/foreign language (CS/FL) learning has gained great attention; numerous research began discussing Chinese learners' learning issues (Wang, 1998; Williams, 2013), but few empirical studies investigated issues in CS/FL teacher training. The development of technology has changed learners' learning behaviors and allowed users easy access to resources, and CSL/FL learners are not exceptional. If Chinese teachers possess knowledge about what digital resources are proper for certain learning purposes, they can effectively apply appropriate resources to students' in-class or after-class learning. Unfortunately, mostly Chinese teachers remain digital immigrants who have perceived technology suspiciously. Research has mentioned that many in-service teachers do not use technology in instruction (Galanouli & McNair, 2001; Sessoms, 2008), and think the impact of technology on in-

DOI: 10.4018/978-1-5225-0483-2.ch011

structional methods is peripheral (Chaptal, 2002; Zhao, Pugh, Sheldon, & Byers, 2002; Koehler, Mishra & Yahya, 2007; Teo, et al., 2008), not to mention CS/FL teachers.

The reason for this type of perspective might be due to the comfort zone with old non-technological based materials, the rapid changes of digital products (Liu & Lan, 2014), possibly the limited technology use in their teaching institutes (Bos, 2011), and age factor (Cheng, 2009; Lee & Tsai, 2010; Yeung, et al, 2014). In real classrooms, CFL/SL language teachers, especially experienced teachers, tend to embrace real objects, gestures, and non-technological materials, which are easier to use in their current language lessons and have been used for years. Yet, the rapid development of technology makes new educational tools available and begins challenging language teachers' old instructional habits. Chinese Teachers facing such complicated challenges nowadays become not only reluctant to apply technology into classroom instruction, but also uneducated about how to apply proper technology into foreign/second language instruction. Such attitudes may affect the perceptions of new teachers in the same working environment toward technology integration in FL/SL instruction. This may be one of the reasons hindering the development of technology-enhanced instruction in CF/SL teaching.

Many educational entities propose guidelines indicating the importance of preparing Chinese language teachers to use technology in educational settings (ACTFL standard, 2015; Chinese Language Association of Secondary-elementary Schools, 2015). However, the controversy between expectation and reality shows technology's integration in CF/SL education is still in its infancy. To resolve this issue, changing teachers' instructional behaviors and developing their professional knowledge of instructional technology become a crucial task that also needs more attention from scholars, educators, and teacher trainers.

TECHNOLOGY AND CHINESE TEACHER EDUCATION

Researchers found that some teacher training programs place ICT (Information and Communication Technology) courses as an elective option (Brown & Warschauer, 2006; Hsu & Sharma, 2006; Lim et al., 2010). Take teaching Chinese as CS/FL institutions in Taiwan as an example. There are approximately seventeen CS/FL teacher training institutions and only forty percent of them (around seven institutions) list this course: *Multimedia Assisted Chinese Instruction* as a requisite for undergraduate pre-service teacher programs. Out of the seven institutions, only one institution offers this course as a requisite at the master level. Considering the larger population of undergraduate students, this reality shows that pre-service Chinese teachers with a bachelor's degree may acquire more knowledge about technology instruction than those with master's degree. In general, insufficient instructional technology training offered through Chinese pre-service teacher programs is certainly evident in Taiwan, even though Taiwan is considered a high-tech country, where the accessibility of technology products for teachers is not a problem.

A successful technology integrated teacher training program should offer teachers opportunities to utilize technology to advance their professional development and promote authentic learning experiences (Hsu & Sharma, 2006). A solid theory orienting pre-service teachers to adopt technology for enhancing student learning in the classroom is necessary. Mishra and Koehler expanded Shulman's (1986) theory of Pedagogical Content Knowledge (PCK) and their new Technological Pedagogical and Content Knowledge (TPACK) framework provided pre-service or in-service teacher education with a lens to examine teachers' training outcomes from a course, workshop, or program. TPACK is a theoretical concept for teacher trainers to plan a training program that allows teachers to develop the knowledge of how to use technology with a proper pedagogical approach in certain learning subjects. The author of this chapter believes that Chinese pre-service teacher training should infuse with the concept of TPACK as both a source of guidance and an evaluation tool in order to construct a better training course that blends the concepts of technology, pedagogy, and Chinese language teaching for future Chinese teachers.

Implementing TPACK into a training curriculum involves several strategies. Matherson, Wilson, and Wright (2014) pointed out that teacher-training programs should engage authentic field instruction practices. Solving authentic instructional problems should be one promising outcome for technology based teacher training (Koehler, Mishra & Yahya, 2007; Jaipal & Figg, 2010), so field practice is an important strategy to encourage pre-service teachers using technology to resolve the authentic instructional and technological issues in specific learning context. Furthermore, real educational settings easily reflect pre-service teachers' TPACK (Gao, et al., 2011).

Regarding Chinese teacher-training programs in Chinese speaking countries, unfortunately, numerous issues hinder implementation of field-based teacher training programs. Local practicum positions are not always sufficient for all student teachers from Teaching Chinese as a Second/Foreign Language (TCS/FL) institutions, to say nothing of expecting student teachers to use technological resources in their Chinese field practices. In order to provide high quality and quantity field practices for student teachers to take advantage of technology resources in Chinese instruction, synchronous cooperation between teacher training programs and language learning programs becomes a necessity for effective teacher training. This type of cooperation establishes a partnership between second language teacher training programs in Chinese speaking countries and Chinese language teaching programs in non-Chinese speaking countries, such as the USA, Japan, and Korea (Xie, 2011; Cheng & Zhan, 2012; Liu & Lan, 2014). In the past five years, it has become a common strategy in Taiwan for Chinese teacher training programs to offer online tutors or teaching positions in conjunction with Chinese overseas learning programs. Currently, some researchers are using discourse analysis to track the teachers' performance (Yeh & Dai, 2015) and investigate the online learners' learning outcomes (Cheng & Chen, 2015), as well as teachers' pedagogical skills (Liu & Lan, 2014). However, few articles discuss teachers' TPACK professional development on using technology in Chinese classes. The author believes that online field practices integrated into pre-service Chinese teacher training courses can maximize the effectiveness of pre-service teachers' TPACK knowledge development.

Since 2010, the author has conducted a longitude pre-service Chinese teacher training study, applying TPACK and found that in addition to field practice, four other strategies—advisors' observations and reflections, peer cooperation, curriculum design, and teaching journals—also play critical roles in constructing pre-service teachers' technological and pedagogical knowledge in online Chinese courses (Cheng, 2014). In the field, unpredictable variables (e.g., student demographics, students' language level, and class sizes) may have an impact on teaching strategies, so Chinese learners' learning outcomes were not considered as a research variable in previous teacher-training research. Chinese teachers genuinely care about students' learning outcomes and perceptions of courses. It is assumed that if the teacher training model blend with well-constructed field practices, training outcomes can be considered as teachers' performances as well as students' learning outcomes. Therefore, the author expanded TPACK based training model and investigated the development of Chinese pre-service teachers' professional knowledge, as well as Chinese learners' learning outcomes after training. The framework of this training design is entitled Teaching and Learning TPACK (TL-TPACK) model. To investigate the effectiveness of TL-TPCK model, this chapter aims to answer the following research questions:

1. What is pre-service teachers' perceived progress in the seven components of TPACK?
2. What are pre-service teachers' self-reported evaluations of their TPACK performances over time?
3. As a reference of TL-TPACK training outcome, how much of Chinese learners' knowledge was retained from online sessions offered by pre-service teachers?

TPACK IN LANGUAGE TEACHER EDUCATION

Koehler and Mishra (2009) point out that teacher preparation programs should rethink teachers' professional knowledge. Knowledge of technology should not be treated as context-free. A good teacher should consider the role of technology associated with content and pedagogy. TPACK is a framework that specifies a set of knowledge that teachers need to have for effective teaching with technology. It emphasizes the connections and interplays among the three core knowledge bases: technological knowledge (TK), pedagogical knowledge (PK), and content knowledge (CK). Therefore, the additional four components are: Technological Content Knowledge (TCK), Technological Pedagogical Knowledge (TPK), Pedagogical Content Knowledge (PCK), and Technological Pedagogical and Content Knowledge (TPACK) (as shown in Figure 1). Clear definition of each component assists teacher trainers in clarifying their training context, especially when the definition is applied to specific subjects. The following section provides definitions of the seven knowledge bases of TPACK, as discussed by Mishra and Koehler. Examples associated with CS/FL training context are included to build connections between theory and application.

Figure 1. TPACK

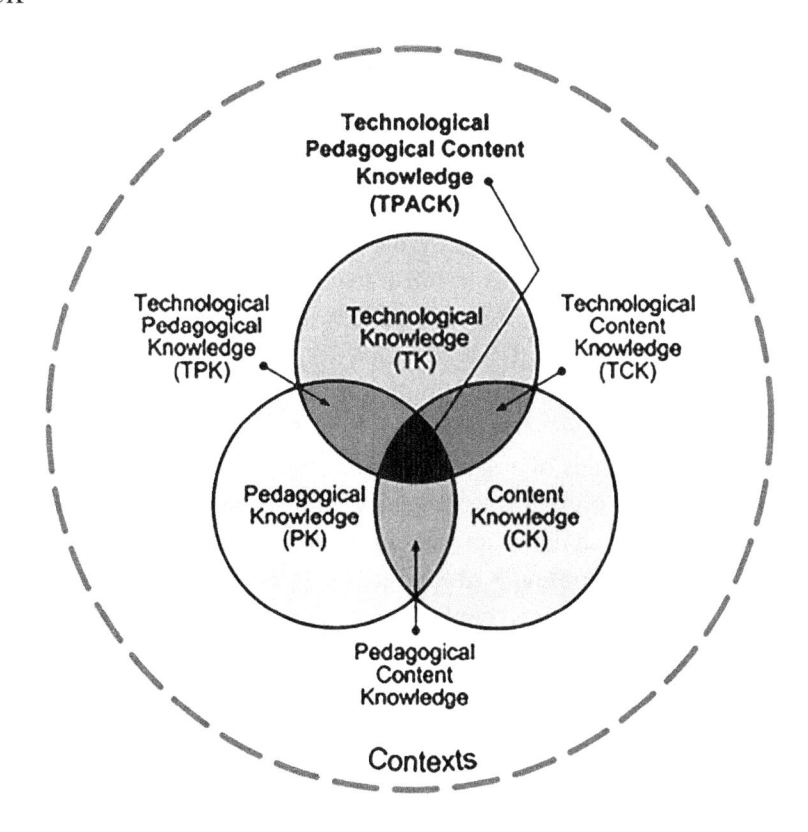

1. **Content Knowledge (CK):** teacher's knowledge of the subject to be learned or taught. Content of different disciplines varies, so learning content of different learning subjects are not covered with the same information. Content knowledge is crucial for teachers, because they are the people who transmit accurate messages regarding the course content. For CSL teachers, content knowledge can be anything associated with what they teach, such as knowledge of vocabulary definitions, grammatical or linguistic forms, knowledge of cross cultural differences, etc.
2. **Pedagogical Knowledge (PK):** teacher's knowledge of the methods and processes of learning and teaching. It can be knowledge of the student learning process, classroom management, or learning assessment. For CSL teachers, pedagogical knowledge should be knowledge of how a foreign language learner acquires another language, what learning behaviors the students may have, what challenges the students may encounter, what kinds of classroom activities or instructional strategies could promote their learning, and how to assess their language performances correctly.
3. **Technological Knowledge (TK):** TK in TPACK is the Fluency of Information Technology (FIT). More than computer technological literacy, technological knowledge refers to a deeper understanding of applying information technology to solve problems, accomplish given tasks, and promote communication. For CSL teachers, TK means knowledge of knowing what information technology can solve instructional tasks, communicate with learners, and develop appropriate learning environments.
4. **Technological Content Knowledge (TCK):** teacher knowledge of knowing the affordances and constraints of technology for the content in their disciplines. For CSL teachers, they should have knowledge of what specific technology can properly address the language content they teach, such as knowing what technological applications are suitable for speaking practices, how to use multimedia to present Chinese characters and pinyin, and how to design learning content with videos.
5. **Technological Pedagogical Knowledge (TPK):** teachers' knowledge of how teaching and learning can change when using technology in a particular way. Teachers with TPK know the affordances and constraints of pedagogical designs and technological tools respectively. Take CSL online teachers for example; videoconferencing platform is a primary tool to present classroom materials. Teachers with TPK know drawing tools allow students to get involved in speaking activities through pointing out the objects displayed on the screen. Therefore, teachers may take advantage of the drawing tools to engage students to finish language interactive tasks through negotiations, such as clarifying directions by drawing the locations and routes students intend to go.
6. **Pedagogical Content Knowledge (PCK):** teachers' knowledge of transforming subject context into teaching. This is the core concept that Shulman claimed in 1986. Teachers with PCK interpret the subjects and find appropriate ways to present the content based on learners' prior knowledge as well as knowing the methods of assessment. For CSL teachers, they know what instructional strategies can appropriately present the content, such as using the radical approach for Chinese character lessons to improve students' abilities of character recognition.
7. **Technological Pedagogical Content Knowledge (TPACK):** teachers' combination of knowledge bases from content, pedagogy, and technology. Teachers with TPACK understand the concept of effectively using technology, know what pedagogical strategies are suitable with certain technology applications for certain content, know when and when not to use technology when learning issues occur, know learners' prior knowledge, and know how technology can and cannot build new knowledge based on prior knowledge. A 21st century teacher is expected to have TPACK professional competencies, which open the door to becoming a great teacher.

Few studies examined TPACK in F/SL education, and most of them are in Teaching English as a Second Language (TESL) context. Several TPACK studies on EFL pre/in-service teachers published in recent years were from Turkey, due to national polices for developing teacher's ICT proficiencies (Oz, 2015). All the studies used surveys to assess pre-service EFL teachers' TPACK, beliefs, or skill development. With a survey from 27 EFL pre-service teachers, Koçoglu (2009) showed that EFL pre-service teachers in their last year of the teacher-training program tended to gain more PCK and TPK than other TPACK components because of increasing of practicum hours. In Ekrem's and Recep's (2014) study, 137 EFL Turkish pre-service teachers' responses were collected through a survey and the results showed that male teachers' TK was better than female teachers', and female teachers' PK was better than male teachers'. This finding was consistent with Oz's (2015) finding. Additionally, TPACK and the seven components were strongly correlated, especially the ones between PCK and CK, and between PCK and PK. Similarly, Oz's (2015) study on 76 EFL pre-service teachers who were simultaneously taking a practicum course during their final semester revealed that teachers' TK and PK were highly developed, as opposed to TCK and PCK. One major flaw of these studies is that very limited information of language teacher training programs was provided.

Liu and Lan (2014) strongly recommended that practices of TPACK should be offered in the real classrooms, where pre-service teachers are able to identify instructional problems, learning issues, and appropriateness of technology use. Kurt et al.'s (2013) TPACK study of 22 Turkish pre-service English teachers within a 12-week training period incorporated course designs, peer reviews, group discussions, and field practices. Those pre-service teacher's TK, TCK, TPK and TPACK scores were significantly different pre and post training course. With real classroom practices, the findings reflected more realistic outputs.

Despite surveys as a robust instrument to assess teacher' TPACK, teacher self-reports may not fully reflect the reality. When pre-service teachers practice in the field, their students' perceptions toward the teacher's TPACK can also be considered as a reference. Tseng (2014) collected 257 high school English learners 'perceptions toward three pre-service teacher's TPACK performance in Taiwan. Students of this study perceived that their teachers' CK was stronger than their TPACK. Unfortunately, this study did not report the validity and reliability of research instruments. Tai (2015) offered a 5-week TPACK-in-Action CALL (Computer assisted Language Learning) workshop for 24 full-time English elementary teachers in Taiwan with 5-step training procedures: modeling, analyzing, demonstrating, application, and reflections. Results showed that TPACK based workshops can positively impact English teachers' CALL competencies. However, this study treated TPACK only as holistic and integrated knowledge, so detailed analysis of other TPACK components were not discussed.

A longitude TPACK Chinese teacher training study was conducted by the author. The major research context of this study was Teaching Chinese as a Second Language in Taiwan. A 12-week long training, incorporated with online field practices, was implemented in 2011 (Cheng & Zhan, 2012) with 14 pre-service teachers, in 2012 with 9 participants (Cheng, 2013 and 2014), and in 2013 with 8 pre-services teachers, respectively. Survey responses showed pre-service teachers rated field practices and intern advisors as the top two promising strategies assisting them in developing TPACK competencies. Pre-service teachers believed CK was gained through online field practices and promoted through peer cooperation. Field practice, intern advisors, and peer cooperation are effective training strategies to develop TK, PK, and CK. Pre-service teachers' journals reflected TPK, PK, PCK, and TK. However, CK and TPACK were missing.

Table 1 Comparisons of TPACK foreign language studies

Studies	TPACK development	Training
Koçoglu (2009)	PCK and TPK	No
Oz (2015)	TK and PK	No
Kurt et al.'s (2013)	TK, TCK, TPK and TPACK	Yes (12 weeks)
Cheng, 2014	TK, PK, CK, TPK, and PCK	Yes (12weeks)

Overall, the results of foreign language pre-service teachers' TPACK studies were inconsistent. As Table 1 shows, the only overlap among the three language pre-service teacher training studies was TK. When considering the two training studies (Kurt et al., 2013; Cheng, 2014), pre-service teacher's TK and TPK were developed. Therefore, TK and TPK are the two competencies that easily presented. However, it is still dangerous to draw such conclusions due to the insufficient number of subsequent studies. Additional empirical data from TPACK studies on language teacher training is required to validate these measurements.

TL-TPACK MODEL

In order to provide a more comprehensive training model for CSL teachers, the author developed the TL-TPACK training model and included authentic tasks during training based on the knowledge components of TPACK. Online instructional design, advising, peer cooperation, reflection, and field practices were all incorporated in this training model.

As showed in Figure 2, the TL-TPACK model was implemented in four phases: preparation, practicum, reflection, and evaluation. The first three phases can be administered repeatedly as a circular process according to numbers of practicum lessons.

Online platforms served as the major channel to deliver technology-enhanced instruction for participants of this study. During the preparation phases, pre-service teachers' TK was first trained to include skills of videoconferencing platform functions and digital multimedia creations. Due to instabilities of Internet speed among participants, two online platforms were employed: Nefsis and WiziQ (Figure 3). The former was the primary platform and the latter served as the backup. Pre-service teachers of this study took two 3-hour in-class sessions and spent approximately 5 hours out of class becoming familiar with the online platforms, including how to schedule an online session, set up auto-recording, upload documents, activate users' audio/video devices, type Chinese characters and phonetic symbols, and use platform tools (pen and drawing) to enhance instruction. Furthermore, locating, editing, and applying multimedia resources, such as graphics, text, audio, and video clips, were part of the requirements for this training course.

Pre-service teachers' CK and PCK were trained through familiarity of the textbook that they were going to teach. Being familiar with the words and grammar listed in the textbook was a key step in designing an effective lesson. In addition, pre-service teachers added 5 to 7 new words associated with the theme of each lessons as supplementary content.

Their PK was trained through discussions of second language acquisition (e.g., Krashen i+1 and spiral design) and writing a lesson plan for oral Chinese training cooperatively with their team member.

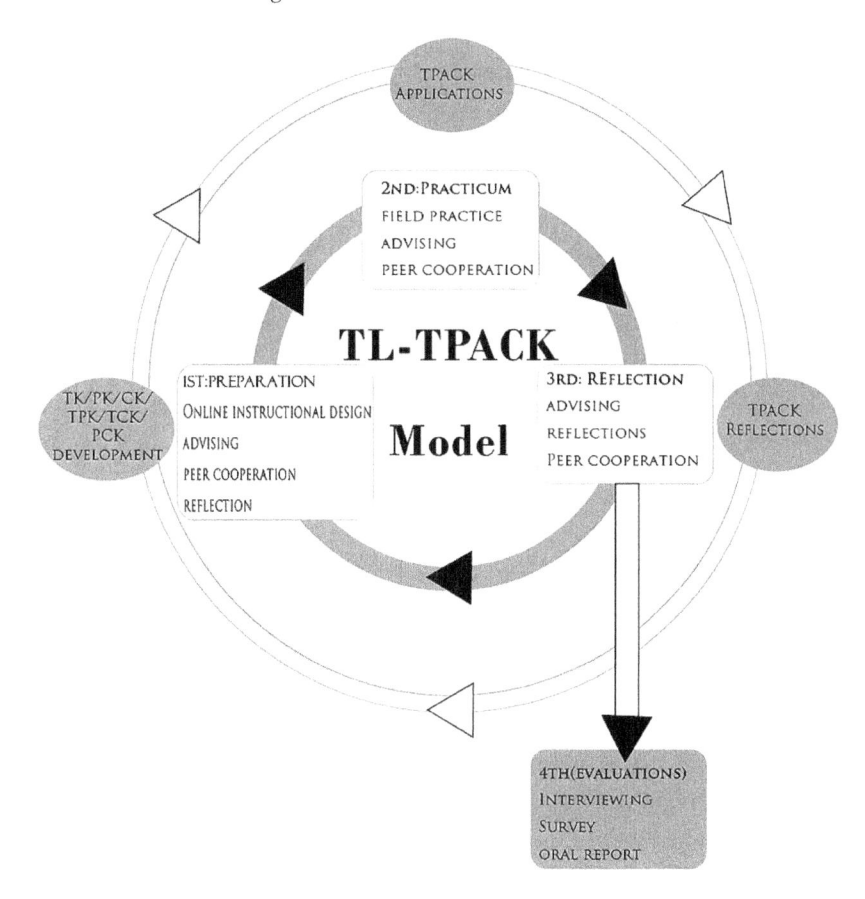

Figure 2. TL-TPACK teacher training model

Pre-service teachers needed follow Krashen's i+1 theory when choosing words and grammatical pattern. Regarding TPK and TCK, they were required to design their multimedia-supported presentations accordingly and used digital multimedia in their questions, tasks, and activities.

During the field practice phase, the pre-service teachers implemented their lesson plans through video conference. A total of five online sessions were arranged every other week during the study. In each session, a pre-service teacher assisted CSL students in practicing oral Chinese based on what students have already learned. During the online teaching session, the peer teacher and advisors (training advisor and master advisor) observed the lessons. In this stage, pre-service teachers performed their TPACK as TPACK application.

During the reflections phase, right after the completion of each online lesson, the training and master advisors shared their immediate feedback. Training advisors collected all of the observation notes and shared important issues during the face-to-face training sessions. The pre-service teachers finished the TPACK structured journals each time. During this stage, pre-service teachers were assessed by advisors, self-assessed their TPACK, and shared their feedback with advisors, collectively constituting a TPACK reflective stage.

During the evaluation phase, pre-service CSL teachers were evaluated through semi-structured interviews and surveys at the end of the training. CSL learners reported what they had learned in Chinese. This stage was aimed to review pre-service teacher participants' overall performance.

Figure 3. Snapshot of Nefsis (left) and WiziQ (right)

*Numbers are referring to the same functions between two platforms.

RESEARCH METHODOLOGY

This study employed a *mixed-method* approach and data were collected from *field practices*, *training procedures*, and *different tools of measurements*. Due to the small sample size of this research, qualitative content analysis of teaching reflections and quantitative calculations from pre-service teacher and learners' responses to surveys were administered. In the fall semester of 2014, this study selected eleven pre-service teachers at a graduate program of a national university in Taiwan and eleven American learners from a mid-west private university in the United States. All of the pre-service teachers were recruited through convenience sampling from those enrolled in *Distance Education* offered by the graduate institute of TCS/FL in Taiwan. Each teacher was paired with an American student for the field practice. Four Chinese learners participated voluntarily and seven Chinese learners were recruited from *Chinese 303* offered by an undergraduate Chinese program in the States. Due to enrollment issues, two American students dropped the course. This change led to an uneven number of pairs. As a solution, S3 and S6 voluntarily took additional sessions offered by T3, T4, T7, and T8 respectively (see Table 2).

Participants

Among these eleven pre-service teachers, nine of them were second-year students, except T4 and T10, who were third year students and had taken a similar training course: *Multimedia Assisted Chinese Instruction*. Regarding their teaching experiences, prior this study, T10 left this item blank. Two pre-service teachers (T3 and T11) had no CS/FL teaching experiences. T7 had 20 teaching hours. Three pre-service teachers (T1, T4, and T8) had forty practicum hours each. T9 had 127 practicum hours. T5 and T6 had

Table 2. The participants

Participants	ID										
Teachers	T1	T2	T3	T4	T5	T6	T7	T8	T9	T10	T11
Students	S1	S2	S3	S3	S4	S5	S6	S6	S7	S8	S9

Table 3. The participants' CSL teaching experiences

Practicum hours prior this study	Pre-service teachers	Short term overseas experience
Not applicable	T10**	
No experience	T3, T11	
10	T2	
20	T7	T7
40	T1, T4**, T8	T1 and T8
127	T9	T9
1year or above	T5, T6	T5* and T6*

*T5 had 1.8 years and T6 had 1 year teaching experience as a CSL instructor or tutor at a language center

** T4 and T10 were in their third graduate year

Table 4. The students' background

Learning years	Students	Learning Text	Themes
1st year learners	S3	Integrated Chinese Level 1, Part 1	Introductions, Hobbies, Travel, Shopping, School life
2nd year learners	S1, S2, S6, S7, S8, S9	Integrated Chinese Leve2 1, Part 1	Introductions, School Life, Friends, Part-Time Jobs, Travel/ Education
3rd year learners	S4, S5	Finished Integrated Chinese Level 2 Part 2	

been instructors and tutors at a Mandarin Learning Center for 1.8 years and 1 year, respectively. Over all, most of them were considered novice teachers. Among those experiences, over half of them had short-term (from two weeks to 1 year) overseas Chinese teaching experiences.

There were nine Chinese learners who fully participated in the online lessons. Participants were divided into three groups according to their learning experiences: 1st, 2nd, and 3rd year learners. S3 was the only first year student who voluntarily joined in the study. Six 2nd year students (S1, S2, S6, S7, S8, and S9) were from the cooperative Chinese course and their online participation was graded. Two 3rd year students (S4 and S5) also voluntarily joined in this study, as shown in Table 4.

The online sessions of this study were considered supplementary lessons for a Chinese learning program in the States. These sessions were considered extracurricular activities. The purpose of the online sessions was to provide Chinese learners with more opportunities to practice their speaking and listening skills, as well as learning several new words corresponding to certain themes. The learning themes for 1st year learners included introductions, hobbies, travel, shopping, and school life. The themes for 2nd and 3rd year learners were introductions, school life, friends, part-time jobs, and travel or education (see Table 4).

Data Collection

To examine pre-service teachers' TPACK development and triangulate the findings, multiple data sources, including surveys, teaching reflections and interviews were used.

1. **TPACK Survey:** Pre- and post-surveys were conducted to collect the pre-service teachers responses associated with the seven components of TPACK after the first online session and after the completion of the last online teaching session. The survey contained two parts: demographic information and professional development of TPACK. The five questions in the demographic information section were gender, ID number, teaching experience and preparation time. Twenty-nine closed questions and two open-ended questions were included in the second part. A five-level Likert scale (1=strongly disagree, 2= disagree, 3=neutral, 4=agree, 5=strongly agree) was applied to collect the data associated with pre-service teachers' professional development. Each TPACK component had at least two related questions (Appendix 1). Most of TPACK surveys in the literature were created for general context, so the survey of this current study was cited from the author's previous study (Cheng, 2015). Cronbach's alpha was calculated through SPSS 20.0, and TPACK had an alpha coefficient of 0.84, indicating that the items had relatively high internal consistency. Pre-survey responses from eight pre-service teachers and the post-survey responses from eleven pre-service teachers were collected. To analyze the data, descriptive analysis was applied to examine the differences of TPACK's seven components. T-test was conducted to examine the differences between the pre and post surveys.

2. **TPACK Reflections:** Previous research pointed out that a structured journal could enhance self-awareness and high level reflections (Cohen-Sayag & Fischl, 2012). The current research aims to adopt a structured journal to enhance the pre-service teachers' awareness of their own TPACK development. The journal first asks pre-service teachers to evaluate their performance of the seven knowledge bases of TPACK by marking down exceed or fail after the completion of each online teaching session. Then, describe the teaching events to support the assessment in Chinese. Three different marks were used: check, X, and triangle (see Figure 4 as an example from T4). The results were analyzed based on the teacher's positive or negative responses. The check mark was converted into 1, referencing this pre-service teacher had developed certain knowledge during certain stages. The X mark was converted to 0, referencing this pre-service teacher had not developed this specific knowledge. The triangle was converted to 0.5, referencing the pre-service teacher had partially developed this specific knowledge. The qualitative data from the reflections were analyzed and cited to support findings. Teachers' reports in the numeric method were meant to monitor TPACK performances over time. Appendix 2 shows the English version. Fifty-five journals were supposed to be collected from eleven teachers. However, due to the absence of students (T3 and T4), only twenty journals were fully collected.

3. **Interviews.** Both pre-service teachers and learners were interviewed. A think-aloud interview approach was used after pre-service teachers completed the questionnaire at the end of the fifth online session (Appendix 3). "Think-aloud is a research method in which participants speak aloud any words in their mind as they complete a task" (Chapters, 2003, p1). The disadvantage of this method is possibly breaking up the flow of survey, but it is more likely to capture respondents' ideas. The researchers suggested that having respondents first answer a question and then think-aloud to the interviewer about their reasoning (Campanelli, 2012). A research assistant of the current study presented the survey questions to each pre-service teacher and read each question in Chinese for them. Interviewees of this study first told their answers and then verbally explained how they came up with each answer. The entire process was administered in Chinese. The interview of eleven pre-service teachers was videotaped and their responses were transcribed.

A TL-TPACK Model on CSL Pre-Service Teachers' Competencies of Online Instruction

Figure 4. The record of T4's evaluations on her TPACK performances on 2nd class

撰述 CK、PK、TK、TPK、TCK、TPK、PCK、TPACK 的表現與反思

	CK	PK	TK	TPK	TCK	PCK	TPACK
達成	∨	∨	∨	∨	∨		

Table 5. The summary of journal collections

ID	T1	T2	T3	T4	T5	T6	T7	T8	T9	T10	T11	Total
# of reflections	5	5	4	3	5	5	5	3	5	4	5	49

A delayed interview was also employed after the learners' completion of the fifth session. Nine CSL American students were interviewed to see how much knowledge they had retained from the previous four online sessions. The questions were showed in Appendix 3. The key graphics about the content of four classes were presented during the interview. Figure 5 shows S1's interview content, and key graphics selected from class materials of the T1-3 session. The selections were decided by the student' online teacher. Interviews were conducted mostly in Chinese, except the guidelines. Followed by the guidelines, questions including *how much do you remember this content?* and *Please describe* were asked in Chinese. Due to students of this study with three levels of Chinese, all interviewers were well-trained 3rd year graduate students of teaching Chinese as second/foreign language. While interviewing, interviewers may adjust their word selections for questioning of "*How much do you remember this content?*" accordingly. For instance, using "Qǐng shuō shuō, zhèxiē zhàopiàn" in Chinese ("tell me about what you see" in English) for lower level students instead of "Qǐngwèn nǐ jìdé zhèxiē zhàopiàn ma? Qǐng shuō shuō kàn" in Chinese (*How much do you remember this content?* and *Please describe*" in English). Students were told to answer in Chinese.

Figure 5. S1's interview content from T1-3 (friends' personalities and appearances)

RESULTS

TPACK Knowledge

Considering each of the seven components individually, all of the means in the post-survey increased from pre-survey (Table 6), but only PK (M=3.94, p=0.48), TCK (M=4.31, p=0.18) and TPACK (M=3.86, p=0.00) were statistically significantly different between pre- and post-survey, indicating that pre-service teachers' believed that their PK, TCK, and TPACK had increased after training.

The survey responses showed that 78% of pre-service teachers thought their PK knowledge had developed by the end of the training, especially on spiral based design, practices of asking open-ended questions, and practices of being aware that lessons need to ensure the learners' oral output. Also, 63% pre-service teachers positively agreed that they had increased TCK by the end of the training. TCK is associated with the adoption of digital multimedia, such as visual and audio aides, as well as tools from online platforms, to explain the new content and ensure the comprehension and output of the students. In terms of TPACK, even though its mean value tended to be lower than other components in the post survey, the differences in gain were significant (Mean different =2.24) (Table 6) and 73% of pre-service teachers positively agreed their TPACK had developed.

However, pre-service Chinese teachers' CK, TK, TPK, and PCK did not demonstrate significant differences after the fifth session. But the mean value of TK (M=4.45), CK (M=4.3), and TPK (M=4.2) still tended to be higher than other TPACK components. 91% of pre-service teachers agreed that their TK had developed by the end of training. The software and hardware that pre-service teachers utilized in this training was not very difficult to operate, and these pre-service teachers had become familiar with the techniques from the very beginning. The pre-survey showed that 78% of pre-service teachers agreed that their TK, associated with online platforms, digital multimedia materials, and Chinese characters and pinyin input, were sufficient. Since they were already familiar with the platform and the multimedia applications at the beginning of the training, there was not much progress to make towards the end of the training. TK were considered as an easy-to-develop skill within an intensive training, which corresponds to the conclusion of previous studies (Kurt et al., 2013; Cheng, 2014).

Table 6. Summary of the mean and results of T test

TPACK items	1st mean	5th mean	% of positive responses at the 1 the session	% of positive responses at the 5 the session	mean differences	Sig.
TK	4.18	4.45	78%	91%	0.27	0.227
PK	3.5	3.94	65%	78%	0.44	0.048*
CK	3.9	4.2	80%	87%	0.3	0.093
TPK	4.1	4.2	72%	84%	0.1	0.826
PCK	3.62	3.74	53%	73%	0.12	0.278
TCK	3.78	4.31	69%	91%	0.53	.018*
TPACK	1.62	3.86	19%	73%	2.24	.000*

* Significant difference

A TL-TPACK Model on CSL Pre-Service Teachers' Competencies of Online Instruction

87% of pre-service teachers agreed they had gained CK by the end of training. However, 80% of them had already developed their CK at the beginning of the training. CK played a critical role in terms of effectiveness of instruction. If pre-service teachers were not familiar with the content they taught in the beginning, they may have encountered more challenges during the online sessions. Additionally, those pre-service teachers' tasks were to accomplish only ten lessons from students textbook and they could partially controlled their own supplementary vocabularies. Therefore, CK was clearly defined with limited scope, so it is also reasonable to have such results that 80% of pre-service teachers tried to become more familiar with the content in the beginning.

Regarding TPK, pre-service teachers acquire knowledge of how to use technology to support pedagogical strategies, such as using drawing tools to enhance the negotiations of learners' communicative skills, using video clips to design speaking or listening practices, and applying Google map to trigger student and teachers' communications. Although it did not show significant differences, about 84% of the pre-service teachers positively thought they could effectively use multimedia and online tools to present the content by the end of the training. More evidences were also showed from journal reflections, see details in next session.

There was no significant difference regarding their PCK. PCK refers to pre-service teachers' knowledge of how to apply proper pedagogical strategies to present the content of the subject area, such as through asking questions, which include words that students have learned to ensure learners' comprehension, so that learners will be able to carry on conversations. 73% of pre-service teachers agreed that they could perform PCK successfully by the end of the training. Researchers (Harris & Hofer, 2011) pointed out PCK requires more field practices to acquire, and only two pre-service teachers, T5 and T6, had more than one year field experiences prior this study, so it is assumed that only five time practicum hours (12 week training) may not have been sufficient for most of the pre-service teachers with limited teaching experiences to develop their PCK. Such results also were found in the past two studies: PCK were not presented in the end of an intensive training program (Kurt et al., 2013; Cheng, 2014). Extending the practicum period may lead to a greater impact; further studies are needed to prove or disprove this hypothesis.

TPACK Performance

Eleven pre-service teachers evaluated their TPACK seven competencies upon finishing each cycle in the TL-TPACK training model. By analyzing teachers' ratings in numeric method, it was clear to check the overall TPACK performances and see the changes in the development of TPACK's seven components during the circular training model. The results first discussed their ratings and then examined pre-service teachers' qualitative journal reports.

In terms of overall TPACK performance ratings, Table 7 shows TCK and PK (Scores = 8.5) were the top skills that pre-service teachers thought they had improved, which partially corresponded to the survey results: PK and TCK were significantly different. According to the journal reflections, 7 pre-service teachers (T1, T3, T5, T7, T9, T10, and T11) marked TCK down more than four sessions. They were satisfied with their TCK due to their students' great oral productions. When they reached the following achievement, TCK was marked: well-design multimedia-enhanced PPT presentation to explain new vocabulary, successfully used the functions of videoconferencing, such as drawing tool, when explaining new information and words, and successfully used Google map to establish nice interactions between student and teacher.

Table 7. The summary of pre-service teachers' TPACK evaluation

TPACK items	1st scores	2nd scores	3rd scores	4th scores	5th scores	Average
TK	7	7	6	9	7	7.2
TCK	9.5	7.5	7.5	8.5	9.5	8.5*
TPK	7.5	7	7	7.5	7.5	7.3
PK	8	8.5	8.5	8.5	9	8.5*
CK	6.5	7	7.5	8.5	10	7.9
PCK	4	5.5	8.5	8	8	6.8
TPACK	2	3.5	4.5	4	4.5	3.5

*Top one

It was my first time using drawing tools from WiziQ to lead the conversation on the topic of school campus with Google map. I liked the results, and my students spoke more, and I would definitely use drawing tools for the following sessions. (T5-3)

I could successfully review old content and encourage my student to perform better production with the support from my PPT design. (T10-2)

I used graphics first to assess what the student had learned, followed by a series of questioning to introduce new vocabulary. According to the transcriptions, I did a nice job in terms of the student's production. (T11-3)

By examining pre-service teachers' PK reflections, 5 pre-service teachers (T1, T5, T6, T7, T10) marked down PK more than four sessions, but there were approximately 6 pre-service teachers who were not fully satisfied with their PK performance. Table 7 shows PK's rating had gradually increased. The journals indicated a successful PK class occurred when pre-service teachers effectively applied i+1 and spiral-based design for their lessons, and asking proper questions to promote students' productions. Otherwise, pre-service teachers did not mark down their PK. Overall, pre-service teachers' rating scores were considered the best, which supported their survey results.

This session was designed based on spiral design. I first reviewed the content I taught in the last session and then introduce this week's topic: boy and girl friends. When I tried to explain new vocabulary, "i+1" theory was applied. At the end of this session, I found that several new words I had taught occurred in my student's output. (T1-3)

Due to the quantity of new vocabulary, I intentionally designed some questions to allow my students to practice new words. From the transcriptions, I found that my students successfully use the new words when provided many chances to speak. (T3-3)

CK (Score = 7.9) was rated as the second best skill. The CK rating had gradually increased according to the evaluation from the 1st to 5th session. 6 pre-service teachers (T1, T3, T5, T6, T9, and T11) marked down CK more than four sessions. Most of them mentioned they could successfully teach the new content they liked to teach. Table 7 shows that pre-service teachers' ratings of CK performances had gradually increased. The author assumes that the more sessions pre-service teachers teach, the more confidence about the content they have owned. In the fifth journal reflections, all pre-service teachers marked down CK. That is, by the end of the training, pre-service teachers could perform CK well. From T2's journal reflections, it was mentioned that, *"This was the last online session, and I became very familiar with the text content my student had learned. This helped me to explain new words by using student' prior knowledge (T2-5)"*. Even though T2 did not show her CK in every online session, by the end of the training, she could show her confidence of CK performance. As mentioned in the survey results session, CK of this training was not too challenging, so mostly pre-service teachers rated their CK nicely from 2nd session. That is, pre-service teachers have become confidence with the content they were planning to teach online earlier in the training, which again supported the survey result.

Due to the effect of Internet connection issues, TK's ratings seem to be predictable. Once either the student or the teacher encountered technical issues, especially with audio/video transmission problems, their course design could not be implemented smoothly. Therefore, the marks of TK were affected by technical conditions. For example, TK's ratings dropped in the 3rd session, and TCK's ratings slightly dropped in the 2nd and 3rd sessions. Those issues included students' internet or computer problems (T4-2, T8-3, T10-1), inability to play video clips (T4-2, T5-3, T7-3, T11-1), delayed/failed transmission of sound (T3-2, T5-5, T7-5, T8-3), and unfamiliarity with the backup platform (T3-5, T9-3). Even though their TK performances were influenced by technical issues, pre-service teachers still rated themselves as high TK teachers, which corresponded to the survey results, pre-service teachers thought they have accomplished the technical skills for online classes in the earlier of training.

PCK (score = 6.8) was rated among the worst. The ratings of last two sessions were higher than the first two sessions. From pre-service teachers' reflections, it can be seen that teachers who did not marked PCK down were aware of their weakness, such as inappropriate questioning (T2-1, T2-2, T5-1, T7-1, T7-2, T8-5, T11-4), incorrect feedback (T2-1), immature class leading (T2-3, T2-3, T3-1,T5-5, T6-3, T9-1), insufficient time for students to respond questions (T9-2, T9-3), and ignoring student's serious language errors (T2-4, T9-4, and T11-4). Questioning and class leading were the main weaknesses among participants of the study. These are important professional PCK knowledge for language pre-service teachers, which need a great amount of practicum hours to develop. This training model helped them to become aware of these weaknesses. Hopefully, they can continue to develop their PK as lifelong learners.

TPACK (score = 3.5) was rated among the worst. However, TPACK's ratings tended to grow over time. Overall, the ratings of last two sessions were higher than the first two sessions. This shows pre-service teachers' confidence in performing TPACK had increased by the end of the training, which is supported by the survey results of significantly different TPACK performances between pre and post training, but with low mean value. According to pre-service teachers' reflections, only T11 marked down TPACK more than four sessions, and the rest of the pre-service teachers did not rate their TPACK performance very high. It was expected that pre-service teachers may rate their TPACK low because it is not easy to perform TPACK in online lessons. Pre-service teachers understood that a successful TPACK performance required no technical issues, great student productions, with the support of proper multimedia assisted materials, and teachers' mature pedagogical design to enhance students' learning.

Learners' Knowledge Retention

Observation of learner's performances was treated as a reference for TL-TPACK model outcomes. Each student had five online sessions arranged every other week, and each session lasted an hour. The pre-service teachers were told not to teach more than seven new vocabulary words each lesson, which needed to be reviewed in the next session. The spiral design principle was the primary concept for training pre-service teachers' PK, TCK, and TPK. By examining student output, pre-service teachers' PK, TCK, and TPK performances could be assessed.

A delayed interview was conducted at the end of the fifth session to see how much information the learners had retained from session 1 to session 4. Analysis of the transcriptions from the nine learners' responses showed that S1 did not remember much information from three online sessions out of four. S5 did not remember the content from 2 sessions, and S2 and S9 could not remember the content from one session. The rest of the students (S3, S4, S6, S7, and S8) could talk about the theme from each session in Chinese.

When analyzing the students' responses, new words they had learned in the online sessions were considered. The results showed that seven learners (S1, S2, S3, S4, S6, S7 and S8) were able to use new words they had learned from the online lessons. However, only two to eight new words, mostly from session 3 had been retained. S3, S4, and S8 were the top three students in terms of knowledge retention. It is not surprising to see such a conclusion for S3 and S4, because S3 volunteered to take two online sessions from T3 and T4 in the middle of training due to enrollment issues; therefore, his learning hours were about 8 hours. S4 was also a volunteer joining in the online sessions and her Chinese level was higher than most others. S8 was from the partnership course. However, another high level volunteer, S5, did not remember any new words in the interview, so controversial results from the cases of S5 and S8 need further investigation. By analyzing T6's (S5's teacher) reflections, it was found that some issues had occurred. T6 had overestimated S5's level in the first session and S5 was a shy student who tended to say, "I don't know" to any questions he did not know or he did not want to answer. A shy student like S5 needed more time to establish the relationship with his teacher and his teacher also should not accept "I don't know for answers".

After examining the teaching reflections and teaching contents from T10 (S8's teacher), it was found that T10 performed her PK nicely, strictly and consciously following the concept of spiral design. New words such as 地圖(map; dìtú), (參加)旅行團 (tour group; (cānjiā) lǚxíng tuán), (當)背包客(backpacker; (dāng) bèibāo kè), 內向(introversive; nèixiàng), 外向(extroversive; wàixiàng), 樂觀(positive; lèguān), and 悲觀(negative; bēiguān), re-occurred in the five lessons, so his responses contained 參加旅行團 (cānjiā lǚxíng tuán), 內向(nèixiàng), 外向(wàixiàng), 開朗(active; kāilǎng), 網站(website; wǎngzhàn), 樂觀(lèguān), 打工(part-time job; dǎgōng), and 度假(vacation; dùjià), which were strongly associated with the repetitions.

These results show that the learners could use their own words to answer the questions, but not all of them could use the new words in their responses, possibly due to some of the PCK and PK issues that pre-service teachers mentioned in their journals, such as insufficient repetition of the new vocabulary that teachers had intended to teach, the insufficient learning hours, and students' unpredictable learning variables (personalities and learning experiences).

After careful identification of the new vocabulary from the interview transcription, it was revealed that seven out of nine learners used a minimum of two new words. Therefore, increasing students' learning hours and improving pre-service teachers' PCK performances to focus strictly on spiral design with the learning content may be critical factors for the effectiveness of the TL-TPACK model.

Table 8. Summary of CSL learners' output

ID	1st session	2nd session	3rd session	4th session	# of new words
S1			2		2
S2			3		3
S3*	1	2	2		5
S4*	1	2	1		4
S5*					0
S6	1	1			2
S7				2	2
S8	2		5	1	8
S9					0
# of students	4	3	5	2	

CONCLUSION

These conclusions have been drawn from pre-service teacher's TPACK performances based on the TL-TPACK training model.

The TL-TPACK training model can promote seven TPACK components. Responses from surveys and journals show pre-service teachers' PK and TCK had certainly developed, and both significantly differ after training. That is, PK and TCK can be promoted within an intensive training program integrated with online practicum, especially for TCK. Online field practice forced pre-service teachers to effectively apply the functions of online platforms and multimedia to explain new information and review old knowledge in a short period of time. Also, the teaching content was clearly defined within limited units and new vocabularies. TCK in this study refers to knowing how to use multimedia and online platforms effectively to present the defined learning content, so that students can comprehend new information based on their prior knowledge, learn more vocabulary, and speak more in online lessons. According the responses from pre-service teachers' surveys and reflections, around 75% of pre-service teachers thought their TCK had developed by the end of the training, and there was a significant difference between pre and post training. These results are very encouraging for a single-course training. In reality, a single-course training cannot guarantee the development of the seven knowledge bases, but TCK was one important knowledge base corresponding with the course objectives.

Teachers' TPACK had a gradually developed. Most of the pre-service teachers did not rate their TPACK high in their journal reflections, because it is a comprehensive achievement among technological, pedagogical and content knowledge. This may be a nice evidence of low mean value from survey. However, the author believes that TL-TPACK model helps pre-service CSL teachers develop their TPACK slowly, with the support of significant difference of TPACK between pre and post training. It could still be considered a skill in progress if more training hours had been provided within the cycle.

CK and TK were easy-to-develop skills in TL-TPACK training model under the conditions of selecting easy-to-accomplished technical applications and limiting scope of instructional content pre-service teachers need to manage. Most of the pre-service teachers were trying very hard to acquire their TK and CK in the earlier of the training, and gained the confidence of their performance of CK and TK.

Therefore, author suggests that teacher trainers who plan to employ a short term TL-TPACK training program should considered defining content and easy to use applications with limitation. Training can be implemented with different contents and technical tools repeatedly to gradually develop pre-service teachers' professional knowledge.

More field experiences are needed for pre-service teachers of current study to develop PCK. This refers to using proper pedagogical strategies to present content, such as through asking questions including words that students had learned during previous lessons to ensure learners' comprehension, or arranging the learning content spirally, so that the learners can practice the new information multiple times, ultimately acquiring the knowledge. However, pre-service teachers did not successfully perform PCK, so some of the lessons were not suitable for the learners' level and their knowledge was not retained. Therefore, successful PCK knowledge requires more field experience, which corresponds to Harris and Hofer's (2011) study.

PK and PCK are important knowledge bases for learning efficiency. Data according to the pre-service teachers' course designs, journal reflections, and students' final oral reports, indicated that teachers' professional knowledge on pedagogical approach and content arrangement was associated with the learners' learning retention. Proper amount of learning content, repetition of the exercises, applying students' priori knowledge, proper questioning, and spiral design all ensure better learning performances. However, more practicing hours from pre-service teachers and students are needed, so it is assumed that when increasing practicum hours and learning hours, both pre-service teachers' TPACK competencies and students learning retentions may improve.

Pedagogical Implication for Teacher Educators

For pre-service teachers' professional development, when teachers are planning to integrate technology into language class, suggestions and implications are stated as follows:

Comparing with other components, TK and CK are quick gain knowledge, which can be developed in a short period of time. TK is the fundamental knowledge for instructional technology. It is suggested that easy-to-access-and-learn tools are nice beginnings. Pre-service teachers can also initiate development of their CK by becoming familiar with a variety of FL/SL learning materials.

The development of TK and CK is related to TCK's performance, which can also be gained in a short period of time by preparing instructional materials well.

However, PK, PCK and TPACK all take time to fully developed, which also requires pre-service teachers' commitment to lifelong learning behaviors. Regarding PK, understanding what pedagogical methods are suitable for certain instructional objectives is easy to achieve, but implementing these strategies needs practice from field experiences. TPK may also be affected by PK's development.

Research Implication

Regarding the validation of measurement tools of this study, unlike the findings from author's previous study (Cheng & Zhan, 2012; Cheng, 2014a), the current study shows that mostly the survey results and journal reflections seems to support with each other. That is, both survey and journal were designed based the TPACK components, so the journal reflections associated with seven TPACK components were fully collected. Therefore, the data from the two resources can be compared.

Overall, the results of this study did not completely correspond with previous studies. The only foreign language study with a similar design was Kurt et al.'s (2013) TPACK study on 22 Turkish pre-service English teachers within a 12-week training period. Those pre-service teacher's TK, TCK, TPK, and TPACK scores were significantly different between the pre and post training course periods. Even though Kurt had arranged teaching practicum hours, it was only a one lesson micro-teaching in the field. Limited practicum hours did not seem to affect their results. However, the practicum hours is considered a crucial factor for current study. Such inconsistent findings needs further investigation.

During the current study, pre-service teachers' TK, TCK, and TPK had increased, but the CSL learners' new knowledge retention was not very stable, which may possibly be associated with pre-service teachers' PK and PCK. Repetition and proper level of learning content are key factors; the content of each pre-service teacher's lessons should be strictly controlled to ensure students' opportunities to practice new knowledge for retaining that information.

Research limitation

In literature, not many TPACK based research had been conducted with a training program. This study tried to fill this void. However, the following limitations can serve as a reference for further investigation.

1. If more training cycles had been implemented, the changes of pre-service teachers' TPACK performances of current study over time may be different.
2. If the students had been selected from same level, all of the pre-service teachers could have received similar training in terms of CK and students' learning content could have been controlled by the researchers. In this way, a knowledge retention test could have been conducted in a similar design.

Therefore, insufficient training cycles and less controlled of students learning content were the major limitations.

FUTURE RESEARCH SUGGESTIONS

TPACK research on foreign language teacher training is still in its infancy. It is strongly suggested that proper training strategies such as sufficient practicum hours should be applied. Trainers should thoughtfully design and concern pre-service teachers' TPACK professional development accordingly when integrating technology into teacher training programs. The current research focused on speaking and listening learning content for adult learners. More research, associated with different themes and learners with different ages are needed to seal the literature void. Additionally, more training cycles need to be applied for further investigation. Finally, a longitudinal study on pre-service teachers' TPACK development is suggested.

REFERENCES

American Council on the Teaching of Foreign Languages (ACTFL). (2015). *2013 Program Standards for the Preparation of Foreign Language Teachers.* Retrieved from http://www.actfl.org/2013-program-standards-the-preparation-foreign-language-teachers#sthash.3jVxFLkl.dpuf

Bos, B. (2011). Professional development for elementary teachers using TPACK. *Contemporary Issues in Technology & Teacher Education, 11*(2), 167–183.

Brown, D., & Warschauer, M. (2006). From the university to the elementary classroom: Students' experiences in learning to integrate technology in instruction. *Journal of Technology and Teacher Education, 14*(3), 599–621.

Campanelli, P. (2012). Testing survey questions. In E. D. De Leeuw, J. J. Hox, & D. A. Dillman (Eds.), International handbook of survey methodology (pp. 176–200). European Association of Methodology Series. New York: Lawrence Erlbaum Associates

Chai, C. S., Chin, C. K., Koh, J. H. L., & Tan, C. L. (2013). Exploring Singaporean Chinese language teachers' technological pedagogical content knowledge and its relationship to the teachers' pedagogical beliefs. *The Asia-Pacific Education Researcher, 22*(4), 657–666. doi:10.1007/s40299-013-0071-3

Chai, C. S., Koh, J. H. L., & Tsai, C.-C. (2010). Facilitating Preservice Teachers' Development of Technological, Pedagogical, and Content Knowledge (TPACK). *Journal of Educational Technology & Society, 13*(4), 63–73.

Chaptal, A. (2002). Is the investment really worth it? *Educational Media International, 39*(1), 87–99. doi:10.1080/09523980210131178

Chapters, E. (2003). The use of think-aloud methods in qualitative research: An Introduction to think-aloud methods. *Brock Education, 12*(2), 68–82.

Cheng, H. (2009). The Investigation of the Relationships between Current Development of CALL-TCSL Teachers and the Training Programs. *Chung Yuan Journal of Teaching Chinese as a Second Language, 3,* 107–127.

Cheng, H. (2013). *A distance education teacher training study on practicum reflections and training strategies.* The 8th International Conference on Internet Chinese Education International Conference on Internet Chinese (ICICE 2013), Pasadena, U.S.A.

Cheng, H. (2014a). The study of CSL online teacher training course and the teachers' development of Technological Pedagogical Content Knowledge. *Journal of Technology and Chinese Language Teaching, 5*(2), 1–18. http://www.tclt.us/journal/2014v5n2/cheng.pdf

Cheng, H. (2014b). *The study of pre-service teachers' TPACK in a distance education teacher training program.* The 11th International Conference of World Chinese Language Association, Taipei: Taiwan

Cheng, H., & Zhan, H. (2012). *Examining Pre-service Teachers' Technological Pedagogical Content Knowledge Instructional Strategies via Video-conferencing Technology, The Journal of Educational Technology Development and Exchange.* JETDE.

Cheng, T., & Chen, H. (2015). *ZaiMei kuaqu hezuo de Huayuwen ji wenhua yuanju jiaoxue zhi shili fenxiang yu tasuo*. The 9th International Conference on Internet Chinese Education International Conference on Internet Chinese (ICICE 2015), Boston, U.S.A

Cohen-Sayag, E., & Fischl, D. (2012). Reflective Writing in pre-service teachers' teaching: What does it promote? *Australian Journal of Teacher Education*, *37*(10), 20–36. doi:10.14221/ajte.2012v37n10.1

Ekrem, S., & Recep, C. (2014). Examining Preservice EFL Teachers' TPACK Competencies in Turkey. *Journal of Educators Online*, *11*(2), 1.

Galanouli, D., & McNair, V. (2001). Students' perceptions of ICT-related support in teaching placements. *Journal of Computer Assisted Learning*, *17*(4), 396–408. doi:10.1046/j.0266-4909.2001.00196.x

Gao, P., Chee, T. S., Wang, L., Wong, A., & Choy, D. (2011). Self reflection and preservice teachers' technological pedagogical knowledge: Promoting earlier adoption of student-centred pedagogies. *Australasian Journal of Educational Technology*, *27*(6), 997–1013. doi:10.14742/ajet.925

Hsu, P.-S., & Sharma, P. (2006). A systemic plan of technology integration. *Journal of Educational Technology & Society*, *9*(4), 173–184.

Jaipal, K., & Figg, C. (2010). Unpacking the "Total PACKage": Emergent TPACK Characteristics from a Study of Preservice Teachers Teaching With Technology.[Chesapeake, VA: AACE.]. *Journal of Technology and Teacher Education*, *18*(3), 415–441.

Koehler, M. J., & Mishra, P. (2005). What happens when teachers design educational technology? the development of technological pedagogical content knowledge. *Journal of Educational Computing Research*, *32*(2), 131–152. doi:10.2190/0EW7-01WB-BKHL-QDYV

Koehler, M. J., & Mishra, P. (2009). What is technological pedagogical content knowledge? *Contemporary Issues in Technology & Teacher Education*, *9*(1), 60–70.

Koehler, M. J., Mishra, P., & Yahya, K. (2007). Tracing the development of teacher knowledge in a design seminar: Integrating content, pedagogy and technology. *Computers & Education*, *49*(3), 740–762. doi:10.1016/j.compedu.2005.11.012

Koehler, M. J., Shin, T. S., & Mishra, P. (2012). How do we measure TPACK? Let me count the ways. In R. N. Ronau, C. R. Rakes, & M. L. Niess (Eds.), *Educational technology, teacher knowledge, and classroom impact: A research handbook on frameworks and approaches* (pp. 16–31). Hershey, PA: IGI Global. doi:10.4018/978-1-60960-750-0.ch002

Koh, J. H. L., Chai, C. S., & Tsait, C. C. (2010). Examining the technological pedagogical content knowledge of Singapore pre-service teachers with a large-scale survey. *Journal of Computer Assisted Learning*, *26*(6), 563–573. doi:10.1111/j.1365-2729.2010.00372.x

Kurt, G., Mishra, P., & Kocoglu, Z. (2013) *Technological pedagogical content knowledge development of Turkish preservice teachers of English*. Paper presented at the meeting of the Society for Information Technology and Teacher Education, New Orleans, LA. Abstract retrieved from http://academicexperts.org/conf/site/2013/papers/38476/

Lee, M.-H., & Tsai, C.-C. (2010). Exploring teachers' perceived self efficacy and technological pedagogical content knowledge with respect to educational use of the World Wide Web. *Instructional Science, 38*(1), 1–21. doi:10.1007/s11251-008-9075-4

Lim, C. P., Chai, C. S., & Churchill, D. (2010). *Leading ICT in education practices: A capacity building toolkit for teacher education institutions in the Asia-Pacific.* Singapore: Microsoft.

Liu, S. H., & Lan, Y. (2014). Pre-service CSL Teachers' Field Experience in the Real and the Virtual Worlds. *Journal of Chinese Language Teaching, 11*(3), 61–90.

Matherson, L. H., Wilson, E. K., Wright, V. H. (2014). *Need TPACK? Embrace Sustained Professional Development.* Delta Kappa Gamma Bulletin, 45-52

Mishra, P., & Koehler, M. J. (2006). Technological Pedagogical Content Knowledge: A new framework for teacher knowledge. *Teachers College Record, 108*(6), 1017–1054. doi:10.1111/j.1467-9620.2006.00684.x

Oz, H. (2015). Assessing Pre-service English as a Foreign Language Teachers' Technological Pedagogical Content Knowledge. *International Education Studies, 8*(5), 119–130. doi:10.5539/ies.v8n5p119

Sessoms, D. (2008). Interactive instruction: Creating interactive learning environments through tomorrow's teachers. *International Journal of Technology in Teaching and Learning, 4*(2), 86–96.

Shulman, L. (1986). Those who understand: Knowledge growth in teaching. *Educational Researcher, 15*(2), 4–14. doi:10.3102/0013189X015002004

Tai, S.-J. (2015). From TPACK-In-Action workshops to classrooms: CALL competency developed and integrated. *Language Learning & Technology, 19*(1), 139–164.

Teo, T., Chai, C. S., Hung, D., & Lee, C. B. (2008). Beliefs about teaching and uses of technology among pre-service teachers. *Asia-Pacific Journal of Teacher Education, 36*(2), 163–174. doi:10.1080/13598660801971641

The Chinese Language Association of Secondary-Elementary Schools. (CLASS)(2015). CLASS Professional Standards for k-12 Chinese Teachers. Retrieved from http://classk12.org/13/ts.htm

Tseng, J.-J. (2014). Investigating EFL teachers' technological pedagogical content knowledge: Students' perceptions. In S. Jager, L. Bradley, E. J. Meima, & S. Thouësny (Eds), *CALL Design: Principles and Practice; Proceedings of the 2014 EUROCALL Conference, Groningen, The Netherlands* (pp. 379-384) doi:doi:10.14705/rpnet.2014.000249 doi:10.14705/rpnet.2014.000249

Wang, S. C. (1998). A Study on the Learning and Teaching of Hanzi-Chinese Characters. *Working Papers in Educational Linguistics, 14*(1), 69-101

Williams, C. (2013). Emerging development of semantic and phonological routes to character decoding in Chinese as a foreign language learners. *Reading and Writing, 26*(2), 293–315. doi:10.1007/s11145-012-9368-5

Xie, T. (2011). *Three Models of Long Distance e-Tutoring: A Pilot Study.* The 7th International Conference on Internet Chinese Education (ICICE 2011). Taipei.

Yeh, P., & Dai, J. H. (2015). *The Implications of Discourse Analysis in an Online Chinese Teacher Training Course*. The 9th International Conference on Internet Chinese Education International Conference on Internet Chinese (ICICE 2015), Boston, U.S.A

Yeung, A. S., Tay, E. G., Hui, C., Lin, J. H., & Low, E. L. (2014). Pre-service teachers' motivation in using digital technology. *Australian Journal of Teacher Education*, *39*(3). doi:10.14221/ajte.2014v39n3.1

Zelkowski, J., Gleason, J., Cox, D. C., & Bismarck, S. (2013). Developing and validating a reliable TPACK instrument for secondary mathematics preservice teachers. *Journal of Research on Technology in Education*, *46*(2), 173–206. doi:10.1080/15391523.2013.10782618

Zhao, Y., Pugh, K., Sheldon, S., & Byers, J. (2002). Conditions for classroom technology innovations. *Teachers College Record*, *104*(3), 482–515. doi:10.1111/1467-9620.00170

KEY TERMS AND DEFINITIONS

Chinese as a Foreign Language (CFL): According to the definition of Longman dictionary of language teaching and applied linguistics (Richards, Platt & Platt, 1998), a foreign language is "a language which is taught as school subjects but which is not used as a medium of instruction in schools nor as a language of communication within a country". Examples of learners' learning Chinese or teachers' teaching Chinese as a foreign language are Chinese learned or taught in the United States, England, Japan, or Korea, where Chinese plays no major role in the countries for communication. Even though the scholars distinguish the definition of CSL and CFL, teacher training programs mostly provide training courses for both CSL and CFL, which aim to train students to become Chinese teachers around the world. The majority of teacher training institutions may use TCSL in their title, but some use TCS/FL to indicate their missions.

Chinese as a Second Language (CSL): According to the definition of Longman dictionary of language teaching and applied linguistics (Richards, Platt & Platt, 1998), a second language is "a language which is not a native language in a country but which is widely used as a medium of communication (e. g. in education and in government)". Examples of learners' learning Chinese or teachers' teaching Chinese as a second language are Chinese learned or taught in Taiwan, China, Hong Kong, and Singapore, where Chinese plays an institutional and social role for people to communicate.

Computer Assisted Language Learning (CALL): CALL refers to language instruction with the assistance of technology. Using a loose definition, CALL means using technology for more individualized practice on specific language learning.

Information and Communication Technology (ICT): ICT refers to an extensive term that includes communication device or application, telecommunications devices, such as mobile phones, computer and network hardware and software as well as videoconferencing and distance learning. ICTs are often used in a particular context, such as ICTs in education, which can be similar to Instructional technology. The term is often used outside of the United States.

Pre-Service Teacher: A pre-service teacher is a college student studying a teacher education program, which offers education of teachers before they enter into service as teacher. In general, a pre-service teacher program offers a collection of unrelated courses and field experiences. A Chinese pre-service teacher program offers training courses related to Chinese education and field practicum.

Technological, Pedagogical and Content Knowledge (TPACK): a framework to understand and describe the knowledge needed by a teacher for effective pedagogical practice in a technology enhanced learning environment. Punya Mishra and Matthew J. Koehler are the major scholars who developed TPACK based on Shulman's (1986) theory of Pedagogical Content Knowledge (PCK). It emphasizes the connections and interplays among the three core knowledge bases: technological knowledge (TK), pedagogical knowledge (PK), and content knowledge (CK). The additional four components are: Technological Content Knowledge (TCK), Technological Pedagogical Knowledge (TPK), Pedagogical Content Knowledge (PCK), and Technological Pedagogical and Content Knowledge (TPACK).

TL-TPACK Model: TL-TPACK model is a teacher training model applied TPACK framework. It concerns about not only teachers' performances but also students' learning performances.

APPENDIX 1: SURVEY FOR PRE-SERVICE TEACHERS

Part 1: Demographic Information

1. **Gender:** Male/Female
2. **Last 3 Digital Number of ID:** _ _ _
3. **My Teaching/Practicum Experiences:** School_____; Background of Students_____; Hours_____
4. **How much time do I spend to prepare this online lesson?** _____ hours
5. **How much time do I spend to familiarize the online platform?** _____ hours

Part 2: Professional Development of TPACK

Please select the best answer for each statement in Table 9.

Table 9. After online teaching...

	Strongly Disagree	Disagree	Neutral	Agree	Strongly Agree
Technological Knowledge					
1. I am familiar with the operations of associated multimedia.					
2. I am familiar with document unloading to the platform.*					
3. I am familiar with audio and video settings of online learners.					
4. I am familiar with input of Chinese characters and pinyin.					
Pedagogical Knowledge					
5. My lesson has followed the spiral design.					
6. I know how to appropriately ask another question for similar questions when students do not understand the current one.*					
7. My lesson have reach the principle of less teacher's talk and more student output.					
8. My questions are mostly open-ended which ensure the student's output.					
9. I have established a great relationship with my student, which encourage the student output.					
Content Knowledge					
10. I am familiar with the content of my student have learned.					
11. I know how to explain the new content to my student.					
12. I understand spiral curriculum very well.					
13. I understand how to ask questions from student's prior knowledge and lead to the new knowledge.					
14. I understand when to use student native language to assist student's comprehension.					

Table 9. Continued

	Strongly Disagree	Disagree	Neutral	Agree	Strongly Agree
Technological Pedagogical Knowledge					
15. I have utilized a great amount of graphics for oral practices in my lesson.*					
16. I first used graphics to lead the oral discussion and then used the text to support the comprehension to ensure the oral output of my student.					
17. I have integrated the pencil function into the graphic-enhanced activities to ensure the interactions with my student.					
18. I have offered the text support such as characters and its pinyin to ensure the effectiveness of student learning.					
PCK					
19. The quantity of new words I taught in my lesson is not overloaded to my student.					
20. I always initialize questions from students prior knowledge to the new language.					
21. To ensure the students' oral output, my questions are mostly open-ended.					
22. The content and the length of my lesson are suitable to my student.					
23. My lesson did not arrange the new words I am teaching appealing over and over again.*					
TCK					
24. I am using text and pinyin to ensure the students comprehension when teaching new words.					
25. When I am using videos in my lesson, the content and language of the videos are suitable to my student.					
26. The graphics I used for my lesson can assist student's oral output.					
27. To ensure students oral input, I mainly used graphics to design my lesson.					
TPACK					
28. I have adopted spiral principle to design my lesson, use proper graphics and text support incorporated with student prior knowledge to lead great amount output of CSL learners.					
29. With the understanding of students' learning difficulties and language level, I offered a proper content engaging the activities supporting the proper tools from online platform to ensure the effective language interactions.					

APPENDIX 2: TPACK REFLECTION GUIDELINES FOR PRE-SERVICE TEACHERS

Please first evaluate your CK, PK, TK, TPK, TCK, TPK, PCK, TPACK performance and provide supporting examples.

Table 10.

	CK	PK	TK	TPK	TCK	TPK	PCK	TPACK
Exceed								

APPENDIX 3 INTERVIEW QUESTIONS FOR CHINESE LEARNERS (ENGLISH VERSION)

This interview aims to see how much you can recall from all of the online sessions. I am going to asking you few questions in Chinese, please answer the questions in Chinese.If you have any questions, please let me know before we begin. (Show students this instruction)

Questions

1. How much do you remember the content from session 1? Please describe. (Show presentation from first session)
2. How much do you remember the content from session 2? Please describe. (Show presentation from first session)
3. How much do you remember the content from session 3? Please describe. (Show presentation from first session)
4. How much do you remember the content from session 4? Please describe. (Show presentation from first session)

Chapter 12
The Technology Segment of a Methods Course:
Its Impact on Teaching Realities and Imagined Needs

Jason D. Hendryx
University of Wyoming, USA

ABSTRACT

This chapter reports a case study with survey data collected from one residency Spanish language teacher completing the final phase of a modern languages education program as well as two current in-service Spanish language teachers who completed the same program the year previously. Specifically, the study examined 1) what the three teachers recall of an overarching framework for embracing technology they were introduced to in their methods course, 2) what technologies they currently employ for language instruction and why, and 3) what characteristics they imagine the model modern language educator of the future will require. Findings revealed that these teachers did not recall in detail the overarching system for embracing technology introduced to them, they utilized a very broad range of technologies for teaching which would prove difficult to train them all in effectively during a methods course, and they saw flexible, engaging, patient, and content-prepared professionals as the future of the profession.

INTRODUCTION

These are interesting times for language teachers and language teacher trainers. Language teachers are being called on to do more and more in their classrooms--: from being experts in the languages and cultures they teach, to knowing and successfully applying second language acquisition theories within context-driven pedagogical rationales, to being able to differentiate instruction within and across their lessons, to aligning what they teach with national and state language proficiency standards, to assessing learners across all language skill areas in multiple modalities, to seamlessly incorporating various technologies appropriately into their lessons to enhance the overall impact on language learning, plus so much more (Brown & Lee, 2015; Burns & Richards, 2009, 2012). With such massive amounts of

DOI: 10.4018/978-1-5225-0483-2.ch012

potentially beneficial content to cover in modern languages education methods courses, language teacher trainers are left to attempt to decide what knowledge is of most worth for their students.

This is certainly no easy task and involves sharing, discussing, and negotiating a broad range of hopefully useful and relevant content with future language teachers. One strand of the many that must be successfully woven into a modern languages methods course is technology. Technology is certainly one component of language teacher training that has been historically, and continues to be currently, a much-considered element (Arnold, 2013). From effectively utilizing resources in language labs of the past, to now knowing how mobile device applications might assist in the language learning process have all been, at some level, incorporated into the language teacher training processes across the decades (Furstenberg & Morgenstern, 1992; Sabbath, 1962; Walker & White, 2013). Meaningful training in technology is especially important for language teachers today. "For student teachers in today's culture of technology, the issue is not whether to use it or not to use it, it is how to use it, when and how much to use it" (Allan, 2015, p. 36).

In order to better understand what students who recently completed their modern languages education methods courses took away from a technology element they encountered in that coursework, this study aimed to investigate the following questions:

1. What do these former students recall, if anything, of a methods course segment on technology and what impact did it have on their teaching?
2. What kinds of technology do these same former students, now teaching or residency teaching, currently utilize in their classrooms and for what purposes?
3. What do they believe to be the essential characteristics future modern language educators will require to be successful?
4. How might these methods courses be further improved for future students?

It is hoped that by obtaining these former students' reflection on past coursework, examination of current practices, and imagination of future possibilities, fruitful advancements can be realized in modern languages methods course content. With such data in place understandings might emerge which could provide language teacher trainers opportunities to present technology for language teaching in methods courses which would be more in alignment with the realities their students go on to face, and resonate more soundly with the futures students imagine about the profession.

BACKGROUND

This study stemmed from a desire to ascertain what, and to some extent how, students who had recently completed their language methods coursework in a teacher preparation program in the Western United States drew on what they had studied in those courses in their residency teaching and first years of teaching. Because so much information is shared with students in their methods classes it seemed potentially very informative to examine a single piece of that mass of information to see how it functioned in students' realities and thinking after the methods courses were completed and they went on to become teachers.

The language methods pedagogy elements of the program these students completed were delivered through two courses: Methods I and Methods II. Methods I is a nuts and bolts course which addresses the fundamentals of teaching speaking, listening, reading, writing, grammar, and culture which has a lesson plan as its culminating project. Methods II meanwhile is a finishing course, which examines principles of second language acquisition, teacher identity development, national foreign language, or world readiness standards, classroom management, advocating for the field, professional development, and technology (there were assignments requiring the use of technology in Methods I as well) with a unit plan as the final project. Methods I and Methods II courses are offered concurrently.

One strand of the modern languages education methods coursework students must complete, and of particular interest to the researcher, was the technology segment. Students had multiple types and kinds of interaction with learning how to utilize technology for teaching throughout their program. Additional program elements included a dedicated course on how to apply technology for teaching and multiple assignments which required the development of teaching activities which were technology based. The technology element of the methods coursework, in particular the Methods II coursework, was chosen to be examined for this study. This decision was based on the multiple points of contact students had with technology in their program by that time, suggesting students might have a more layered and comprehensive understanding of how technology might be employed for teaching, and the current relevance of technology in teaching today.

In both of the methods courses the primary text was Brandl's (2008) work titled, *'Communicative language teaching in action: Putting principles to work.'* To establish that the students in these classes would have found additional purchase for thinking about technology for language teaching in their textbook, Arnold (2013), in an examination of how texts used in language teacher training courses presented technology to future language teachers, commented that,

Brandl (2008) explicitly recognizes this need for a unique CALL pedagogy. Since online texts are often organized and laid out differently than traditional texts (e.g., integration of multimedia, which can cause cognitive overload), Brandl urges that 'numerous pedagogical issues need to be compensated for'... (p. 238)

The actual overarching framework these students were introduced to in their Methods II course is called the 3Ds, standing for Directional, Developmental, and Decisive. This framework was developed from over a decade of language classroom observations of over a hundred language teachers teaching more than 25 different languages at five different institutions (both high school and university). From classroom observations it became apparent that teachers employing technology who embraced one or more of the Ds in their uses of technology appeared to generate more student language output and more student engagement and interest. In the 3D approach ordering is relevant and the first D is the most important in the framework.

Directional simply means that the technology resource is aimed at the students in the classroom, making the language being conveyed by the technology relevant to the students in some way. One way to unpack the directional component of the 3Ds approach is to think of it as projecting the language embedded in technology into the specific contexts and physical spaces of the students. One example might be to have a PowerPoint of a particular item as well as that actual item, or representation of that item, in the physical classroom space. This takes a representation of language provided by technology and projects it into the classroom with the real object technology is representing.

Another example of the directional D is to provide a rich context for something being provided through technology that makes more meaningful connections with students' lives in some way. This

The Technology Segment of a Methods Course

might mean introducing a musical band from a target language speaking region and providing background information as to how old the musicians are, how large the crowds they are playing for are, how many albums they have sold, and how that places them in comparison with comparable U.S. bands, instead of just playing a music video on YouTube.

The second D is Developmental. Most technology, one could say, is not intended for language instruction specifically and even technologies intended for that purpose have their shortcomings. This D emerged from observing teachers not allowing the limits of the technology they were using to take away from the richness of the language being taught. This would mean that teachers would augment what technology could not fully capture about the language being shared with additional in-class materials, discussions, and resources. For example, some technologies may only support certain types, numbers, and kinds of text. Embracing this D would mean that teachers would not allow those limitations with technology to impact the meanings, cultural and linguistic, of the target language they were in the process of teaching.

The third and final D of the 3D approach is Decisive. Teachers who were observed using technology for maximum learning impact did not allow the pace of technology use, that being either too fast or too slow, to influence their teaching in a counterproductive manner, instead they were able to regulate the pace of the technology they were utilizing to further enhance their overall teaching effectiveness. Careful scrutiny of the 3D approach reveals that the letter D was not selected at random. Indeed the D in the approach stands for "distortions" caused by technology, specifically in space (Directional), content (Developmental), and time (Decisive).

The teacher trainer teaches the 3D approach to technology for teaching in the Methods II course because the trainer is not aware of another comparable overarching approach for utilizing technology for language teaching. The teacher trainer also does not offer trainings in specific technologies in either of the methods courses for three fundamental reasons—meaningful future application, time, and possible redundancy. The first reason is that the exact technologies graduating students will encounter in the states and districts where they take their future teaching assignments cannot be determined in advance and therefore such specific trainings may have no meaningful future applications for the students whatsoever. The second is time. To take time in an already overfilled curriculum for the training of specific technologies which students may never use in their future careers is frustrating for teacher and students alike, as such coursework cannot be proven in advance to have practical value for all students and therefore no justifications can be offered for the time in class spent on teaching those technologies. Lastly, when these students arrive in methods courses they have already taken a technology course which provided them with training in a broad range of technologies aimed specifically at language teaching and learning. If specific technology training was offered in the methods classes there is the possibility that similar content to what was already offered might be covered and leave students with a feeling of redundancy in terms of content across courses (which they are already very vocal about encountering in the program).

In terms of providing a rationale for examining the impact and possible use of an isolated component of a particular course after the course had completed, it would seem that only if the content to be studied had some tangible links to current scholarship would such an endeavor be sufficiently supported. With that in mind we now turn our attention to the relevant literature.

LITERATURE REVIEW

Much has been written recently about how technology might be applied for language teaching and learning, how language teachers might be trained in employing technology for teaching, and how language teachers or student language teachers conceptualize and utilize technologies for teaching purposes (Blake, 2013; Boehm & Aniola-Jedrzejek, 2009; Cetto, 2010; Chapelle, 2004; DuBravac, 2013; Evans, 2009; Heift & Chapelle, 2012; Hoopingarner, 2009; Kern, 2006, 2014; Lafford & Lafford, 2005; Li & Swanson, 2014; Luke & Britten, 2007; Luke, 2011; Reinders, 2009; Schmid & Whyte, 2012; Walker & White, 2013; Zhang, Zhao, & Li, 2014). A number of general works on employing technology for education and how to utilize technology successfully have also been published recently (Jonassen, Howland, Marra, & Crismond, 2008; Morgan & Olivares, 2012; Oviatt, 2013).

In this literature review, instead of providing a nuanced framing of each of the works listed above in a manner which supports and adds depth to the justification for this study, only two of them will be examined briefly to situate the two primary thrusts which most of these works share in common: Providing a comprehensive overview of current technologies and how they can be applied to language teaching contexts, or how particular groups have utilized, or reacted to, technology enhanced instruction. For the former DuBravac (2013) will be presented and for the latter Kern (2014).

DuBravac (2013), as so many of these kinds of works do, provides an excellent, and very thorough, overview of how a multitude of technologies can be effectively utilized for language teaching. DuBravac, however, takes his scrutiny of the field a step further than many of the other similar efforts in this area and provides meaningful links between technology and second language acquisition as well as national and international language proficiency standards. In the chapter headings of the table of contents words like "software", "web", "computer", "acquisition", "(language proficiency) standards", "eportfolios" and so on can be found.

It is in the "Theories of second language acquisition" chapter which we may be able to forward some tentative connections between that work and the aforementioned 3D approach. This is because of how the author chooses to frame second language acquisition theories as being property (internalization), transition (interaction), and environmental (distance) focused. In such an orientation one might consider the possibility of bridging language acquisition understandings of environmental with directional, transition with decisive, and property with developmental. Indeed, environments can provide learners and teachers with specific contexts which they become familiar with through rich, focused, multilayered immersions and speak to issues of space. Meanwhile, transition stresses in-the-moment functionality and use and talks to time, while property suggests ownership and in that understanding, maintenance and continuing development as well.

DuBravac (2013) also does not allow us to forget that technology "…is a rapidly changing field" (p. 221). Interestingly enough however, it seems that no matter how far technology might be able to take us we cannot remove, or replace, the fundamental concern of language teaching, "Future endeavors in language instruction must focus on the issue of helping students realize the importance of communicating with others in the target language" (p. 223).

Kern (2014) meanwhile offers the other commonly encountered type of work in this field, in which a particular type of technology being employed for language teaching is carefully examined with an eye toward better understanding what is actually happening during the process for those involved. Of particular interest to this study are the first three suggestions from his "relations pedagogy" section,

The Technology Segment of a Methods Course

which find both traction and resonance with the 3D system students were introduced to in their Methods II coursework. Kern presents them as,

How do linguistic elements interact with nonlinguistic elements to produce particular meanings?

How have conventional semiotic resources been appropriated, adapted, or recontextualized for individual or collective purposes?

How are time (e.g., rhythm, timing) and space (e.g., visual layout, movement) used to create particular meanings or effects? (p. 353)

In these three suggestions we find that both the first and second are aimed at what in the 3D approach has been labeled as developmental. Teachers who embrace this concept do not allow the limits, or influences, of technology, to adversely impact how and what language they want to teach. The last suggestion addresses issues of time and space directly. Albeit with slightly different lenses than introduced in the 3Ds, there is enough of an overlap to see meaningful linkages.

With representative examples of the two commonly encountered types of literature in this area offered in this review, there is certainly room to suggest a level of connectedness between both kinds of works and the overarching 3D approach students were introduced to in their Methods II class.

METHODOLOGY

To answer the questions proposed in this study, students who had completed their modern languages education methods coursework within the past 2 years and who were either currently teaching modern languages or completing their residency teaching at high schools throughout the state in the northwestern region of the country were contacted by e-mail to determine if they would be willing to participate. In total, five students fit the above criteria and were contacted. Of those, three agreed to participate. All institutional policies and procedures concerning working with individuals for a research project were followed in the collection of data presented in this chapter.

Participation for this study involved completing a short survey which was sent and returned by e-mail. One of the participants did not have time to complete the survey electronically so a time was arranged when the participant could complete the survey with the researcher over the phone. The survey instrument was comprised of three sections. The first section called for participants to write in ten technologies they were currently using in their classrooms and why, the second section asked for ten characteristics or traits they believed as essential for future model language educators to possess, as well as how these future language educators might best be trained, and the final section presented nine questions which probed what they remembered about the technology segment they had experienced in their Methods II coursework.

Participants

All participants were from a 4-year secondary education program in modern languages education at a mid-sized research university located in the northwest region of the United States. The modern languages education program currently has national accreditation with restrictions and approximately three students complete the program each year. The participants in this study were Becky, Debra, and Rick (all pseudonyms). Becky was working on her residency teaching in Spanish at a high school to complete her program requirements and obtain her teaching certificate. Debra and Rick had completed the same program a year earlier and both were teaching Spanish, Debra at a middle school, Rick at a high school.

All were language teachers (residency or in-service) and in their 20s at the time of this study and all had spent time in regions where Spanish was the primary spoken language. Becky was the oldest and Debra the youngest of the participants. Becky had taught Spanish at the university level for several years and had also taught English for a time in an online setting as well. While neither Debra nor Rick had the type of teaching experience Becky had, they were both excellent students and often proved to be more flexible in their thinking than Becky for in-class and out-of-class assignments. Debra was especially good at producing outstanding work while Rick would need more time to process information. However, once he processed information Rick would put a very creative and unique spin on what he learned, often with very insightful results. Based on the experiences of the teacher trainer Becky, Debra, and Rick would be ranked in the top 10% of pre-service language teachers he has worked with over the past decade. All were reflective, caring, dedicated, and inspiring teaching professionals.

For this study Debra was the first to complete the survey and provided the greatest amount of detail in her responses. Becky was sent a reminder e-mail about the study and the second participant to complete the survey. Becky also provided a number of reflective comments in her data. Rick was sent several reminder e-mails about the study and finally, because of his teaching and coaching loads, a time when the survey could be given over the phone was arranged. Because the survey was administered to Rick over the phone, after he had finished coaching, but before scheduled parent conferences, his answers to the survey items were not as detailed as either Debra or Becky's.

Data Analysis

The data collected for this study through a survey (and for Rick in a phone interview) were examined for common themes in relation to the four stated questions of interest to this study. Because of the extremely small number of participants, data were not coded and no statistical analyses on the data were made. The data will be presented in the following manner. First, how and if participants remember the 3D segment of their Methods II course will be examined. This will be followed by exploring what technologies the participants employ in their current language teaching environments. Next the characteristics seen by participants as essential for future world language teachers will be offered. Finally, how these participants believe that the modern languages methods course they completed might be improved for future students will be shared.

IMPACT

The first question this study sought to investigate was what impacts the overarching 3D approach for utilizing technology these teachers encountered in their Methods II course had on their current uses of technology? The answers these teachers provided were very enlightening. Not one of them could recall the 3D approach with any clarity as part of their coursework. Even Becky, who had just completed her Methods II coursework a few months before starting her residency teaching assignment, did not remember it in specific detail. However she did comment that it had an impact, "Yes. Even if I don't remember the exact details of specific theories, the process of learning them and discussing them plants a seed that I often refer to as I plan for instruction, instruct, and reflect on instruction." Meanwhile Debra commented about the 3D approach that,

Unfortunately, I do not remember all that much about the 3-D approach from my methods course, other than that we had discussed the importance of not using technology for technology's sake, but rather to achieve a certain purpose and to support student learning in an effective way.

But Debra also added,

While it is not the guiding principle in my use of technologies in the classroom, I do try to keep in mind when using different technologies that it should have a purpose and should not just be so that students are doing something new and that they would think of as 'fun'.

Rick, meanwhile commented about the impact of the 3D approach on his current teaching as being nonexistent as he was now, "doing my own thing."

In terms of being provided the option of being exposed to just an overarching approach for technology use or an overarching approach as well as trainings in specific technologies, Becky, Debra, and Rick all would have liked to have had both kinds of content in their methods coursework. However, Rick did mention that, "it would have been hard for the teacher to bring in the exact technologies students would be working with in the future into the class." Debra meanwhile offers a very clear argument, and fitting summary for this section, as to why an overarching approach for embracing technology as well as trainings in some specific technologies would work very well together,

…it would probably be helpful to learn about some new technologies that seem promising for the near future in classrooms….Having some discussion and instruction on how to use these types of technologies may help guide teachers when they actually begin to use them in the classroom. They may also work as more concrete examples of how to apply the overarching principles, which seem more important since they carry over to more situations.

TEACHING REALITIES

The second question of this study set out to answer was what kinds of technology these teachers utilize in their classrooms and for what purposes? Of the 25 technologies employed for language teaching identified by the participants in this study, Smart Boards and interactive online apps and language practice programs appeared most frequently followed by the use of PowerPoints (See Table 1). In commenting on the pedagogical rationales for the various types of technology she employed in the classroom Becky remarked,

This makes language learning more engaging and relevant because students are able to see the language at work in the real world, and it is a nice interactive platform where the possibilities are endless. This is useful because the teacher can then listen to each dialogue individually. Their responses are projected in real time and students compete for points.

Table 1. Specific technologies currently utilized for teaching languages

	Becky	**Debra**	**Rick**
1	PowerPoint	SMART board	SMART board
2	Projector	Online textbook	PowerPoint
3	Speakers	Online videos (such as those from YouTube)	I-Movies
4	SMART board	Classroom wiki	Prezi
5	Recorders	Online "games" (such as Kahoot)	I-Pad
6	Smartphones	Online dictionaries	Screen chomp app
7	Vimeo	Grammar and vocabulary practice sites	Whiteboard
8	Quizlet		Little whiteboards
9			Cell phone
10			Phones

Meanwhile, Debra commented that the technologies she employs provide enhanced engagement between learners and the content being covered, "They can interact with the learning more by writing, typing, clicking, or dragging and dropping", "…can follow along more easily", "…are far more engaged" and "they are all completely engaged and interested." She adds that,

…students can access videos that are more realistic and relevant to them, and they can feel that they are truly learning the language because they are getting material that a native speaker would listen to. This also provides further input and allows students to hear the language as spoken by different speakers with different accents, something that they would be likely to encounter in real-life with the language.

Debra also remarked on the ability of technology to provide opportunities for practice, "…[It] allows for them to follow links there to further resources should they wish to do more practice outside of class" and "Students are able to practice their vocabulary, grammar, and other concepts quickly and this also gives instant feedback on those…" She further adds that,

…this practice is left to students to practice outside of class. This way, in-class instruction can focus on being more communicative (since this is harder to achieve outside of the classroom), while students are still getting the practice at home to help them use the language more accurately in their communication.

Rick on the other hand sees the majority of the technologies he employs in the classroom as being outlets for student products in the target language as well as ways for them to practice with the language both inside and outside the classroom.

With an understanding of what kinds of technology these teachers currently utilize in their classrooms and for what purposes in place, let us now turn our attention to the third and fourth questions this study sought to investigate.

Table 2. Essential characteristics future model modern languages educators will require for success

	Becky	**Debra**	**Rick**
1	Kind	Passion	Engaging
2	Patient	Approachability	Oral communication skills
3	Hardworking	Willingness to experiment	Technology
4	Able to collaborate with colleagues	Content-area knowledge	Patience
5	Curious about the world	Desire to keep learning	Rapport
6	Reflective of their own teaching	Humor	Time abroad
7	Interested in learning new ways of teaching	Creativity	Defend the profession
8	Resourceful	Patience	
9	Has a positive attitude		
10	Self-critical		

LOOKING TO THE FUTURE

The final two questions this study set out to investigate were what characteristics and traits future modern language educators will need to possess to be successful and how the methods courses these participants completed can be improved upon? For the first of these questions, from the 25 characteristics that study participants forwarded (See Table 2), all mentioned patience, and all spoke to a desire for continuous learning as essential (Rick imbedded this in his understanding of how technology would be used).

The future realities participants imagine for language teachers share both similarities and differences. Becky for example imagines a future in which,

World language teaching will change as it always has changed....I foresee that as the world becomes more and more connected, there will be a greater emphasis on culture and even travel than language classrooms of the past. I also foresee a greater use of technology in the classroom.

Meanwhile, Debra remarks that,

I suspect that world language teaching will continue to change at an even faster rate than it has up to this point. Being on the inside and seeing what is going on, I can see how technology will play an even greater role both inside and outside of the classroom. It is likely that the push will be towards being even more communicative and less grammar-based and that there will be further pressure to limit the use of L1 as much as possible.

Rick simply states about the future of the profession that, "It will be positive and continue to grow."

As for the role technology will play in these imagined language teaching futures, participants do not envision a future without technology. Becky comments that,

Technology will continue to be incorporated into the language classroom as long as it keeps helping us fulfill our goals. When I compare my high school Spanish classroom fifteen years ago to the Spanish classroom today, the role of technology has greatly increased. I foresee that it will continue to increase.

Debra adds,

Technology will become more and more prevalent and important in the language-learning environment. Students will be able to do far more outside of the classroom and will become more independent learners. It will become easier to differentiate instruction by providing students with materials appropriate to their levels. Students will also be able to interact with native speakers of the language more readily via video messaging applications.

But it is perhaps Rick who puts the future role of technology for language teaching most succinctly, "It is a must have. It is critical—it provides exposure to current language. It does a better job than books in staying current and it offers more than just the views of the teacher."

When asked to situate themselves in the future realities they see for language teaching Becky said,

I foresee that I will be open to teaching in a classroom where more technology is employed as long as it helps us meet our goals and keeps students engaged in language learning. I don't want to use technology only for the sake of using it, but I will use it if it helps us make language learning more interesting and dynamic for our students and helps us teach better.

Debra contributed the following,

As a teacher, I see myself as someone who facilitates and guides students more as they become more independent learners. Instead of providing them with the information, students will probably do more of their own self-teaching, with feedback and clarification provided by the teacher. I do not see technology being able to replace the world language teacher completely in the near future...but I do see the language teacher role changing even more as time goes on.

And Rick remarked that, "A lot of it will be about continuing to grow and adapt to embrace an approach with a constant element of change."

When asked what a model language teacher would be like and be able to do Becky stated that, "She will be able to adapt to a variety of environments and types of classrooms and schools." Debra suggested that,

The model world language teacher will be one that promotes language learning as much as possible, making it relevant to students' lives and making them see the importance of it in their futures....She will be able to engage students in their learning and help them grow as much as they possibly can in the language in the time she has with them....She will both teach students and learn from them, letting them know that she is just as much a student as they are, rather than some omniscient greater being. She will be open with her students and allow them to make mistakes, take risks, and experiment with their learning. She will not only teach the language, but will teach students those things that they most need to know. She will teach wherever there is a need for her to teach.

The Technology Segment of a Methods Course

Table 3. Preparing and training future language teachers

	Becky	Debra	Rick
1	If it is possible, more time in actual classrooms before the student teaching experience	It would likely be beneficial to teachers-in-training to have some type of instruction on SLA methods and theories earlier on in their training program…	Expose students to the realities of the profession ASAP. Require the local conference for networking and reality check purposes
2	One or two more micro teaching sessions	Further opportunities to observe other world language teachers in action, especially those that employ different methods in their teaching	More opportunities for student teachers to interact with current teachers
3	A model lesson assignment where students create a 15-30 lesson for an interview committee	It would also likely be useful to have more practice with mock teaching scenarios to become more comfortable with this earlier on.	
4	Mock interviews?		

Rick meanwhile had a much more focused understanding that a model language teacher should be able, "To be engaging with reading and writing and have a nuanced way of utilizing authentic resources. (I want to be) a person who can teach world language and critical thinking (skills). I am not here yet, but I am trying!"

TRAINING FUTURE TEACHERS

The final question put to participants was regarding what they would have liked to have experienced differently in their own program, specifically in their methods instruction (See Table 3). Of the nine comments they provided, four were directed at providing more substantive interactions with current in-service language teachers while students were in the program and two were aimed at offering students more practice teaching opportunities. While none of the comments speak specifically to technology, they do all suggest that, through more time spent with in-service teachers, or in mock teaching or preparing for teaching exercises, they would be exposed to more technology utilized by in-service teachers in their actual classrooms, and provided more opportunities to imagine and or practice how they might embrace technology in their own teaching later on.

DISCUSSION

In regards to the first question this study examined, it is not surprising that students had little or no memory of the 3Ds approach to employing technology for language teaching introduced to them in their Methods II course. It is hoped however, that the seeds for utilizing technology had been planted, which may still at some later day sprout into view. A similar conceptual framing was offered by Becky when she responded to whether she remembered the 3Ds or not as part of her methods' coursework. Indeed, as Watzke (2007) suggests, "…theoretical underpinnings, develop as pedagogical content knowledge through a process of teaching, conflict, reflection, and resolution specific to the classroom" (p. 74). Perhaps then these newly minted language teachers are still processing how they can and will utilize and interact with technology for language teaching purposes and their understandings of how to use it, and how it can be used, will evolve as they teach with it in their classrooms.

As for the technologies teachers identified as using for language teaching purposes there was a great deal of variation as to what constituted as a teaching technology and this variation proved very interesting. That small, individual whiteboards, audio recorders, and projectors were all captured under the term technology, offers language teacher trainers some insights into how teachers conceive technology operating in the classroom and perhaps an access point for instruction and layered learning moments for students in modern languages education programs. For example, a language teacher trainer might provide a number of slips of paper for students; each with a different possible technology they might encounter in their future classrooms and ask students to imagine how these technologies might be used for teaching and why. Then hand these same students some blank slips of paper and ask them to write down what they consider technology in the classroom and how they would use those technologies for language teaching as well.

As for why participants utilized technology for language teaching and learning, their answers are similar to findings found in earlier studies. To be sure, increased student engagement, providing additional opportunities for practice, immediate feedback, a vehicle for showcasing student target language work, increased access to native speakers and authentic language, as well as not just something to be used for its own sake, are important aspects for utilizing technology for language teaching and learning endeavors.

For example, in terms of not just using technology for technology's sake, Hoopingarner (2009) states, "…teaching languages with technology must take into account good language pedagogy, and that the introduction of technology neither replaces nor transforms the nature of good teaching" (p. 232). A sentiment echoed by Luke (2011),

It is safe to say that technology is not a panacea for all of the common educational elements. Simply changing the method, the venue, or the instructor does not guarantee a change in student motivation, student behavior, or student achievement. (p. 69)

As for the potential of technology to engage language learners, Allan (2015) states it has "... huge potential to bring your classroom alive" (p. 37). Loewen (2015) adds to this by remarking, "In particular, it can help keep learners interested in the learning process, and it can provide additional, engaging exposure to the L2, which can increase the learners' time on task…" (p. 153).

Comments made by Debra and Rick about technology providing enhanced access to resources are also found in Loewen (2015), who said, "…it is possible for learners to have much more exposure to the L2. Today, learners in foreign language contexts can have considerable access to authentic L2 materials and L2 native speakers with just a few clicks of a mouse" (p. 152). Loewen's insights into technology being "…a way of providing individualized instruction…" (p. 152) are also found in statements made by Debra. However, Loewen's view that technology "…can also be used to create additional social and interactive contexts for L2 learning…" (p. 153) was not found explicitly stated in participant data for this study. In addition to the fact that participants did not mention the potential impact of technology on classroom interaction, they also did not mention its possible role in language extensions, the post- elements of a learning cycle in which learners are pushed to use new language in the most open and free way possible. There were also no comments offered as to how students' target-language technology products, which Rick mentioned as being a primary use for technology in the language classroom, would be utilized or integrated for later classroom applications.

The Technology Segment of a Methods Course

Luke (2011) seems to sum up much of what participants in this study remarked on as being why they employ technology for language teaching, "Learners become invested in a process that empowers them by providing control over time, access, flexibility, individuality, and resources" (p. 72). And it is Luke's suggestions for the future of technology for language teaching which also find purchase with what participants shared in this study, "Computer and Internet technology are not likely to vanish any time soon from K-16 education" (p. 77). There are those who, "…view modular computer-based education as the future of the U.S. education system, primarily because it allows for individualization, differentiation, flexibility and adaptability" (p. 77).

For the question which asked for participants to share their vision for the traits and characteristics which future of language teachers will require to be successful, it was certainly interesting that only Rick mentioned knowledge of, and about, technology as an essential requirement. Even so, Becky and Debra both mentioned the need for a desire to keep learning and keep developing as a teacher which would probably include an ever-evolving understanding and utilization of technology.

Other traits identified by participants in this study as essential for future language educators are found in recently published works. For example, an examination of Lopez-Burton and Minor's (2014) work reveals that patience, engagement, humor, creativity, effective use of technology, and others are all qualities, traits, and skills currently viewed as being exhibited in outstanding modern language instructors. Items like continuing to be inquisitive and being flexible are not mentioned in that text but represent more of the entire experience of being a language teacher, which, as these participants provided with their data, does not end at the classroom door but extends well beyond the walls of the classroom.

In the last question participants were asked how the language methods courses they took might be improved so that future students taking those classes might benefit. One suggestion all participants had in common was for there to be more opportunities to interact with, and observe, current in-service teachers. While on the surface this suggestion does not specifically mention technology, it would certainly not be misleading to say that during these proposed additional interactions and observations with in-service language teachers, how those teachers use technology, and which technologies they use, would be a big part of what methods' students would take away from those kinds of experiences.

FUTURE RESEARCH DIRECTIONS

While data from this study has provided some insights into how this set of teachers processed a technology segment in their modern languages education program content, captured a glimpse of what technologies they currently employ for language teaching and why, and what they see as the required skills and abilities for future language teachers, many more questions emerged from this study than were answered. For example, how do current language teachers actually conceptualize technology functioning in their day-to-day teaching of languages at a deep level? Wright (2012) makes a powerful argument for an investigation into how teachers are embracing technologies and why when stating,

The current information revolution inevitable affects formal education…These new technologies do not simply exist, waiting neutrally to be used, either. Teachers often experience intense pressure to adopt technological solutions to learning problems, even when a case for adoption has not been made. (p. 64)

Further questions include, what roles and functions can an overarching approach for understanding technology serve in a language methods course? How do teachers make their primary assumptions as to how technology is to be utilized? What are the key abilities of an outstanding language teacher and where and how might abilities to use technology intersect with that understanding? And of course how do teachers utilize technology in an effective and informed matter for students in their classrooms when they must be cognizant that not every student has access to the same technologies or any technology at all. As Debra mentioned,

Even with all this, I do try to limit the amount of required work that I assign that necessitates the use of technology because I do still have students who do not have access to the internet or a computer at home and who would be at a disadvantage in completing their work.

In addition, because the number of participants in this study was so small, it may also prove useful to ask a similar set of questions of a larger group of language teachers to determine if their answers would reveal similar findings. Finally, Luke's (2011) proposed four professional "hats" language teachers need to wear; "invested expert", "curriculum developer", "technology expert", and "risk taker" could be an interesting framing for examining what professional skills language teachers see themselves as needing to have and how they might order those skills in terms of overall importance for success in classroom language teaching environments.

CONCLUSION

The majority of data gathered in this study confirms much of what has been found and discussed in earlier works: from the observation that students may not take in every element of what happens in their language education methods courses until a possible later time when that knowledge is required out of classroom need, to the benefits of technology for language teaching which involve enhancing engagement, increasing access to authentic resources, and providing opportunities for practice, to successful language teachers of tomorrow needing to be patient and having a desire to keep learning in rapidly changing teaching and learning environments.

While the data offered here do not break much new ground, they do offer confirmation of much of what has come before, and therefore, serve to bolster earlier claims as well as provide much needed data to further situate the actual thinking of language teachers about the roles and uses of technology through the lenses of their past coursework, current teaching contexts, and imagined futures. One possible take away from this study for the technology segment of future methods courses is that combinations of overarching and specific approaches for utilizing technologies for language teaching, embedded in current teaching realities and imagined future possibilities, may offer a very powerful platform from which to provide this kind of instruction. And such instruction is certainly of great value, as Jones and Coffey (2013) comment, "…studies have consistently confirmed that the role of the teacher is the single most important factor in determining the success of technologies contribution to learning" (p. 115).

In closing, data from this study can be added to the discussion about the perceived uses of technology for language teaching from the perspectives of language teachers. Data which, as Zhang, Zhao and Li (2014) mention, can help us move toward realizing more robust models for how to more effectively train teachers in the uses and roles of technology for language teaching,

If it is to be acknowledged what teachers do at the level of the classroom shapes the kinds of knowledge that students acquire and leads to educational change, achieving the desired effects of learning through ICT integration necessitates consideration of teachers' attitudes and beliefs and the contextual factors that shape them. (p. 252)

Just as in language teaching itself, for learning to occur you must begin the process of instruction from where the learners actually are developmentally and conceptually, not from where one might think they should be.

REFERENCES

Allan, S. (2015). *Teach now! Modern foreign languages: Becoming a great teacher of modern foreign languages*. London: Routledge.

Arnold, N. (2013). The role of methods textbooks in providing early training for teaching with technology in the language classroom. *Foreign Language Annals*, *46*(2), 230–245. doi:10.1111/flan.12020

Blake, R. J. (2013). *Brave new digital classroom: Technology and foreign language learning* (2nd ed.). Washington, DC: Georgetown University Press.

Boehm, D., & Aniola-Jedrzejek, L. (2009). Seven principles of good practice for virtual international collaboration. In M. Chang & C.-W. Kuo (Eds.), *Learning culture and language through ICTs: Methods for enhanced Instruction* (pp. 298–317). Hershey, PA: Information Science Reference. doi:10.4018/978-1-60566-166-7.ch018

Brandl, K. (2008). *Communicative language teaching in action: Putting principles to work*. Upper Saddle River, NJ: Pearson.

Brown, H. D., & Lee, H. (2015). *Teaching by principles: An interactive approach to language pedagogy*. White Plains, NY: Pearson.

Burns, A., & Richards, J. C. (Eds.). (2009). *The Cambridge guide to second language teacher education*. Cambridge, UK: Cambridge University Press.

Burns, A., & Richards, J. C. (Eds.). (2012). *The Cambridge guide to pedagogy and practice in second language teaching*. Cambridge, UK: Cambridge University Press.

Bush, M. D. (1997). Implementing technology for language learning. In M. D. Bush (Ed.), *Technology-enhanced language learning* (pp. 287–349). Lincolnwood, IL: National Textbook Company.

Cetto, M. (2010). Technology and second language teaching. *Brújula*, *8*, 119–121.

Chapelle, C. A. (2004). Technology and second language learning: Expanding methods and agendas. *System*, *32*(4), 593–601. doi:10.1016/j.system.2004.09.014

DuBravac, S. (2013). *Technology in the L2 curriculum*. Boston: Pearson.

Evans, M. (Ed.). (2009). *Foreign language learning with digital technology*. London: Continuum.

Fisher, L. (2009). Trainee teachers' perceptions of the use of digital technology in the languages Classroom. In M. J. Evans (Ed.), *Foreign Language Learning with Digital Technology* (pp. 60–79). London: Continuum.

Furstenberg, G., & Morgenstern, D. (1992). Technology for language learning and teaching: Designs, products, perspectives. In W. Rivers (Ed.), *Teaching languages in college: Curriculum and content* (pp. 117–140). Lincolnwood, IL: NTC.

Heift, T., & Chapelle, C. A. (2012). Language learning through technology. In S. M. Gass & A. Mackey (Eds.), *The routledge handbook of second language acquisition* (pp. 555–570). London: Routledge.

Hoopingarner, D. (2009). Best practices in technology and language teaching. *Language and Linguistics Compass*, *3*(1), 222–235. doi:10.1111/j.1749-818X.2008.00123.x

Jonassen, D., Howland, J., Marra, R. M., & Crismond, D. (2008). *Meaningful learning with technology* (3rd ed.). Upper Saddle River, NJ: Pearson.

Jones, J., & Coffey, S. (2013). Modern foreign languages 5-11: A guide for teachers (2nd ed.). London: Routledge.

Kern, R. (2006). Perspectives on technology in learning and teaching languages. *TESOL Quarterly*, *40*(1), 183–210. doi:10.2307/40264516

Kern, R. (2014). Technology as *Pharmakon*: The promise and perils of the internet for foreign language education. *Modern Language Journal*, *98*(1), 340–357. doi:10.1111/j.1540-4781.2014.12065.x

Lafford, P. A., & Lafford, B. A. (2005). CMC technologies for teaching foreign languages: What's on the horizon? *CALICO Journal*, *22*(3), 679–709.

Li, S., & Swanson, P. (Eds.). (2014). *Engaging language learners through technology integration; Theory, applications, and outcomes*. Hershey, PA: Information Science Reference.

Loewen, S. (2015). *Introduction to instructed second language acquisition*. New York: Routledge.

Lopez-Burton, N., & Minor, D. (2014). *On being a language teacher: A personal and practical guide to success*. New Haven, CT: Yale University Press. doi:10.12987/yale/9780300186895.001.0001

Luke, C. (2011). Crossing the digital divide: Language learning in virtual environments. In D. Schwarzer, M. Petrón, & C. Luke (Eds.), *Research informing practice—practice informing research: Innovative teaching methodologies for world language teachers* (pp. 59–85). Charlotte, NC: Information Age Publishing.

Luke, C. L., & Britten, J. S. (2007). The expanding role of technology in foreign language teacher education programs. *CALICO Journal*, *24*(2), 253–267.

Morgan, R. K., & Olivares, K. T. (Eds.). (2012). *Quick hits for teaching with technology: Successful strategies by award-winning teachers*. Bloomington, IN: Indiana University Press.

Oviatt, S. (2013). *The design of future educational interfaces*. New York: Routledge.

Reinders, H. (2009). Technology and second language teacher education. In A. Burns & J. C. Richards (Eds.), *The Cambridge guide to second language teacher education* (pp. 230–237). Cambridge, UK: Cambridge University Press.

Sabbath, M. (1962). Some aspects of teacher training in laboratory techniques. *Journal of Educational Sociology*, *35*(6), 271–272. doi:10.2307/2264339

Schmid, E. C., & Whyte, S. (2012). Interactive whiteboards in state school settings: Teacher responses to socio-constructed hegemonies. *Language Learning & Technology*, *16*(2), 65–86.

Walker, A., & White, G. (2013). *Technology enhanced language learning: Connecting theory and practice*. Oxford, UK: Oxford University Press.

Watzke, J. L. (2007). Foreign language pedagogical knowledge: Toward a developmental theory of beginning teacher practices. *Modern Language Journal*, *91*(1), 63–82. doi:10.1111/j.1540-4781.2007.00510.x

Wright, T. (2012). Managing the classroom. In A. Burns & J. C. Richards (Eds.), *The Cambridge guide to pedagogy and practice in second language teaching* (pp. 60–67). Cambridge, UK: Cambridge University Press.

Zhang, D., Zhao, S., & Li, L. (2014). Teachers' perceptions and use of information and communication technologies (ICTs) in Chinese language education. In S. Li & P. Swanson (Eds.), *Engaging language learners through technology integration; Theory, applications, and outcomes* (pp. 237–256). Hershey, PA: Information Science Reference.

ADDITIONAL READING

Hubbard, P. (2008). CALL and the future of language teacher education. *CALICO Journal*, *25*(2), 175–188.

Kern, R. (2011). Technology for language learning. In J. Simpson (Ed.), *The Routledge handbook of applied linguistics* (pp. 200–214). New York: Routledge.

Motteram, G., Slaouti, D., & Onat-Stelma, Z. (2013). Second language teacher education for CALL: An alignment of practice and theory. In M. Thomas, H. Reinders, & M. Warschauer (Eds.), *Contemporary computer-assisted language learning* (pp. 55–71). London: Bloomsbury.

Stevenson, I. (2008). Tool, tutor, environment or resource: Exploring metaphors for digital technology and pedagogy using activity theory. *Computers & Education*, *51*(2), 836–853. doi:10.1016/j.compedu.2007.09.001

KEY TERMS AND DEFINITIONS

3D System: An overarching system for successfully employing technology for language teaching and learning which speaks to the three primary distortions technology can cause (i.e., space, content, time). Expressed by the terms Directional (Space), Developmental (Content), and Decisive (Time).

Decisive: One aspect in a system for successfully employing technology for language teaching and learning which speaks to the distortion in time which technology can cause (The third D in the 3D system).

Developmental: One aspect in a system for successfully employing technology for language teaching and learning which speaks to the distortion in content (i.e., language) which technology can cause (The second D in the 3D system).

Directional: One aspect in a system for successfully employing technology for language teaching and learning which speaks to the distortion in space which technology can cause (The first D in the 3D system).

Extension: Part of a language lesson which offers language learners the opportunity to play with the language elements which have just been taught, allowing them more freedom in how and what they choose to do with the language. Extensions also provide language teachers with one type of comprehension check on learner uptake by observing the level at which learners can successfully employ these language elements.

Interaction: Opportunities created by the teacher allowing learners to engage each other, the teacher, and the content in meaningful ways, typically at the sentence-level, in the target language.

Product: Target-language materials students create (spoken or written) which are then folded back into the existing curriculum in meaningful ways.

Technology: Broadly understood as any resource, physical or virtual, which can be utilized for the enhancement of language teaching and learning (e.g., blackboard, blog…) .

Chapter 13
Mentoring Teacher Assistants to Use Online Tools

Grisel M. Garcia Perez
University of British Columbia – Okanagan, Canada

ABSTRACT

This chapter indicates how a group of Teaching Assistants (TAs) was trained in the use of technology to help students enrolled in large first year Spanish classes excel in learning of Spanish as a foreign language. Framed by the Communities of Practice theory proposed by Wenger (1998), this study supports the theory that by examining their practices, trainees may become more effective in what they learn. Six TAs participated in the study and their reflection-on-action logs were examined and compared to the trainer's personal observations. Interpretation of the results was then carried out by comparing parallel and dissimilar ideas which were then used as focus for discussion. Outcomes support the theory that communities of practice and reflective inquiry are valuable teacher training tools.

INTRODUCTION

The twenty-first century has brought a new challenge: preparing teacher candidates to guide learning with technology. The methods used to train teachers before have gone from classroom management, teaching strategies, lesson planning and evaluation to ways to teach, practice and evaluate the same content using different tools that entail ever-emerging electronic technological changes. In second/foreign language teaching and learning this reality has also become apparent. The introduction of voice tools, e-books, e-language labs, Skype, videos, and more, has opened exciting and creative ways to promote interaction among language learners. The value that these new tools have added to the teaching and learning language experiences constitutes a key issue that needs to be addressed in training students who want to become language teachers. First, they need to be armed with an excellent knowledge of technology, and second, they need to be able to use it as an integrated guiding tool in the teaching-learning process.

In this study, theory and practice were combined to achieve the training goals. To accomplish these goals, the teaching assistants (TAs) of a university-based Spanish program examined their practices in order to become more effective in what they were learning. They planned, monitored, observed, assessed

DOI: 10.4018/978-1-5225-0483-2.ch013

and reflected on their practices. Trainees were given tasks which they solved and discussed in groups; they observed how their individual group gave feedback to the students they were assigned, and then came together to discuss their observations. Finally, they reflected on what they had learned from their study group. Framed by the Communities of Practice theory proposed by Wenger (1998), this case study is used as evidence to support the theory that by examining their practices, trainees can become more effective in learning about technology and its value in second/foreign language teaching and learning. Drawing upon the theoretical framework, the following objectives were formulated:

1. To examine how teaching assistants could benefit from a learning community with respect to using technology to teach
2. To assess how reflective learning impacts their effectiveness in assisting students learning Spanish as a foreign language.

CONNECTING TRAINEES AND STUDENTS WITH TECHNOLOGY

Over the years, the need to be more technologically literate has become prevalent among educators. Besides basic teaching practices like lesson planning and classroom management, the curriculum in pre-service teaching has been incorporating courses like Connecting Technology with Learning, Technology and Second/Foreign Language Learning, and Educational Technology. These additions have prompted researchers to conduct studies that investigate, for example, pre-service teacher's self efficacy beliefs about technology integration (Abbit, 2011; and Wang, Ertmer, & Newby, 2004). They argue that if self-efficacy beliefs lead to increased performance, they can help pre-service teachers increase their self belief so that, in turn, their use of technology can improve. However, both studies fail to prove this relationship. Abbit (2011) concludes that his study results represent perceptions of knowledge and beliefs and not evidence of demonstrated knowledge and ability.

Other researchers have studied the value of e-mail exchanges between pre-service teachers and students to open up dialogue between them (Cook-Sather, 2007), or to build skills for teaching writing (Davenport, 2006). Cook-Sather investigated how weekly e-mail exchanges between trainees and their teachers and trainees and their students create a unique space for teaching and learning for all participants. Participants in her study reported that e-mail exchanges are beneficial because they create a space that allows for instant, regular, individualized communication, careful analysis and reflection, and insight into others' point of view.

The fact that Cook-Sather (2007) gives special consideration to self reflection in her investigation is very relevant for this study. In teacher training, conscious development of insights into what the trainees are learning and experimenting with is paramount, and technology can be used to facilitate this practice and to guide the students' learning process.

Computer Assisted Language Learning (CALL)

The idea to guide learning with technology has represented a shift in education from the twentieth to the twenty first century (Fernández, García-Pérez, & Santiago, (2014); Fernández, Santiago, Tomaino, del Río, & Casaravilla, 2011; García-Pérez, 2014; 2011; Harmer, 2008; 2007; Niess, Lee, & Kajder,

2008; Wang, Ertmer, & Newby, 2004; and Willis & Willis, 2007). In second or foreign language teaching, Computer Assisted Language Learning (CALL) has been in practice since the 60's and has gone through three main stages: the structural/behavioral stage, the communicative stage, and the integrative stage (Koike & Klee, 2013; Yang, 2010).

CALL's first stage (structural/behavioral) was based on the behaviorist theory and was characterized by repetitive language drills which the students completed following computer commands. The second stage (communicative) was based on the communicative approach. At this stage, computer exercises were more centered on the communicative use of forms than on the grammatical forms themselves. Grammatical rules were not explained in class, and students were given more opportunities to be more creative in using the target language. Software was designed with the flexibility to allow students to work either alone or in groups to complete tasks like a language game or reconstruction of a text. With technological advances in the 90's, these communicative computer programs were slowly left behind and the integrative stage appeared. This third stage established a link between the four main skills in language teaching (listening, speaking, reading and writing) with technology in order to improve the language learning process. Elements like video, sound, animation and graphics were combined with the text to enrich the learning environment. However, in spite of all the advances of this integrative stage, Koike & Klee (2013) stated that there were still controversies in regards to "whether or not computer programs were intelligent enough to allow a true interaction" (p. 210); and others argued that there was not a single universally accepted Second Language Acquisition (SLA) theory supporting current technological materials (Levy, 1997).

In order to better understand the value that computers brought to SLA, Kern & Warschauer (2000) proposed the socio-cognitive approach. This model provided alternative contexts to facilitate negotiation of meanings in collaborative situations, and ultimately created authentic discourse communities through realistic communicative tasks. Based on this approach, different studies were launched to enhance listening, speaking, reading and writing. For example, through Skype sessions, studies were carried out to promote authentic interactions with native speakers, thus promoting authentic practice of these four main skills (Fernández, García-Pérez, & Santiago, 2014; Fernández, Santiago, Tomaino, del Río, & Casaravilla, 2011). Besides these four main skills, some of these studies tried to determine the relationship between language learning and intercultural communication. Using virtual exchanges, these researchers argued that by providing the students with virtual contacts with native speakers, their language proficiency and their intercultural awareness could improve. Through e-mail exchanges, research was also conducted to facilitate the development of reading and writing (García-Pérez & Fernández, 2011; Lawrence, 2002; Liaw & Johnson, 2001; Porter, 1997; Schueller, 2007; Sipe, 2000; Yang, 2010). All these studies incorporated CALL to develop language learning but it was apparent that those involved in the teaching process needed to be able to acquire more skills to obtain the most from these technological advances and better guide students' learning.

Taking this into account, the Spanish Program at the University of British Columbia, Okanagan Campus (UBCO) designed a series of training activities for students who had been granted a position as Spanish TAs. These TAs were hired to work 6 hours a week (during 13 weeks) assisting the instructors in class (3 hours), marking online journals, uploading and troubleshooting online vocabulary and grammar quizzes, and giving feedback to students on iLrn (3 hours). The training was focused upon the importance of reflective practice in the learning process, so a case study framed by the Communities of Practice theory was designed.

Communities of Practice

The notion that learning entails a profound process of participation in a community of practice has increased significantly in the past few years (Dede, 2004; Gómez-Blancarte & Miranda Viramontes, 2014; Hoadley, 2012; Saint-Onge & Wallace 2011, Wenger, 2004; 1998; Wenger, McDermott, & Snyder, 2002; Wenger & Snyder, 2000). In particular, the Communities of Practice framework provides opportunities for ongoing practical learning for its members, "communities of practice are groups of people who share a concern or a passion for something they do and who interact regularly to learn how to do it better" (Wenger, 1988).

According to Wenger's theory, a community of practice must have three main characteristics: the domain, the community and the practice. The first refers to the fact that the group needs to share the same area of interest. In this case study, six TAs were hired to assist first year large language classes. Most learned Spanish as a foreign language, were proficient in the language, and had a passion to assist in the language learning process. This group was easily distinguished from remaining TAs in the department: they were the "Spanish TAs" with their own identity and similar interests. The second characteristic is the community. To meet this criterion, members should assist each other in sharing information in the process of learning, so a course (Spanish Applied Linguistics- Span 441) was designed to provide the space the TAs needed to build relationships that allowed them to learn from each other. During weekly in-class sessions, TAs had the opportunity to talk about their experiences when uploading online vocabulary quizzes designed by the researcher. They could discuss their concerns, and assist each other with feedback. More advanced TAs mentored less advanced ones in uploading these quizzes on *Blackboard Connect*, the enterprise level online Learning Management System used at the University of British Columbia, which professors can use to expand the classroom, engage the students, and enhance learning. They also served as mentors on marking first year students' online journals, and in providing feedback to first year students on *iLrn*, a course management system created specifically for languages and used to provide students the opportunity to develop their skills in listening, speaking, reading, and writing at their own pace. Unconsciously, they were actually assessing other students which is a "valuable working tool in teacher education because it supports student teachers to acquire skills that are essential in their professional working life" (Sluijsmans & Prins, 2006, p. 6).

The last characteristic is the practice. This refers to the fact that the group needs to share hands-on experiences. Interaction is a key here, and the development of resources, solving problematic tasks, and sharing stories is vital. In order to organize this shared practice, sessions were organized in three different areas: online vocabulary quizzes, online journals, and *iLrn*. During week one, the TAs became acquainted with the Span 101 class they were assigned to, so in-class discussions focused on this topic. Week two was devoted to online vocabulary quizzes, week three to online journals, and week four to *iLrn*. Reflective logs were collected each week, commencing week five again with online quizzes, week six with online journals, etc., until a cycle of three discussion sessions per area were completed. The idea was to examine whether the assignments became more manageable through hands-on experience and whether the students' sense of confidence when giving feedback to first year language students grew over time as they reflected upon their learning within their study group.

CONTEXT

Currently, the Spanish Program at UBCO has an intake of over one thousand students annually who either want to satisfy the language other than English requirement or want to pursue a major or minor in Spanish or a combined major or minor in Spanish and French. It is possible to satisfy the language other than English requirement through different options, including successful completion of examinations or demonstrating competency in any language other than English with presentation of official transcripts. Other options are:

1. Successful completion of an approved Grade 12 course in a language other than English before entering UBC Okanagan
2. GREK 111 and 121, and LATN 300
3. Secondary school in their first language in case of students whose first language is other than English,
4. All four levels of the American Sign Language Basic Certificate offered through an accredited institution.
5. Either French 104, German 210, Japanese 201, Spanish 202, Spanish 204, Spanish 252 or its equivalent.
6. Successful completion of Okanagan Language (NSYL 110 and NSYL 111) offered through the Nicola Valley Institute of Technology at the En'owkin Centre or the UBC Okanagan campus.

The Spanish Program is housed in the Faculty of Creative and Critical Studies (FCCS) and offers twelve courses per school year not counting two first and two second year language courses that are offered in the summer. From these twelve courses, six are devoted to teaching the Spanish language and are yearly at nearly full capacity: ten beginner language classes (Span 101-102: sixty students per class); seven intermediate language level classes (Span 201-202: forty students per class); and two advanced language classes (Span 301-302: thirty five students per class) for a total of nineteen language classes with around 950 students. The other six courses are offered at the third or fourth year levels and cover specializations such as literature, linguistics, or translation. The maximum capacity in these classes is usually twenty five, and there are around 100 students enrolled at these levels. The tendency is to see the number of students per class decrease as the level increases.

Monitoring the students' learning was being compromised because immediate individual feedback was not logically possible in these large face-to-face classes. In second or foreign language learning, feedback is understood as any communication between the instructor and the student that provides information about the student's performance in a given task. If feedback is absent or reduced, the learning process is affected. As a result, the Spanish Program started mentoring TAs in the use of technology as a means of monitoring first year students' learning.

METHOD

Participants

Six TAs participated in the study: one graduate teaching assistant, two undergraduate teaching assistants and three work-study students. All were female students and were housed in the Faculty of Creative and Critical Studies. There were three trainers: Trainer 1 was from the Center of Teaching and Learning who trained the TAs on *Blackboard Connect*. Trainer 2 was a specialist from *iLrn Heinle Learning Center*, and Trainer 3 was the Head of the Spanish Program, an assistant professor in the same faculty who teaches Span-441, and the person conducting the study. Trainer 3 participated in all training sessions and was the only one keeping a log aside from the TAs.

The Training

Integrating technology into the training of TAs involved three stages. The first two stages occurred one week prior to the start of the semester. The third stage lasted 9 weeks for a total of 10 weeks of training. During the first stage, six TAs were trained in the general use of *Blackboard Connect,* an online Learning Management System used to expand the classroom, engage the students, and enhance learning. Technological training related to language activities included:

1. Uploading and trouble-shooting online vocabulary and grammar quizzes
2. Becoming familiar with giving feedback to students' online journals following the Program's rubrics.
3. Familarizing themselves with keeping grades updated

Training at this stage was provided by Trainers 1 and 3. First, a two-hour workshop was given to all TAs by Trainer 1 where the basic features of the platform were explained. Second, a language related session (one hour) was arranged to address uploading a sample vocabulary quiz and giving feedback to students' online journals. This session was conducted by Trainer 3.

The second stage included a one hour workshop given by Trainer 2 where all TAs were trained in the use of *iLrn Heinle Learning Center,* an online system used to provide students with the opportunity to develop their skills in listening, speaking, reading, and writing at their own pace. This workshop was done through a teleconference where the basic features of this e-learning platform were explained. Again, Trainer 3 offered individual training sessions in the use of *iLrn Heinle Learning Center.* This system has assignable integrated textbook activities that allow TAs to give students individual feedback on their language learning. The students taking beginner and intermediate language courses are required to buy a package containing the Spanish textbook *¿Cómo se dice...? 10th Edition*, an *iLrn* access card, and a bilingual dictionary.

The third stage was a related to taking *Spanish Applied Linguistics (Span 441).* TAs were invited to take this 36-hour course and all 6 accepted the invitation. In this course, theoretical linguistic concepts were introduced, and the experiential learning approach was used to provide those taking the course with opportunities to enact the concepts learned through classroom observations and in class assistance to first-year students. All TAs were given the opportunity to integrate the technological tools learned in Stages 1 and 2 in Span 441. Weekly vocabulary and grammar quizzes were given to the study group to upload on connect, and each TA was assigned to a section of Spanish 101 to assist a Spanish instructor in giving feedback to first year students' online journals and *iLrn* exercises.

TAs and Trainer 3 Logs

Because this study examines the impact that the Communities of Practice theory has on TAs' learning while they were being trained in the use of technology, Trainer 3 encouraged the TAs to address the following questions in their study group and personal logs:

1. How difficult is it to upload online quizzes on *BlackBoard Connect*? How long did it take you to test the quiz?
2. Do you get any support from your study group? What are your major concerns?
3. How difficult is it to give feedback on students' online journals? How long does it take? Do you get any support from your study group? What are your major concerns?
4. How difficult it is to give feedback to students' *iLrn* exercises? How long does it take? Do you get any support from your study group? What are your major concerns?

The study group was formed by the six TAs who were asked keep their personal logs from the moment they started uploading online quizzes on *Blackboard Connect*. Trainer 3 encouraged the study group to interact in Spanish and through the process of negotiation of meaning, the TAs reached a clear understanding of each other in their interactions. However, all TAs had the choice to keep personal logs either in English or Spanish.

ANALYSIS

In order to analyse the TAs progress, the ten weeks of training were divided into three periods: Time 1 (Weeks 1-4), Time 2 (Weeks 5-7) and Time 3 (Weeks 8-10).

Time 1 (Weeks 1 to 4)

The trainer's notes reveal that most TAs who took part in this case study reported having major difficulties uploading online quizzes on *Blackboard Connect*. It took them an average of 35 minutes to upload the first quiz which consisted of ten multiple choice questions (All vocabulary and grammar quizzes had the same number of questions). The TAs explained that problems arose when they started testing and saw that they had to be really meticulous in spelling, punctuation, and clicking the right boxes for the quiz to work as expected. Five TAs said that they had received enormous help from the only graduate TA in the group. This TA was doing her Doctorate degree in Translation and was very skillful in technological issues. Another concern was timing. The TAs had been instructed to program the quiz for only ten minutes without backtracking to change errors. While the study group was troubleshooting the quizzes, they reported that ten minutes was not enough for first year students to complete the task. They unanimously proposed changing the timing to fifteen minutes.

Regarding giving feedback to students' online journals, all TAs reported that the activity was enjoyable. They spent an average of two minutes per student. Four out of the six TAs were non-native speakers of Spanish and expressed some insecurity when carrying out the task, something observed by Trainer 3. All four TAs stressed the immense assistance received by the two native Spanish-speaking TAs in the group. In this first round, online journals were supposed be submitted on *Blackboard Connect* in a dropbox, and students were supposed to write from twenty five to thirty words where they introduced themselves because the topic of the lesson was *Getting to know each other*. For this activity, trainees had to highlight the students' mistakes; and according to the rubrics provided (Appendix 1), they had to decide which acronym to write to guide the students' corrections. Based on the feedback provided, students could resubmit their journals to get a higher mark. It was interesting to note that five TAs out of the six were amazed at the fact that some first year students made the same mistake when they said what their name was: *Me llamoesAntonio* instead of *Me llamo Antonio*. In their study group discussion, contrastive error analysis led them to conclude that the students were just transferring the syntax from English *My nameisAntonio*. So, taking advantage of opportunistic teaching, topics like fozzilization and ways to address negative transfer from the learner's first language were brought up by the instructor during one of the Spanish 441 lessons.

Regarding *iLrn*, the study group reported that it was an extremely easy and enjoyable activity. Most of the exercises are self corrected, and the ones assigned that needed the TAs' attention required few corrections. The TAs' concerns were more related to the exercises themselves because in some cases, correct but dispreferred answers were not accepted. The instructor advised them to relay that information to the study group leader who could contact the publisher directly with these types of discrepancies encountered on *iLrn*.

Time 2 (Weeks 5 to 7)

During week five, the study group reported that uploading quizzes on *Blackboard Connect* had become easier. It took its members an average of ten minutes to upload and troubleshoot each quiz. By this time, the TAs had already uploaded and tested six quizzes, three vocabulary and three grammar. Quiz uploading and testing was conducted as in the study group, but TAs took turns keying in the data. Trainer 3 was always present when they were carrying out the task, which occurred in the trainer's office. During the first four weeks, online quizzes were released on Saturday morning at 8:00am and made available until midnight Sunday. The TAs agreed that it was better to release the quizzes on Friday afternoon (2:00 pm) to accommodate students who had other commitments on weekends. The window of time was expanded as per their recommendations.

Online journals became progressively more challenging because the students had to write more for each subsequent entry. In total, Span 101 students are required to write four journal entries organized by themes. The first one, as already mentioned, is *Getting to know each other* (25 words), the second *At the University* (50 words), the third one *On the phone* (75 words), and the last one *Customs and Traditions* (100 words). As structures became more complex, some TAs felt unsure about their ability to provide students with correct feedback. In particular, two TAs reported not feeling confident about correcting students' mistakes, notably prepositions *a* and *en*, "to" and "in" respectively. They immediately requested assistance from two other group members and the instructor (Trainer 3) adjusted her office hours to meet the needs of these TAs.

Regarding *iLrn*, the TAs reported that many students were not completing all the exercises. One TA recommended creating alerts on *BlackBoard Connect* which could remind the classes when the online exercises were due. Another TA said that sending an e-mail reminder as well could be beneficial. Both suggestions were put into practice after consulting faculty members teaching first year classes. All instructors were very supportive at all times and accommodated all of the TAs' needs.

Time 3 (Weeks 8 to 10)

By this time, the TAs required minimal supervision and assistance with online quizzes. They felt very comfortable uploading them. However, the number of TAs being uncomfortable with correcting online journal entries increased to three. These three TAs were encouraged to come to the instructor's office and there, they completed the task collaboratively without difficulty. All TAs reported that the alert on *Blackboard Connect* had worked because more students were completing the assigned *iLrn* exercises. Another TA thought that it was better to do the *¿Qué dijiste?* (What did you say?) and the *Para decirlo en Español* (How do you say this in Spanish) exercises in class because the exercises were difficult. To complete *¿Qué dijiste?*, for example, an answer is provided and the students have to come up with a question; in *Para decirlo en Español,* the students have to translate mini dialogues that include the vocabulary and grammar studied in the lesson. These observations were taken into consideration for future courses and were passed on to the Faculty in the Spanish Program.

CHALLENGES

The hiring of TAs was a response to an increase in student enrolment in the Spanish program at UBC Okanagan. This increase was good news but brought with it challenges. Concerns among the Faculty in the Spanish program grew because manpower remained the same; there was no money for new hires. Thus, four full time professors plus a sessional instructor had to share the increased workload. Formative evaluation in second/foreign language teaching is of outmost importance, and it was evident that it would be impossible to give individual feedback to students in these large language classes, so monitoring the students' learning was compromised.

Training these new TAs in the use of technology as a means to provide such monitoring appeared to be a viable solution. However, the Department did not have the means to hire enough assistants. At that time, the Spanish Program had only been allocated funds for two graduate students (twelve hours a week each) to be TAs, but six were needed. One graduate student withdrew from the program due to personal reasons, so the money allocated to this student was split into two undergraduate teaching assistant positions at six hours per week each. The Head of the Spanish program applied for three TA positions for work study students.

The Work Study Program at UBC Okanagan offers a minimum wage subsidy to faculty who commit to provide the TAs they hire with enriched educational employment opportunities. Applications are very competitive and students are usually allowed to work a maximum of twelve hours per week. Full-time graduate, undergraduate, international, exchange, or unclassified students may apply. At the time of this study, one international student (a native Spanish speaker) was hired, and two undergraduates who were majoring in Spanish. The composition of the TAs participating in the study was thus mixed and this had serious implications. First, not all students were hired to work the same number of hours weekly: graduate students had 12 hours; undergraduate 6 hours; and work study 10 hours. The trainer needed to take varying pay scales and work/contact hours into consideration when assigning tasks to these TAs.

The second challenge was classroom configuration and available equipment. Once hired and trained on *Blackboard Connect* and *iLrn*, TAs were assigned to a specific Span 101 class taking into consideration the time the class was taught and the TAs' own schedule. Not all classrooms at UBC Okanagan are the same. Language programs have three designated language classrooms with a maximum capacity of 40 students. This meant that professors teaching first year Spanish could not be assigned to those classrooms because their class size was 60. Hence, they had to teach in classrooms that still kept the basic arrangement which had been used for years (a board where the teachers and students write with a chalk or markers, an overhead projector or a projector, textbooks and a CD player). The TAs were trained to assist the instructors in class whenever they needed to show the videos included in *iLrn*. Many of the instructors are accustomed to use e-books and follow the links to carry out the listening activities that come along with the e-book, but this was not possible if they were assigned to classrooms that were not equipped with their technological needs. Other professors were more fortunate because they were assigned to lecture style classrooms which were then used as electronic laboratory style classrooms. These classrooms are equipped with two projectors, a computer, two projection screens, and excellent speakers but the seating arrangement is not ideal for language teaching. The seats are pinned to the floor and it is thus very difficult to promote collaboration and group work. Social learning in these classrooms was mainly achieved when the students worked in pairs but it was physically impossible to give individual feedback to students in lecture style classrooms. This means that the TAs were exposed to mixed hands-on experience for actual use of technology in the classrooms.

Another challenge was related to the fact that TAs had varying language proficiency levels. Two of the six TAs were born in Mexico and had come to Canada early in their lives. They had native like command of Spanish, but English was their dominant language. The other four TAs were Canadian students who had learned Spanish at UBC Okanagan. From these four, one had an excellent command of Spanish grammar, but the other three hesitated quite a bit when they had to give feedback to the students' online journals. Even though all concerns were solved in the study group, the whole situation represented a bit of frustration and perhaps demotivated the less proficient TAs.

The last challenge was that not all students taking Span 441 were TAs. This meant that even though a physical space was provided in the classroom for the TAs to share their experiences in online learning within their study group, time had to be allotted to the rest of the class to share other kinds of experiences which the students taking Span 441 had had in their assigned classes. From the point of view of classroom management, this reality was very challenging. Nevertheless, this enriched the class dialogue, and contributed to the activities they had to complete for the course in general, which were:

1. To support first year students in their Spanish learning: Each Span 441 student was assigned five first year students whom they monitored closely throughout the semester.
2. Observations: Students of Span 441 were asked to complete four classroom observation tasks on specific grammatical aspects taught to first year students.
3. Reflective Journal: concerns arising from their encounters with first year students and classroom observations.
4. Teaching materials: Resources Span 441 students created to facilitate language learning.

5. Research project: Span 441 students were assigned three possible topics for a research project: learning strategies, assessment and testing in Second Language Teaching, and Computer Assisted Language Learning. They could select one of the three and specific guidelines were posted on *Blackboard Connect* for successful completion of this task.

SOLUTIONS AND RECOMMENDATIONS

Redesigning Span 441 as a two semester course combining technological training, classroom observations, and hands-on activities in the classroom may provide a sustainable solution to the current problem the Spanish Program is facing with large language classes. Students in Span 441 have demonstrated their willingness to assist first year students pursuing Spanish language learning, and the potential to use these students in their pre-service training as human resources to the fullest and best potential is there without financial costs. Theory can be introduced in class, allowing the students to enact the concepts learned outside the classroom. The course itself may be used to support their community of practice where its members, sharing the same values and learning from each other, can examine their practices and raise awareness of their own strengths and weaknesses.

At the moment, the Spanish program has secured financial support for three undergraduate TAs working six hours a week. Based on previous experience regarding mixed language proficiency levels, TAs are going to be assessed using the Common European Framework of Reference for Languages (CEFR), a guideline used to describe achievements of learners of foreign languages mostly in Europe. TA candidates should be able to get a level of B2 or above to be considered for a position of Spanish TA. This measure should improve the teaching assistants' performance when giving feedback on online journals to first year students. Another proposed solution is to make Span-441 a required course for those students applying for a TA position in the Spanish program.

Regarding class size, the Spanish Program at UBCO has the largest language class size in the province of British Columbia, Canada. The Department Head has been asked to lower the maximum capacity in first year language classes to 45 and approval is pending. Training TAs to use technology effectively in monitoring students' learning could diminish the negative impact of large classes where opportunities are limited to otherwise provide formative evaluation.

FUTURE DIRECTIONS IN TEACHER TRAINING

For optimal learning to take place, many factors need to be taken into consideration. In particular, three stand out in this study. One is the on-going assessment of students' performance. When teachers observe students' performance in class, they collect evidence that reflects the way students progress towards the goals of instruction, helping them check the current status of their learning process and the steps they need to take to achieve their goals. This informal diagnosis is called formative assessment. In large language classes, formative assessment may be compromised, but a possible solution may be for teachers to start considering new ways of using online learning resources to assess their students' learning. The need to combine formative and summative assessment is imperative in language classes because the students can use the teacher's on-going feedback to improve their learning, while teachers can make use of summative evaluations to evaluate the students' learning. More qualitative and quantitative research is needed to examine the role that technology can play in shaping and adjusting what may happen next in the classroom. In other words, more statistical data should exist supporting the validity of the correlation between technology and formative evaluation. But even more important than this is the need to examine effective ways in which pre-service and language teachers can be trained to use technology and the effects their training may have on their practices regarding formative assessment.

A related factor is guiding learning with technology. Teachers need to make important decisions when selecting training programs that involve technology. In teacher training, the idea is to have trainees learn about technology while they learn with it. However in order to be successful, trainers need to be knowledgeable about technology. This means that they need to have a diverse range of strategies and approaches to be able to choose the most effective ones ultimately meeting their desired training objectives. Research in this area should be more focused on finding out what the trainees' perceptions are regarding the best practices in technology training.

The last factor is experiential learning. Creating Communities of Practice, that is, groups who come together with the same interests, who want to share their knowledge, reflect upon their learning, and learn from each other while putting theory into practice seems to be an excellent approach in successful educational technology. In teacher training, there is a need to gain a deeper understanding of virtual learning environments to promote the importance of having students collaborate in virtual communities of practice. In this regard, virtual forums on using technology to support language learning may allow teacher candidates and others to form communities of practice at a distance.

CONCLUSION

This case study was guided by the conceptual framework proposed by Wenger (1988) regarding Communities of Practice. It constitutes a compelling form of enquiry and theory building that helped reveal that by reflecting on their practices through sharing and discussions in study groups or learning communities, trainees' effectiveness in learning about technology and its valuable use in second/foreign language teaching and learning may improve. Based on the trainees' notes, the benefits of functioning in a community of practice become apparent.

"Me gusta mi grupo. Me encanta que nos ayudamos y aprendemos mutuamente"
Translation: *"I like my group. I love that we help each other and learn from each other"*

The fact that communication through technology can become time and place independent allowed the students to receive asynchronous individual assistance from all of the TAs. Moreover, the technological tools allowed TAs to reach out to all the students, something which was almost impossible in a face-to-face class. In most cases, reflective learning positively impacted the effectiveness of the TAs in assisting students learning Spanish as a foreign language. As in most case studies, results are difficult to generalize due to small sample size. However, preliminary findings do build on the theory that reflective inquiry is a valuable tool in teacher training.

REFERENCES

Abbitt, J. T. (2011). An investigation of the relationship between self-efficacy beliefs about technology integration and technological pedagogical content knowledge (TPACK) among preservice teachers. *Journal of Digital Learning in Teacher Education, 27*(4), 134–143. doi:10.1080/21532974.2011.10784670

Cook-Sather, A. (2007). Using email to connect pre-service teachers, experienced teachers, and high school students within an undergraduate teacher preparation program. *Journal of Technology and Teacher Education, 15*(1), 11–37.

Davenport, N. A. M. (2006). Connecting pre-service teachers with students: Using email to build skills for teaching writing. *Journal of Reading Education, 31*(2), 13–19.

Dede, C. (2004). Enabling Distributed-Learning Communities via Emerging Technologies. *Proceedings of the 2004 Conference of the Society for Information Technology in Teacher Education (SITE)*. Charlottesville, VA: American Association for Computers in Education.

Dewey, J. (1938). *Experience and Education*. Indianapolis, IN: Kappa Delta Pi.

Fernández, T., García-Pérez, G., & Santiago, J. (2014). A Language Exchange Program: Sustainability Innovation in Language and Culture Engagement. *Journal of Science, 12*(2), 8–12.

Fernández, T., Santiago, J., Tomaino, A., del Río, M., & Casaravilla, A. (2011). A Virtual Challenge: English-Spanish learning exchange between Australian and Spanish university students. *Proceedings of the 5th International Technology, Education and Development Conference, (INTED2011)*.

García-Pérez, G. (2011). Effectiveness of formative e-assessment in large language classes. *Proceedings of the 6th International Conference on e-Learnin*. Academic Publishing Limited.

García-Pérez, G. (2014). *Learning by doing: Spanish Applied Linguistics as a Living Lab*. 2nd International Scientific Forum, Albania.

García-Pérez, G., & Fernández, T. (2011). When three cultures meet: Enhancing intercultural communication through virtual story telling. *The 9th International Conference on Education and Information Systems, Technologies and Applications*.

Gómez-Blancarte, A., & Miranda Viramontes, I. (2014). Communities of practice: A theoretical framework to design for teachers' statistical learning. In K. Makar, B. de Sousa, & R. Gould (Eds.), *Sustainability in statistics education: Proceedings of the Ninth International Conference on Teaching Statistics (ICOTS9)*.

Harmer, J. (2007). *The Practice of English Language Teaching* (4th ed.). Pearson Education Limited.

Harmer, J. (2008). *How to teach English (New Edition)*. Pearson Education Limited.

Hoadley, C. (2012). What is a community of practice and how can we support it? In Theoretical foundations of Learning Environments. Routledge, Taylor and Frances Group.

Koike, D. A., & Klee, C. A. (2013). *Lingüística aplicada: Adquisición del español como segunda lengua*. New York, NY: John Wiley and Sons, Inc.

Lawrence, G. (2002). The use of E-mail as a tool to enhance second language education programs: An example from a core French classroom. *Canadian Modern Language Review*, *58*(3), 465–472. doi:10.3138/cmlr.58.3.465

Liaw, M. L., & Johnson, R. J. (2001). E-mail writing as a cross-cultural learning experience. *System*, *29*(2), 235–251. doi:10.1016/S0346-251X(01)00013-6

Niess, M. L., Lee, J. K., & Kajder, S. B. (2008). *Guiding Learning with Technology*. John Wiley and Sons, Inc.

Porter, L. R. (1997). *Creating the virtual classroom, distance learning with the Internet*. John Wiley & Sons, Inc.

Saint-Onge, H., & Wallace, D. (2011). *Leveraging Communities of Practice for Strategic Advantage*. Abingdon, UK: Routledge.

Schueller, J. (2007). One good turn deserves another: Sustaining an intercultural E-mail exchange. *Die Unterrichtspraxis*, *40*(2), 184–196.

Sipe, R. B. (2000). Virtually Being There: Creating Authentic Experience through Interactive Exchanges. *English Journal*, *90*(2), 104–111. doi:10.2307/821226

Sluijsmans, D. M. A., & Prins, F. (2006). A conceptual framework for integrating peer assessment in teacher education. *Studies in Educational Evaluation*, *32*(1), 6–22. doi:10.1016/j.stueduc.2006.01.005

Wang, L., Ertmer, P. A., & Newby, T. J. (2004). Increasing preservice teachers' self-efficacy beliefs for technology integration. *Journal of Research on Technology in Education*, *36*(3), 231–250. doi:10.1080/15391523.2004.10782414

Wenger, E. (1998). *Communities of Practice: Learning, Meaning, and Identity*. Cambridge, UK: Cambridge University Press. doi:10.1017/CBO9780511803932

Wenger, E. (2004). Knowledge management is a donut: Shaping your knowledge strategy with communities of practice. *Ivey Business Journal*, *68*(3), 1–8.

Wenger, E., McDermott, R., & Snyder, W. (2002). *Cultivating communities of practice: a guide to managing knowledge*. Boston, MA: Harvard Business School Press.

Wenger, E., & Snyder, W. (2000). Communities of practice: The organizational frontier. *Harvard Business Review*, *1*(78), 139–145.

Willis, D., & Willis, J. (2007). *Doing Task-based Teaching*. Oxford, UK: Oxford University Press.

Yang, Y. (2010). Computer-assisted Foreign Language Teaching: Theory and Practice. *Journal of Language Teaching and Research*, *1*(6), 909–912. doi:10.4304/jltr.1.6.909-912

KEY TERMS AND DEFINITIONS

Communities of Practice: Groups of people who have similar interests and work together to learn how to perform a task in a better way.

Experiential learning: Learning that occurs through hands on experience.

Feedback: any communication between the teacher and the student that provides information about the student's performance in a given task.

Foreign Language Learning: Learning a language in an area where the language is not spoken.

Formative assessment: On-going assessment of students' performance which does not usually requires grading.

IT: Information technology (computers, software, educational platforms, and other communication devices relying on microchips).

Negotiation of meaning: A process that second or foreign language students go through to reach a clear understanding of each other.

Reflective learning: A process of learning that leads the students to be more aware of their strengths and weaknesses.

Second Language Learning: Learning a second language in an area where the language being learnt is spoken.

Virtual learning: Learning over the Internet.

APPENDIX

The Rubrics shown in Table 1 and Table 2 were used by trainees to provide students with feedback on their online journals.

Errors	Mark in percentage
0-2	100
3-5	90
5-7	80
8-10	60
10-15	40
15+	20
Unreadable	redo

VC: Verb Conjugation	Wrong: Yo es estudiante.
	Right: Yo soy estudiante.
WW: Wrong Word:	Wrong: La mapa es de Cuba. Berta estudia a la universidad.
	Right: El mapa es de Cuba. Berta estudia en la universidad.
O: Omit (You should omit the highlighted word or expression)	Wrong: Me llamo es Grisel.
	Right: Me llamo Grisel.
WM: Word Missing	Wrong: Yo soy ___ estudiante inteligente.
	Right: Yo soy un estudiante inteligente.
A: Agreement	Wrong: Los estudiantes son inteligente_.
	Right: Los estudiantes son inteligentes.
SP: Spelling Error	Wrong: Los estudiantes son inteligentes. ¿Cuál es tu número de teléphono?
	Right: Los estudiantes son inteligentes. ¿Cuál es tu número de teléfono?
WO: Word Order	Wrong: Grisel's estudiantes.
	Right: Los estudiantes de Grisel.
C: Comprehensibility, English Structure used	Wrong: Mi liamo is Antonio. Mi ser estudiante at la university UBCO.
	Right: Me llamo Antonio. Soy estudiante de la Universidad de la Columbia Británica en el Okanagan.

Chapter 14
Social Media and Foreign Language Teacher Education:
Beliefs and Practices

Jiahang Li
Michigan State University, USA

ABSTRACT

This chapter will focus on examining how instructors who are preparing foreign language teachers, both pre-service and in-service, integrate social media in their teaching practices to gain more insights on what beliefs these instructors hold and what differences and similarities between their beliefs and actual teaching practices about social media integration in foreign language teacher education. The chapter will first provide a literature review about the general beliefs that instructors held on the integration of social media and foreign language teacher education. Next, promising examples of the integration of social media in foreign language teacher education will be provided. Last but not least, affordances and challenges of the integration of social media and foreign language teacher education will be discussed, followed by implications and future directions.

INTRODUCTION

Social media has emerged and been widely adopted in many areas including education. *Social media*, a term often used interchangeably with *Web 2.0*, refers to online applications that promote users, their interconnections, and user-generated content (Cormode & Krishnamurthy 2008). In this chapter, the term social media refers to online applications that promote users, their interconnections, and user-generated content (Cormode & Krishnamurthy 2008), including *social network sites* (SNS) like Facebook and MySpace; video-sharing sites like YouTube; image-sharing sites like Flickr, Tumblr and Pinterest; collaborative knowledge development through wikis; and microblogging sites like Twitter (Greenhow & Gleason, 2012).

Based on survey results (Moran, Seaman, & Tinti-Kane, 2012), *social media* usage in the United States has increased noticeably: 65% of adult Internet users claim they use *social media* like MySpace,

DOI: 10.4018/978-1-5225-0483-2.ch014

Facebook. The *social media* adoption rate has increased 4% from 2011 (61%) and more than doubled comparing with the results reported in 2008 (29%). Moreover, major *social media* (e.g., Facebook and Twitter) have gained increase in the number of active users. For instance, Facebook, at the end of 2011, had 133 million users in the United States and 845 million active users globally — about 54% of the world's online population; Twitter, with over 24 million active users in the United States, has also increased over 30% from 2011. All these increasing numbers suggest that *social media* becomes more and more popular and even a part of people's lives globally, which, in turn, calls for attention from educators and researchers to explore the affordances and challenges of using social media in- and outside of classroom settings.

In the field of education, many researchers have started to explore how to incorporate *social media* into teaching and learning. In terms of students' learning, many scholars argue that *social media* practices can facilitate new forms of collaborative knowledge construction (Cress & Kimmerle, 2008; Greenhow, 2011; Greenhow & Li, 2013; Larusson & Alterman, 2009), communication (Greenhow & Robelia, 2009a), identity work (Greenhow & Robelia, 2009b), social capital (Greenhow & Burton, 2011; Ellison, Steinfield, & Lampe, 2007; Valenzuela, Park, & Kee, 2009), and civic participation in the online-offline community (Greenhow, 2011; Robelia, Greenhow & Burton, 2011). Moreover, faculty members are adopting *social media* increasingly for both their personal and professional purposes. Based on a large survey conducted by Moran, Seaman, and Tinti-Kane (2011), over 90% of faculty members were aware of *social media*, such as Myspace, Facebook, Twitter, YouTube, and blogs, and over 90% of all higher education teaching faculty members are using *social media* in courses they're teaching or for their professional careers outside the classroom.

However, the increasing awareness and adoption of *social media* does not necessarily indicate effectiveness or value in education. Just like Levy (2009) argued, "effective transfer depends, to a large degree, on the affordances of the particular technology and the ways its strengths and limitations may be coordinated and managed as a pedagogical tool (p. 778)." Due to the evolution of technology and the increasing need for preparing teachers with a better understanding of how to use technology in their classrooms, educational researchers have been exploring the integration of *social media* and what affordances and challenges can be identified in teaching and learning. Amongst various areas of interests in education, foreign language teacher education has been researched in the relationship between technology and pedagogy, especially for foreign language teachers who teach language other than English (Garrett, 2009).

In the field of foreign language teacher education, research has been focused more on pre-service teachers' beliefs, attitudes, technological knowledge construct, and learning outcomes, including: 1) evaluating programs for technology integration (Mayo, Kajs, & Tanguma 2005); 2) audits of pre-service teachers' technological skill (Banister & Vannatta, 2005); 3) assessing the conceptualization of the complicated relationship between pedagogy, technology and discipline specific content knowledge (Mishra & Koehler, 2006; Rienties, Brouwer, & Lygo-Baker, 2013); and 4) pre-service teachers' confidence (Topper, 2004). Only a few studies (e.g., Georgina & Hosford, 2009) examined how instructors integrate technology in foreign language teacher education. Admittedly, some researchers have begun to use *social media* tools, such as Blogs, Wikis, to cultivate language teachers' writing skills in various languages with a focus on self-expression, creativity, ownership, and community building (Ducate & Lomicka, 2008; Kessler, 2009). However, these studies do not provide enough information about what beliefs instructors held about the integration of *social media* and foreign language teacher education.

Social Media and Foreign Language Teacher Education

Teacher beliefs, including foreign language teachers and instructors who teach foreign language teachers, is an important construct that needs further exploration and clarification (Parajes, 1992). In this chapter, teacher belief is defined as "an integrated system of personalized assumptions about teaching and learning" (Artzt & Armour-Thomas, 1998, p. 8) which shape the way teachers perceive and interpret classroom interaction and influence their construction of intentions in response to those interactions. Despite the complex relationship between teachers' beliefs and practices, researchers have argued that teacher beliefs can guide teacher decisions (Smith, 2005) and help further develop teachers' repertoire after being aware of their beliefs (Cochran-Smith & Lytle, 1999; Shulman, 1996). With the increasing adoption of *social media*, it is worthwhile to examine instructors' beliefs about the integration of *social media* and foreign language teacher education.

This chapter focuses on examining how one instructor who taught foreign language teachers using *social media* to gain more insights on what beliefs the instructor held and what differences and similarities between her beliefs and actual teaching practices about *social media* integration in foreign language teacher education. This chapter first provides a literature review about the general beliefs that instructors held on the integration of *social media* and foreign language teacher education. Next, promising examples of the integration of *social media* in foreign language teacher education are provided. Last but not least, affordances and challenges of the integration of *social media* and foreign language teacher education are discussed, followed by implications and future directions.

Literature Review

Many researchers have discovered potential benefits of using *social media* for academic purposes and argued that: the use of social media in teaching could 1) possibly connect informal learning to the formal learning environment (Greenhow & Li, 2013); 2) provide engaging channels to facilitate student-student, student instructor, and student-content interactions in multimedia formats (Hughes, 2009; Nellison, 2007). However, current research tends to pay more attention on the learners' rather than the instructors' perspectives. Although some researchers (Mazer, Murphy, & Simonds, 2007, 2009) have noticed the gap and conducted studies on how instructors use *social media* in teaching, little empirical research can be found explaining instructors' beliefs and practices of integrating *social media* and foreign language teacher education. In this session, a review of literature is presented from three perspectives to demonstrate the importance of exploring instructors' beliefs and practices about integrating *social media* and foreign language teacher education: teacher beliefs, instructors' general beliefs about *social media*, and instructors' general integration of *social media*.

Teacher Beliefs

Many researchers agreed on the argument that it is important to encourage teachers to compare their beliefs about teaching and their teaching practices (Norton, Richardson, Hartley, Newstead, & Mayes, 2005; Trigwell & Prosser, 2004). However, teachers' beliefs do not always align with their teaching practices (Ajzen, 2002; Norton et al., 2005; Rienties, Brouwer, & Lygo-Baker, 2013). For instance, Ertmer, Gopalakrishnan, and Ross (2001) argued that teachers' beliefs about classroom technology use did not always align with their classroom teaching practices. Because of the mismatch between teachers' beliefs and their teaching practices, it is worthwhile to explore why such discrepancies exist. A primary reason for the inconsistency might be the contextual constraints (e.g., curricular requirements, social pressure from parents, peers, or administrators). Moreover, teachers' beliefs are often understood by others based on what teachers say, intend, and do (Kagan, 1992; Kane et al., 2002), which makes it more difficult to compare teachers' beliefs and practices. For example, although teachers may express the belief that *social media* is helpful in teaching language in a communicative approach (e.g., practicing the language with native speakers via Facebook), their daily teaching practice may not include any *social media*, because they hold another belief that using Facebook might be a distraction for students in the process of learning the language. Therefore, it is important to explore what beliefs teachers have and how these beliefs align with their teaching practices. Since instructors who teach foreign language teachers also hold beliefs, it is reasonable to examine their beliefs and practices in relation with *social media*.

Instructors General Beliefs about Social Media

Instructors, in general, have mixed feelings about using *social media* for various purposes. While agreeing the benefits of using *social media* for personal uses, faculty members have different perceptions about the value of using *social media* as a professional tool for both in and outside of classroom. Moran, Seaman, & Tinti-Kane (2011, 2012) conducted a series of surveys to examine both the personal and professional impacts of *social media* on teaching faculty. In the 2011 study, a total of 1,920 responses were included as participants whereas a total of 3,875 responses were included in the 2012 study. In both surveys, Moran et al. differentiated various purposes of using *social media* by faculty members: for personal use only, with no relationship to professional and/or teaching responsibilities; for professional (nonteaching) use; and for use in the classes they teach.

In a 2011 survey, Moran et al. report that 38% faculty members agreed with the argument that educators should use *social media* to reach students where they are, while 24% disagreed and 39% kept neutral. When participants were asked whether or not they agree with the statement of "social networks take more time than they are worth", 19% disagreed, 38% chose neutral, and 43% agreed. Faculty members were concerned about using *social media*, such as "lack of integrity of online submissions", "privacy concerns", "takes too much faculty time", "lack of faculty training, faculty not confident with *social media*", "lack of integration with schools' learning management system", "lack of support at my institution". Among these concerns, on a scale of "somewhat important", "important", and "very important", 43% of faculty members believed that the lack of integrity of online submissions and privacy were "very important" issues that need to be considered when using *social media* in class; 27% of faculty member believed that the lack of training for faculty members to use *social media* in class was a "very important" barrier in preventing the integration of *social media* and classroom teaching; 20% of faculty members concurred that the "very important" barrier was "faculty not confident with *social media*"; almost 40% of faculty members claimed that the lack of support from their institutions or schools was a "very important" issue in preventing faculty members from using *social media*. In the 2012 survey, Moran et al. reported that faculty continued to consider a number of issues to be serious barriers. However, they also showed a noticeable change in the overall pattern of faculty perceptions of the barriers to the use of *social media* for their teaching. Every factor measured in both 2011 and 2012 showed a decline in the level of faculty concern for 2012 as compared to the previous year. The results for 2012 showed the same two concerns topping the list as were noted for 2011—privacy and the integrity of student submissions. Over 70 percent report that "lack of integrity of student submissions" is an "important" or "very important" barrier, and over 60 percent say privacy concerns are an "important" or "very important" barrier. The faculty concern with the integrity of student submissions was seen as the most serious barrier in both 2011 and 2012. Older faculty members held a greater level of concern with the issue of integrity of student submissions than did younger faculty. Virtually the same pattern of level of concern by age is seen when privacy issue was examined. Those aged 45 to 55 that had the greatest level of concern, and again they are the most likely to rate that level as "very important."

Instructors' General Integration of Social Media

Instructors' use of *social media* changed dramatically over time. In 2009, the Faculty Survey of Student Engagement (FSSE, 2010) conducted a national survey over 4,600 faculty members from 50 U.S. colleges and universities. Results showed that over 80% of the surveyed faculty members did not know or never used *social media* technologies such as blogs, wikis, Google docs, and video conferencing tools. However, Moran et al. (2011) found that almost all higher education teaching faculty are aware of the major *social media* sites; more than 75% visited a social media site within the past month for their personal use; and nearly 50% posted content. More importantly, over 90% of all faculty members are using *social media* in courses they're teaching or for their professional careers outside the classroom. Nearly 65% of all faculty members have used *social media* during a class session, and 30% have posted content for students to view or read outside class. Over 40% of faculty members have required students to read or view *social media* as part of a course assignment, and 20% have assigned students to comment on or post to *social media* sites. Online video is by far the most common type of *social media* used in class, posted outside class, or assigned to students to view, with 80% of faculty reporting some form of class use of online video. Based on the results describe above (Moran et al., 2011), faculty members already integrated *social media* into teaching in classroom settings.

At least two major implications can be drawn from both Moran et al.'s survey results: first, faculty members are not familiar with *social media* and how to use it in classroom teaching. They did not receive enough training on how to use *social media* in classroom teaching, nor did they receive sufficient support from their institutions or schools, which may be part of the reason why they claimed that they were not confident enough to use *social media*. The unfamiliarity of using *social media* requires instructors to explore best practices and effective ways to use *social media* in their classrooms. Second, some faculty members were concerned about too much personal (students and/or faculty members) information exposed on *social media* in classroom teaching. Admittedly, using *social media* does involve personal information sharing when subscribing. However, all *social media* tools allow users to control how their information will be shared and viewed publicly. Some faculty members may not know the appropriate functions or features that all *social media* provided for user control and setting. This, again, points to the need for training and professional development opportunities specifically focusing on how to integrate *social media* in teaching.

Although it is difficult to find empirical studies exploring instructors' beliefs about using *social media* in foreign language teacher education, many researchers have examined teachers' beliefs with a broader term "technology" (Kim, Kim, Lee, Spector, & Demeester, 2013). Ertmer (2005) argued that for lasting successful integration of technology in education, it is necessary to change teachers' beliefs about the implementation of technology in education towards a more student-centered orientation. Because technology provides ample opportunities for students to learn in a collaborative and participatory way, it is important for teachers, then, to be aware of the learning environment and style is leaning towards a student-centered approach rather than a traditional teacher-centered knowledge transmission approach.

Next, a promising case of one instructor from a STARTALK teacher training program is provided to illustrate the beliefs, practices, affordances, and challenges of *social media* integration.

Foreign Language Teacher Education Program: STARTALK

STARTALK is a widely known foreign language teacher preparation program. Starting in 2006 as a component of the 2006 National Security Language Initiative (NSLI), the STARTALK program has its unique focus on promoting the teaching and learning of Less Commonly Taught Languages (LCTLs). The STARTALK program provides professional development opportunities for over 1400 language teachers across the United States in 2012 (see STARTALK website). The format of STARTALK teacher programs range from basic professional development courses to credit-bearing method courses for teachers from novice to veteran levels. Currently STARTALK programs are offered in 11 languages: Chinese, Arabic, Hindi, Russian, Urdu, Persian, Portuguese, Swahili, Turkish, Dari, and Korean. STARTALK ran programs in 48 states and District of Columbia, missing Louisiana and North Dakota, but have participants from all 50 states.

STARTALK's long-term goals are to initiate and sustain interest and to foster proficiency in strategically important languages. The mission of the STARTALK program initiative is to increase the number of Americans learning, speaking, and teaching LCTLs by offering students (K–16) and teachers of these languages creative and engaging summer experiences that strive to exemplify best practices in language education and in language teacher development, forming an extensive community of practice that seeks continuous improvement through outcomes-driven program design; standards-based curriculum planning; learner-centered approaches; excellence in selection and development of materials; and meaningful assessment of outcomes (STARTALK website, startalk.umd.edu, 2013). Many STARTALK instructors in teacher programs have integrated technology component into teaching practices. Based on the survey report provided by Center for Applied Linguistics (Sugarman, Di Silvio, & Malone, 2012), over 56 percent of instructors who participated (N=73) in STARTALK summer teacher training programs claimed that they used websites designed for language learning, nearly 33 percent used computer software designed for language learning, almost 18 percent used video conference (e.g. Skype), and almost 25 percent used virtual learning environment such as Moodle or Blackboard in their programs. Although statistics can't be found about how many STARTALK instructors in teacher programs have used social media in their teaching, it is clear that these instructors are integrating technology into language teacher preparation practices and certain social media (e.g. Skype, Blog) are identified as useful tools in preparing teachers. With the widely adoption of *social media*, many instructors of these teacher training programs have started either using *social media* (formally or informally) as a pedagogical tool to teach or introducing *social media* as a theme in their curricula.

To summarize, there is a huge gap between the increasing adoption of *social media* in foreign language teacher program (e.g., STARTALK) and the lack of empirical research on what beliefs instructors have about *social media* integration and how they actually use *social media* in training foreign language teachers. The integration of *social media* and foreign language teacher education requires more research to identify the affordances and challenges. As one of the nationwide intensive teacher training programs, STARTALK provides many foreign language teachers with professional development opportunities. With the increasing trend of using *social media* in these programs, it is necessary to explore how instructors in these teacher training programs integrate *social media* in their teaching practice. Therefore, the research questions of the following case are: 1) what beliefs STARTALK teacher program instructors have on the integration of social media and foreign language teacher education, and 2) what are the similarities and differences between instructor's beliefs and practice about the integration of social media and foreign language teacher education. Next, Hong's case is described to illustrate instructor's beliefs and practices of *social media* integration.

SOCIAL MEDIA INTEGRATION: THE CASE OF HONG'S STARTALK PROGRAM

In this session, Hong (pseudonym), the instructor from one STARTALK teacher training program in 2013, is introduced. First, data collection and analysis method are explained. Then, background information about Hong and her STARTALK teacher program is provided. Following that, a detailed description of how Hong adopted social media in her program is illustrated. Lastly, the affordances and challenges of the integration of social media and foreign language teacher education are discussed.

Method

Adopting a qualitative case study (Yin, 2009) design, all the data regarding Hong and her STARTALK teacher training program that are presented in this chapter were collected by the author in the summer of 2013. After IRB was approved, the author sent out email to all STARTALK teacher program directors and lead instructors in May 2013. Hong voluntarily participated in this study. Hong was then asked to complete an online questionnaire designed to collect demographic information and beliefs about social media and foreign language teacher education. From July to September 2013, the author conducted three interviews (two Skype and one phone) with one before the teacher program started, one after the teacher program ended, and one after the author finished analyzing the data from Hong. In addition, the author conducted two online observations using Skype and collected video recordings from Hong while she was teaching in her teacher program. Lastly, all teaching materials (curriculum, assignments, and photos), and social media usage records were collected to triangulate with other data.

Background Information of Hong

Hong is a Chinese female in her early 30s who was born in China (Online Questionnaire). She got her BA degree in English Education from China. After working as an English teacher teaching college students, she decided to pursue doctoral degree in Curriculum and Instruction in the United States. After graduated in 2012, she worked as a Chinese Immersion Instructional Specialist for the Department of Education in a northeastern state in the United States. Hong has various experiences in teaching foreign languages (Chinese and English) in both the United States and China. Interested in helping other Chinese teachers, Hong also became involved in foreign language teacher education in many areas. She worked as Chinese Language Student Teacher Supervisor since September 2009 at the College of Education in a university in the northeastern United States. Her duties included conducting classroom observations and evaluations for preservice teachers, providing feedback and mentorship for preservice teachers, and assisting preservice teachers to complete their teaching portfolios. She also worked for a Chinese after school program as a teacher trainer where she provided many professional workshops for Chinese teachers. With her current job at the [State] Department of Education, Hong is in charge of developing

Chinese curriculum, providing professional development for Chinese language teacher, and promoting the Chinese immersion programs in the local area (Hong's Resume).

Regarding the beliefs about the integration of social media and foreign language teacher education, Hong embraced the idea that social media had many benefits and were inevitably woven into everyone's life. When integrated into foreign language teacher education, Hong believed that social media could be helpful in a spontaneous way where teachers could seek for support and guidance virtually. Admittedly, Hong also thought that foreign language teachers and teacher educators had to be aware of the challenges that could impact the social media integration, such as the lack of technical support and internet access, and lack of training and guidance in how to use social media in foreign language teaching. Considering the inevitability of the integration of social media, Hong believed that specific training about how to use social media in foreign language teaching and teacher education were underdeveloped and needed further attention (Online Questionnaire).

Background Information of Hong's Teacher Program

Hong's program was proposed by the [State] Department of Education in the northeastern United States which consisted of two programs: elementary student program and teacher program. The student program offered a two-week summer camp for 38 Kindergarten to Second Grade students. Students participated in a morning camp for four days each week as an introduction to Chinese language and culture learning and get familiarized with the immersion program in which they enrolled beginning in the Fall semester of 2013. The teacher program was designed to provide a standards-based and feedback-rich learning experience for elementary Chinese language teachers through a combination of methods seminars, practicum experiences, and instructional coaching sessions for 96 hours over the course of 16 instructional days from July 18th, to August 2nd, 2013. The teacher program included two parts: first, teacher participants received an intensive three-day mini-methods course before the student program started, and second, teacher participants worked as teachers in the student program. As a result of these trainings and experiences, teacher participants were expected to be able to: 1) provide comprehensible input for students while remaining in the target language; 2) engage all learners all the time using active participation to check for understanding; and 3) design and deliver instruction that was standards and proficiency-based. However, the teacher program didn't include social media as a topic to teach all participants. There were 9 teacher participants attending PC's teacher program who were all native Chinese. Among these teacher participants, 8 were preservice teachers and only one was experienced teacher.

The Integration of Social Media and Hong's Program

Using her own experiences with various technology (computers, smartphone, IPad) and social media (Facebook, Twitter, QQ), Hong was absolutely aware of different *social media* and had been using them frequently for her personal purpose. Without a detailed curriculum and lesson plan to incorporate *social media*, Hong confirmed, in her follow-up interview that the actual use of *social media* in her program was a spontaneous idea. Hong just picked up *social media* because they needed to share some Power-Points with the teacher participants. According to Hong, *social media* was widely used by instructors and teacher participants due to its benefits in file sharing, reducing the physical distance, and enhancing communication and connection within the group. Therefore, *social media* became essential to the pro-

Social Media and Foreign Language Teacher Education

Figure 1. Facebook Posting

gram even though it was not originally planned to be integrated. Based on interviews and observations, Hong's program adopted many *social media*, including Facebook, QQ, YouTube.

From Figure 1, it was evident that about 30 Facebook users interacted virtually with the person who posted the group phone by clicking "Like". Moreover, many users posted comments about the photo and made connections with the people that were tagged in the photo. By communicating virtually in Facebook, teacher participants and instructors could build personal bounds within the group and support each other. Although none of the comments were really focusing on the content of the teacher program, it seemed that teacher participants were actively involved in using social media, like Facebook, to interact and get to know each other better.

Figure 2 is an example of one of the embedded functional areas that QQ has, called QQ Zone, where users can upload pictures and videos to share with their friends through QQ. The user in Figure 2 was one of the teacher participants that Hong trained in her program. She posted the pictures of the kids that she taught in the student program in the summer of 2013. One of the pictures (the third one on the third row) was the screenshot of the local online news that described the success of the program. Through sharing these pictures with her friends, the impact and positive results of the program were promoted across the continent. This is a good case in point to demonstrate the spontaneous integration of *social media* by the teacher participants to share their ideas about teaching. In addition, Hong also integrated other *social media*, such as YouTube, to further enhance the learning by uploading videos of teacher participants' teaching in the student program (see *Figure 3*).

Figure 3 showed one of the lessons that two teacher participants were teaching. This kind of resource, supported by social media (YouTube), can be seen by all the teacher participants and the general public.

269

Figure 2. QQ Zone

Teacher participants can watch their teaching videos to reflect upon their instructions to find out what needs to be improved at any time outside of classroom. Moreover, teacher participants may also receive comments and suggestions from the general public who see this video clip. Allowing teacher participants to self-reflect and gain possible feedback from others, *social media* makes the learning more participatory and engaging.

Comparing Hong's Beliefs and Practice

Based on data collected from interviews and online questionnaire, Hong believed that *social media* had many benefits and were inevitably woven into everyone's life. When integrated into foreign language teacher education, Hong agreed that *social media* could be helpful in a spontaneous way where teachers could seek for support and guidance virtually. Admittedly, Hong also thought that foreign language teachers and teacher educators had to be aware of the challenges that could impact the *social media* integration, such as the lack of technical support and internet access, and lack of training and guidance in how to use *social media* in foreign language teaching. Hong's beliefs about the integration of *social*

Figure 3. YouTube Video Clip Screenshot

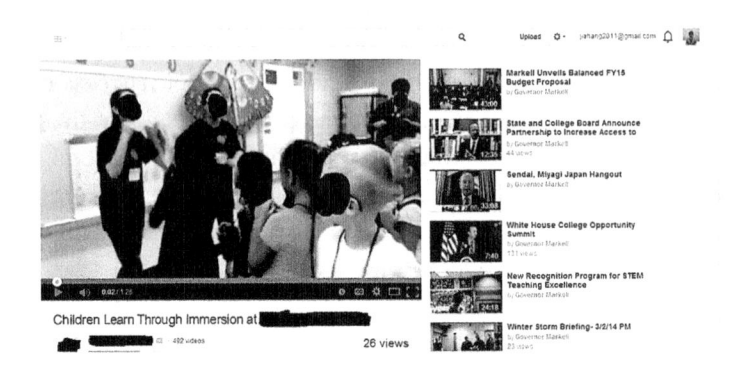

media and foreign language teacher education was largely impacted by her beliefs about foreign language teaching, learning, and teacher education. Hong extremely valued the importance of learning a foreign language which could increase individual's global competency. Further, she advocated foreign language teachers must provide comprehensible input in the target language using various activities to engage learners, which could be enhanced by adopting *social media*. Along with these beliefs about foreign language learning and teaching, Hong thought that a systematic approach was needed for the current foreign language teacher education where instructors design the training based on foreign language teachers' real needs. Considering the inevitability of the integration of *social media*, Hong believed that specific training about how to use *social media* in foreign language teaching and teacher education were underdeveloped and needed further attention.

Drawing upon the online observation data, Hong's actual teaching practice were aligned with her beliefs about the integration of *social media* and foreign language teacher education. Hong's case is particularly interesting in that the spontaneous adoption of various *social media* enhanced her beliefs about the integration of *social media* and foreign language teacher education. From this case, it is clear that Hong's beliefs were reinforced when she identified the benefits that *social media* brought to the teacher participants both formally and informally. Thus, it suggests that teacher beliefs can be reinforced by teaching practice. In other words, if positive results about a certain belief are found, teachers may feel more confident about that belief. Therefore, if foreign language teachers have the opportunity to explore the advantages of using *social media* by seeing its application and purposeful integration, they will be more likely to incorporate *social media* in their teaching. Hong's case coincides with previous literature in that beliefs that aligned with teaching practices can encourage teaching practices. Hong's beliefs about *social media* integration aligned with her teaching practices, which further guided her to embrace the adoption of various *social media* in her teaching training program.

Affordances and Challenges of the Integration of Social Media

The affordances that *social media* contributes to Hong's STARTALK teacher program include: 1) collaborative learning opportunities to engage learners; 2) access information resources in a virtual community regardless of distance and time; and 3) connect formal and informal learning through technology. These benefits enhanced learning outcomes by providing more participatory and collaborative ways of learning, which was also supported by previous literature. Through a sociocultural approach of learning, individuals engaged in and became active members of "communities of practice", where they learned behaviors and formed belief systems of their social groups and eventually started acting in accordance with their norms. For instance, by forming and participating in a Facebook, QQ, and YouTube, all participants of Hong's program were able to maintain existing relationships, share photographs, and communicate within the virtual community. Hong's case suggests that *social media* spaces can provide an ideal context for teachers' professional learning where individuals actively engage in the practices of a collaborative global online community. Virtual communities of practice constructed through *social media* enable learners to connect, construct a shared understanding, engage in discussions, and share resources, while forming a community of practice through technological affordances.

Despite all the benefits that *social media* could bring to foreign language teacher education, Hong also identified some challenges including the lack of technical support, and limited equipment and access to the internet. Hong noted in the interview that internet access was a challenge to the integration of *social media*. The lack of internet connection in the first few days and the poor signal strength after internet access was provided made it difficult for teacher participants and instructors to use internet. In Hong's opinion, the lack of technical support, especially the lack of authorization to install software on the computer was a huge challenge to her integration of *social media*. Hong also pointed out that teacher training for the specific use of *social media* in foreign language teaching was scarce. Without the necessary guidance from instructors, foreign language teachers were lost in figuring out which and in what ways *social media* could be used in their classrooms. This specific challenge suggested that professional development workshops were necessary in preparing foreign language teachers for *social media* integration. In terms of solutions, Hong suggested that the first step would be train instructors about the practices and strategies of using *social media*. Starting from there, teacher education programs, even certification programs, could be established to further prepare more foreign language teachers about how to adopt *social media* in their teaching. Another potential challenge Hong identified was the lack of connection between using *social media* and teaching foreign language in an immersion classroom. Hong believed that for young learners who were in kindergarten and first grade, *social media* could not be integrated easily with a meaningful purpose. These young leaners didn't have the access or spend much time in using *social media*. Therefore, foreign language teachers who were going to teach in immersion settings might not be interested in exploring the benefits of using *social media* in their teaching.

CONCLUSION AND FUTURE RESEARCH DIRECTION

The findings from Hong's case reinforced the argument that if teachers conscientiously aligned their beliefs about teaching with their actual teaching practice, instructional goals were more likely to be accomplished (Saroyan & Amundsen, 2001). Hong emphasized the value of *social media* integration in foreign language teacher education. She considered *social media* as a useful tool in connecting foreign language teachers and encourage sharing and learning beyond classroom setting. In her teaching practice, although Hong didn't make plans for *social media* integration before the program, a variety of *social media* were used formally and informally throughout the program. This spontaneous integration indicates that her beliefs guided her teaching practice in the natural adoption of *social media*.

Hong's case provides future directions for research as well as foreign language teacher education practice. Future research on teachers' beliefs about the integration of social media and foreign language teacher education needs to identify mismatch and discrepancies between beliefs and practices. In so doing, researchers could have better understanding about why certain beliefs could or could not impact teaching practices. Furthermore, it will be interesting to explore how instructors make decisions especially when facing situations that are contrary to their beliefs. It will also be valuable to find out what kinds of situations and practices could change instructors' beliefs. Considering the relatively short duration of STARTALK teacher programs and the complex nature of teacher belief, longitudinal studies are also needed to fully understand the construct of teacher beliefs.

Regarding practices, foreign language teacher education administrators and instructors need to develop a more focused program with substantial support and training when integrating *social media* in foreign language teacher education. Although spontaneous adoption might be successful like Hong's case, it is necessary to make specific plans and careful selections when integrating *social media* in foreign language teacher education. By analyzing potential challenges, necessary steps need to be developed to maximize opportunities for a successful integration of *social media* and foreign language teacher education. In addition, instructors must be familiar with various *social media* tools and their affordances and challenges before making the integration. It would be impossible for her to adopt *social media* if Hong didn't know and use any prior to her STARTALK teacher program.

Using STARTALK teacher program as an individual case, this chapter connects *social media* and foreign language teacher education by identifying the instructor's beliefs and practices of integrating various *social media* into teacher education programs. *Social media* can be beneficial in building community of practice and enhancing collaborative learning. On the other hand, specific challenges also exist when integrating *social media* into teacher education, such as the lack of adequate training and technical support. Future research needs to further determine what kinds of beliefs foreign language teachers have about various *social media* and their effectiveness in foreign language teacher education. With deeper understanding of foreign language teachers' beliefs about *social media*, instructors may improve the quality and effectiveness of professional development programs by providing what foreign language teachers really need.

REFERENCES

Ajzen, I. (2002). Perceived behavioral control, self-efficacy, locus of control, and the theory of planned behavior. *Journal of Applied Social Psychology, 32*(4), 665–683. doi:10.1111/j.1559-1816.2002.tb00236.x

Artzt, A. F., & Armour-Thomas, E. (1998). Mathematics teaching as problem solving: A framework for studying teacher metacognition underlying instructional practice in mathematics. *Instructional Science, 26*(1/2), 5–25. doi:10.1023/A:1003083812378

Banister, S., & Vannatta, R. (2005). Dynamic virtual instruction: Enhancing online courses and connection. *Proceedings of the Computers and Advanced Technology in Education International Conference.* Retrieved on April 28, 2013, from: http://www.actapress.com/Abstract.aspx?paperId=21561

boyd, d. m., & Ellison, N.B. (2007). Social network sites: Definition, history, and scholarship. *Journal of Computer-Mediated Communication, 13*(1), article 11.

Cochran-Smith, M., & Lytle, S. L. (1999). Relationships of knowledge and practice: Teacher learning in communities. Review of Research in Education, 24, 249–305.

Cormode, G., & Krishnamurthy, B. (2008). Key differences between Web 1.0 and Web 2.0. *First Monday, 13*(6). doi:10.5210/fm.v13i6.2125

Ducate, L. C., & Lomicka, L. L. (2008). Adventures in the blogosphere: From blog readers to blog writers. *Computer Assisted Language Learning, 21*(1), 9–28. doi:10.1080/09588220701865474

Ellison, N., Steinfield, C., & Lampe, C. (2007). The benefits of Facebook "friends": Exploring the relationship between college students' use of online social networks and social capital. *Journal of Computer-Mediated Communication, 12*(3), article 1. Retrieved on April 28, 2013, from http://jcmc.indiana.edu/vol12/issue4/ellison.html

Ertmer, P. A. (2005). Teacher pedagogical beliefs: The final frontier in our quest for technology integration? *Educational Technology Research and Development, 53*(4), 25–39. doi:10.1007/BF02504683

Ertmer, P. A., Gopalakrishnan, S., & Ross, E. M. (2001). Technology-using teachers: Comparing perceptions of exemplary technology use to best practice. *Journal of Research on Technology in Education, 33*(5), 1–26.

Fang, Z. (1996). A review of research on teacher beliefs and practices. *Educational Research, 38*(1), 47–65. doi:10.1080/0013188960380104

FSSE. (2010, July 25). Professors' use of technology in teaching. *The Chronicle of Higher Education.* Retrieved on April 29, 2013, from http://chronicle.com/article/Professors-Useof/123682/?sid=wc&utm_source=wc&utm_medium=en

Garrett, N. (2009). Computer-assisted language learning trends and issues revisited: Integrating innovation. *Modern Language Journal, 93*, 719–740. doi:10.1111/j.1540-4781.2009.00969.x

Georgina, D. A., & Hosford, C. C. (2009). Higher education faculty perceptions on technology integration and training. *Teaching and Teacher Education, 25*(5), 690–696. doi:10.1016/j.tate.2008.11.004

Greenhow, C. (2011). Online social networks and learning. *On the Horizon, 15*(1), 4–12. doi:10.1108/10748121111107663

Greenhow, C., & Burton, L. (2011). Help from my "Friends:" Social capital in the social network sites of low-income high school students. *Journal of Educational Computing Research, 45*(2), 223–245. doi:10.2190/EC.45.2.f

Greenhow, C., & Gleason, B. (2012). Twitteracy: Tweeting as a new literacy practice. *The Educational Forum, 76*(2).

Greenhow, C., & Li, J. (2013). Like, comment, share: Collaboration and civic engagement within social network sites. For inclusion. In C. Mouza & N. Lavigne (Eds.), *Emerging technologies for the classroom: A learning sciences perspective* (pp. 127–241). New York: Springer.

Greenhow, C., & Robelia, E. (2009a). Old communication, new literacies: Social network sites as social learning resources. *Journal of Computer-Mediated Communication, 14*(4), 1130–1161. doi:10.1111/j.1083-6101.2009.01484.x

Greenhow, C., & Robelia, E. (2009b). Informal learning and identity formation in online social networks. *Learning, Media and Technology, 34*(2), 119–140. doi:10.1080/17439880902923580

Hughes, G. (2009). Social software: New opportunities for challenging social inequalities in learning? *Learning, Media and Technology, 34*(4), 291–305. doi:10.1080/17439880903338580

Janus, L. (1998). *Less commonly taught languages of emerging importance: Major issues, cost problems, and their national implications*. International education in the new global era proceedings of a national policy conference on the Higher Education Act, Title VI, and Fulbright-Hays programs less commonly taught language. Retrieved January 15, 2013 from http://www.international.ucla.edu/pacrim/title6/Break6-Janus.pdf

Kagan, D. M. (1992). Implications of research on teacher belief. *Educational Psychologist, 27*(1), 65–90. doi:10.1207/s15326985ep2701_6

Kane, R., Sandetto, S., & Heath, C. (2002). Telling half the story: A critical review of research on the teaching beliefs and practices of university academics. *Review of Educational Research*, *72*(2), 177–228. doi:10.3102/00346543072002177

Kessler, G. (2009). Student-initiated attention to form in Wiki-based collaborative writing. *Language Learning & Technology*, *13*(1), 79–95.

Kim, C., Kim, M. K., Lee, C., Spector, J. M., & DeMeester, K. (2013). Teacher beliefs and technology integration. *Teaching and Teacher Education*, *29*, 76–85. doi:10.1016/j.tate.2012.08.005

Larusson, J., & Alterman, R. (2009). Wikis to support the "collaborative" part of collaborative learning. *International Journal of Computer-Supported Collaborative Learning*, *4*(4), 371–402. doi:10.1007/s11412-009-9076-6

Lawless, K. A., & Pellegrino, J. W. (2007). Professional development in integrating technology into teaching and learning: Knowns, unknowns, and ways to pursue better questions and answers. *Review of Educational Research*, *77*(4), 575–614. doi:10.3102/0034654307309921

Levy, M. (2009). Technologies in use for Second Language learning. *Modern Language Journal*, *93*, 769–782. doi:10.1111/j.1540-4781.2009.00972.x

Mayo, N., Kajs, K., & Tanguma, J. (2005). Longitudinal study of technology training to prepare future teachers. *Educational Research Quarterly*, *29*(1), 3–15.

Mazer, J. P., Murphy, R. E., & Simonds, C. J. (2007). I'll see you on "Facebook": The effects of computer-mediated teacher self-disclosure on student motivation, affective learning, and classroom climate. *Communication Education*, *56*(1), 1–17. doi:10.1080/03634520601009710

Mishra, P., & Koehler, M. J. (2006). Technological pedagogical content knowledge: A framework for integrating technology in teachers' knowledge. *Teachers College Record*, *108*(6), 1017–1054. doi:10.1111/j.1467-9620.2006.00684.x

Moran, M., Seaman, J., & Tinti-Kane, H. (2011). *Teaching, learning, and sharing: How today's higher education faculty use social media*. Boston, MA: Pearson Learning Solutions and Babson Survey Research Group.

Moran, M., Seaman, J., & Tinti-Kane, H. (2012). *Blogs, Wikis, Podcasts and Facebook: How today's higher education faculty use social media*. Boston, MA: Pearson Learning Solutions and Babson Survey Research Group.

Nellison. (2007, December 11). ECAR: Facebook as a teaching tool? *Blog*. Retrieved March 18, 2013, from http://nellison.blogspot.com/2007/12/ecar-facebook-as-teachingtool.html

Norton, L., Richardson, J. T. E., Hartley, J., Newstead, S., & Mayes, J. (2005). Teachers' beliefs and intentions concerning teaching in higher education. *Higher Education*, *50*(4), 537–571. doi:10.1007/s10734-004-6363-z

Pajares, M. F. (1992). Teachers' beliefs and educational research: Cleaning up a messy construct. *Review of Educational Research*, *62*(3), 307–332. doi:10.3102/00346543062003307

Rhodes, N. C., & Pufahl, I. (2009). *Foreign language teaching in U.S. schools: Results of a national survey*. Washington, DC: Center for Applied Linguistics.

Rienties, B., Brouwer, N., & Lygo-Baker, S. (2013). The effects of online professional development on teachers' beliefs and intentions towards learning facilitation and technology. *Teaching and Teacher Education, 29*, 122–131. doi:10.1016/j.tate.2012.09.002

Robelia, B., Greenhow, C., & Burton, L. (2011). Adopting environmentally responsible behaviors: How learning within a social networking application motivated students to act for the environment. *Environmental Education Research, 17*(4), 553–575. doi:10.1080/13504622.2011.565118

Saville-Troike, M. (2012). *Introducing second language acquisition*. Cambridge University Press. doi:10.1017/CBO9780511888830

Shulman, L. S. (1996). Paradigms and research programs in the study of teaching: A contemporary perspective. In M. C. Wittrock (Ed.), *Handbook of research on teaching* (3rd ed., pp. 3–36). New York: Macmillan.

Smith, L. K. (2005). The impact of early life history on teachers' beliefs: In-school and out-of-school experiences as learners and knowers of science. *Teachers and Teaching: Theory and Practice, 11*(1), 5–36. doi:10.1080/1354060042000337075

STARTALK website (2015). startalk.umd.edu

Sugarman, J., Di Silvio, F., & Malone, M. E. (2012). *2012 STARTALK participant survey report: Teacher trainees*. Washington, DC: Center for Applied Linguistics.

Topper, A. (2004). How are we doing? Using self-assessment to measure changing teacher technology literacy within a graduate educational technology program. *Journal of Technology and Teacher Education, 12*(3), 303–317.

Trigwell, K., & Prosser, M. (2004). Development and use of the Approaches to Teaching Inventory. *Educational Psychology Review, 16*(4), 409–424. doi:10.1007/s10648-004-0007-9

Valenzuela, S., Park, N., & Kee, K. F. (2009). Is there social capital in a Social Network Site?: Facebook use and college students' life satisfaction, trust, and participation. *Journal of Computer-Mediated Communication, 14*(4), 875–901. doi:10.1111/j.1083-6101.2009.01474.x

Yin, R. K. (2009). *Case study research: Design and methods* (4th ed.). Thousand Oaks, CA: Sage.

Young, S. F. (2008). Theoretical frameworks and models of learning: Tools for developing conceptions of teaching and learning. *The International Journal for Academic Development, 13*(1), 41–49. doi:10.1080/13601440701860243

KEY TERMS AND DEFINITIONS

Foreign Language: refers to a language that is "not widely used in the learners' immediate social context which might be used for future travel or other cross-cultural communication situations, or studied as a curricular requirement or elective in school, but with no immediate or necessary practical application" (Saville-Troike, 2012, p.4).

Less Commonly Taught Languages (LCTLs): Refers to all of the world's languages that are currently taught in the United States, except for English, French, German, and Spanish (Janus, 1998).

Social Media: refers to online applications which promote users, their interconnections, and user-generated content (Cormode & Krishnamurthy 2008), which includes *social network sites* (SNS) like Facebook and MySpace; video-sharing sites like YouTube; image-sharing sites like Flickr, Tumblr and Pinterest; collaborative knowledge development through wikis; and microblogging sites like Twitter (Greenhow & Gleason, 2012).

Teacher Belief: in this study, teacher belief is defined as "an integrated system of personalized assumptions about teaching and learning" (Artzt & Armour-Thomas, 1998, p. 8) which shape the way teachers perceive and interpret classroom interaction and influence their construction of intentions in response to those interaction.

Compilation of References

Abbitt, J. T. (2011). An investigation of the relationship between self-efficacy beliefs about technology integration and technological pedagogical content knowledge (TPACK) among preservice teachers. *Journal of Digital Learning in Teacher Education, 27*(4), 134–143. doi:10.1080/21532974.2011.10784670

ACTFL Foreign Language Teacher Standards Writing Team. (2013). *Program Standards for the Preparation of Foreign Language Teachers*. Retrieved from http://www.actfl.org/sites/default/files/pdfs/ACTFL-Standards20Aug2013.pdf

Ahmad, W. M. A. W., Halim, N. B. A., Aleng, N. A., Mohamed, N., Amin, W. A. A. W. M., & Amiruddin, N. A. (2013). Quantitative analysis on the level of acceptance, usage and problems of e-books among school teachers in Terengganu. *The International Journal of Social Sciences, 7*(1), 89–101.

Ajzen, I. (1991). The theory of planned behavior. *Organizational Behavior and Human Decision Processes, 50*(2), 179–211. doi:10.1016/0749-5978(91)90020-T

Ajzen, I. (2002). Perceived behavioral control, self-efficacy, locus of control, and the theory of planned behavior. *Journal of Applied Social Psychology, 32*(4), 665–683. doi:10.1111/j.1559-1816.2002.tb00236.x

Allaire, S., & Laferriere, T. (2005). The knowledge-building oriented virtual practicum. In C. Crawford et al. (Eds.), *Proceedings of Society for Information Technology & Teacher Education International Conference 2005* (pp. 800-804). Chesapeake, VA: AACE.

Allan, S. (2015). *Teach now! Modern foreign languages: Becoming a great teacher of modern foreign languages*. London: Routledge.

Alsofyani, M. M., Aris, B. B., Eynon, R., & Majid, N. A. (2012). A preliminary evaluation of short blended online training workshop for TPACK development using technology acceptance model. *Turkish Online Journal of Educational Technology-TOJET, 11*(3), 20–32.

American Council on Teaching of Foreign Languages (ACTFL). (2011). *21st Century Skills Map for World Languages*. Retrieved October 25, 2015, from https://www.actfl.org/sites/default/files/pdfs/21stCenturySkillsMap/p21_worldlanguagesmap.pdf

American Council on the Teaching of Foreign Languages (ACTFL). (2013). *Program Standards for the Preparation of Foreign Language Teachers*. Retrieved from: http://www.actfl.org/sites/default/files/pdfs/ACTFL-Standards20Aug2013.pdf

American Council on the Teaching of Foreign Languages (ACTFL). (2015). *2013 Program Standards for the Preparation of Foreign Language Teachers*. Retrieved from http://www.actfl.org/2013-program-standards-the-preparation-foreign-language-teachers#sthash.3jVxFLkl.dpuf

American Council on the Teaching of Foreign Languages (ACTFL). (2015). *National standards for foreign language education*. Retrieved from: http://www.actfl.org/sites/default/files/pdfs/WorldReadinessStandardsforLearningLanguges.pdf

Compilation of References

American Council on the Teaching of Foreign Languages. (2012). *ACTFL proficiency guidelines*. Alexandria, VA: Author.

Anderson, N., & Nunan, D. (2003, March). *Strategies for successful listening and reading development*. Paper presented in the 37th Annual TESOL Convention, Baltimore, MD.

Anderson-Levitt, K. (2002). *Teaching cultures*. Cresskill, NJ: Hampton Press.

Archambault, L. M., & Barnett, J. H. (2010). Revisiting technological pedagogical content knowledge: Exploring the TPACK framework. *Computers & Education*, *55*(4), 1656–1662. doi:10.1016/j.compedu.2010.07.009

Arnold, N. (2007). Technology-mediated learning 10 years later: Emphasizing pedagogical or utilitarian applications? *Foreign Language Annals*, *40*(1), 161–181. doi:10.1111/j.1944-9720.2007.tb02859.x

Arnold, N. (2013). The role of methods textbooks in providing early training for teaching with technology in the language classroom. *Foreign Language Annals*, *46*(2), 230–245. doi:10.1111/flan.12020

Artzt, A. F., & Armour-Thomas, E. (1998). Mathematics teaching as problem solving: A framework for studying teacher metacognition underlying instructional practice in mathematics. *Instructional Science*, *26*(1/2), 5–25. doi:10.1023/A:1003083812378

Atkins, N. E., & Vasu, E. S. (2000). Measuring knowledge of technology usage and stages of concern about computing: A study of middle school teachers. *Journal of Technology and Teacher Education*, *8*(4), 279–302.

Bandura, A., Barbaranelli, C., Caprara, G. V., & Pastorelli, C. (1996). Multifaceted impact of self-efficacy beliefs on academic functioning. *Child Development*, *67*(3), 1206–1222. doi:10.2307/1131888 PMID:8706518

Banister, S., & Vannatta, R. (2005). Dynamic virtual instruction: Enhancing online courses and connection. *Proceedings of the Computers and Advanced Technology in Education International Conference*. Retrieved on April 28, 2013, from: http://www.actapress.com/Abstract.aspx?paperId=21561

Barnett, M. (2006). Using a web-based professional development system to support preservice teachers in examining authentic classroom practice. *Journal of Technology and Teacher Education*, *14*(4), 701–729.

Bax, S. (2003). CALL - Past, Present and Future. *System*, *31*(1), 13–28. doi:10.1016/S0346-251X(02)00071-4

Becker, H. J. (1994). How exemplary computer-using teachers differ from other teachers: Implications for realizing the potential of computers in schools. *Journal of Research on Computing in Education*, *26*(3), 291–321. doi:10.1080/08886504.1994.10782093

Beijing Normal University Teacher Education Research Center. (2012). *Report of teachers' development of middle and elementary schools in China*. Beijing: Social Science Literature Press.

Bell, T. R. (2015). The flipped German classroom. In A. Moeller (Ed.), *Learn languages, explore cultures, transform lives*. Richmond, VA: Terry.

Bennett, D., McMillan Culp, K., Honey, M., Tally, B., & Spielvogel, B. (2001). It all depends: Strategies for designing technologies for change in education. *Methods of evaluating educational technology*, 105-124.

Bergmann, J., & Sams, A. (2012). *Flip your classroom: Reach every student in every class every day*. International Society for Technology in Education. Retrieved from: https://www.iste.org/resources/product?ID=2285

Bergmann, J., & Sams, A. (2012). *Flip your classroom: Reach every student in every class every day*. Eugene, OR: International Society for Technology in Education.

Bertin, J.-C., & Sarré, C. (2014). New approaches to CALL. *Arab World English Journal*, 2-8.

Bingimlas, K. A. (2009). Barriers to the successful integration of ICT in teaching and learning environments: A review of the literature. *Eurasia Journal of Mathematics, Science & Technology Education, 5*(3), 235–245.

Bitchener, J., & Knoch, U. (2009). The relative effectiveness of different types of direct written corrective feedback. *System, 37*(2), 322–329. doi:10.1016/j.system.2008.12.006

Bitner, N., & Bitner, J. (2002). Integrating technology into the classroom: Eight keys to success. *Journal of Technology and Teacher Education, 10*(1), 95–100.

Blake, R. J. (2013). *Brave new digital classroom: Technology and foreign language learning* (2nd ed.). Washington, DC: Georgetown University Press.

Blanco, J., & Redwine Donley, P. (Eds.). (2013). *Panorama* (4th ed.). Vista Higher Learning.

Blattner, G., & Lomicka, R. (2012). Facebook-ing and the Social Generation: A new era of language learning. *ALSIC, 15*(1), 1–25.

Blin, F., & Appel, C. (2011). Computer Supported Collaborative Writing in Practice: An Activity Theoretical Study. *CALICO Journal, 28*(2), 473–497. doi:10.11139/cj.28.2.473-497

Boehm, D., & Aniola-Jedrzejek, L. (2009). Seven principles of good practice for virtual international collaboration. In M. Chang & C.-W. Kuo (Eds.), *Learning culture and language through ICTs: Methods for enhanced Instruction* (pp. 298–317). Hershey, PA: Information Science Reference. doi:10.4018/978-1-60566-166-7.ch018

Borg, S. (2003). Teacher cognition in language teaching: A review of research on what language teachers think, know, believe, and do. *Language Teaching, 36*(2), 81–109. doi:10.1017/S0261444803001903

Bos, B. (2011). Professional development for elementary teachers using TPACK. *Contemporary Issues in Technology & Teacher Education, 11*(2), 167–183.

Bosley, C., Krechowiecka, I., & Moon, S. (2005). *Review of literature on the use of information and communication technology in the context of careers education and guidance.* Centre for Guidance Studies, University of Derby. Commissioned by BECTA. Retrieved September 20, 2015, from http://www.derby.ac.uk/files/icegs_review_of_literature_on_the_use_of_ict2005.pdf

boyd, d. m., & Ellison, N.B. (2007). Social network sites: Definition, history, and scholarship. *Journal of Computer-Mediated Communication, 13*(1), article 11.

boyd, d., & Ellison, N. (2007). Social networking sites: definition, history, and scholarship. *Journal of Computer Mediated Communication, 13*(1). Retrieved from http://jcmc.indiana.edu/vol13/issue1/boyd.ellison.html

Bradley, G., & Russell, G. (1997). Computer experience, school support and computer anxieties. *Educational Psychology, 17*(3), 267–284. doi:10.1080/0144341970170303

Brandl, K. (2008). *Communicative language teaching in action: Putting principles to work.* Upper Saddle River, NJ: Pearson.

Brantley-Dias, L., & Ertmer, P. A. (2013). Goldilocks and TPACK: Is the construct 'just right?'. *Journal of Research on Technology in Education, 46*(2), 103–128. doi:10.1080/15391523.2013.10782615

British Educational Communication and Technology Agency (BECTA). (2004). *A review of the research literature on barriers to the uptake of ICT by teachers.* Retrieved September 17, 2015, from http://dera.ioe.ac.uk/1603/1/becta_2004_barrierstouptake_litrev.pdf

Compilation of References

Brown, D., & Warschauer, M. (2006). From the university to the elementary classroom: Students' experiences in learning to integrate technology in instruction. *Journal of Technology and Teacher Education, 14*(3), 599–621.

Brown, H. D., & Lee, H. (2015). *Teaching by principles: An interactive approach to language pedagogy*. White Plains, NY: Pearson.

Bruce, C. S. (2004). *Information literacy as a catalyst for educational change. A background paper*. Retrieved October 21, 2015, from http://eprints.qut.edu.au/4977/1/4977_1.pdf

Bull, P. (2009). Self-efficacy and technology integration: perceptions of first year teaching fellows to technology integration in education. *In Society for Information Technology & Teacher Education International Conference, 2009*(1), 1768-1776.

Burns, A., & Richards, J. C. (Eds.). (2009). *The Cambridge guide to second language teacher education*. Cambridge, UK: Cambridge University Press.

Burns, A., & Richards, J. C. (Eds.). (2012). *The Cambridge guide to pedagogy and practice in second language teaching*. Cambridge, UK: Cambridge University Press.

Bush, M. D. (1997). Implementing technology for language learning. In M. D. Bush (Ed.), *Technology-enhanced language learning* (pp. 287–349). Lincolnwood, IL: National Textbook Company.

Butler, D., & Sellbom, M. (2002). Barriers to adopting technology for teaching and learning. *EDUCAUSE Quarterly, 25*(2), 22–28.

Butzin, S. M. (2004). *Project CHILD: A proven model for the integration of computer and curriculum in the elementary classroom*. Retrieved August 18, 2015, from http://www.acec-journal.org/archives_archives.php

Cabanatan, P. (2003, June). *Integrating Pedagogy and Technology: The SEAMEO INNOTECH Experience*. Proposal presented to Experts Meeting on Teachers/Facilitators Training in Technology-Pedagogy Integration, Bangkok, Thailand.

Cambridge, D., Kaplan, S., & Suter, V. (2005). *Community of practice design guide: A step-by-step guide for designing & cultivating communities of practice in higher education*. Retrieved from: http://net.educause.edu/ir/library/pdf/nli0531.pdf

Campanelli, P. (2012). Testing survey questions. In E. D. De Leeuw, J. J. Hox, & D. A. Dillman (Eds.), International handbook of survey methodology (pp. 176–200). European Association of Methodology Series. New York: Lawrence Erlbaum Associates

Cao, W., Hu, Z., Li, H., & Xu, X. (2015). Status quo of computer-assisted ELT in basic education in China. *Computer-Assisted Foreign Language Education, 4*, 41–46.

CECR. (2007). *College English curriculum requirements*. Shanghai: Shanghai Foreign Language Publishing Press.

Cetto, M. (2010). Technology and second language teaching. *Brújula, 8*, 119–121.

Chai, C. S., Chin, C. K., Koh, J. H. L., & Tan, C. L. (2013). Exploring Singaporean Chinese language teachers' technological pedagogical content knowledge and its relationship to the teachers' pedagogical beliefs. *The Asia-Pacific Education Researcher, 22*(4), 657–666. doi:10.1007/s40299-013-0071-3

Chai, C. S., Koh, J. H. L., & Tsai, C. C. (2010). Facilitating preservice teachers' development of technological, pedagogical, and content knowledge (TPACK). *Journal of Educational Technology & Society, 13*(4), 63–73.

Chai, C. S., Koh, J. H. L., Tsai, C. C., & Tan, L. L. W. (2011). Modeling primary school pre-service teachers' technological pedagogical content knowledge (TPACK) for meaningful learning with information and communication technology (ICT). *Computers & Education, 57*(1), 1184–1193. doi:10.1016/j.compedu.2011.01.007

Chai, C. S., Koh, J. H. L., & Tsai, C.-C. (2010). Facilitating Preservice Teachers' Development of Technological, Pedagogical, and Content Knowledge (TPACK). *Journal of Educational Technology & Society, 13*(4), 63–73.

Chambers, A., & Bax, S. (2006). Making CALL work: Towards normalisation. *System, 34*(4), 465–479. doi:10.1016/j.system.2006.08.001

Chapelle, C. (2003). *English language learning and technology: Lectures on applied linguistics in the age of information and communication technology*. Amsterdam: John Benjamins. doi:10.1075/lllt.7

Chapelle, C. A. (2004). Technology and second language learning: Expanding methods and agendas. *System, 32*(4), 593–601. doi:10.1016/j.system.2004.09.014

Chaptal, A. (2002). Is the investment really worth it? *Educational Media International, 39*(1), 87–99. doi:10.1080/09523980210131178

Chapters, E. (2003). The use of think-aloud methods in qualitative research: An Introduction to think-aloud methods. *Brock Education, 12*(2), 68–82.

Chen, C. H., & Chan, L. H. (2011). Effectiveness and impact of technology-enabled project-based learning with the use of process prompts in teacher education. *Journal of Technology and Teacher Education, 19*(2), 141–167.

Cheng, H. (2013). *A distance education teacher training study on practicum reflections and training strategies*. The 8th International Conference on Internet Chinese Education International Conference on Internet Chinese (ICICE 2013), Pasadena, U.S.A.

Cheng, H. (2014b). *The study of pre-service teachers' TPACK in a distance education teacher training program*. The 11th International Conference of World Chinese Language Association, Taipei: Taiwan

Cheng, T., & Chen, H. (2015). *ZaiMei kuaqu hezuo de Huayuwen ji wenhua yuanju jiaoxue zhi shili fenxiang yu tasuo*. The 9th International Conference on Internet Chinese Education International Conference on Internet Chinese (ICICE 2015), Boston, U.S.A

Cheng, H. (2009). The Investigation of the Relationships between Current Development of CALL-TCSL Teachers and the Training Programs. *Chung Yuan Journal of Teaching Chinese as a Second Language, 3*, 107–127.

Cheng, H. (2014). The study of CSL online teacher training course and the teachers' development of technological pedagogical content knowledge. *Journal of Technology and Chinese Language Teaching., 5*(2), 1–18.

Cheng, H. (2014a). The study of CSL online teacher training course and the teachers' development of Technological Pedagogical Content Knowledge. *Journal of Technology and Chinese Language Teaching, 5*(2), 1–18. http://www.tclt.us/journal/2014v5n2/cheng.pdf

Cheng, H., & Zhan, H. (2012). *Examining Pre-service Teachers' Technological Pedagogical Content Knowledge Instructional Strategies via Video-conferencing Technology, The Journal of Educational Technology Development and Exchange*. JETDE.

Chenoweth, N., Ushida, E., & Murday, K. (2013). Student learning in hybrid French and Spanish courses: An overview of language online. *CALICO, 24*(1), 115–146.

Chien, Y. T., Chang, C. Y., Yeh, T. K., & Chang, K. E. (2012). Engaging pre-service science teachers to act as active designers of technology integration: A MAGDAIRE framework. *Teaching and Teacher Education, 28*(4), 578–588. doi:10.1016/j.tate.2011.12.005

Compilation of References

Chinese Language Association of Secondary-Elementary Schools. (2007). *An Overview of the Twelve Professional Standards for K-12 Chinese Language Teachers.* Retrieved from https://nealrc.osu.edu/sites/nealrc.osu.edu/files/teacher-k-12-class-teachers-standards.pdf

Chizmar, J. F., & Williams, D. B. (2001). What do faculty want? *EDUCAUSE Quarterly, 24*(1), 18–24.

Chong, C. K., Puteh, M., & Goh, S. C. (2015). Framework to Integrate Spreadsheet into the Teaching and Learning of Financial Mathematics. *Electronic Journal of Mathematics & Technology, 9*(1), 92–106.

Cochran-Smith, M., & Lytle, S. L. (1999). Relationships of knowledge and practice: Teacher learning in communities. Review of Research in Education, 24, 249–305.

Cohen-Sayag, E., & Fischl, D. (2012). Reflective Writing in pre-service teachers' teaching: What does it promote? *Australian Journal of Teacher Education, 37*(10), 20–36. doi:10.14221/ajte.2012v37n10.1

Compton, L. K. (2009). Preparing language teachers to teach language online: A look at skills, roles, and responsibilities. *Computer Assisted Language Learning, 22*(1), 73–99. doi:10.1080/09588220802613831

Conole, G., & Alevizou, P. (2010). *A literature review of these of Web 2.0 tools in higher education.* Milton Keynes, UK: Open University.

Cook-Sather, A. (2007). Using email to connect pre-service teachers, experienced teachers, and high school students within an undergraduate teacher preparation program. *Journal of Technology and Teacher Education, 15*(1), 11–37.

Copley, J., & Ziviani, J. (2004). Barriers to the use of assistive technology for children with multiple disabilities. *Occupational Therapy International, 11*(4), 229–243. doi:10.1002/oti.213 PMID:15771212

Corbeil, R. J., & Corbeil, V. E. M. (2007). Are you ready for mobile learning? *Educase Quarterly Magazine, 30*(2), 51–58.

Corbin, J., & Strauss, A. (2007). *Basics of qualitative research: Techniques and procedures for developing grounded theory* (3rd ed.). Thousand Oaks, CA: Sage Publications.

Corbin, J., & Strauss, A. (2008). *Basics of Qualitative Research: Techniques and Procedures for Developing Grounded Theory* (3rd ed.). Thousand Oaks, CA: Sage.

Cormode, G., & Krishnamurthy, B. (2008). Key differences between Web 1.0 and Web 2.0. *First Monday, 13*(6). doi:10.5210/fm.v13i6.2125

Cuban, L. (1999). The technology puzzle. *Education Week, 18*(43), 68–69.

Cuban, L., Kirkpatrick, H., & Peck, C. (2001). High access and low use of technologies in high school classrooms: Explaining an apparent paradox. *American Educational Research Journal, 38*(4), 813–834. doi:10.3102/00028312038004813

Dai, W., & Wang, X. (2012). The content and approach for EFL teachers' professional development in informational technological context. *Computer-Assisted Foreign Language Education, 6*, 8–13.

Davenport, N. A. M. (2006). Connecting pre-service teachers with students: Using email to build skills for teaching writing. *Journal of Reading Education, 31*(2), 13–19.

Davis, F. D. (1989). Perceived usefulness, perceived ease of use, and user acceptance of information technology. *Management Information Systems Quarterly, 13*(3), 319–340. doi:10.2307/249008

Debski, R. (2006). Theory and practice in teaching project-oriented CALL. In P. Hubbard & M. Levy (Eds.), *Teacher education in CALL* (pp. 99–114). Amsterdam: John Benjamins. doi:10.1075/lllt.14.10deb

Decision, C. (2005). *Science and technology basic plan.* Tokyo: The Japan Science and Technology Agency.

Dede, C. (2004). Enabling Distributed-Learning Communities via Emerging Technologies. *Proceedings of the 2004 Conference of the Society for Information Technology in Teacher Education (SITE)*. Charlottesville, VA: American Association for Computers in Education.

Derwing, T. M., & Munro, M. J. (2009). Putting accent in its place: Rethinking obstacles to communication. *Language Teaching*, *42*(04), 276–490. doi:10.1017/S026144480800551X

Develotte, C., Guichon, N., & Vincent, C. (2010). The use of the webcam for teaching a foreign language in a desktop videoconferencing environment. *ReCALL*, *22*(3), 293–312. doi:10.1017/S0958344010000170

Dewey, J. (1938). *Experience and Education*. Indianapolis, IN: Kappa Delta Pi.

Dhonau, S., McAlpine, D. C., & Shrum, J. L. (2010). What is taught in the foreign language methods course? *NECTFL Review*, *66*, 73–95.

Doering, A., Veletsianos, G., Scharber, C., & Miller, C. (2009). Using the technological, pedagogical and content knowledge framework to design online learning environments and professional development. *Journal of Educational Computing Research*, *41*(3), 319–346. doi:10.2190/EC.41.3.d

Domalewska, D. (2014). Technology-supported classroom for collaborative learning: Blogging in the foreign language classroom. *International Journal of Education and Development using Information and Communication Technology*, *10*(4), 21-30.

Dooly, M. (2009). New competencies in a new era? Examining the impact of a teacher training project. *ReCALL*, *21*(3), 352–369. doi:10.1017/S0958344009990085

Dooly, M., & Masats, D. (2011). Closing the loop between theory and praxis: New models in EFL teaching. *ELT Journal*, *65*(1), 42–51. doi:10.1093/elt/ccq017

Dooly, M., & Sadler, R. (2013). Filling in the gaps: Linking theory and practice through telecollaboration in teacher education. *ReCALL*, *25*(1), 4–29. doi:10.1017/S0958344012000237

DuBravac, S. (2013). *Technology in the L2 curriculum*. Boston: Pearson.

Ducate, L. C., & Lomicka, L. L. (2008). Adventures in the blogosphere: From blog readers to blog writers. *Computer Assisted Language Learning*, *21*(1), 9–28. doi:10.1080/09588220701865474

Egbert, J. (2006). Learning in context: Situating language teacher learning in CALL. In P. Hubbard & M. Levy (Eds.), *Teacher education in CALL* (pp. 167–190). Amsterdam: John Benjamins. doi:10.1075/lllt.14.15egb

Egbert, J., Paulus, T. M., & Nakamichi, Y. (2002). The impact of CALL instruction on classroom computer use: A foundation for rethinking technology in teacher education. *Language Learning & Technology*, *6*(3), 108–126.

Ekanayake, S. Y., & Wishart, J. (2014). Integrating mobile phones into teaching and learning: A case study of teacher training through professional development workshops. *British Journal of Educational Technology*. doi:10.1111/bjet.12131

Ekrem, S., & Recep, C. (2014). Examining Preservice EFL Teachers' TPACK Competencies in Turkey. *Journal of Educators Online*, *11*(2), 1.

Ellison, N., Steinfield, C., & Lampe, C. (2007). The benefits of Facebook "friends": Exploring the relationship between college students' use of online social networks and social capital. *Journal of Computer-Mediated Communication*, *12*(3), article 1. Retrieved on April 28, 2013, from http://jcmc.indiana.edu/vol12/issue4/ellison.html

Elola, I., & Oskoz, A. (2010). Collaborative Writing: Fostering Foreign Language and Writing Conventions Development. *Language Learning & Technology*, *14*(3), 51–71.

Compilation of References

Embong, A. M., Noor, A. M., Ali, R. M. M., Bakar, Z. A., & Amin, A. R. M. (2012a). Teachers' perceptions on the use of e-books as textbooks in the classroom. *World Academy of Science. Engineering and Technology, 6*(10), 580–586.

Embong, A. M., Noor, A. M., Hashim, H. M., Ali, R. M., & Shaari, Z. H. (2012b). E-books as textbooks in the classroom. *Procedia: Social and Behavioral Sciences, 47,* 1802–1809. doi:10.1016/j.sbspro.2012.06.903

Erben, T. (1999). Constructing learning in a virtual immersion bath: LOTE teacher education through audiographics. In R. Debski & M. Levy (Eds.), *WORLDCALL: Global perspectives on computer-assisted language learning* (pp. 229–248). Lisse, The Netherlands: Swets & Zeitlinger Publishers.

Ertmer, P. A. (1999). Addressing first- and second-order barriers to change: Strategies for technology integration. *Educational Technology Research and Development, 47*(4), 47–61. doi:10.1007/BF02299597

Ertmer, P. A. (2005). Teacher pedagogical beliefs: The final frontier in our quest for technology integration? *Educational Technology Research and Development, 53*(4), 25–39. doi:10.1007/BF02504683

Ertmer, P. A., Gopalakrishnan, S., & Ross, E. M. (2001). Technology-using teachers: Comparing perceptions of exemplary technology use to best practice. *Journal of Research on Technology in Education, 33*(5), 1–26.

Ertmer, P. A., & Ottenbreit-Leftwich, A. T. (2010). Teacher technology change: How knowledge, confidence, beliefs, and culture intersect. *Journal of Research on Technology in Education, 42*(3), 255–284. doi:10.1080/15391523.2010.10782551

Ertmer, P. A., Ottenbreit-Leftwich, A. T., Sadik, O., Sendurur, E., & Sendurur, P. (2012). Teacher beliefs and technology integration practices: A critical relationship. *Computers & Education, 59*(2), 423–435. doi:10.1016/j.compedu.2012.02.001

Evans, L. S., & Gunn, A. A. (2011). It's not just the language: Culture as an essential component in preservice teacher education. *Journal of Multiculturalism in Education, 7*(1), 1–30.

Evans, M. (Ed.). (2009). *Foreign language learning with digital technology*. London: Continuum.

Fabrigar, L. R., Wegener, D. T., MacCallum, R. C., & Strahan, E. J. (1999). Evaluating the use of exploratory factor analysis in psychological research. *Psychological Methods, 4*(3), 272–299. doi:10.1037/1082-989X.4.3.272

Fabry, D., & Higgs, J. (1997). Barriers to the effective use of technology in education. *Journal of Educational Computing, 17*(4), 385–395. doi:10.2190/C770-AWA1-CMQR-YTYV

Facebook. (2015, May 5). In *Wikipedia, the free encyclopedia*. Retrieved from http://en.wikipedia.org/wiki/Facebook

Fang, Z. (1996). A review of research on teacher beliefs and practices. *Educational Research, 38*(1), 47–65. doi:10.1080/0013188960380104

Felix, U. (2005). Analyzing recent CALL effectiveness research: Towards a common agenda. *Computer Assisted Language Learning, 18*(1-2), 1–32. doi:10.1080/09588220500132274

Fernández, T., Santiago, J., Tomaino, A., del Río, M., & Casaravilla, A. (2011). A Virtual Challenge: English-Spanish learning exchange between Australian and Spanish university students. *Proceedings of the 5th International Technology, Education and Development Conference, (INTED2011)*.

Fernández, T., García-Pérez, G., & Santiago, J. (2014). A Language Exchange Program: Sustainability Innovation in Language and Culture Engagement. *Journal of Science, 12*(2), 8–12.

Ferris, D. R. (1999). The case for grammar correction in L2 writing classes. A response to Truscott (1996). *Journal of Second Language Writing, 8*(1), 1–10. doi:10.1016/S1060-3743(99)80110-6

Finger, G., Jamieson-Proctor, R., & Albion, P. (2010). *Beyond pedagogical content knowledge: The importance of TPACK for informing preservice teacher education in Australia. In Key competencies in the knowledge society* (pp. 114–125). Springer Berlin Heidelberg.

Fisher, L. (2009). Trainee teachers' perceptions of the use of digital technology in the languages Classroom. In M. J. Evans (Ed.), *Foreign Language Learning with Digital Technology* (pp. 60–79). London: Continuum.

Flipped Learning Network. (n.d.). Retrieved from http://flippedlearning.org

Fox, R., & Henri, J. (2005). Understanding teacher mindsets: IT and change in Hong Kong schools. *Journal of Educational Technology & Society*, *8*(2), 161–169.

Freeman, D. (2002). The hidden side of the work: Teacher knowledge and learning to teach. *Language Teaching*, *35*(01), 1–13. doi:10.1017/S0261444801001720

Freeman, D., & Johnson, K. E. (1998). Reconceptualizing the knowledge-base of language teacher education. *TESOL Quarterly*, *32*(3), 397–417. doi:10.2307/3588114

Frey, T. (2008). Determining the impact of online practicum facilitation for inservice teachers. *Journal of Technology and Teacher Education*, *16*(2), 181–210.

FSSE. (2010, July 25). Professors' use of technology in teaching. *The Chronicle of Higher Education*. Retrieved on April 29, 2013, from http://chronicle.com/article/Professors-Useof/123682/?sid=wc&utm_source=wc&utm_medium=en

Fuchs, C., & Akbar, F. S. (2013). Use of technology in an adult intensive English program: Benefits and challenges. *TESOL Quarterly*, *47*(1), 156–167. doi:10.1002/tesq.80

Funkhouser, B. J., & Mouza, C. (2013). Drawing on technology: An investigation of preservice teacher beliefs in the context of an introductory educational technology course. *Computers & Education*, *62*, 271–285. doi:10.1016/j.compedu.2012.11.005

Furman, N., Goldberg, D., & Lusin, N. (2007). *Enrollments in languages other than English in United States institutions of higher education, fall 2006*. Retrieved from http://www.mla.org/pdf/06enrollmentsurvey_final.pdf

Furstenberg, G., & Morgenstern, D. (1992). Technology for language learning and teaching: Designs, products, perspectives. In W. Rivers (Ed.), *Teaching languages in college: Curriculum and content* (pp. 117–140). Lincolnwood, IL: NTC.

Galanouli, D., & McNair, V. (2001). Students' perceptions of ICT-related support in teaching placements. *Journal of Computer Assisted Learning*, *17*(4), 396–408. doi:10.1046/j.0266-4909.2001.00196.x

Gao, P., Chee, T. S., Wang, L., Wong, A., & Choy, D. (2011). Self reflection and preservice teachers' technological pedagogical knowledge: Promoting earlier adoption of student-centred pedagogies. *Australasian Journal of Educational Technology*, *27*(6), 997–1013. doi:10.14742/ajet.925

García-Pérez, G. (2011). Effectiveness of formative e-assessment in large language classes. *Proceedings of the 6th International Conference on e-Learnin*. Academic Publishing Limited.

García-Pérez, G. (2014). *Learning by doing: Spanish Applied Linguistics as a Living Lab*. 2nd International Scientific Forum, Albania.

García-Pérez, G., & Fernández, T. (2011). When three cultures meet: Enhancing intercultural communication through virtual story telling. *The 9th International Conference on Education and Information Systems, Technologies and Applications*.

Garrett, N. (1991). Technology in the service of language learning: Trends and issues. *Modern Language Journal*, *75*(1), 74–101. doi:10.1111/j.1540-4781.1991.tb01085.x

Compilation of References

Garrett, N. (2009). Computer-assisted language learning trends and issues revisited: Integrating innovation. *Modern Language Journal, 93*, 719–740. doi:10.1111/j.1540-4781.2009.00969.x

Garrison, D. R., & Kanuka, H. (2004). Blended learning: Uncovering its transformative potential in higher education. *The Internet and Higher Education, 7*(2), 95–105. doi:10.1016/j.iheduc.2004.02.001

Gedera, D. (2012). The dynamics of blog peer feedback in ESL classroom. *Teaching English with Technology, 12*(4), 16-30.

Gentry, L. B., Denton, C. A., & Kurz, T. (2008). Technologically-based mentoring provided to teachers: A synthesis of the literature. *Journal of Technology and Teacher Education, 16*(3), 339–373.

Georgina, A. D., & Hosford, C. C. (2009). Higher education faculty perceptions on technology integration and training. *Teaching and Teacher Education, 25*(5), 690–696. doi:10.1016/j.tate.2008.11.004

Gibson, J. (1979). *The ecological approach to visual perceptions*. Boston: Houghton Mifflin.

Gick, B., Bernhardt, B., Bacsfalvi, P., Wilson, I., Hansen Edwards, J. G., & Zampini, M. L. (2008). Ultrasound imaging applications in second language acquisition. In J. G. Hansen Edwards & M. L. Zampini (Eds.), Phonology and second language acquisition (pp. 315-328). Philadelphia, PA: John Benjamins. doi:10.1075/sibil.36.15gic

Goertler, S. (2012). Students' readiness for and attitudes toward hybrid foreign language instruction: Multiple perspectives. *CALICO Journal, 29*(2), 297–320. doi:10.11139/cj.29.2.297-320

Goktas, Y., Yildirim, Z., & Yildirim, S. (2008). A review of ICT related courses in pre-service teacher education programs. *Asia Pacific Education Review, 9*(2), 168–179. doi:10.1007/BF03026497

Goldburg, D., Looney, D., & Lusin, N. (2015). Enrollments in languages other than English in *United States institutions of higher education, fall 2013*. Retrieved from http://www.mla.org/pdf/2013_enrollment_survey.pdf

Gómez-Blancarte, A., & Miranda Viramontes, I. (2014). Communities of practice: A theoretical framework to design for teachers' statistical learning. In K. Makar, B. de Sousa, & R. Gould (Eds.), *Sustainability in statistics education: Proceedings of the Ninth International Conference on Teaching Statistics (ICOTS9)*.

Goodhue, D. L., & Thompson, R. L. (1995). Task-technology fit and individual performance. *Management Information Systems Quarterly, 19*(2), 213–236. doi:10.2307/249689

Goodson, I. F., & Mangan, J. M. (1995). Subject cultures and the introduction of classroom computers. *British Educational Research Journal, 21*(5), 613–628. doi:10.1080/0141192950210505

Greenhow, C. (2011). Online social networks and learning. *On the Horizon, 15*(1), 4–12. doi:10.1108/10748121111107663

Greenhow, C., & Burton, L. (2011). Help from my "Friends:" Social capital in the social network sites of low-income high school students. *Journal of Educational Computing Research, 45*(2), 223–245. doi:10.2190/EC.45.2.f

Greenhow, C., & Gleason, B. (2012). Twitteracy: Tweeting as a new literacy practice. *The Educational Forum, 76*(2).

Greenhow, C., & Li, J. (2013). Like, comment, share: Collaboration and civic engagement within social network sites. For inclusion. In C. Mouza & N. Lavigne (Eds.), *Emerging technologies for the classroom: A learning sciences perspective* (pp. 127–241). New York: Springer.

Greenhow, C., & Robelia, E. (2009a). Old communication, new literacies: Social network sites as social learning resources. *Journal of Computer-Mediated Communication, 14*(4), 1130–1161. doi:10.1111/j.1083-6101.2009.01484.x

Greenhow, C., & Robelia, E. (2009b). Informal learning and identity formation in online social networks. *Learning, Media and Technology, 34*(2), 119–140. doi:10.1080/17439880902923580

Grosbois, M. (2014). Practicum experience in teacher education: is experience the best teacher? In J. Martínez Agudo (Ed.), *English as a foreign language teacher education: Current perspectives and challenges* (pp. 107–126). Amsterdam, New York: Editions Rodopi.

Grosbois, M. (in press). Computer supported collaborative writing and language learning. In F. Fiarr & L. Murray (Eds.), *Handbook of Language Learning and Technology*. London: Routledge.

Gu, X. Q., &Fu, S. R. (2011). Research of users' technology acceptance of mobile learners. *E-education,* (6), 48-55.

Gu, H. (2012). The strategic reaction to the new curriculum reform in basic education: A case of the EFL teacher education program in Henan Province. *Educational Review, 4*, 87–89.

Guha, S. (2000). *Are we all technically prepared?Teachers' perspectives on the causes of comfort or discomfort in using computers at elementary grade teaching*. Paper presented at the Annual Meeting of the National Association for the Education of Young Children, Atlanta, GA.

Guichon, N. (2009). Training future language teachers to develop online tutor's competence through reflective analysis. *ReCALL, 21*(2), 166–185. doi:10.1017/S0958344009000214

Guichon, N. (2012). *Vers l'intégration des TIC dans l'enseignement des langues*. Paris: Didier.

Guichon, N., & Hauck, M. (2011). Editorial: Teacher education research in CALL and CMC: More in demand than ever. *ReCALL, 23*(03), 187–199. doi:10.1017/S0958344011000139

Guidry, K. R., Cubillos, J., & Pusecker, K. (2013). *The connection between self-regulated learning and student success in a hybrid course*. Paper presented at the Association for Institutional Research Annual Forum, Long Beach, CA. Retrieved from: http://www.mistakengoal.com/docs/Self-regulated_learning_hybrid_course.pdf

Halvorsen, A. (2014). *Facebook usage in Thailand: The plurilingual competencies of Thai high school students and teachers* (Doctoral Dissertation). Retrieved from http://hdl.handle.net/2142/49516

Hampel, R., & Stickler, U. (2005). New skills for new classrooms: Training tutors to teach languages online. *Computer Assisted Language Learning, 18*(4), 311–326. doi:10.1080/09588220500335455

Harmer, J. (2007). *The Practice of English Language Teaching* (4th ed.). Pearson Education Limited.

Harmer, J. (2008). *How to teach English (New Edition)*. Pearson Education Limited.

Harris, J., Grandgenett, N., & Hofer, M. (2010). Testing a TPACK-based technology integration assessment rubric. In *Society for Information Technology & Teacher Education International Conference* (Vol. 2010, No. 1, pp. 3833-3840).

Hayashi, A., Chen, C., Ryan, T., & Wu, J. (2004). The role of social presence and moderating role of computer self-efficacy in predicting the continuance usage of e-learning systems. *Journal of Information Systems Education, 15*(2), 139–154.

Haydn, T. A., & Barton, R. (2007). Common needs and different agendas: How trainee teachers make progress in their ability to use ICT in subject teaching. Some lessons from the UK. *Computers & Education, 49*(4), 1018–1036. doi:10.1016/j.compedu.2005.12.006

He, B., Puakpong, N., & Lian, A. (2015). Factors affecting the normalization of CALL in Chinese senior high schools. *Computer Assisted Language Learning, 28*(3), 189–201. doi:10.1080/09588221.2013.803981

Hegelheimer, V. (2006). When the technology course is required. In P. Hubbard & M. Levy (Eds.), *Teacher education in CALL* (pp. 117–133). Amsterdam: John Benjamins. doi:10.1075/lllt.14.12heg

Compilation of References

Heift, T., & Chapelle, C. A. (2012). Language learning through technology. In S. M. Gass & A. Mackey (Eds.), *The routledge handbook of second language acquisition* (pp. 555–570). London: Routledge.

Heining-Boynton, A. L., LeLoup, J. W., & Cowell, G. S. (2013). *Anda! Curso intermedio*. Pearson.

Hennessy, S., Ruthven, K., & Brindley, S. (2005). Teacher perspectives on integrating ICT into subject teaching: Commitment, constraints, caution, and change. *Journal of Curriculum Studies*, *37*(2), 155–192. doi:10.1080/0022027032000276961

Hew, K. F., & Brush, T. (2007). Integrating technology into K-12 teaching and learning: Current knowledge gaps and recommendations for future research. *Educational Technology Research and Development*, *55*(3), 223–252. doi:10.1007/s11423-006-9022-5

Hill, P. (2014). *Online educational delivery models: A descriptive view*. Retrieved from: http://er.dut.ac.za/bitstream/handle/123456789/56/Hill_2012_Online_Educational_Delivery_Models.pdf?sequence=1&isAllowed=y

Hirano, H. (2014). *"Soogoo Nihongo" no jugyoo de okonau zero shokyuu kara no onsee kyooiku no jissen: Akusento, intoneeshon no shizensei wo juushishita shikakuka hojo kyoozai no shiyoo* [Practice of Japanese prosody education for beginners in an integrated Japanese course: Use of visualized Japanese accent and intonation learning material]. Retrieved from http://www.ninjal.ac.jp/publication/papers/07/pdf/NINJAL-Papers0703.pdf

Hoadley, C. (2012). What is a community of practice and how can we support it? In Theoretical foundations of Learning Environments. Routledge, Taylor and Frances Group.

Holmes, K. (2009). Planning to teach with digital tools: Introducing the interactive whiteboard to pre-service secondary mathematics teachers. *Australasian Journal of Educational Technology*, *25*(3), 351–365. doi:10.14742/ajet.1139

Hong, K. H. (2010). CALL teacher education as an impetus for L2 teachers in integrating technology. *ReCALL*, *22*(1), 53–69. doi:10.1017/S095834400999019X

Hoopingarner, D. (2009). Best practices in technology and language teaching. *Language and Linguistics Compass*, *3*(1), 222–235. doi:10.1111/j.1749-818X.2008.00123.x

Hoven, D. (2007). The affordances of technology for student teachers to shape their teacher education experience. In M. A. Kassen, L. R. Lavine, K. Murphy-Judy, & M. Peters (Eds.), *Preparing and Developing Technology Proficient L2 Teachers* (pp. 133–163). San Marcos, TX: CALICO.

Howard, J. (2002). Technology-enhanced project-based learning in teacher education: Addressing the goals of transfer. *Journal of Technology and Teacher Education*, *10*(3), 343–364.

Hsu, P.-S., & Sharma, P. (2006). A systemic plan of technology integration. *Journal of Educational Technology & Society*, *9*(4), 173–184.

Huang, H. M., & Liaw, S. S. (2007). Exploring learners' self-efficacy, autonomy, and motivation toward e-learning. *Perceptual and Motor Skills*, *105*(2), 581–586. doi:10.2466/pms.105.2.581-586 PMID:18065082

Hubbard, P. (2008). CALL and the future of language teacher education. *CALICO Journal*, *25*(2), 175–188.

Hubbard, P., & Levy, M. (2006). The scope of CALL education. In P. Hubbard & M. Levy (Eds.), *Teacher education in CALL* (pp. 3–21). Amsterdam: John Benjamins. doi:10.1075/lllt.14.04hub

Hughes, G. (2009). Social software: New opportunities for challenging social inequalities in learning? *Learning, Media and Technology*, *34*(4), 291–305. doi:10.1080/17439880903338580

Hughes, J. (2005). The role of teacher knowledge and learning experiences in forming technology-integrated pedagogy. *Journal of Technology and Teacher Education*, *13*(2), 277–302.

Hughes, J. (2013). Descriptive indicators of future teachers' technology integration in the PK-12 classroom: Trends from a laptop-infused teacher education program. *Journal of Educational Computing Research*, *48*(4), 491–516. doi:10.2190/EC.48.4.e

Huhn, C. (2012). In search of innovation: Research on effective models of foreign language teacher preparation. *Foreign Language Annals*, *45*(1), 163–183. doi:10.1111/j.1944-9720.2012.01184.x

Hunter, J. (2015). *Technology integration and high possibility classrooms: Building from TPACK*. New York: Routledge.

Hu, Z., & McGrath, I. (2011). Innovation in higher education in China: Are teachers ready to integrate ICT in English language teaching? *Technology, Pedagogy and Education*, *20*(1), 41–59. doi:10.1080/1475939X.2011.554014

International Society for Technology in Education (ISTE). (2015). *Standards for teachers*. Retrieved from: http://www.iste.org/standards/ISTE-standards/standards-for-teachers

International Society for Technology in Education. (2008). *ISTE standards teachers*. Retrieved from http://www.iste.org/standards/iste-standards/standards-for-teachers

Interstate New Teacher Assessment and Support Consortium INTASC Foreign Language Standards Committee. (2002). *Model standards for licensing beginning foreign language teachers: A resource for state dialogue*. Retrieved from http://programs.ccsso.org/content/pdfs/ForeignLanguageStandards.pdf

Interstate New Teacher Assessment and Support Consortium. (2013). *InTASC: Model core teaching standards and learning progressions for teachers 1.0*. Washington, DC: Council of Chief State School Officers.

Jaipal, K., & Figg, C. (2010). Unpacking the "Total PACKage": Emergent TPACK Characteristics from a Study of Preservice Teachers Teaching With Technology.[Chesapeake, VA: AACE.]. *Journal of Technology and Teacher Education*, *18*(3), 415–441.

Jang, S. J. (2008). The effects of integrating technology, observation and writing into a teacher education method course. *Computers & Education*, *50*(3), 853–865. doi:10.1016/j.compedu.2006.09.002

Jang, S. J., & Chen, K. C. (2010). From PCK to TPACK: Developing a transformative model fro pre-service science teachers. *Journal of Science Education and Technology*, *19*(6), 553–564. doi:10.1007/s10956-010-9222-y

Janus, L. (1998). *Less commonly taught languages of emerging importance: Major issues, cost problems, and their national implications*. International education in the new global era proceedings of a national policy conference on the Higher Education Act, Title VI, and Fulbright-Hays programs less commonly taught language. Retrieved January 15, 2013 from http://www.international.ucla.edu/pacrim/title6/Break6-Janus.pdf

Jenkins, H. (2008). *Confronting the challenges of participatory culture: Media education for the 21st century (John D. and Catherine T. MacArthur Foundation Reports on Digital Media and Learning)*. Chicago, IL: MacArthur Foundation.

Jiao, B., & Wei, H. (2012). A survey on the EFL teachers' informational literacy at elementary and secondary levels. *Journal of Heilongjiang Educational Institute*, *31*(10), 35–35.

Jimoyiannis, A. (2010). Designing and implementing an integrated technological science knowledge framework for science teachers professional development. *Computers & Education*, *55*(3), 1259–1269. doi:10.1016/j.compedu.2010.05.022

Jiyoon, Y. (2008). Cyber practicum: A future practicum classroom. *British Journal of Educational Technology*, *39*(1), 163–165.

Johnson, D. W., & Johnson, R. T. (2009). An educational psychology success story: Social interdependence theory and cooperative learning. *The Journal of Educational Research*, *38*(5), 365–379.

Johnson, E. M. (2002). The role of computer-supported discussion for language teacher education: What do the students say? *CALICO Journal, 20*(1), 59–80.

Jonassen, D., Howland, J., Marra, R., & Crismond, D. (2008). *Meaningful learning with technology* (3rd ed.). Upper Saddle River, NJ: Pearson.

Jones, J., & Coffey, S. (2013). Modern foreign languages 5-11: A guide for teachers (2nd ed.). London: Routledge.

Jung, I. (2005). ICT-Pedagogy integration in teacher training: Application cases worldwide. *Journal of Educational Technology & Society, 8*(2), 94–101.

Jung, I., & Latchem, C. (2011). A model for e-education: Extended teaching spaces and extended learning spaces. *British Journal of Educational Technology, 42*(1), 6–18. doi:10.1111/j.1467-8535.2009.00987.x

Kagan, D. M. (1992). Implications of research on teacher belief. *Educational Psychologist, 27*(1), 65–90. doi:10.1207/s15326985ep2701_6

Kane, R., Sandetto, S., & Heath, C. (2002). Telling half the story: A critical review of research on the teaching beliefs and practices of university academics. *Review of Educational Research, 72*(2), 177–228. doi:10.3102/00346543072002177

Kang, J., Ni, X., & Li, G. (2010). Preparing foreign language teachers to implement a technology-rich curriculum. In D. Gibson & B. Dodge (Eds.), *Proceedings of Society for Information Technology & Teacher Education International Conference 2010* (pp. 3876-3879). Chesapeake, VA: Association for the Advancement of Computing in Education.

Kang, Y., & Cheng, X. (2014). Teacher learning in the workplace: A study of the relationship between a novice EFL teacher's classroom practices and cognition development. *Language Teaching Research, 18*(2), 169–186. doi:10.1177/1362168813505939

Kao, C. P., & Tsai, C. C. (2009). Teachers' attitudes toward web-based professional development, with relation to Internet self-efficacy and beliefs about web-based learning. *Computers & Education, 53*(1), 66–73. doi:10.1016/j.compedu.2008.12.019

Katz, A., & Snow, M. A. (2009). Standards and second language teacher education. In A. Burns & J. C. Richards (Eds.), *The Cambridge guide to second language teacher education* (pp. 66–76). Cambridge, UK: Cambridge University Press.

Kennedy, K., & Archambault, L. (2012). Design and Development of Field Experiences in K-12 Online Learning Environments. *The Journal of Applied Instructional Design, 2*(1), 35–48.

Kern, R. (2006). Perspectives on technology in learning and teaching languages. *TESOL Quarterly, 40*(1), 183–210. doi:10.2307/40264516

Kern, R. (2014). Technology as *Pharmakon*: The promise and perils of the internet for foreign language education. *Modern Language Journal, 98*(1), 340–357. doi:10.1111/j.1540-4781.2014.12065.x

Kerr, S. T. (1996). Visions of sugarplums: The future of technology, education, and the schools. In S. T. Kerr (Ed.), *Technology and the future of schooling: Ninety-fifth yearbook of the National Society for the Study of Education* (pp. 1–27). Chicago: University of Chicago Press.

Kessler, G. (2009). Integrating technology in the foreign language classroom. In K. Cennamo (Ed.), S. Ross, J. D., & Ertmer, P. A. (Eds.), Technology Integration for Meaningful Classroom Use: A Standards-Based Approach (pp. 351–367). Wadsworth.

Kessler, G. (2006). Assessing CALL teacher training. In P. Hubbard & M. Levy (Eds.), *Teacher education in CALL* (pp. 23–42). Amsterdam: John Benjamins. doi:10.1075/lllt.14.05kes

Kessler, G. (2009). Student-initiated attention to form in Wiki-based collaborative writing. *Language Learning & Technology, 13*(1), 79–95.

Kessler, G. (2013). Collaborative language learning in co-constructed participatory culture. *CALICO Journal, 30*(3), 307–322. doi:10.11139/cj.30.3.307-322

Kim, C., Kim, M. K., Lee, C., Spector, J. M., & DeMeester, K. (2013). Teacher beliefs and technology integration. *Teaching and Teacher Education, 29*, 76–85. doi:10.1016/j.tate.2012.08.005

Kirkwood, M., Kuyl, T. V. D., Parton, N., & Grant, R. (2000, September). *The New Opportunities Fund (NOF) ICT training for teachers programme: Designing a powerful online learning environment.* Paper presented at the European conference on educational research, Edinburgh, UK.

Kitade, K. (2015). Second language teacher development through CALL practice: The emergence of teachers' agency. *CALICO Journal, 32*(3), 396–425.

Knapczyk, D. R., Hew, K. F., & Frey, T. J. (2005). Evaluation of online mentoring of practicum for limited licensed teachers. *Teacher Education and Special Education: The Journal of the Teacher Education Division of the Council for Exceptional Children, 28*(3-4), 207–220. doi:10.1177/088840640502800407

Koehler, M. J., & Mishra, P. (2005). What happens when teachers design educational technology? The development of technological pedagogical content knowledge. *Journal of Educational Computing Research, 32*(2), 131–152. doi:10.2190/0EW7-01WB-BKHL-QDYV

Koehler, M. J., & Mishra, P. (2009). What is technological pedagogical content knowledge? *Contemporary Issues in Technology & Teacher Education, 9*(1), 60–70.

Koehler, M. J., Mishra, P., & Cain, W. (2013). What is technological pedagogical content (TPACK)? *Journal of Education, 193*(3), 13–19.

Koehler, M. J., Mishra, P., & Yahya, K. (2007). Tracing the development of teacher knowledge in a design seminar: Integrating content, pedagogy and technology. *Computers & Education, 49*(3), 740–762. doi:10.1016/j.compedu.2005.11.012

Koehler, M. J., Shin, T. S., & Mishra, P. (2012). How Do We Measure TPACK? Let Me Count the Ways. In R. Ronau, C. Rakes, & M. Niess (Eds.), *Educational Technology, Teacher Knowledge, and Classroom Impact: A Research Handbook on Frameworks and Approaches* (pp. 16–31). Hershey, PA: Information Science Reference. doi:10.4018/978-1-60960-750-0.ch002

Koehler, M., & Mishra, P. (2009). What Is Technological Pedagogical Content Knowledge? *Contemporary Issues in Technology & Teacher Education, 9*(1), 60–70.

Koh, J. H. L., & Chai, C. S. (2011). Modeling pre-service teachers' technological pedagogical content knowledge (TPACK) perceptions: The influence of demographic factors and TPACK constructs. In G. Williams, P. Statham, N. Brown & B. Cleland (Eds.), Changing Demands, Changing Directions (pp. 735-746). ASCILITE.

Koh, J. H. L., Chai, C. S., & Tsait, C. C. (2010). Examining the technological pedagogical content knowledge of Singapore pre-service teachers with a large-scale survey. *Journal of Computer Assisted Learning, 26*(6), 563–573. doi:10.1111/j.1365-2729.2010.00372.x

Koh, J. H. L., & Divaharan, S. (2011). Developing pre-service teachers' technology integration expertise through the TPACK-developing instructional model. *Journal of Educational Computing Research, 44*(1), 35–58. doi:10.2190/EC.44.1.c

Koike, D. A., & Klee, C. A. (2013). *Lingüística aplicada: Adquisición del español como segunda lengua.* New York, NY: John Wiley and Sons, Inc.

Compilation of References

Kozma, R., & Anderson, R. E. (2002). Qualitative case studies of innovative pedagogical practices using ICT. *Journal of Computer Assisted Learning*, *18*(4), 387–394. doi:10.1046/j.0266-4909.2002.00250.doc.x

Kurt, G., Mishra, P., & Kocoglu, Z. (2013) *Technological pedagogical content knowledge development of Turkish preservice teachers of English*. Paper presented at the meeting of the Society for Information Technology and Teacher Education, New Orleans, LA. Abstract retrieved from http://academicexperts.org/conf/site/2013/papers/38476/

Lafford, P. A., & Lafford, B. A. (2005). CMC technologies for teaching foreign languages: What's on the horizon? *CALICO Journal*, *22*(3), 679–709.

Lan, Y. J., Chang, K. E., & Chen, N. S. (2012). CoCAR: An online synchronous training model for empowering ICT capacity of teachers of Chinese as a foreign language. *Australasian Journal of Educational Technology*, *28*(6), 1020–1038. doi:10.14742/ajet.808

Larusson, J., & Alterman, R. (2009). Wikis to support the "collaborative" part of collaborative learning. *International Journal of Computer-Supported Collaborative Learning*, *4*(4), 371–402. doi:10.1007/s11412-009-9076-6

Lavy, I., & Shriki, A. (2008). Investigating changes in prospective teachers' views of a 'good teacher' while engaging in computerized project-based learning. *Journal of Mathematics Teacher Education*, *11*(4), 259–284. doi:10.1007/s10857-008-9073-0

Lawless, K. A., & Pellegrino, J. W. (2007). Professional development in integrating technology into teaching and learning: Knowns, unknowns, and ways to pursue better questions and answers. *Review of Educational Research*, *77*(4), 575–614. doi:10.3102/0034654307309921

Lawrence, K. S. (1999). Standards for Foreign Language Learning in the 21st Century. *Np: Allen*.

Lawrence, G. (2002). The use of E-mail as a tool to enhance second language education programs: An example from a core French classroom. *Canadian Modern Language Review*, *58*(3), 465–472. doi:10.3138/cmlr.58.3.465

Lay, J. G., Chi, Y. L., Hsieh, Y. S., & Chen, Y. W. (2013). What influences geography teachers' usage of geographic information systems? A structural equation analysis. *Computers & Education*, *62*(3), 191–195. doi:10.1016/j.compedu.2012.10.014

Lee, D. (1997). Factors influencing the success of computer skills learning among in-service teachers. *British Journal of Educational Technology*, *28*(2), 139–141. doi:10.1111/1467-8535.00018

Lee, M.-H., & Tsai, C.-C. (2010). Exploring teachers' perceived self efficacy and technological pedagogical content knowledge with respect to educational use of the World Wide Web. *Instructional Science*, *38*(1), 1–21. doi:10.1007/s11251-008-9075-4

Lenhart, A. (2015). Teens, social media and technology overview 2015. Washington, DC: Pew Research Center. Retrieved from http://www.pewinternet.org/files/2015/04/PI_TeensandTech_Update2015_0409151.pdf

Levy, M. (2009). Technologies in use for second language learning. *Modern Language Journal*, *93*(1), 769–782. doi:10.1111/j.1540-4781.2009.00972.x

Lewis, C. L. (2015). Preservice teachers' ability to identify technology standards: Does curriculum matter? *Contemporary Issues in Technology & Teacher Education*, *15*(2), 235–254.

Liaw, M. L., & Johnson, R. J. (2001). E-mail writing as a cross-cultural learning experience. *System*, *29*(2), 235–251. doi:10.1016/S0346-251X(01)00013-6

Li, G., & Ni, X. (2011). Primary EFL teachers' technology use in China: Patterns and perceptions. *RELC Journal, 42*(1), 69–85. doi:10.1177/0033688210390783

Li, L. (2014). Understanding language teachers' practice with educational technology: A case from China. *System, 46*, 105–119. doi:10.1016/j.system.2014.07.016

Li, L., & Walsh, S. (2011). Technology uptake in Chinese EFL classes. *Language Teaching Research, 15*(1), 99–125. doi:10.1177/1362168810383347

Limayem, M., Hirt, S. G., & Chin, W. W. (2001). Intention does not always matter: The contingent role of habit on IT usage behavior.*Proceedings of the 9th European Conference on Information Systems.*

Lim, C. P., Chai, C. S., & Churchill, D. (2010). *Leading ICT in education practices: A capacity building toolkit for teacher education institutions in the Asia-Pacific.* Singapore: Microsoft.

Li, S., & Swanson, P. (Eds.). (2014). *Engaging language learners through technology integration; Theory, applications, and outcomes.* Hershey, PA: Information Science Reference.

Liu, S. H. (2011). Modeling pre-service teachers' knowledge of, attitudes toward, and intentions for technology integration. In T. Bastiaens & M. Ebner (Eds.), *Proceedings of EdMedia: World Conference on Educational Media and Technology 2011* (pp. 3350-3355). Association for the Advancement of Computing in Education (AACE).

Liu, M., Moore, Z., Graham, L., & Lee, S. (2002). A look at the research on computer-based technology use in second language learning: A review of the literature from 1990–2000. *Journal of Research on Technology in Education, 34*(3), 250–273. doi:10.1080/15391523.2002.10782348

Liu, S. H. (2011). Factors related to pedagogical beliefs of teachers and technology integration. *Computers & Education, 56*(4), 1012–1022. doi:10.1016/j.compedu.2010.12.001

Liu, S. H., & Lan, Y. (2014). Pre-service CSL Teachers' Field Experience in the Real and the Virtual Worlds. *Journal of Chinese Language Teaching, 11*(3), 61–90.

Lo Bianco, J. (2011). Chinese: The gigantic *up-and-comer*. In L. Tsung & K. Cruickshank (Eds.), *Teaching and learning Chinese in global contexts: CFL worldwide* (pp. xiii–xxiv). London: Continuum.

Loewen, S. (2015). *Introduction to instructed second language acquisition.* New York: Routledge.

Lopez, M. H., & Gonzalez-Barrera, A. (2013). *What is the future of Spanish in the United States?* Retrieved from: http://www.pewresearch.org/fact-tank/2013/09/05/what-is-the-future-of-spanish-in-the-united-states/

Lopez-Burton, N., & Minor, D. (2014). *On being a language teacher: A personal and practical guide to success.* New Haven, CT: Yale University Press. doi:10.12987/yale/9780300186895.001.0001

Luke, C. (2011). Crossing the digital divide: Language learning in virtual environments. In D. Schwarzer, M. Petrón, & C. Luke (Eds.), *Research informing practice—practice informing research: Innovative teaching methodologies for world language teachers* (pp. 59–85). Charlotte, NC: Information Age Publishing.

Luke, C. L., & Britten, J. S. (2007). The expanding role of technology in foreign language teacher education programs. *CALICO Journal, 24*(2), 253.

Luke, C. L., & Britten, J. S. (2013). The expanding role of technology in foreign language teacher education programs. *CALICO, 24*(2), 253–268.

Mao, M. (2007). An investigation of college English teachers' competence on web-based teaching. *Foreign Language World, 2*, 26–31.

Compilation of References

Marinova-Todd, S. H., Marshall, D. B., & Snow, C. E. (2001). Missing the point: A response to Hyltenstam and Abrahamsson. *TESOL Quarterly*, *35*(1), 171–176. doi:10.2307/3587864

Marshall, J. A., Petrosino, A. J., & Martin, T. (2010). Preservice teachers' conceptions and enactments of project-based instruction. *Journal of Science Education and Technology*, *19*(4), 370–386. doi:10.1007/s10956-010-9206-y

Martel, J., & Wang, A. (2014). Language teacher identity. In M. Bigelow & J. Ennser-Kananen (Eds.), *The Routledge Handbook of Educational Linguistics*. New York: Routledge.

Martin, S., & Vallance, M. (2008). The impact of synchronous inter-networked teacher training in Information and Communication Technology integration. *Computers & Education*, *51*(1), 34–53. doi:10.1016/j.compedu.2007.04.001

Matherson, L. H., Wilson, E. K., Wright, V. H. (2014). *Need TPACK? Embrace Sustained Professional Development*. Delta Kappa Gamma Bulletin, 45-52

Matsuzaki, H. (2012). Onsee ninshiki gijutsu wo mochiita nihongo inritsu renshuuyoo sofuto no kaihatsu [The Development of Software to Study Japanese Prosody Using an Automatic Speech Recognition System]. *Bungee Gengo Kenkyuu: Gengo Hen* [Studies in language and literature. Language], *61*, 177-190.

Mayo, N., Kajs, K., & Tanguma, J. (2005). Longitudinal study of technology training to prepare future teachers. *Educational Research Quarterly*, *29*(1), 3–15.

Mazer, J. P., Murphy, R. E., & Simonds, C. J. (2007). I'll see you on "Facebook": The effects of computer-mediated teacher self-disclosure on student motivation, affective learning, and classroom climate. *Communication Education*, *56*(1), 1–17. doi:10.1080/03634520601009710

McDonald, K., & Smith, C. M. (2013). The flipped classroom for professional development: Part I. Benefits and strategies. *Journal of Continuing Education in Nursing*, *44*(10), 437–438. doi:10.3928/00220124-20130925-19 PMID:24098988

McGrail, E. (2007). Laptop technology and pedagogy in the English language arts classroom. *Journal of Technology and Teacher Education*, *15*(1), 59–85.

McKeeman, L., & Oviedo, B. (2015). 21st century world language classrooms: Technology to support cultural competence. *Learn Language, Explore Cultures, Transform Lives*. Retrieved from: http://www.csctfl.org/documents/2015Report/Chapter%206.pdf

Mercer, S. (2011). Understanding learner agency as a complex dynamic system. *System*, *39*(4), 427–436. doi:10.1016/j.system.2011.08.001

Merriam, S. B. (2009). *Qualitative research: A guide to design and implementation*. San Francisco, CA: Jossey-Bass.

Mertens, D. M. (2010). *Research and evaluation in education and psychology* (3rd ed.). Thousand Oaks, CA: Sage.

Mills, N. (2011). Situated learning through social networking communities: The development of joint enterprise, mutual engagement, and shared repertoire. *CALICO Journal*, *28*(2), 345–368. doi:10.11139/cj.28.2.345-368

Minematsu, N., Nakagawa, C., & Tagawa, Y. (2012). Kooritsutekina nihongo inritsu kyooiku no jitsugen ni muketa infurasutorakucha no koochiku: akusento no koopasu bunseki + onrain akusento jiten no koochiku + inritsu kyooiku jissen [Development of the infrastructure to implement an effective and efficient methodology of teaching/learning Japanese prosody: Corpus-based analysis of word accents, development of an on-line accent dictionary, and practical methodology of prosody education]. In *Proceedings of the 9th International Symposium for Japanese Language Education and Japanese Studies*. Retrieved from http://www.japanese-edu.org.hk/sympo/upload/manuscript/20121015080146.pdf

Miniwatts Marketing Group. (2015). *Internet world stats*. Retrieved from: http://www.internetworldstats.com/stats7.htm

Mishra, P., & Koehler, M. (2006). Technological pedagogical content knowledge: A framework for teacher knowledge. *Teachers College Record, 108*(6), 1017–1054. doi:10.1111/j.1467-9620.2006.00684.x

Mishra, P., & Koehler, M. J. (2009). Too cool for school? No way! Using the TPACK framework: You can have your hot tools and teach with them, too. *Learning and Leading with Technology, 36*(7), 14–18.

MOE (Ministry of Education). (2001). *English Curriculum Standards for Fulltime Common Senior High Schools*. Beijing: Beijing Normal University Press.

Moeller, A. J., & Park, H. (2003). Foreign language teacher education and technology: Bridging the gap. *Faculty Publications: Department of Teaching, Learning and Teacher Education.* Retrieved from http://digitalcommons.unl.edu/teachlearnfacpub/175/

Moran, M., Seaman, J., & Tinti-Kane, H. (2011). *Teaching, learning, and sharing: How today's higher education faculty use social media*. Boston, MA: Pearson Learning Solutions and Babson Survey Research Group.

Moran, M., Seaman, J., & Tinti-Kane, H. (2012). *Blogs, Wikis, Podcasts and Facebook: How today's higher education faculty use social media*. Boston, MA: Pearson Learning Solutions and Babson Survey Research Group.

Morgan, B. (2004). Teacher identity as pedagogy: Towards a field-internal conceptualization in bilingual and second language education. *Bilingual Education and Bilingualism, 7*(2-3), 172-188.

Morgan, R. K., & Olivares, K. T. (Eds.). (2012). *Quick hits for teaching with technology: Successful strategies by award-winning teachers*. Bloomington, IN: Indiana University Press.

Moser, K., & Ivy, J. (2013). World language teachers: Self-perceptions of their TPACK. *Modern Journal of Language Teaching Methods, 3*(2), 167–190.

Mouza, C. (2002). Learning to teach with new technology: Implications for professional development. *Journal of Research on Computing in Education, 35*(2), 272–289.

Mouza, C., Karchmer-Klein, R., Nandakumar, R., & Ozden, S. Y. (2014). Investigating the impact of an integrated approach to the development of preservice teachers' technological pedagogical content knowledge (TPACK). *Computers & Education, 71*, 206–221. doi:10.1016/j.compedu.2013.09.020

Muldrow, K. (2013). A new approach to language instruction: Flipping the classroom. *Language and Education, 8*, 28–31.

Müller-Hartmann, A. (2012). The Classroom-Based Action Research Paradigm in Telecollaboration. In M. Dooly & R. O'Dowd (Eds.), *Research Methods for Online Interaction and Exchange* (pp. 156–192). Bern: Peter Lang.

Mumtaz, S. (2000). Factors affecting teachers' use of information and communications technology: A review of the literature. *Journal of Information Technology for Teacher Education, 9*(3), 319–341. doi:10.1080/14759390000200096

Murphy-Judy, K., & Youngs, B. (2006). Technology standards for teacher education, credentialing, and certification. In P. Hubbard & M. Levy (Eds.), *Teacher education in CALL* (pp. 45–60). Amsterdam: John Benjamins. doi:10.1075/lllt.14.06mur

Nakamura, N. (2007). Hatsukon kurasu jugyou houkoku [The report from the pronunciation class]. Tokyo Gaikokugo Daigaku ryuugakusei nihongo kyooiku sentaa ronshuu [Collection of theses from Japanese Education Center, Tokyo University of Foreign Studies], 33(1), 179-189.

National Board for Professional Teaching Standards. (2010). *World language standards* (2nd ed.). Retrieved from http://www.nbpts.org/sites/default/files/documents/certificates/nbpts-certificate-eaya-wl-standards.pdf

Compilation of References

National East Asian Languages Resource Center at the Ohio State University and Chinese Language Association of Secondary-elementary Schools. (2007). *CLASS professional standards for K-12 Chinese teachers.* Retrieved from https://nealrc.osu.edu/sites/nealrc.osu.edu/files/teacher-k-12-class-teachers-standards.pdf

National Standards in Foreign Language Education Project. (1999). *Standards for foreign language learning in the 21st century.* Lawrence, KS: Allen Press.

National Standards in Foreign Language Education. (2006). *Standards for foreign language learning: Preparing for the 21st century.* Retrieved from http://www.actfl.org/sites/default/files/pdfs/public/StandardsforFLLexecsumm_rev.pdf

Nellison. (2007, December 11). ECAR: Facebook as a teaching tool? *Blog.* Retrieved March 18, 2013, from http://nellison.blogspot.com/2007/12/ecar-facebook-as-teachingtool.html

Ng, W., & Nicholas, H. (2013). A framework for sustainable mobile learning in schools. *British Journal of Educational Technology, 44*(5), 695–715. doi:10.1111/j.1467-8535.2012.01359.x

Nicholson, S. A., & Bond, N. (2003). Collaborative reflection and professional community building: An analysis of pre-service teachers' use of an electronic discussion board. *Journal of Technology and Teacher Education, 11*(2), 259–279.

Niess, M. L. (2011). Investigating TPACK: Knowledge growth in teaching with technology. *Journal of Educational Computing Research, 44*(3), 299–317. doi:10.2190/EC.44.3.c

Niess, M. L., Lee, J. K., & Kajder, S. B. (2008). *Guiding Learning with Technology.* John Wiley and Sons, Inc.

Norton, B. (1990). Language, identity, and the ownership of English. *TESOL Quarterly, 31*(3), 409–429. doi:10.2307/3587831

Norton, L., Richardson, J. T. E., Hartley, J., Newstead, S., & Mayes, J. (2005). Teachers' beliefs and intentions concerning teaching in higher education. *Higher Education, 50*(4), 537–571. doi:10.1007/s10734-004-6363-z

O'Reilly, T. (2005). *What is Web 2.0?* Retrieved from http://www.oreilly.com/go/web2

Office for Standards in Education. (1998). *Information technology: a review of inspection findings 1993/4.* London: HMSO.

Officiel de l'Éducation Nationale, B. (2013). *Référentiel des compétences professionnelles des métiers du professorat et de l'éducation.* BOEN n°30. Retrieved from http://www.education.gouv.fr/pid285/bulletin_officiel.html?cid_bo=73066

Ogawara, Y., & Kono, T. (2002). Kyooshi no onsee kyooikukan to shidoo no jissai [The influence of teachers' beliefs toward pronunciation teaching on their teaching practices]. *Nihongo kyooiku hoohoo kenkyuukaishi* [Journal of Japanese Language Education Methods], *9*(1), 28-29.

Olapiriyakul, K., & Scher, J. M. (2006). A guide to establishing hybrid learning courses: Employing information technology to create a new learning experience, and a case study. *The Internet and Higher Education, 9*(4), 287–301. doi:10.1016/j.iheduc.2006.08.001

Ottenbreit-Leftwich, A. T., Brush, T. A., Strycker, J., Gronseth, S., Roman, T., Abaci, S., & Plucker, J. et al. (2012). Preparation versus practice: How do teacher education programs and practicing teachers align in their use of technology to support teaching and learning? *Computers & Education, 59*(2), 399–411. doi:10.1016/j.compedu.2012.01.014

Oviatt, S. (2013). *The design of future educational interfaces.* New York: Routledge.

Oxford, R. L., & Jung, S. (2007). National guidelines for technology integration in TESOL programs: Factors affecting (non) implementation. In M. A. Kassen, R. Z. Lavine, K. Murphy-Judy, & M. Peters (Eds.), *Preparing and developing technology-proficient L2 teachers* (pp. 23–48). San Marcos, TX: CALICO.

Ozdamli, F., & Uzunboylu, H. (2014). M-learning adequacy and perceptions of students and teachers in secondary schools. *British Journal of Educational Technology, 46*(1), 159–172. doi:10.1111/bjet.12136

Oz, H. (2015). Assessing Pre-service English as a Foreign Language Teachers' Technological Pedagogical Content Knowledge. *International Education Studies, 8*(5), 119–130. doi:10.5539/ies.v8n5p119

Pachler, N., Daly, C., & Turvey, A. (2010). Teacher professional development practices: The case of the Haringey transformation teachers programme. In J. O. Lindberg & A. D. Olofsson (Eds.), *Online learning communities and teacher professional development* (pp. 77–95). Hershey, PA: Information Science Publishing. doi:10.4018/978-1-60566-780-5.ch005

Pajares, M. F. (1992). Teachers' beliefs and educational research: Cleaning up a messy construct. *Review of Educational Research, 62*(3), 307–332. doi:10.3102/00346543062003307

Palak, D., & Walls, R. T. (2009). Teachers' beliefs and technology practices: A mixed-methods approach. *Journal of Research on Technology in Education, 41*(4), 417–441. doi:10.1080/15391523.2009.10782537

Pamuk, S. (2012). Understanding preservice teachers' technology use through TPACK framework. *Journal of Computer Assisted Learning, 28*(5), 425–439. doi:10.1111/j.1365-2729.2011.00447.x

Partnership for Century (P21). (2011). *21st Century Skills Map*. Retrieved from: https://www.actfl.org/sites/default/files/pdfs/21stCenturySkillsMap/p21_worldlanguage map.pdf

Pelgrum, W. (2001). Obstacles to the integration of ICT in education: Results from a worldwide educational assessment. *Computers & Education, 37*(2), 163–178. doi:10.1016/S0360-1315(01)00045-8

Peng, W., & He, J. (2007). An integrated model of technology and curriculum for EFL teacher training: Issues and Strategies. *Foreign Language World, 2*, 18–25.

Peters, M. (2006). Developing computer competencies for pre-service language teachers: Is one course enough? In P. Hubbard & M. Levy (Eds.), *Teacher education in CALL* (pp. 153–165). Amsterdam: John Benjamins. doi:10.1075/lllt.14.14pet

Pierson, M. E., & McNeil, S. (2000). Preservice technology integration through collaborative action communities. *Contemporary Issues in Technology & Teacher Education, 1*(1), 189–199.

Pillot-Loiseau, C., Antolík, T. K., & Kamiyama, T. (2013). Contribution of ultrasound visualisation to improving the production of the French/y/-/u/contrast by four Japanese learners. In *Proceedings of Phonetics, phonology, languages in contact: Varieties, multilingualism, second language learning* (pp. 86–89). Paris: Fance.

Pina, A., & Harris, B. (1993). *Increasing teachers' confidence in using computers for education*. Paper presented at the Annual Meeting of the Arizona Educational Research Organisation, Tucson, AZ.

Polly, D., Mims, C., Shepherd, C. E., & Inan, F. (2010). Evidence of impact: Transforming teacher education with preparing tomorrow's teachers to teach with technology (PT3) grants. *Teaching and Teacher Education, 26*(4), 863–870. doi:10.1016/j.tate.2009.10.024

Porter, L. R. (1997). *Creating the virtual classroom, distance learning with the Internet*. John Wiley & Sons, Inc.

Project Tomorrow. (2008). *21st century learners deserve a 21st century education*. Selected National Findings of the Speak Up 2007 Survey. Retrieved March 28, 2015, from http://www.tomorrow.org/speakup/speakup_congress_2007.html

Puentedura, R. (2006). *Transformation, Technology and Education*. Retrieved from http://hippasus.com/resources/tte/

Pufahl, I., & Rhodes, N. (2011). Foreign language instruction in U.S. Schools: Results of a national survey of elementary and secondary schools. *Foreign Language Annals, 44*(2), 258–288. doi:10.1111/j.1944-9720.2011.01130.x

Compilation of References

Ravitz, J., Becker, H., & Wong, Y. (2000). *Constructivist-compatible beliefs and practices among U.S. teachers*. Retrieved December 20, 2015, from http://www.crito.uci.edu/TLC/FINDINGS/REPORT4/REPORT4.PDF

Reinders, H. (2009). Technology and second language teacher education. In A. Burns & J. C. Richards (Eds.), *The Cambridge guide to second language teacher education* (pp. 230–237). Cambridge, UK: Cambridge University Press.

Reinhardt, J., & Zander, V. (2011). Social networking in an intensive English program classroom: A language socialization perspective. *CALICO Journal*, *28*(2), 326–344. doi:10.11139/cj.28.2.326-344

Rhodes, N. C., & Pufahl, I. (2009). *Foreign language teaching in U.S. schools: Results of a national survey*. Washington, DC: Center for Applied Linguistics.

Richards, J. C., & Nunan, D. (Eds.). (1990). Second Language Teacher Education. New York: Cambridge University Press.

Rienties, B., Brouwer, N., & Lygo-Baker, S. (2013). The effects of online professional development on teachers' beliefs and intentions towards learning facilitation and technology. *Teaching and Teacher Education*, *29*, 122–131. doi:10.1016/j.tate.2012.09.002

Rilling, S., Dahlman, A., Dodson, S., Boyles, C., & Pazvant, O. (2005). Connecting CALL theory and practice in preservice teacher education and beyond: Processes and products. *CALICO Journal*, *22*(2), 213–235.

Robelia, B., Greenhow, C., & Burton, L. (2011). Adopting environmentally responsible behaviors: How learning within a social networking application motivated students to act for the environment. *Environmental Education Research*, *17*(4), 553–575. doi:10.1080/13504622.2011.565118

Roessingh, H., & Chambers, W. (2011). Project-based learning and pedagogy in teacher preparation: Staking out the theoretical mid-ground. *International Journal of Teaching and Learning in Higher Education*, *23*(1), 60–71.

Sabbath, M. (1962). Some aspects of teacher training in laboratory techniques. *Journal of Educational Sociology*, *35*(6), 271–272. doi:10.2307/2264339

Sahin, I., Akturk, A. O., & Schmidt, D. (2009, March). Relationship of preservice teachers' technological pedagogical content knowledge with their vocational self-efficacy beliefs. *In Society for Information Technology & Teacher Education International Conference, 2009*(1), 4137-4144.

Saint-Onge, H., & Wallace, D. (2011). *Leveraging Communities of Practice for Strategic Advantage*. Abingdon, UK: Routledge.

Salehi, H., & Salehi, Z. (2012). Challenges for using ICT in education: Teachers' insights. *International Journal of e-Education, e-Business, e- Management Learning*, *2*(1), 40–43.

Sarré, C. (2013). Technology-mediated tasks in English for Specific Purposes (ESP): Design, implementation and learner perception. *International Journal of Computer-Assisted Language Learning and Teaching*, *3*(2), 1–16. doi:10.4018/ijcallt.2013040101

Saville-Troike, M. (2012). *Introducing second language acquisition*. Cambridge University Press. doi:10.1017/CBO9780511888830

Schmid, E. C., & Whyte, S. (2012). Interactive whiteboards in state school settings: Teacher responses to socio-constructed hegemonies. *Language Learning & Technology*, *16*(2), 65–86.

Schmid, E., & Hegelheimer, V. (2014). Collaborative research projects in the technology-enhanced language classroom: Pre-service and in-service teachers exchange knowledge about technology. *ReCALL*, *26*(3), 315–332. doi:10.1017/S0958344014000135

Schmidt, D. A., Baran, E., Thompson, A. D., Mishra, P., Koehler, M. J., & Shin, T. S. (2009). Technological pedagogical content knowledge (TPACK): The development and validation of an assessment instrument for preservice teachers. *Journal of Research on Technology in Education, 42*(2), 123–149. doi:10.1080/15391523.2009.10782544

Schoepp, K. W. (2005). Technology integration barriers in a technology-rich environment. *Learning and Teaching in Higher Education: Gulf Perspectives, 2*(1), 1-24. Retrieved from http://www.zu.ac.ae/lthe/vol2no1/lthe02_05.pdf

Schueller, J. (2007). One good turn deserves another: Sustaining an intercultural E-mail exchange. *Die Unterrichtspraxis, 40*(2), 184–196.

Seo, K. K., Templeton, R., & Pellegrino, D. (2008). Creating a ripple effect: Incorporating multimedia-assisted project-based learning in teacher education. *Theory into Practice, 47*(3), 259–265. doi:10.1080/00405840802154062

Sessoms, D. (2008). Interactive instruction: Creating interactive learning environments through tomorrow's teachers. *International Journal of Technology in Teaching and Learning, 4*(2), 86–96.

Shibata, T., & Matsuzaki, H. (2012). Onsee to shuutoku: Sooron. [Phonology and acquisition] In K. Hatasa, Y. Hatasa, M. Kudara, & T. Shimizu (Eds.), *Daini gengo shuutoku to gengo kyooiku* [Second language acquisition and language education] (pp. 196–213). Tokyo, Japan: Kurosio Publishers.

Shrum, J. L., & Glisan, E. W. (2016). *Teacher's handbook: Contextualized language instruction* (5th ed.). Boston: Heinle & Heinle.

Shulman, L. (1986). Those who understand: Knowledge growth in teaching. *Educational Researcher, 15*(2), 4–14. doi:10.3102/0013189X015002004

Shulman, L. (1987). Knowledge-base and teaching: Foundations of the new reform. *Harvard Educational Review, 57*(1), 1–22. doi:10.17763/haer.57.1.j463w79r56455411

Shulman, L. S. (1996). Paradigms and research programs in the study of teaching: A contemporary perspective. In M. C. Wittrock (Ed.), *Handbook of research on teaching* (3rd ed., pp. 3–36). New York: Macmillan.

Silverman, D. (2006). *Interpreting qualitative data: Methods for analyzing talk, text, and interaction* (3rd ed.). London: SAGE Publications.

Sipe, R. B. (2000). Virtually Being There: Creating Authentic Experience through Interactive Exchanges. *English Journal, 90*(2), 104–111. doi:10.2307/821226

Slaouti, D., & Motteram, G. (2006). Reconstructing practice: Language teacher education and ICT. In P. Hubbard & M. Levy (Eds.), *Teacher Education in CALL* (pp. 80–97). Philadelphia: John Benjamins. doi:10.1075/lllt.14.09sla

Sluijsmans, D. M. A., & Prins, F. (2006). A conceptual framework for integrating peer assessment in teacher education. *Studies in Educational Evaluation, 32*(1), 6–22. doi:10.1016/j.stueduc.2006.01.005

Smith, J. A., & Sivo, S. A. (2012). Predicting continued use of online teacher professional development and the influence of social presence and sociability. *British Journal of Educational Technology, 43*(6), 871–882. doi:10.1111/j.1467-8535.2011.01223.x

Smith, L. K. (2005). The impact of early life history on teachers' beliefs: In-school and out-of-school experiences as learners and knowers of science. *Teachers and Teaching: Theory and Practice, 11*(1), 5–36. doi:10.1080/1354060042000337075

Smith, S. J., & Robinson, S. (2003). Technology integration through collaborative cohorts preparing future teachers to use technology. *Remedial and Special Education, 24*(3), 154–160. doi:10.1177/07419325030240030401

Snoeyink, R., & Ertmer, P. A. (2001). Thrust into technology: How veteran teachers respond. *Journal of Educational Technology Systems*, *30*(1), 85–111. doi:10.2190/YDL7-XH09-RLJ6-MTP1

Sockett, J., & Toffoli, D. (2012). Beyond learner autonomy: A dynamic systems view of the informal learning of English in virtual online communities. *ReCALL*, *24*(2), 138–151. doi:10.1017/S0958344012000031

So, H. J., & Kim, B. (2009). Learning about problem based learning: Student teachers integrating technology, pedagogy and content knowledge. *Australasian Journal of Educational Technology*, *25*(1), 101–116. doi:10.14742/ajet.1183

Song, D. (2004). A reflection on the ICT training of elementary and secondary school teachers. *e-. Education Research*, *2*, 75–77.

STARTALK website (2015). startalk.umd.edu

Statistics Canada. (2011). *Focus on Geography Series, 2011 Census: Census metropolitan area of Vancouver, British Columbia*. Retrieved from http://www12.statcan.gc.ca/census-recensement/2011/as-sa/fogs-spg/Facts-cma-eng.cfm?LANG=Eng&GK=CMA&GC=933

Stepp-Greany, J. (2002). Student perceptions on language learning in a technological environment: Implications for the new millennium. *Language Learning & Technology*, *6*(1), 165–180.

Stevenson, M., & Liu, M. (2010). Learning a language with Web 2.0: Exploring the use of social networking features of foreign language learning websites. *CALICO Journal*, *27*(2), 233–259. doi:10.11139/cj.27.2.233-259

Sugarman, J., Di Silvio, F., & Malone, M. E. (2012). *2012 STARTALK participant survey report: Teacher trainees*. Washington, DC: Center for Applied Linguistics.

Sutherland, L., Howard, S., & Markauskaite, L. (2010). Professional identity creation: Examining the development of beginning preservice teachers' understanding of their work as teachers. *Teaching and Teacher Education*, *26*(3), 455–465. doi:10.1016/j.tate.2009.06.006

Tai, S.-J. (2015). From TPACK-In-Action workshops to classrooms: CALL competency developed and integrated. *Language Learning & Technology*, *19*(1), 139–164.

Tanno, K. (2013). A case study of implementing flipped-teaching in a beginning Japanese course.*Proceedings of the 20th Princeton Japanese Pedagogy Forum*.

Teo, T. (2009a). Modeling technology acceptance in education: A study of pre-service teachers. *Computers & Education*, *52*(1), 302–312. doi:10.1016/j.compedu.2008.08.006

Teo, T. (2009b). Is there an attitude problem? Reconsidering the role of attitude in the TAM. *British Journal of Educational Technology*, *40*(6), 1139–1141. doi:10.1111/j.1467-8535.2008.00913.x

Teo, T. (2010). A path analysis of pre-service teachers' attitudes to computer use: Applying and extending the technology acceptance model in an educational context. *Interactive Learning Environments*, *18*(1), 65–79. doi:10.1080/10494820802231327

Teo, T. (2011). Factors influencing teachers' intention to use technology: Model development and test. *Computers & Education*, *57*(4), 2432–2440. doi:10.1016/j.compedu.2011.06.008

Teo, T. (2014). Unpacking teachers' acceptance of technology: Tests of measurement invariance and latent mean differences. *Computers & Education*, *75*, 127–135. doi:10.1016/j.compedu.2014.01.014

Teo, T., Chai, C. S., Hung, D., & Lee, C. B. (2008). Beliefs about teaching and uses of technology among pre-service teachers. *Asia-Pacific Journal of Teacher Education*, *36*(2), 163–174. doi:10.1080/13598660801971641

Teo, T., & Noyes, J. (2010). Exploring attitudes towards computer use among pre-service teachers from Singapore and the UK: A multi-group invariance test of the technology acceptance model (TAM). *Multicultural Education & Technology Journal*, *4*(2), 126–135. doi:10.1108/17504971011052331

Thang, S. M., Hall, C., Murugaiah, P., & Azman, H. (2011). Creating and maintaining online communities of practice in Malaysian smart schools: Challenging realities. *Educational Action Research*, *19*(1), 87–105. doi:10.1080/09650792.2011.547724

The Chinese Language Association of Secondary-Elementary Schools. (CLASS)(2015). CLASS Professional Standards for k-12 Chinese Teachers. Retrieved from http://classk12.org/13/ts.htm

The Council of Chief State School Officers. (2011). *Research synthesis*. Retrieved from http://www.ccsso.org/Resources/Publications/InTASC_Research_Synthesis.html

The Council of Chief State School Officers. (2013). *InTASC model core teaching standards and learning progressions for teachers 1.0*. Retrieved from http://www.ccsso.org/documents/2013/2013_intasc_learning_progressions_for_teachers.pdf

Theisen, T. (2013). What are the possibilities for "student voice" in the 21st century? *Language and Education*, *8*(4), 7.

Thomas, M. (2015). Introduction. In M. Thmas & H. Reinders (Eds.), *Contemporary Task-Based Language Teaching in Asia* (pp. 1–6). London: Bloomsbury Publishing.

Thoms, J. (2011). Hybrid language and learning: Assessing pedagogical and curricular issues. In C. Wilkerson & P. Swanson (Eds.), *Dimension* (pp. 21–34). Valdosta, GA: SCOLT Publications.

Toda, T. (2008). *Nihongo Kyooiku to Onsee* [Japanese Language Education and Phonology]. Tokyo: Kurosio.

Toda, T. (2009). Nihongo kyooiku ni okeru gakushuusha onsee no kenkyuu to onsee kyooiku jissen[Learners' pronunciation and practices of pronunciation education in the field of Japanese language education]. *Nihongo Kyooiku*, *143*, 47–57.

Tondeur, J., Van Braak, J., Sang, G., Voogt, J., Fisser, P., & Ottenbreit-Leftwich, A. (2011). Preparing pre-service teachers to integrate technology in education: A synthesis of qualitative evidence. *Computers & Education*, *59*(1), 134–144. doi:10.1016/j.compedu.2011.10.009

Topper, A. (2004). How are we doing? Using self-assessment to measure changing teacher technology literacy within a graduate educational technology program. *Journal of Technology and Teacher Education*, *12*(3), 303–317.

Trent, J., & Shroff, R. H. (2013). Technology, identity, and community: The role of electronic teaching portfolios in becoming a teacher. *Technology, Pedagogy and Education*, *22*(1), 3–20. doi:10.1080/1475939X.2012.720416

Trigwell, K., & Prosser, M. (2004). Development and use of the Approaches to Teaching Inventory. *Educational Psychology Review*, *16*(4), 409–424. doi:10.1007/s10648-004-0007-9

Truscott, J. (1996). The case against grammar correction in L2 writing classes. *Language Learning*, *46*(2), 327–369. doi:10.1111/j.1467-1770.1996.tb01238.x

Tseng, J.-J. (2014). Investigating EFL teachers' technological pedagogical content knowledge: Students' perceptions. In S. Jager, L. Bradley, E. J. Meima, & S. Thouësny (Eds), *CALL Design: Principles and Practice*; *Proceedings of the 2014 EUROCALL Conference,Groningen, The Netherlands* (pp. 379-384) doi:doi:10.14705/rpnet.2014.000249 doi:10.14705/rpnet.2014.000249

Tsui, A. B. M., & Tollefson, J. W. (2007). Language policy and the construction of national cultural identity. In A. B. M. Tsui & J. Tollefson (Eds.), *Language Policy, Culture, and Identity in Asian Contexts* (pp. 1–21). Mahwah, NJ: Lawrence Erlbaum Associates.

Compilation of References

Twitter. (2015, May 8). In *Wikipedia, the free encyclopedia*. Retrieved from http://en.wikipedia.org/wiki/Twitter

U.S. Department of Education, Office of Educational Technology. (2010). *Transforming American education: Learning powered by technology*. Retrieved December 12, 2015, from http://www2.ed.gov/about/offices/list/os/technology/netp-executive-summary.pdf

United Nations Educational, Scientific and Cultural Organization (UNESCO). (2009). *World Report on Investing in Cultural Diversity and Intercultural Dialogue*. Retrieved from http://unesdoc.unesco.org/images/0018/001852/185202e.pdf

Urakami, F. (2004). Nihongo kyooiku ni okeru onsee shidoo[Speech sound in teaching foreign languages]. *Chuugoku Gakuen Kiyoo, 3*, 27–34.

Valenzuela, S., Park, N., & Kee, K. F. (2009). Is there social capital in a Social Network Site?: Facebook use and college students' life satisfaction, trust, and participation. *Journal of Computer-Mediated Communication, 14*(4), 875–901. doi:10.1111/j.1083-6101.2009.01474.x

Vallance, M. (2007). An information and communications technology (ICT)-enabled method for collecting and collating information about pre-service teachers' pedagogical beliefs regarding the integration of ICT. *Research in Learning Technology, 15*(1), 51–65. doi:10.1080/09687760601129851

Van Olphen, M. (2008, March). *World language teacher education and educational technology: A look into CK, PCK, and TPCK*. Annual Meeting of the American Educational Research Association, New York, NY.

van Olphen, M. (2007). Digital portfolios: Balancing the academic and professional needs of world language teacher candidates. In M. Kassen, R. Lavine, K. Murphy-Judy, & M. Peters (Eds.), *Preparing and developing technology-proficient L2 teachers* (pp. 265–294). San Marcos, TX: CALICO.

van Olphen, M. (2007). Perspectives of foreign language preservice teachers on the use of a web-based instructional environment in a methods course. *CALICO Journal, 25*(1), 91–109.

Van Olphen, M. (2008). World language teacher education and educational technology: A Look into CK, PCK, and TPCK. In *Annual Meeting of the American Educational Research Association*.

Vannatta, R., Beyerbach, B., & Walsh, C. (2001). From teaching technology to using technology to enhance student learning: Preservice teachers' changing perceptions of technology infusion. *Journal of Technology and Teacher Education, 9*(1), 105–127.

Veen, W. (1993). The role of beliefs in the use of information technology: Implications for teacher education, or teaching the right thing at the right time. *Journal of Information Technology for Teacher Education, 2*(2), 139–153. doi:10.1080/0962029930020203

Venkatesh, V., Morris, M. G., Davis, F. D., & Davis, G. B. (2003). User acceptance of information technology: Toward a unified view. *Management Information Systems Quarterly, 27*(3), 425–478.

W3Techs. (2015). *Usage of content languages for websites*. Retrieved from: http://w3techs.com/technologies/overview/content_language/all

Waheed, M., & Jam, F. A. (2010). Teacher's Intention to Accept Online Education: Extended TAM Model. *Interdisciplinary Journal of Contemporary Research in Business, 2*(5), 330–344.

Walker, A., & White, G. (2013). *Technology enhanced language learning: Connecting theory and practice*. Oxford, UK: Oxford University Press.

Wang, S. C. (1998). A Study on the Learning and Teaching of Hanzi-Chinese Characters. *Working Papers in Educational Linguistics, 14*(1), 69-101

Wang, L., Ertmer, P. A., & Newby, T. J. (2004). Increasing preservice teachers' self-efficacy beliefs for technology integration. *Journal of Research on Technology in Education, 36*(3), 231–250. doi:10.1080/15391523.2004.10782414

Wang, S., & Vasquez, C. (2012). Web 2.0 and second language learning: What does the research tell us? *CALICO, 29*(3), 412–430. doi:10.11139/cj.29.3.412-430

Wang, Y., Chen, N. S., & Levy, M. (2010). Teacher training in a synchronous cyber face-to-face classroom: Characterizing and supporting the online teachers' learning process. *Computer Assisted Language Learning, 23*(4), 277–293. doi:10.1080/09588221.2010.493523

Warschauer, M., & Healey, D. (1998). Computers and language learning: An overview. *Language Teaching, 31*(02), 57–71. doi:10.1017/S0261444800012970

Warschauer, M., & Meskill, C. (2000). Technology and second language learning. In J. Rosenthal (Ed.), *Handbook of undergraduate second language education* (pp. 303–318). Mahwah, New Jersey: Lawrence Erlbaum.

Watson, D. M. (2001). Pedagogy before technology: Re-thinking the relationship between ICT and teaching. *Education and Information Technologies, 6*(4), 251–266. doi:10.1023/A:1012976702296

Watzke, J. L. (2007). Foreign language pedagogical knowledge: Toward a developmental theory of beginning teacher practices. *Modern Language Journal, 91*(1), 63–82. doi:10.1111/j.1540-4781.2007.00510.x

Wenger, E., McDermott, R., & Snyder, W. M. (2002). Cultivating communities of practice. Cambridge, MA: Harvard University Press.

Wenger, E. (1998). *Communities of Practice: Learning, Meaning, and Identity*. Cambridge, UK: Cambridge University Press. doi:10.1017/CBO9780511803932

Wenger, E. (2004). Knowledge management is a donut: Shaping your knowledge strategy with communities of practice. *Ivey Business Journal, 68*(3), 1–8.

Wenger, E., McDermott, R., & Snyder, W. (2002). *Cultivating communities of practice: a guide to managing knowledge*. Boston, MA: Harvard Business School Press.

Wenger, E., & Snyder, W. (2000). Communities of practice: The organizational frontier. *Harvard Business Review, 1*(78), 139–145.

Whyte, S. (2014). Bridging the gaps: Using social media to develop techno-pedagogical competences in pre-service language teacher education. *Recherche et pratiques pédagogiques en langues de spécialité, 33*(2), 143-169.

Wiersma, W., & Jurs, S. G. (2010). *Research Methods in Education*. Beijing: Social Science Literature Press.

Wild, M. (1996). Technology refusal: Rationalising the failure of student and beginning teachers to use computers. *British Journal of Educational Technology, 27*(2), 134–143. doi:10.1111/j.1467-8535.1996.tb00720.x

Wildner, S. (1999). Technology integration into preservice foreign language teacher education programs. *CALICO Journal, 17*(2), 223–250.

Williams, C. (2013). Emerging development of semantic and phonological routes to character decoding in Chinese as a foreign language learners. *Reading and Writing, 26*(2), 293–315. doi:10.1007/s11145-012-9368-5

Compilation of References

Williams, D., Coles, L., Wilson, K., Richardson, A., & Tuson, J. (2000). Teachers and ICT: Current use and future needs. *British Journal of Educational Technology*, *31*(4), 307–320. doi:10.1111/1467-8535.00164

Willis, D., & Willis, J. (2007). *Doing Task-based Teaching*. Oxford, UK: Oxford University Press.

Winke, P., & Goertler, S. (2013). Did we forget someone? Students' computer access and literacy for CALL. *CALICO*, *25*(3), 482–509.

Wong, L. H., Chai, C. S., Zhang, X., & King, R. B. (2015). Employing the TPACK framework for researcher-teacher co-design of a mobile-assisted seamless language learning environment. *IEEE Transactions on Learning Technologies*, *8*(1), 31–42. doi:10.1109/TLT.2014.2354038

Wright, T. (2012). Managing the classroom. In A. Burns & J. C. Richards (Eds.), *The Cambridge guide to pedagogy and practice in second language teaching* (pp. 60–67). Cambridge, UK: Cambridge University Press.

Wu, Z. (2002). *Teachers' knowledge and curriculum change: a critical study of teachers' exploratory discourse in a Chinese university*. (Unpublished Doctoral dissertation). University of Lancaster, Lancaster, UK.

Wu, M. L. (2010). *SPSS statistical analysis practice*. Chongqing, China: Chongqing University Press.

Xie, T. (2011). *Three Models of Long Distance e-Tutoring: A Pilot Study*. The 7th International Conference on Internet Chinese Education (ICICE 2011). Taipei.

Yang, G. (2010). The pattern on EFL's professional development in rural area: A perspective from the " New Curriculum Standards[Education education]. *Journal of Hebei Normal University*, *12*(4), 62–65.

Yang, P., Zhang, Q., & Yi, X. (2004). On the construction of teachers' autonomy training model. e-. *Education Research*, *2*, 25–27.

Yang, Y. (2010). Computer-assisted Foreign Language Teaching: Theory and Practice. *Journal of Language Teaching and Research*, *1*(6), 909–912. doi:10.4304/jltr.1.6.909-912

Yeh, P., & Dai, J. H. (2015). *The Implications of Discourse Analysis in an Online Chinese Teacher Training Course*. The 9th International Conference on Internet Chinese Education International Conference on Internet Chinese (ICICE 2015), Boston, U.S.A

Yeung, A. S., Tay, E. G., Hui, C., Lin, J. H., & Low, E. L. (2014). Pre-service teachers' motivation in using digital technology. *Australian Journal of Teacher Education*, *39*(3). doi:10.14221/ajte.2014v39n3.1

Yin, R. (2009). *Case study research: Design and methods* (5th ed.). Los Angeles, CA: Sage.

Yonemoto, K., Noguchi, M., Hayashi, H., Tsuda, A., & Yamane, N. (2014). Chooompa eezoo wo ooyooshita nihongo hatsuon shidoo no kanoosee [Ultrasound application to the empowerment of pronunciation teaching and learning]. In *Proceedings of Annual Conference of the Canadian Association for Japanese Language Education* (pp. 248-257). Retrieved from http://www.cajle.info/wp-content/uploads/2014/09/Yonemoto_CAJLE2014_Proceedings_248-257.pdf

Young, J. R., Young, J. L., & Shaker, Z. (2012). Describing pre-service teacher technological pedagogical content knowledge (TPACK) literature using confidence intervals. *TechTrends*, *56*(5), 25–33. doi:10.1007/s11528-012-0600-6

Young, S. F. (2008). Theoretical frameworks and models of learning: Tools for developing conceptions of teaching and learning. *The International Journal for Academic Development*, *13*(1), 41–49. doi:10.1080/13601440701860243

Zelkowski, J., Gleason, J., Cox, D. C., & Bismarck, S. (2013). Developing and validating a reliable TPACK instrument for secondary mathematics preservice teachers. *Journal of Research on Technology in Education*, *46*(2), 173–206. doi:10.1080/15391523.2013.10782618

Zhai, H. (2008). Discussion on elementary and secondary EFL teachers' information literacy education at the information age. *Journal of Qiqihaer Teachers'. College, 3*, 119–121.

Zhang, D., Zhao, S., & Li, L. (2014). Teachers' perceptions and use of information and communication technologies (ICTs) in Chinese language education. In S. Li & P. Swanson (Eds.), *Engaging language learners through technology integration; Theory, applications, and outcomes* (pp. 237–256). Hershey, PA: Information Science Reference.

Zhang, J. X., & Schwarzer, R. (1995). Measuring optimistic self-beliefs: A Chinese adaptation of the General Self-Efficacy Scale. *Psychologia, 38*(3), 174–181.

Zhang, J., Shi, S., Miao, F., & Yang, W. (2003). A performance criteria study on elementary and secondary school teachers' educational informational technology. *China Educational Technology, 2*, 104–113.

Zhang, X., & Niu, G. (2009). Strategies on improving college English teachers' professional development on information technology application. *Continuing Education Research, 5*, 44–46.

Zhao, J. (2013). The role of network technology in the development of college English teachers. *Journal of Changchun University, 23*(4), 483–487.

Zhao, Y. (2003). Recent developments in technology and language learning: A literature review and meta-analysis. *CALICO, 21*(1), 7–27.

Zhao, Y. (2003). Recent developments in technology and language learning: A literature review and meta-analysis. *CALICO Journal, 21*(1), 7–27.

Zhao, Y., Pugh, K., Sheldon, S., & Byers, J. (2002). Conditions for classroom technology innovations. *Teachers College Record, 104*(3), 482–515. doi:10.1111/1467-9620.00170

Zhong, Z., Wang, Y., Huang, Y., & Shi, H. (2003). An investigation on the elementary and secondary school teachers' information literacy. *e-. Education Research, 1*, 65–69.

About the Contributors

Chin-Hsi Lin is an Assistant Professor in the department of Counseling, Educational Psychology, and Special Education and Confucius Institute at Michigan State University. His primary research interest is emerging technologies in language education, especially new forms of social media. He investigates the process and outcome of social learning and authentic communications on a social network site developed for language learning.

Dongbo Zhang holds a PhD in Second Language Acquisition from Carnegie Mellon University. He is currently an Assistant Professor of Second Language Education in the Department of Teacher Education at Michigan State University where he also coordinates the Chinese Teacher Certification Program and the Graduate Certificate in English Language Learner Education. Dr. Zhang's research interests include second language reading, biliteracy, and language teacher education. His publications have appeared in such journals as Applied Linguistics, Applied Psycholinguistics, Modern Language Journal, Reading and Writing, among others.

Binbin Zheng is an Assistant Professor in the department of Counseling, Educational Psychology, and Special Education and Confucius Institute at Michigan State University. She received her Ph.D. in Language, Literacy, and Technology from the University of California, Irvine in 2013. Dr. Zheng's research focuses on new technologies and students' language and literacy development, as well as educational program evaluations. She is particularly interested in investigating the effect of social media on at-risk learners' language learning.

* * *

Hsiu-Jen Cheng is currently an Assistant Professor in the graduate institution of Teaching Chinese as a Second/Foreign Language at National Kaohsiung Normal University, Taiwan. Her current research projects focus on online Chinese pre-service teacher training. The areas of expertise include pre-service teacher training on mobile devices and digital multimedia integration.

Matthew Deroo is a PhD student at Michigan State University. His research interests are at the intersection of language teaching, student learning, and technology.

Liying Feng is a doctoral student in Curriculum and Instruction with a specialization in Foreign and Second Language Education (FSLE) in the College of Education at the Florida State University. She teaches Chinese as a foreign language (CFL) in the Department of Modern Language and Linguistics. Her research interests include teaching and learning CFL with comprehensible input strategies, identity development of Chinese heritage college students, and comparative studies of Chinese textbooks.

Grisel M. Garcia Perez has a PhD in Applied Linguistics and is a tenured professor who has been teaching languages for 38 years and still says she genuinely enjoys what she does. She considers teaching to be a privileged position that demands humility, respect, and love. Her primary research interest is in the area of second/foreign language teaching and learning. Within this area, she has carried out investigations on e-learning, speech analysis, text analysis, and most recently on intercultural communication and intercultural awareness. At present she is investigating how intercultural development, sensitivity, competence, and communication are interconnected with language learning.

Sarah Gretter is a doctoral candidate in the Educational Psychology and Educational Technology program at Michigan State University. Her research focuses on the implementation of media and information literacy in educational settings, along with teacher training in media and information literacy through pedagogical case studies.

Muriel Grosbois is an Associate Professor in Applied Linguistics at the School of Education of the University Paris-Sorbonne (ESPE), France. She is head of the didactic research team within the CeLiSo research unit (Centre de Linguistique en Sorbonne). She is in charge of the center for digital resources in languages and cultures and chief editor of the ALSIC journal (Apprentissage des Langues et Systèmes d'Information et de Communication). Her research and teaching focus on language learning in a technology-enhanced context.

Hisako Hayashi holds a Ph.D in the Department of Curriculum Theory and Implementation in Education at Simon Fraser University. Her research interests include multilingual students academic, transnational and sociocultural identity construction, Japanese language education (curriculum, instruction and pedagogy) and qualitative research.

Jason D. Hendryx received his Ph.D. in Curriculum and Instruction with a focus on Second Language Acquisition from the University of Washington, Seattle in 2008. Hired in 2008 to teach Chinese at the United States Air Force Academy, he went on to train Chinese language teachers at National Taiwan Normal University and is now in charge of the Modern Languages Education program at the University of Wyoming, where his program graduates go on to teach French, Spanish, and German in middle and high schools in the United States. He has presented at conferences and provided professional development workshops for language teachers around the globe. He has published articles concerning Chinese heritage language learners, student grouping approaches, and teaching Chinese culture. His primary research areas are related to enhancing world language teaching practices and understandings, and language play.

Jiahang Li is an assistant professor and the associate director at the Confucius Institute at Michigan State University. Dr. Li earned a Ph.D. degree in Reading Education from University of Maryland College Park, his research interests include the impacts that social media has on teaching and learning, educational technology, teacher education, teaching Chinese as a foreign language, and multicultural

About the Contributors

literature. He earned M.A. and B.A degrees in Chinese Classical Philology from Department of Chinese Language and Literature at Peking University, China.

Haixia Liu received her MA degree from Sun Yat-sen University in China in 2005. She has worked in the School of Foreign Language, Beijing Normal university Zhuhai Campus since her graduation in 2005. She is currently a PhD student in the Department of Counseling, Education Psychology and Special Education at the College of Education, Michigan State University. Her research interests include teacher adoption of technology, computer-assisted language learning, language teachers' educational technology professional development, and comparative education.

Mei-Hui Liu is currently an associate professor in the Department of Foreign Languages and Literature at Tunghai University, Taiwan. Her research focus is mainly on EFL teacher professional development, technology-enhanced language learning, and online learning community. She has published book chapters and academic articles in domestic and international journals. Her recent publications include articles in Computers & Education: An International Journal, Teaching and Teacher Education: An International Journal of Research and Studies, English Teaching & Learning, and Language Learning & Technology.

Cédric Sarré is an associate professor in English as a Foreign Language (EFL) and English Language Teaching (ELT) at Université Paris-Sorbonne, ESPE (School of Education), France. He is a member of the CeLiSo research team (Centre de Linguistique en Sorbonne) and his research interests include language course development in online settings, the integration of technology – especially CMC – in language learning and teaching, and teacher education.

Yanjiang Teng is a Ph.D. candidate in Curriculum, Instruction and Teacher Education at Michigan State University. His research interests are literacy, second language acquisition, and teacher education. He is currently working on a project on the relationship between teacher belief and teaching practice from the perspective of classroom interactions. He has published articles on second language teacher preparation.

Asami Tsuda received her MA in Japanese Linguistics and Pedagogy from the University of Toronto, and has taught beginner to advanced Japanese language courses in Japan, Canada and the USA. Her interests include development of learning materials to support and promote student autonomy in Japanese language learning. She is currently teaching Japanese at Columbia University. She was also a core member of a project called "Multimodal approaches to the empowerment of pronunciation teaching and learning: Creating online interactive tutorial videos". The materials are open to public and can be found at: http://enunciate.arts.ubc.ca/

Wenxia Wang is Assistant Professor of second and foreign language education at the Florida State University. Her research focuses on second/foreign language teacher education, especially on Chinese language education in the U.S. She directed several STARTALK programs to prepare teachers of critical languages, including Arabic, Chinese, Korean, Portuguese, Russian, and Swahili. At the Florida State University, she teaches undergraduate, Master's, and doctoral courses in second and foreign language education.

Kazuhiro Yonemoto is Assistant Professor in the International Exchange Center of Tokyo Medical and Dental University. His research interests include educational sociolinguistics, education for language minority students, and affective dimensions of second language teaching and learning particularly in the contexts of Japanese as a second language.

Yining Zhang is currently a doctoral student studying educational technology at Michigan State University. Her research interests include self-regulated learning in online and foreign language settings, and CALL.

Index

3D System 231, 243, 244

A

Accomplished Teachers 45, 46, 54
American Council on the Teaching of Foreign Languages (ACTFL) 3, 15, 20, 42-57, 69, 92-97, 107-112, 199, 218
Assessment 5, 15, 33, 35, 43-52, 64-73, 89, 90, 108, 150, 159, 177-194, 202, 208, 255-259, 266

B

Blended Learning 93, 111, 129, 168, 172

C

CEAP 45, 46
CFL Teachers 38-51
Chinese as a Foreign Language (CFL) 38-54, 192, 199, 220, 221
Chinese as a Second Language (CSL) 51, 198-209, 215-221
CLASS 3-18, 25-30, 44-67, 93-150, 164, 168, 177-188, 200-220, 229-234, 247-256, 264, 265
Cloud-Based Practicum 175, 187, 189
College English Curriculum Requirements (CECR) 24-28, 34
Communities of Practice 4, 109-113, 169, 193, 245-259, 271
Complexity 108, 148, 160-172
Computer Assisted Language Learning (CALL) 2, 20, 21, 31-37, 48-53, 59, 70, 71, 92-95, 111-116, 130, 131, 150, 153, 168-171, 179, 182, 193, 203, 220, 221, 228, 243-247, 255, 273, 274
Computer Literacy 25, 37, 186
Curriculum Reform 23, 25, 33, 34
Cycle of Learning 114, 122, 129

D

Digital Divide 32, 37, 242

E

English as a Foreign Language (EFL) 23-37, 52, 72, 79, 154, 160, 161, 168, 175-190, 203, 219, 220
English Language 20-39, 52, 61, 62, 74-87, 95, 110-125, 133-158, 169-188, 195-197, 203-209, 217-225, 232, 249-267, 277
English Language Education 120, 196
English Language Teaching 34, 153, 154, 257
ePortofolio 22
Experiential learning 1, 132, 250, 256, 259
Extension 102, 244
External Barriers 56-73

F

Facebook (FB) 131-150
Face-to-Face Discussion 180, 187
Feedback 1, 5, 13, 30, 96-116, 124, 125, 142, 156-170, 187, 205, 213, 234-238, 246-260, 267, 270
Field-Based Experience 177, 194
Field Practices 198-211
Flipped Classroom 31, 93, 97, 114-129, 188-192
Flipped Learning 92, 115-127
Foreign Language 1-7, 17-24, 34-57, 70, 72, 79, 92-121, 127, 133, 134, 148-154, 170-178, 188-209, 217-221, 228, 238-276
Foreign Language Learning 2, 17, 42, 52-57, 72, 93, 94, 107, 121, 133, 134, 148, 149, 241-249, 259, 271
Foreign Language Teacher Education 1-5, 21, 22, 39, 40, 112, 170, 176, 242, 261-273
Foreign Language Teaching 3, 5, 52, 79, 94, 105, 245-247, 253-261, 268-276
Formative Assessment 255-259
Formative Evaluation 245, 253-256

H

Hanban 38, 39, 46-54
High-Stakes Test 28, 37
Hybrid education 92, 94

I

ICT Integrated Teaching 23-33
Identity 36, 130-132, 147-150, 193, 228, 248, 258, 262, 274
Innovation 12, 20, 25, 34, 41, 143, 168-172, 257, 274
In-Service Teacher 199
Instruction 1-33, 39-60, 67, 70, 93-96, 102-117, 123-134, 140-148, 175-211, 218-241, 255, 267-273
InTASC 43-53
Interaction 1, 86, 93-106, 131, 132, 142-150, 171, 193, 195, 228, 230, 238, 244-248, 263, 277
Internal Barriers 56, 60, 66-73
Interviews 1, 7, 8, 14, 18, 28, 30, 87, 122, 130-145, 151, 160, 182, 183, 205-209, 267-270
ISTE 3, 24, 33, 41, 42, 48-54, 94, 95, 107-111
IT 1-75, 84, 86, 93-178, 184-187, 197-273

K

Knowledge of Technology (TK) 40-50, 75-87, 201-204, 210-224

L

Language Input 24-29, 37
Language-Teaching Methods Course 22
Learning Management System (LMS) 142, 148, 150
Less Commonly Taught Languages (LCTLs) 266, 277
Linguistic Forms 26, 37, 202

M

Mishra and Koehler 39-50, 199, 201
Mobile Learning 74-90

N

National Board for Professional Teaching Standards (NBPTS) 45-53
Negotiation of Meaning 251, 259
New English Curriculum (NEC) 24
New Teachers 15, 50, 54, 107, 199

O

Observations 30, 104, 122, 130-145, 200, 228, 239, 245-255, 267, 269
Online Discussion 12, 94, 177
Online Field Experience 175
Online Instruction 107, 180-188, 198
Online Mentoring 175-177, 186-191, 197
Online Practicum 176-194, 215
Online Tutoring 153-174, 180, 182

P

Pedagogical Beliefs 30, 56-73, 118, 167, 170, 193, 218, 273
Pedagogy 3, 23-40, 48, 69-76, 84, 89, 95-97, 109-119, 128-132, 145-155, 161, 176, 191-202, 219, 227-230, 238-243, 262
Peer Assessment 177, 194, 258
Practice 1-5, 14-46, 58, 59, 66, 72, 91, 97-147, 157-162, 169-172, 178-222, 233-276
Pre-Service Teacher 3, 20, 26, 27, 153-161, 193-208, 215-221, 246
Pre-Service Teacher Education 20, 27, 153, 157
Pre-Service Teachers 1-27, 76, 77, 85-90, 153-171, 190-224, 246, 257, 262
Product 104, 110, 148, 244
Professional Development 13, 19-45, 51-58, 69-75, 86-90, 96, 108, 118, 155-161, 169, 175-200, 208, 216-228, 265-276
Project-Based Instruction 179-185, 192, 194
Pronunciation Teaching and Learning 114, 115, 128

Q

Qualitative 6, 21, 35, 61, 100, 108, 122, 130-135, 149, 157-159, 171, 175, 182, 190, 193, 206-211, 218, 255, 267

R

Reflection 3, 5, 16-19, 31, 35, 41, 46, 153-156, 169, 172, 182-185, 192-197, 204, 219-227, 237, 245, 246
Reflective learning 4, 246, 256, 259
Research 2-7, 14-24, 34-79, 85-97, 105-123, 130-160, 168-208, 216-221, 231, 239-247, 255-266, 272-276
Role Model 177, 194

S

Second Language Learning 15, 21, 22, 71, 115, 128, 149, 156, 241, 259, 275
Self-Efficacy 74-77, 87-91, 160, 178, 246, 257, 258, 273
Self-Reflection 177, 189, 194
Situated Learning 4, 132, 146, 149, 155, 168, 172
Situative Learning 22
Social Media 13, 109, 112, 136, 172, 261-277
Social Networking Sites (SNSs) 130-150, 261, 277
Spanish Language 92-110, 226, 249, 255
Stakeholders 28, 29, 37, 50
Standards 3, 13-18, 24, 33-57, 64, 72, 92-97, 105-111, 133, 134, 218, 220, 226-230, 268
Structural Equation Model 74, 81, 85
Student-Centered Teaching 92, 178

T

Teacher Belief 37, 263, 272-277
Teacher Certification 40, 41, 54
Teacher Knowledge 35-54, 71, 76, 89-95, 112, 191, 202, 219, 220
Teacher Licensing 43, 54
Teachers' Beliefs 27, 30, 69, 72, 128, 133, 155, 262-265, 272-276
Teacher Training 3, 5, 20, 21, 28-35, 51, 88, 97, 144, 175, 178, 184, 192-205, 217-228, 243-246, 255, 256, 266-272
Teacher Training Model 198-205, 222
Teaching Assistants 180, 245-249, 255
Teaching Pedagogy 26-31
Teaching Philosophy 26-32, 118, 178
Technical Support 30, 31, 56, 58, 64-73, 108, 268-273
Technological Pedagogical and Content Knowledge (TPACK) 24-41, 48-53, 74-96, 105-112, 176, 190-224, 257, 275
Technology 1-203, 211-276
Technology Acceptance Model 59, 74, 77, 88, 90
Technology Course 1-10, 17, 20, 191, 229
Technology Infusion 176, 177, 183, 189-194
Technology Instruction 1-10, 17-19, 199
Technology Professional Development 175-189, 197
Technology-Related Knowledge 15, 56, 64, 67, 73
Technology Resources 56, 73, 200
Technology Standards 3, 13-18, 24, 38-53, 107, 109
Technology Use 3-21, 27-35, 41, 47, 56-77, 84, 96, 107, 130, 132, 140, 142, 151, 155, 178, 192, 199, 203, 229, 233, 263, 274
TL-TPACK Model 198, 204, 214, 215, 222
TPACK 24-31, 38-41, 48-52, 74-96, 105-112, 190-224, 257
Training 2-6, 17-36, 51-59, 68-77, 88, 89, 97, 107, 136, 144, 153-229, 237-256, 264-275

U

Ultrasound Images 114, 120-129

V

Virtual learning 154, 161, 168-172, 256, 259, 266

W

Web 2.0 132, 147, 149, 156, 261, 273

Receive Free Lifetime E-Access or Free Hardcover

Purchase a print book or e-book through the IGI Global Online Bookstore and receive the alternate version for free! Shipping fees apply.

www.igi-global.com

Recommended Reference Books

Take **20% Off** through the IGI Global Online Bookstore

Campus Support Services, Programs, and Policies for International Students
ISBN: 978-1-4666-9752-2
© 2016; 324 pp.
Take 20% Off:* $148

Exploring the Social and Academic Experiences of International Students in Higher Education Institutions
ISBN: 978-1-4666-9749-2
© 2016; 318 pp.
Take 20% Off:* $148

Global Perspectives and Local Challenges Surrounding International Student Mobility
ISBN: 978-1-4666-9746-1
© 2016; 354 pp.
Take 20% Off:* $148

Handbook of Research on Emerging Priorities and Trends in Distance Education
ISBN: 978-1-4666-5162-3
© 2014; 480 pp.
Take 20% Off:* $252

Handbook of Research on Teaching Methods in Language Translation and Interpretation
ISBN: 978-1-4666-6615-3
© 2015; 458 pp.
Take 20% Off:* $260

E-Learning as a Socio-Cultural System
ISBN: 978-1-4666-6154-7
© 2014; 349 pp.
Take 20% Off:* $156

*IGI Global now offers the option to purchase hardcover, e-access, or hardcover + e-access for one price! You choose the format that best suits your needs. This offer is only valid on purchases made directly through IGI Global's Online Bookstore and not intended for use by book distributors or wholesalers. Shipping fees will be applied for hardcover purchases during checkout if this option is selected. E-Access will remain available for the lifetime of the publication and will only allow access to the edition purchased. Free Lifetime E-Access is only available to individuals and single institutions that purchase printed publications directly through IGI Global. Sharing the Free Lifetime E-Access is prohibited and will result in the termination of e-access. **20% discount cannot be combined with any other offer. Only valid on purchases made directly through IGI Global's Online Bookstore and not intended for use by book distributors or wholesalers. Not applicable on databases.

Publishing Progressive Information Science and Technology Research Since 1988

IGI GLOBAL
DISSEMINATOR OF KNOWLEDGE

www.igi-global.com | Sign up at www.igi-global.com/newsletters | facebook.com/igiglobal | twitter.com/igiglobal